An Introduction to
Philosophical Logic

An Introduction to Philosophical Logic

A.C. Grayling

Magdalen College, Oxford

THE HARVESTER PRESS · SUSSEX

BARNES & NOBLE BOOKS · NEW JERSEY

First published in Great Britain in 1982 by
THE HARVESTER PRESS LIMITED
Publisher: John Spiers
16 Ship Street, Brighton, Sussex

and in the USA by
BARNES & NOBLE BOOKS
81 Adams Drive, Totowa, New Jersey 07512

© *A. C. Grayling, 1982*

British Library Cataloguing in Publication Data
Grayling, A.C.
    An introduction to philosophical logic. -(Harvester studies in
    philosophy; 15)
    1. Logic
    I. Title
    160   BC51

ISBN 0-85527-514-6
ISBN 0-7108-0421-1 Pbk

Library of Congress Cataloging in Publication Data
Grayling, A.C.
    An introduction to philosophical logic.

    1. Logic   2. Languages – Philosophy.   I. Title.
BC71.G7   1982   160   82-6854
ISBN 0-389-20299-1   AACR2
ISBN 0-389-20300-9 (pbk.)

Typeset in Times by Granada Graphics Ltd, Redhill
and printed in Great Britain by
The Thetford Press Ltd, Thetford, Norfolk

Dedicated to
my father, H. C. Grayling, *sine quo non*,
and
my children, Jolyon and Georgina, *quibus omnia*.

Contents

Preface

Philosophers are fond of pointing out that there is no shallow-end in philosophy. This is true. Philosophy is a subject which is often complex and sometimes difficult. Books which try to purvey shallow-end philosophy invariably purvey shallow philosophy instead, and in consequence distort and falsify the issues. Because philosophy is, in William James' phrase, among other things a dogged struggle to achieve clarity, offering shallow-end treatment of philosophical topics is, therefore, worse than useless: it is counterproductive. Accordingly I have not tried, in this book, to pretend that the philosophical problems I deal with are simple, or that they can be simplified to the extent that no effort is needed to master them. The problems in question are challenging problems, and demand careful study.

All this said, and philosophy's deep-endedness acknowledged, it remains that new swimmers must, somehow, be helped into the flood. There are various ways of introducing philosophy, the best of which is by means of tutorials rather than the printed page, which latter furnishes no more than a cold monologue in contrast to the former's potential for heated dialogue. Still, books have important uses; one can mull over them, linger on this or that point, pencil insights and objurgations in the margins – *scripta manent, verba volant* after all.

My choice has been to adopt the primer method. Philosophical debates can be mastered *only* by reading the original literature which gives them their content; therefore I have conceived my task to be one of providing prefaces to a number of important issues – that is, as providing some of the background to them, and a sketch of the options concerning them, in order to orientate the beginner. However, although what I say is decidedly *not* intended as a substitute for the literature, my procedure has been to discuss a good part of that literature, for to discuss the literature is to discuss the issues. This has the concomitant virtue of familiarising the neomath with who said what, why, and where. In this way a map of the region is drawn up, with competing theories and their espousers located upon it.

In the way authors are apt to be, I am painfully aware of the shortcomings in what follows. Nevertheless it seems to me that trying to equip students with an overview of important philosophical topics is a worthwhile task, because half the student's battle in achieving understanding comes down to being able to locate given topics in a more general spread of concerns, and, in so doing, to grasp the point of efforts to solve them.

Writing introductory books is much more difficult than one might expect. The drive to clarity and simplicity of exposition has an impressive tendency to produce exactly the opposite result, and a constant worry bedevilling the drive to economy of exposition arises from the question, how little is too little? These difficulties notwithstanding, the aim here has been to say enough, clearly enough, to give a preliminary view of some of the main problems in philosophical logic, while at the same time saying little enough to whet curiosity further − in regard to which, abundant references have been supplied.

It is worth pointing out the following. Some sections in these chapters will appear more difficult to grasp than others. Some contain technicalities, although I have tried to keep these to a minimum. Difficult sections are followed by easier ones, however, and it is almost always the case that the matter treated in difficult sections is treated again, in different but related connections, in later chapters. A measure of patience, and a little faith, will carry the reader through darker stretches of the way. It is the interrelatedness of the topics which generates this dialectic of alternating complexity and straightforwardness; but light, I hope, scatters back and forth across the chapters as one proceeds. At the same time, each chapter is largely self-contained, for this is not a treatise but a textbook; anyone working on a particular topic can use the relevant chapter as a preface or a supplement to his studies, without having to tramp too far afield in other chapters for illumination. One thing: the notes contain references in the standard way, but they also contain a number of asides and amplifications, so I urge their use. It is irritating to have the notes listed at the end of chapters rather than at the foot of the page, I appreciate; but the exigencies of publication in the twilight of a failing economic order so demand.

I have assumed in places that the reader is acquainted with a little basic logic. This assumption had to be made because it is not within the scope and objectives of what follows that it should serve as an introduction to logic as well as to philosophical logic. However, the places where logical technicalities are invoked are few, and I have sought simplicity there as everywhere else.

My aim in this book, in sum, has been to provide an introductory overview of the nature and background of some central problems in philosophy. Introductory books stand to their subject-matter as maps to actual terrain; this one is no exception. I have not sought to provide a comprehensive review of the debates on the problems introduced here — that would be a task for a keeper of minutes. What I have tried to do is to situate the first few rungs of a ladder. The rest of the ladder is for the reader's fashioning.

In the course of writing this book I studied the methods of a number of other introductory writers, to see what lessons might be learned from their approach. In doing so I came to applaud the achievement in this respect of two authors, Susan Haack of Warwick University (*Philosophy of Logics*, Cambridge University Press, 1978) and Bernard Harrison of Sussex University (*Introduction to the Philosophy of Language*, Macmillan, 1979), the first for her clarity, facility and range, and the second for his integrity and passionate involvement with the issues. I have deliberately chosen to be less commital and programmatic than either, and, unlike them, I take Teucer's hint and fire my arrows behind the shield of Ajax. Nevertheless, their commitments far from vitiate what they say. Although their books differ in content from what follows, there are overlaps too; and in picking out additional introductory material for the reader I recommend both these authors.

Prefaces are an author's private property, and provide him with an opportunity to speak his thanks. Mine go to those whose friendship has been an encouragement, not so much in particular connection with this book as in general philosophical and personal ways: Timothy Sprigge, Freddie Ayer, Bernard Harrison, Bill and Gail Stine, Joe Palumbo, Dory Scaltsas, Richard Shusterman, and Jim Austin are chief among them. I am indebted also to Professor Sir Peter Strawson for the educative reception afforded by him to my fortnightly papers in student days; to David McNaughton of Keele University, who kindly read a great part of the final draft of this book and made helpful comments; and to Susan Whitfield for help with the proofs. I have also to thank Wolsey Hall for allowing me to use material which first appeared as a study-aid written by me for students taking the external Honours degree in Philosophy of the University of London.

Finally, it is a deep pleasure to record thanks for the more intimately personal helps which brightened the way. My dear friends Duncan and Elspeth Harvey and Isaac and Ilana Ben Mayor aided the bidding of this small slam far more than they know. I am grateful too to those Magdalen friends who variously supplied the Daubeney, companionable miles around Addison's and Christ Church meadow, and much good talk of many things, all which abetted the outcome.

My most profound dues of all are paid in the Dedication.

A. C. Grayling,
Magdalen College, Oxford,
Trinity 1981

1   *Philosophical Logic, the Philosophy of Logic, Philosophy and Logic*

PHILOSOPHICAL LOGIC AND THE PHILOSOPHY OF LOGIC

The various branches of philosophy are closely interdependent. In thinking about metaphysics, for example, one is obliged to deal with epistemological and logical questions, and in the same way metaphysical issues arise in epistemology, and logical problems recur. This kind of interpenetration links all the philosophical specialisms, which makes it difficult to draw sharp boundaries between them. One's ability to distinguish between the philosophical specialisms rests mainly on having an appreciation of what set of problems is focal to each. Acquiring such an appreciation involves doing philosophy; there are no short cuts.

Nevertheless, it is possible to give an advance sketch of the kind of topics to be dealt with in a philosphical study. In this chapter I do just that with respect to philosophical logic. I also, and therefore, look at the question in what sense philosophical logic is philosophical, and in what sense logical; and again, at slightly more length, I consider the wider issue this raises concerning the relation between philosophy and logic. I deal with both these issues briefly.

The topics to be discussed are: the proposition, analyticity, necessity, existence, truth, meaning and reference. These, at least, are the topics mentioned in chapter headings. In fact the list is more extensive, for in the course of these chapters there also occur discussions of identity, possible worlds, realisms of related sorts, antirealism, and other issues. It would not have been possible to give an overview of philosophical logic without ranging fairly widely in this way, but it will be clear, I think, that because each topic invites, and indeed commands, whole volumes to itself, the discussions I give do not pretend to be more than prefaces to the detailed treatments to be found in original literature.

These topics are collected under a unifying label in contemporary philosophy to mark their interrelatedness, for properly understanding any of them requires understanding the others. It also marks their central importance in all the main philosophical pursuits, where they appear and create difficulties with great frequency.

A third reason, and probably the most important, is the fact of developments in logic since the turn of the century. These have afforded an access of power in dealing with many problems afresh, not only because we have become technically better equipped for the task, but also because developments in logical machinery have promoted and facilitated a certain methodological style, which has turned out to be extraordinarily fruitful in philosophy. That methodological style is analysis.

The invention of symbolic calculi would not have impelled philosophical developments by itself had it not been for the fact, quickly spotted by Frege and Russell, that they immediately prompt a range of philosophical questions, centrally among them questions concerning the nature of meaning and truth − which is in short to say, language; and language vitally interests philosophers because it provides our route to a philosophical understanding of thought and the world. The greatest single impetus to current preoccupations with philosophical logic comes indeed from interest in language, to understand which we simply have to have decisions in this area.

The role played by 'logic' in 'philosophical logic' could be misleading. Philosophical logic is not *about* logic; neither *is* it logic, in the sense in which logic is the study of formal representations and regimentations of inference. Matters might best be put this way: logicians devise calculi which are strict paraphrases of the forms (not the content) of reasoning. They seek to construct simple but powerful languages in which the forms of inference can be expressed and investigated. They test such languages for completeness and consistency, studying the tools required for the task by looking at arithmetic and set theory, and undertaking a precise exploration of the concepts deployed − such as variable freedom and bondage, axiomatisation, regular substitution in quantification theory, and the like.

There then comes a point − never too far away − when thinking about logic involves having to raise certain philosophical issues. The problem of entailment, the significance of the Löwenheim-Skolem theorem, quantification theory's scope and limits, the relationship between logic and set theory, and the nature of set theory itself; these are issues, among others, which are properly the domain of the philosopher of logic. Philosphy of logic is thus an enterprise in which philosophical questions about the nature and some of the implications of logic constitute the subject matter.

But such questions, in their turn again, rapidly and naturally spill over into, or draw attention to, substantial and important philosophical issues of more general concern. The moment the concern widens in this way, and logic as such is no longer the object of the enquiry, but is bound up with philosophical problems about the nature of language, and thought, and the structure and contents of the world, then the enterprise in hand is philosophical logic. Thus philosophical logic is *philosophy,* philosophy logic-informed and logic-sensitive albeit, but philosophy notwithstanding; and the contrast between philosophical logic and the philosophy of logic can accordingly be put like this: when one does philosophy of logic, one is philosophising about logic; but when one does philosophical logic, one is philosophising.

Some, like Haack, hold that 'philosophy of logic' and 'philosophical logic' mean the same thing, *viz.,* the former.[1] For the reasons just given I do not think this a useful view. There is an informative distinction to be drawn here, which helps one to be clear about what tasks there are to be done under either label. Nevertheless, it would be fruitless to insist on making the distinction too sharp; it is useful, but so also is it useful to bear in mind the rich overlaps and interconnections between the two pursuits.

PHILOSOPHY AND LOGIC

Distinguishing between the philosophy of logic and philosophical logic does nothing to explain what relation subsists between philosophy as such and logic as such. The point is not trivial, for at least one major figure in recent philosophy held that philosophy as such just *is* logic as such, and such a view complicates our understanding of the difference and relation between the two. The philosopher in question is Russell.

Russell took the position, during what is generally regarded as his most important philosophical period (before 1920), that if any philosophical problem is a genuine one, then it reduces upon analysis to a problem of logic as such: 'every philosophical problem, when it is subjected to the necessary analysis and purification, is found either to be not really philosophical at all, or else to be . . . logical'.[2] This is a proposal which looks as though it sets the pattern for much of the philosophy done this century. It is superficially (but only superficially) similar to Wittgenstein's later view, expressed in the *Philosophical Investigations,* to the effect that all philosophical

puzzles need only to be unravelled to be resolved, having arisen in
the first place merely because we have made mistakes in our use of
language.[3]

What prompted Russell to take the view he did is explained by
noting two elements in the development of his earlier thought. The
first is that the governing preoccupation of Russell's beginning work
in philosophy and logic related to mathematics; specifically, to the
attempt to demonstrate that 'all pure mathematics follows from
purely logical premises and uses only concepts definable in logical
terms'.[4] Attempts to reduce mathematics to logic are known as
'logicist' programmes, and the received view now is that, owing to
the work of Gödel in the 1930s, such a programme for mathematics
is unfeasible. Nevertheless, Russell's work had an important philosophical dimension over and above the purely logicist ambition for
mathematics. From the former arose those of Russell's views
expressed in *Our Knowledge of the External World*, and 'The
Philosophy of Logical Atomism'.[5] Russell's celebrated Theory of
Descriptions (cf. Chapter 4) is exemplary both of the nature and the
results of his approach to philosophical problems in the light of
these convictions about methodology.

More specifically – and this is the second element in the
development of his thought – the use of logical analysis seemed to
Russell to sweep away the sources of confusion which in his view
had hitherto bedevilled philosophers, chiefly because, he believed,
they had been misled by the surface forms of language. Russell
made much of the notion that to think there can only be subject-
predicate propositions results in 'bad metaphysics', for the reason
that it seduces philosophers into constructing ontologies of, for
example, the Scholastic sort, in which there are substances and their
attributes, or of the Absolute Idealist sort, in which all propositions,
even relational ones, are to be construed as disguised predications on 'reality taken as a whole'.

Moreover, Russell believed that if there is to be knowledge of
anything more than that with which we are immediately acquainted
in episodes of perception, it has to be inferential. Most of what we
know, in fact, is not 'knowledge by acquaintance' but 'knowledge
by description'. Logic, which is the science of inference, is what
enables us to demonstrate how we have such descriptive
knowledge; for, to show what truths can be known about the world
beyond the immediate deliverances of the senses, we have to be
able to understand the structure of molecular or complex propositions, all of which are truth-functionally compounded out of
atomic or simple propositions by the logical glue of the constants

not, all, if-then, or, and so on. Inference, in fact, depends on molecular propositions; we have to be able to connect propositions together if we are to traverse the limits of mere acquaintance, and the science of connecting propositions is logic. Russell sometimes used the expression 'general knowledge' in place of 'descriptive knowledge', and thus his dictum, 'general knowledge belongs to logic'.

It is clear, and I earlier acknowledged, that developments in logic have provided much help in the handling of traditional philosophical problems, and in revealing the existence of new problems; nevertheless, Russell's view is not wholly convincing, and few would be inclined to agree that philosophical problems are all of them reducible to – or, more strongly, just are, although in woolly and preliminary form – logical problems. To state one obvious and not too question-begging objection, one is inclined to say that it is a great deal clearer that problems in ethics are philosophical problems than that they are reducible to, or covertly just are, disguised logical problems in the sense intended by Russell.

A more subtle, not to say more colourful, characterisation of the relation between logic and philosphy was given by Ryle, and his view provides a useful contrast to Russell's outlook.[6]

Ryle both drew a distinction between logic and philosophy (or, as he put it, between 'formal logic' and 'informal logic'; nothing much turns on the choice of terminology), and specified a relation between them. For Ryle, 'formal logic' consists in the study and manipulation of formal symbolised calculi and their elements, whereas 'informal logic' consists in the quite different enterprise of plotting the 'logical geography' of concepts, an enterprise often if not always conducted – to employ Ryle's picturesque metaphors – in the jungles and on the wild frontiers of thought, where the neat, straight railway tracks of formal logic have not yet reached, or where they cannot reach. In another metaphor Ryle said that formal is to informal logic as geometry is to cartography. In the latter, the irregular features of a landscape or continent have to be plotted to scale, and the success of the enterprise depends upon the cartographer's being able to employ, or be guided by, the idealised regularities of Euclidean plane geometry. In just the same way as the cartographer is the 'client' of the geometer, so the philosopher or 'informal logician' is the client of the formal logician. But the stock-in-trade of the formal logician does not and cannot solve philosophical problems, any more than a greengrocer's owning a pocket calculator can determine for him what price to charge for his lettuces.

Ryle's conception of the differences and relation between formal and informal logic is, on the face of it, a convincing one. If his characterisation of this difference and relation is correct, then an unbridgeable gulf lies between the methods respectively involved, a gulf best characterised by remarking the difference between the method we would employ in solving the problem of, say, free will, and that involved in solving a differential equation. Depending upon one's point of view, that there is a marked difference of method between these two enterprises may seem an unfortunate state of affairs; but if Ryle is right, things are ineluctably so.

What Ryle's views incline one to remember is that more goes on in philosophy than is amenable to the straightforward application of logic, still less to direct translation into logic. The point is well made by Passmore: philosophy is not solely concerned with proving something or disproving it 'at every step', as, for example McTaggart thought;[7] but consists just as often in attempts to classify, define, analyse, disambiguate, and assemble reminders, concerning concepts and the expressions by which we communicate and discuss them. Much philosophical work, far from exclusively consisting in strings of deductive transitions like those Spinoza set out to formulate *more geometrico* in his *Ethics,* are more like catalogues, collections, or display-cabinets, where notions are sorted and their connections shewn, in an effort to get us to grasp how our conceptual scheme works. Wittgenstein's *Philosophical Investigations* is a classic of this genre, and so is Alexander's *Space, Time, and Deity.* (Alexander indeed claimed to have an aversion to argument, and described his method as wholly descriptive.[8])

Taken too far, these thoughts can distort the picture; they make philosophy seem to like a retired gentleman's preoccupation with his butterfly collection. In fact the drive to precision and rigour in philosophy is paramount, and if proof is not at issue at *every* step, then it is so at every second step. Indeed, none of the above says that logic has no place in activities of thought outside proof. The rules of consistency and demonstration apply as demandingly to the processes of disambiguating and classifying as they do to straight argument. What these comments about philosophical method say is that philosophy does not *exclusively* consist in searching out formal relationships between elements of an argument; but that, in addition, it involves properly and exhaustively grasping the contents of the argument, where much explication or analysing may need to be done long before it is clear what relationship of logic obtains between the argument's parts.

It is interesting, by way of aside, to note that one of the motivations for the briefly flourishing school of 'ordinary language philosophy' in the decade or so after 1945 was a rejection of the *over-logical* approach to philosophy adopted before the war. Formal efforts in philosophy, like Carnap's *Der Logische Aufbau Der Welt* (*The Logical Structure of the World*),[9] and the work of Goodman and Lesniewski and his followers,[10] had been prosecuted with some vigour chiefly before the Second World War, and the impulse to their kind of programme remains in the work of Quine, with his view, characteristic of his programmatic preferences, that there is a lot to be gained in the direction of clarity and rigour by making a 'canonical ascent' over the vaguaries of common parlance.[11]

A characterisation of contemporary philosophical method would reflect a certain balance between these poles. However, philosophy is governed at every step by the need for precision, clarity and consistency; and even although most would agree with Kripke's dictum to the effect that 'there is no mathematical substitute for philosophy',[12] logic is, consequently, of the greatest importance to philosophy.

Consider how direct applications of logical analysis can be fruitful in philosophical enquiry. When arguments are at issue, one can, by the clean expedient of inspecting their logical credentials, determine their formal validity or otherwise; and in those cases where the form is evidently invalid, one has settled that the conclusion is unacceptable — a major gain. Note, for example, the simple logical insight underlying the main tenet of Popper's views in the philosophy of science.[13] Popper noted that a traditionally received view of the structure of scientific reasoning involves a logical fallacy — specifically, the fallacy of affirming the consequent. Suppose I say: I hypothesise that molecules in a gas move randomly. If this is right, then I should be able to observe motes of smoke in a glass phial being randomly displaced by the molecules constituting the gas in the phial. I conduct the experiment; indeed note that the smoke motes are randomly displaced; and conclude that my hypothesis is established. The logical form of this piece of reasoning is:

$$p \rightarrow q$$
$$q$$
$$\overline{}$$
$$\therefore p$$

Here p stands for: 'molecules in a gas move randomly', and q stands for: 'it is observable that motes of smoke in a glass phial are randomly displaced'.

Now, a different pair of stubstituends will demonstrate the invalidity of this reasoning. Let p stand for: 'it is raining' and q stand for: 'the streets are wet'. Then on this form of argument we get: 'If it is raining, the streets are wet; the streets *are* wet; therefore it is raining', which is a *non sequitur*. Accordingly, Popper argued that no scientific hypothesis can ever be proved; at best such hypotheses can be corroborated by the failure of the most rigorous efforts to falsify them. From the point of view of attaining to conclusiveness in science, outright refutations alone are possible. Conclusive refutations are possible along the lines of the above fallacy's valid cousin, *modus tollens*:

$$p \rightarrow q$$
$$- q$$
$$\overline{}$$
$$\therefore - p$$

If the experimental results turn out otherwise (*viz.* that q), the most this means is that the hypothesis has received some support; it is still liable to overthrow in the light of new evidence.

In at least this respect, then, formal procedures can be utilised in philosophy to effect. There are plenty of other cases. Even if Ryle would allow this, on the grounds that this constitutes a case (to use yet another of his metaphors) of parade-ground discipline helping to hold the line on the battlefield, then we can point to other kinds of applications in which logic is philosophically informative. Consider the point made by Russell; to some philosophers in the past, owing to their having underdeveloped or impoverished logical resources, it seemed self-evident that the proposition has one basic form, from which substantial metaphysical consequences appeared to them to flow. Russell was somewhat ungenerous in his assessment of the logical skills of the medievals, among others, but the point has force. It points to a wider use of logical techniques in philosophy: formalisations can show how sections of language could, or even do, work in the light of some formal description; and postulating certain structures for our conceptual scheme, even idealised ones, can clarify it. Yet again, we learn about our thought and language by looking at how certain entrenched doctrines of logic arise from them. These are all issues of profound philosophical importance, and logic is a crucial element in the work done upon them.

In viewing the question of the relation between philosophy and logic, then, a balance is required. On the whole Ryle's view invites agreement, so long as one adds the riders implicit in the remarks above concerning the enormous utility of logical techniques and applications in philosophical research. It would of course be more than merely pleasant if Leibniz's dream of a universal calculus[14] – by the mechanical application of which we could solve philosophical problems – were true; but so much is a pipe-dream. Yet saying this does not belittle the importance of logic to philosophy. In much the same way as Ryle's cartographer would be nigh helpless without geometry, so the insights and the rigour which logic furnishes to philosophy are indispensable to it. How this works, particularly in connection with the chief concerns of philosophical logic, will become more apparent as the sequel unfolds.

CONTENTS OF THIS BOOK

The layout of the rest of this book is as follows. In chapter 2 I consider the question whether there are propositions, and, if so, what they are. It is important to have a clear idea of the distinction between sentences and propositions, and in the course of discussing this distinction I am able to introduce and explain several concepts which are fundamental to philosophical logic. These are: sense and reference; referential opacity; the principle of intersubstitutivity *salva veritate,* which is defining of extensional contexts; and nominalism and realism concerning abstract entities. There is nothing especially alarming about these concepts despite their long names, and I introduce them with a proper nonchalance, because they will recur frequently during the following chapters, and familiarity with them will ultimately breed comprehension.

In chapter 3 I consider a set of three extremely important distinctions which serve to classify a) truths, b) the propositions in which truths are expressed, and c) the ways we can come to know truths. These distinctions are respectively a') the necessary-contingent distinction, b') the analytic-synthetic distinction, and c') the *a priori-a posteriori* distinction. In the course of discussing a') I shall take a long and interesting detour through the issues of possible worlds and essentialism, which lie at the heart of much recent philosophical work.

Questions of existence concern me in chapter 4. I look at the two related matters of a) our talk about existence and b) the existential presuppositions of the way we talk. Quine's views on ontological commitment and Russell's Theory of Descriptions, together with Strawson's and Donnellan's responses, figure here.

In two chapters – chapters 5 and 6 – I discuss the main theories of truth. Chapter 5 contains discussions of the Pragmatic and Coherence theories of truth, and I try to do them more justice than is customary in recent philosophical literature, partly because they are important theories in their own right, and partly because they are enjoying, or are about to enjoy, renewed interest as a result of recent new work in the philosophy of language. Thus the Pragmatic theory has features which are interesting to anyone persuaded by Dummett's antirealism (see chapters 8 and 9), and the Coherence theory has features which are interesting to those attracted by, for example, Davidson's holistic truth-theoretic view of language (again, see chapter 8 and 9).

Chapter 6 continues the discussion of truth, and consists in examinations of the Correspondence, Redundancy, and Semantic theories. This last, which owes itself to Tarski, is very influential in contemporary philosophy, and after explaining it I discuss some of its wider philosophical consequences. Some technicalities are involved in understanding Tarski, but I go over that part of the ground twice, the first time informally and the second time technically.

The question of meaning now moves to centre-stage, having obtruded itself persistently throughout earlier chapters. In chapter 7, partly as a preparation for chapters 8 and 9, and partly because of their intrinsic importance and interest, I provide sketches of some 'traditional' theories of meaning, together with certain contemporary extensions of them. Among other things, the discussion touches upon Positivist verificationism, Wittgenstein's 'use' theory, Quine's behavioural theory, and the 'causal theory of reference' originated by Kripke and Putnam.

In chapter 8 I discuss truth-conditional theories of meaning, particularly Davidson's theory, and Dummett's antirealist criticism of the crucial idea that truth can explain meaning. This issue is extraordinarily important in modern philosophy, and repays close study. I have sought especially to make Dummett's thought accessible.

The consequences for metaphysics and epistemology of the views discussed in chapter 8 are so important that, in chapter 9, I explore some of them, and suggest lines of thought which might have to be followed if one makes certain choices in the theory of meaning. In this chapter I doff the impartiality which I try to preserve throughout chapters 2–8, and give brief expression to some of my own preferences.

This book discusses *issues*. However, it is possible to use the discussions provided here to get a picture of a particular *philosopher's* overall view, by consulting the index and looking at what he or she says about the various topics canvassed here. If, for example, one collects all the discussions throughout the book of the views of, say, Quine, or Strawson, or Russell, and reads them together, one will get a fair picture of that individual's philosophical outlook. This is a function of the enormous contribution to twentieth-century philosophy made by these and the other thinkers whose names occur in any two or more of the chapters in this book.

NOTES

1 Haack, S., *Philosophy of Logics,* Cambridge, 1978, p.2.
2 Russell, B., *Our Knowledge of the External World,* London, 1914, p.42. (pp.42-69 are reprinted in Copi, I. M. and Gould, J. A., *Readings on Logic,* New York, 1964, under the title 'Logic as the Essence of Philosophy'.)
3 Wittgenstein, L., *Philosophical Investigations* (trans. Anscombe, G. E. M, Oxford, 1958). cf. §§ 123, 133, 255, 309.
4 Russell, B., *My Philosophical Development,* London, 1959, p.74.
5 Russell, B., 'The Philosophy of Logical Atomism', in Marsh, R. C. (ed.), *Logica and Knowledge,* London, 1956, *passim.*
6 Ryle, G., 'Formal and Informal Logic', in *Dilemmas,* Cambridge, 1960, *passim;* reprinted in Copi and Gould, *op. cit.*
7 Passmore, J., *Philosophical Reasoning,* London, 1961, p.7.
8 cf., *ibid*
9 Carnap, R. *The Logical Structure of the World,* Los Angeles, 1961.
10 cf. Kung's review and bibliography in Kung, G., *Ontology and the Logistic Analysis of Language,* Reidel, rev. ed.1967.
11 Quine, W. V., *Word and Object,* MIT, 1960, esp. ch.5 *passim*; pp.157 *et seq.*
12 Kripke, S., 'Is There A Problem About Substitutional Quantification?; in Evans, G. and McDowell, J. *Truth and Meaning,* Oxford, 1976.p.416.
13 Popper, K., *The Logic of Scientific Discovery,* London 1972 (3rd. Ed.)
14 cf. e.g., Leibniz, G. 'Of Universal Synthesis and Analysis', in *Leibniz: Philosophical Writings,* (trans. and ed. Parkinson, G. H. A.), London, 1973, p.10.

2 The Proposition

INTRODUCTION

Truth is an important topic in philosophy, especially in contemporary philosophy. The complexities which surround the notion of truth are numerous and vexing, not least because, at the very outset of discussion on the matter, there is no consensus among philosophers as to what sorts of thing are truth-bearers. Traditionally, the entity which is said to be capable of truth-value is the proposition, which philosophers have distinguished from sentences in various ways and for various reasons. But propositions are controversial items, and the business of settling on a theory of the proposition – or even, indeed, on a theory which dispenses with them altogether – involves one in having to make decisions about a number of important issues in metaphysics and elsewhere first. In this chapter, the questions to be discussed are: what are propositions? Do we need to employ the concept of the proposition in philosophy, or can we dispense with it?

SENTENCES AND WHAT THEY SAY

In order to be clear about the nature of propositions, one has first to be clear about sentences. A sentence is a word or set of words in some language. The language in question may be a natural language like English or Swahili, or an artificial language like logic. In intuitive senses of 'grammatical' and 'meaningful', it can be said that sentences have to be grammatically well-formed, but do not have to be meaningful, to be sentences; one can quite well talk of 'nonsense sentences' without paradox. Examples of such sentences would be Carroll's 'Twas brillig, and the slithy toves/Did gyre and gimble in the wabe', or the sentence beloved of grammarians, 'Green ideas sleep furiously'.

Moreover, a sentence may have different meanings: 'I gave a hand' may mean that I helped someone, or literally donated a human or ape-hand (to some museum), or that my opponent in an equestrian competition had a horse taller by one hand than my own.

Again, the same sentence may be used in a variety of ways: 'You hold the reins' may be a statement of fact, or a command. In some cases, according to Austin's view of performative utterances, a particular use of a sentence may constitute an action, for example when one says 'I do thee wed' or 'I promise'.[1] It has been argued that utterance of the sentence 'It hurts' constitutes a sophisticated piece of behaviour replacing wincing and groaning; this is a view taken by Wittgenstein.[2]

In general, philosophers have been concerned with declarative sentences, those which are used to make assertions; it is this class of sentences which are said to *express propositions,* to state that some predicate holds of some subject or that certain items are related in a certain way.[3]

The distinction between propositions and declarative sentences is drawn by philosophers for a variety of reasons.[4] First, sentences may be, as noted, meaningless or nonsensical, and so express nothing. Secondly, the same sentence can be used by different people, or by the same person on different occasions, to state what is true on certain of those occasions but false on others. Thus 'I have a headache' is true or false depending upon who utters it, or true for a given person at one time, but false for the same person at another time.[5] Thirdly, something is common to the sentences 'It's raining', 'Il pleut', and 'Es regnet'; a way of characterising their common content is required. It is this common content which is said to be the proposition.

Propositions, then, and not sentences, are either true or false, and only 'significant' or 'meaningful' sentences can express propositions. By appeal to talk of propositions the problems of n-way ambiguity and nonsense are avoided. Propositions are what get asserted by the utterance of sentences; and it is propositions which enter into logical relations with each other — sentences do not entail one another, or contradict one another; it is what is proposed by a particular declarative use of a sentence which entails or contradicts some other particular declarative proposal. Moreover, propositions, *qua* the 'what is said' by assertions of sentences, can be usefully regarded as the content, or object, of the so-called 'propositional attitudes', like believing, wishing, hoping, judging — that is (where p is any proposition) as the object of the propositional attitudes 'I believe that p', 'I wish that p', and so on.

So much for some of the general reasons there are for distinguishing propositions from sentences. I shall shortly canvass in more detail other and more fundamental reasons motivating adoption of talk about propositions; which it is important to do, for on the basis of this sketch a problem can be seen to present itself. The problem concerns the ontological status of propositions.

A long-standing metaphysical dispute lurks behind this issue. Throughout most of the history of philosophy, and particularly since medieval times, there have been two schools of thought about abstract entities, proponents of which have been respectively called 'realists' and 'nominalists'. Broadly speaking, realism in this context is the view that abstract entities, like propositions, numbers and universals, *really* exist, just as do tables and trees. Plato's doctrine of Forms constitutes the earliest systematic theory of realism. In Plato's view, Forms in the 'realm of being' exist much more fully and really than do tables and trees, which are merely imperfect and ephemeral instances (or copies) of their Forms.[6] Nominalists, on the other hand, take the view that abstract entities exist in name only, that is *nominally*; so that they do not exist in at all the same sense as do tables and trees, but merely as concepts attaching to a name. The nominalist tendency is to reduce abstract entities, to get rid of them by analysis; and it is precisely nominalist scepticism over abstract entities which lends force to the debate about propositions, giving rise to the questions: Do propositions exist? If they do, what are they? How does one individuate them? If there are no satisfactory answers to these questions, what is the best way to dispense with talk of them?

It naturally runs closer to common-sensical notions of the world to dispute the existence of occult entities like propositions, and to say there is nothing over and above the actual sentences we utter or write down which is somehow the 'content' or the 'what is said' of them, than to say that there are propositions. But as I shall now endeavour to show, the motives there are for entertaining realism about propositions, or, more weakly, retaining appeal to them under a suitable account, are compelling if arguable ones; and, as a further complication, it is somewhat difficult to see how the notion can be dispensed with in practice, because alternatives more to a nominalist taste are equally, if differently, problematic. Accordingly it is worth seeing whether, despite nominalist qualms about propositions, one is obliged, or even just best advised, to make use of them. I revert to the realism-nominalism issue shortly.

In setting out the more fundamental reasons there might be for commitment to propositions, it will be useful to follow a suggestion made by Ryle, to the effect that the motives for such commitment arise from two connected assumptions in the thought of philosophers with broadly realist sympathies. The first of these is a view concerning the intentionality or directedness of consciousness; the second is the denotative theory of meaning.[7]

THE INTENTIONALITY OF CONSCIOUSNESS

The idea that consciousness is intentional is the idea that all acts of consciousness are directed towards an object. Thus, whenever I think, I think about something; when I hope, wish, believe, wonder, fear, then I hope that something, wish that something, and so on. This directedness of my acts of consciousness is the 'intentional relation' obtaining between these acts and the objects they 'intend' (are directed towards). The objects of my intendings are often called the 'accusatives' or 'intentions' of these acts. Such verbs as 'think', 'hope', 'wish', 'believe', 'judge', 'guess', 'consider' are called propositional verbs, and the mental activities they signify are called propositional attitudes or acts.

Propositional attitudes consist in a two-place relation between a mind, on the one hand, and on the other a complex entity named by the 'that' clause in such sentences as 'I believe that he has arrived', which constitutes the intention of the mind's propositional act.

That propositional attitudes, and their intentions, or objects, appear to be distinct from one another may be seen from the fact that what can be said of one, namely the acts, cannot always be said of the other, namely the intentions or objects of those acts. For example, my propositional act of believing that the Norman Conquest took place in the eleventh century AD, is something which occurs in the twentieth century AD, whereas what it is I believe, namely that the Norman Conquest took place when it did, has nothing to do with my act of believing anything whatever about it.

What it is I believe or hope when I believe that something or hope that something, is – a proposition; *viz.*, the proposition expressed by the sentence embedded in the 'that' clause of the whole. There is something of a circle here; the fact that propositions consistute the intentions of propositional acts is something already contained in the idea of a *propositional* act or attitude itself. Nevertheless, the circle is informative, for the reason why propositions have to be invoked as the objects of intentional acts becomes manifest upon examination of the details relating to the independence from such acts of their intentions, as follows.

Suppose that you and I concur in believing that the Norman Conquest took place in 1066 AD. Then we both believe the same thing; we have the same belief. It is logically impossible that you and I should have numerically the same (act of) belief in this respect, for your believings are yours, and mine are mine. What is the same is *what* we believe, not the act of belief; and what we believe is the proposition that, the Norman Conquest took place in 1066 AD'. Therefore propositions must be independent of any acts of consciousness intending them.

Moreover, since I can believe 'that the Norman Conquest took place in 1066 AD' at different times of my life, that proposition must be temporally neutral with respect to my temporally several and various propositional attitudes towards it. So, indeed, does the consideration that I might have different propositional attitudes to the same proposition at different times; as when at one period of my life I believe in the existence of Santa Claus, and at another disbelieve in it. Here I am taking different propositional attitudes, at different times, to the same objective proposition 'that Santa Claus exists'. The same holds for cases where you and I disagree over the questions of Santa Claus' existence: we take different attitudes to the same proposition, therefore the proposition is independent of our attitudes towards it.

Another, related, argument to the objectivity and independence of propositions derives from the timeless nature of many truths and falsehoods. That $5+7=12$, that lambda particle decay produces a proton and a pion, and that a war ended in 1918, are truths which do not become true when I start thinking about them, and cease to be true when I stop thinking about them. They are eternally true, if true; I personally do not create them merely by assuming a propositional attitude towards them. My believing that George Eliot wrote *Middlemarch* is a feature of my own intellectual history, and so is a datable episode or series of episodes in that history; whereas George Eliot's authorship of *Middlemarch* is not part of my or anyone else's intellectual history (except, perhaps, her own), but is independent of anyone's having any propositional attitude towards the issue. Once again, the conclusion is that propositions are independent of the acts of consciousness intending them.

Propositions as the intentions of propositional attitudes must be distinguished from 'images' and 'facts'. What it is I believe when I believe that the Norman Conquest took place in 1066 AD is not a picture in my mind. Nor is it a 'fact', for however one understands the notion of facts, at very least they must be what is the case, and unfortunately it often happens that the intentions of those propositional attitudes which are described as 'wishful thinking', 'false hopes' and so on, are not anywhere near being what is the case. But even wishful thinking and vain hopes are wishes that p, hopes that p; and in each case p is a proposition. Accordingly, propositions are not to be identified with facts. Facts, however, may be true propositions; or perhaps they are those states of affairs which true propositions somehow signify, 'name', or describe. This is a matter of ontology.

PROPOSITIONS AS INTENTIONS CRITICISED

It will be evident to anyone who has read some philosophy of mind that the intentionality thesis invites objections on more grounds than just that it hypostasises the objects of mental acts. I shall however restrict comment to this issue alone.

A distinction can be drawn between the propositional verbs listed earlier – 'believe', 'judge', 'hope' and the rest – and another class of verbs, often called 'cognitive' verbs, namely 'know', 'see', 'smell', 'taste', 'feel' and 'hear'. These share an important feature with propositional verbs, in that both classes of verbs demand a grammatical accusative. In just the same way as a cognitive verb like 'see' demands an accusative, as in 'I see x', so does a propositional verb like 'hope', as in 'I hope that p'. But this shared feature at the level of grammar is philosophically misleading, for whereas something in reality must answer to the grammatical accusative of a cognitive verb, the same does not hold true of propositional verbs. This can be verified readily enough by a comparison of the following:

(1) Tom tastes the sweet, but there is no sweet there.

(2) Tom hopes that Santa Claus exists, but Santa Claus does not exist.

Leaving aside cases of hallucinatory experiences, in which case it would be more appropriate to recast the cognitive verb case (1) into a 'believes that' idiom, it is evident that one is involved in contradiction if one seriously asserts (1); that is, one would be meddling with the sense of the language if one said that Tom tasted, felt, or saw something which was not there to be tasted, seen or felt, unless one specifically had it in mind to report a case of hallucination. By contrast, no contradiction attaches itself to (2) Tom's hoping something which is false, non-existent, or impossible. The contrast most forcefully displays itself when the cognitive verb 'knows' is set alongside the propositional verb 'believes'. A's knowing that p entails that p is the case; but if A believes that p, nothing follows as to whether p is or is not the case, and A's believing that p is quite consistent with p's not being the case. Other contrasts work just as well: leaving aside hallucinatory cases again, if A sees x then there must be an x, whereas if A fears x, it is open whether there is x or not, and, as psychiatrists know only too well, A's fearing x is quite consistent with either or both of the physical and logical impossibilities of x.

The difference between propositional and cognitive verbs can be made out more clearly still if one considers cases of mistake. Suppose (the cognitive verb case) I say 'I see a dog', and then on closer inspection discover that it was a fox. Here I am bound to retract my claim to have seen a dog, by saying something like 'I thought I saw a dog, but what in fact I saw was a fox'. But (the propositional verb case) if I judge or believe that it is a dog, and then discover that it is a fox, I cannot retract my claim to have judged or believed that it was a dog. I cannot say: 'I only thought I judged it was a dog'. To put it another way: my cognitive attitudes are defeasible − that is, they may be mistaken, and if so can be withdrawn subsequently; but my propositional attitudes are not defeasible, and I cannot withdraw the fact that I judged or believed what it was that I judged or believed, or the fact that I did so.

Upholders of the claim that propositions are the objects of mental acts might therefore be seen as having committed themselves to the thesis on the misleading grounds of their noting a feature shared by cognitive and propositional verbs, namely the demand for an accusative which both of them make. Because cognitive verbs require that something in fact answer to their accusatives, realist philosophers took it that the accusatives of propositional verbs must behave likewise. This is not the case. One moral of the story is that grammatical considerations are no sure guide to ontological ones, a Russellian point indeed.

However, it is worth noting that the most this criticism does is to throw doubt on the idea, implicit in the construal which the intentionality thesis demands for propositions, that propositions are objective entities having a real (in the realist sense of real) existence independently of the sentences which express them and the propositional attitudes which intend them. This criticism shows that it is a mistake to say that when I hope or believe something, there is something − namely, a proposition − which I hope or believe, and that *therefore,* on analogy with the things which exist if I truly say I see or feel them, propositions exist.

This is by no means the only criticism which can be levelled at the intentionality construal of propositions. If the suspect philosophical psychology underlying the thesis is rejected, it follows that the thesis ceases to be an argument for using the notion of the proposition. More to the present point, the thesis is unintuitive, for it leaves it open that there are myriads of as yet unentertained or unintended propositions waiting to be discovered – indeed, every problem invited by the notion of an abstract entity is invited by this view of propositions, and the thesis itself does nothing to provide an account of their nature which secures them from those difficulties.

Some of the more fundamental difficulties raised by abstract object talk also underlie criticisms of the second motive to be discussed. I shall come to them in due course, turning first to the motive in questions.

PROPOSITIONS AS MEANINGS

An initially attractive and plausible idea about meaning is that the meaning of a word is the object it denotes. This theory is known as the denotative or referential theory. I shall have cause to mention it more than once in later chapters, and so shall be brief here. The theory constitutes the second motive for invoking propositions, for just as it has it that the meaning of a word is the object denoted by it, so the meaning of a sentence is the proposition it expresses. This looks to be a very useful view, for it permits ready characterisation of certain semantical features of language. Consider, for example, synonymity. The theory has it that a relation of synonymity obtains between two sentences when they both express the same proposition. Thus, suppose Jane has a husband, one brother, and no other siblings. If Jane says 'my husband is having a migraine attack' and her brother says 'my brother-in-law has a severe prolonged headache', then they are saying the same thing; which is to say, the sentences are synonymous because they both express the same proposition.[8]

Earlier I stated some of the general reasons why sentences and propositions have been distinguished from one another, which reasons render unattractive any simple identification of propositions with sentence tokens.[9] A further important reason is this. Many of the things which can be predicated of sentences cannot be predicated of propositions, for a sentence is an uttered or inscribed string of words having particular spatial and temporal properties – as, for example, being said in Oxford or printed in a Boston newspaper; taking so many seconds to say, or being so many centimetres long; being high-pitched or low-pitched; consisting of ink marks or chalk marks; and so on. It is the very point of saying that propositions are abstract that they are none of these things; they are non-physical and atemporal. Moreover, their objectivity is demanded by the fact that they must be available to more than one user of the language, and so cannot be dependent for their existence on this or that particular utterer. They are thus both abstract and objective, precisely what nominalists least like about them.

Regarding propositions as the meanings of sentences provides a forceful way of illustrating their abstractness and objectivity, particularly if one considers cases of translation of belief sentences. When I render the sentence (a) 'I believe he is here' into German, I translate it as 'Ich glaube er ist hier'. Now, if I take it that the object of my belief is the sentence 'he is here', then I am in effect saying (b) 'I believe the sentence "he is here",' which would have to be translated 'Ich glaube den Satz "he is here".' But of course we do not do this; even if we talked naturally, and we do not, of 'believing sentences', we should translate (b) into 'Ich glaube den Satz "er ist hier".' This gives the game away; it is not the sentence which is the object of my belief, but what the sentence means, that is, the proposition.[10]

This example is drawn from Church. In arguing like this for abstract propositions as the meanings of sentences, Church was defending the views of Frege, who painstakingly distinguished between (a) a written or uttered sentence, (b) the accompanying mental idea or ideas, and (c) the proposition (or 'thought', *Gedanke*) expressed by the sentence.[11] Whereas (b) is wholly subjective to the hearer, reader, utterer, or inscriber of the sentence, (c) is an objective abstract entity enjoying the same Platonic reality as numbers, classes, and Plato's own Forms. For Frege, propositions inhabit a 'Third Realm' with other abstract objects; the 'Third Realm' is atemporal, non-physical, and non-mental. To understand a sentence is to grasp the proposition it expresses; propositions are truth-bearers, and sentences have truth-value only in the derivative sense that they are true or false according as to the truth or falsity of the propositions they express.[12]

SENSE, REFERENCE, AND OPACITY

Fleshing out an account of Frege's view requires a technical detour. In connection with his views on the proposition, Frege drew a distinction which has come to enjoy considerable subsequent importance in philosophy: the distinction between sense and reference.[13] Here one needs to introduce and explain three pairs of terms: 'sense'-'reference', 'connotation'-'denotation', and 'intension'-'extension'. As these terms are standardly employed, 'sense', 'connotation' and 'intension' form a related family on one hand,

and their respective pairings 'reference', 'denotation' and 'extension' form a related family on the other hand.[14] Roughly speaking, the first family of terms has to do with the 'meaning' of a term, and the second has to do with the range of items to which a term applies.

The standard characterisation of these distinctions is given in terms of the intension-extension pair, thus: The extension of the term, say, 'prime number' is the class of all prime numbers. What qualifies a number for membership of this class is its being a *prime* number; so the intension of the term 'prime number' is that property, primeness, in virtue of possessing which a number is a member of the class. Or consider the expression 'green plant'. The extension of the expression is the class of all green plants there are, that is, all the plants in the world which are green. The intension of the expression is the set of properties, being a plant and being green, possession of which makes an item a member of the class.

The sense-reference distinction is allied to this. The classic example used is the planet Venus, which the Greeks thought was not one planet but two stars, namely the evening star Hesperus and the morning star Phosphorus. Because the evening and morning stars are the same entity, it is evident that both expressions denote the same entity, *viz.*, Venus. But clearly the expressions 'morning star' and 'evening star' differ in *sense* despite having the same reference, which follows from the fact that if one says 'the morning star is identical with the morning star', the truth of what one says is a simple matter of logic and can be determined by inspecting the sentence itself; but if one says 'the morning star is identical with the evening star', the truth of what one says is a matter of astronomy, not logic. No one could discover that the morning and evening stars are in fact one and the same entity merely by inspecting the expressions 'the morning star' and 'the evening star' alone. It follows that although these two expressions are coreferential, which is to say, refer to the same thing, they differ in sense.

It is noteworthy in passing that words or expressions which have the same meaning, that is are synonymous, are called 'intensionally equivalent'; and likewise, words or expressions which have the same reference or extension are called 'extensionally equivalent'. The foregoing remarks show that words or expressions may be extensionally equivalent without being intensionally equivalent; but if two terms are intensionally equivalent, then they are extensionally equivalent as well.

Frege applied his sense-reference distinction in the following way. For Frege the sense of a sentence is the proposition it expresses; but he held that sentences have references too, and this is the complicated part of his view. The reference or denotation of the name 'Joe Bloggs' is, unproblematically, the individual – Joe Bloggs – who goes by and answers to that name. In a general intuitive way there seems to be no difficulty about names having references; but the notion of the reference of a sentence is less clear. Frege's view was that the references of sentences are *truth-values*. All true sentences have the same reference, namely The True; and all false sentences, similarly, have as their references The False.

This odd-looking doctrine – odd especially because 'The True' and 'The False' constitute difficult objects to believe in – was motivated by Frege's desire to treat sentences as complex species of names. The motive underlying this motive, in turn, was his wish to preserve the notion, first articulated by Leibniz, of the intersubstitutivity of coreferential terms *salva veritate* – by which is meant that if two terms A and B have the same reference, then term A can be substituted for term B in any sentence in which B occurs, without changing the truth-value of the sentence. (*Salva veritate* means 'saving the truth', that is, 'preserving the truth-value'.) Thus in the sentence 'Hesperus is the plant Venus' one can substitute, *salva veritate,* the term 'Phosphorus' for 'Hesperus' because they are coreferential terms. Frege was concerned to develop an extensional logic – and it is defining of extensional contexts that Leibniz's Law holds, that is, that intersubstitution of coreferential terms occurs *salva veritate*. Accordingly, just as with names, atomic coreferring sentences (coreferring in the sense of having the same truth-value) can be substituted for one another in molecular sentences truth-functionally compounded out of them, without change in the molecular sentences' truth-values, even when the substituted atomic sentence differs in sense from the atomic sentence it replaces.

However, in the case of sentences in which an embedded 'that' clause follows a propositional verb, as in 'Ptolemy believed that the earth was flat' or 'Philip is unaware that Tully is Cicero', the context is nonextensional, for the reason that the truth-value of the whole sentence is not a function of the sentence in the subordinate clause. Frege dealt with problem sentences of this kind by saying that the reference of the embedded sentence following 'that' is the proposition it expresses; which is to say, its reference is what its sense would be if it appeared in an extensional context. Because a sentence has a reference only if it has a sense, Frege made the move of identifying the sense of sentences used nonextensionally with the sense of the words 'the proposition that. . .'. Church's view, to the effect that the reference of nonextensionally occurring sentences is its meaning or sense, is Fregean in just this way.

These manoeuvres are perplexing, and Quine has discussed the difficulties which arise in nonextensional contexts, in particular where reference is 'opaque', with important results, as follows.[15]

Intersubstitutivity does not always occur *salva veritate*, and such failure is characteristic of intensional contexts. Consider the statements (using Quine's original numbering):

(3) Cicero = Tully
(4) 'Cicero' contains six letters.

If 'Tully' is substituted for 'Cicero' in (4), the resulting statement is false, because (4) does not contain a referential use of 'Cicero' but merely mentions that name.[16] Now evidently the principle of intersubstitutivity must not be used in contexts such as this, where the name one might misguidedly wish to replace occurs without referring straightforwardly to the object; which happens not only when the name is mentioned, as above, but whenever it occurs in a non-referential, or non-directly referential, context. Consider

(9)   Philip is unaware that Tully denounced Catiline.
(11) Philip is unaware that Cicero denounced Catiline.

If (9) is true, then, substituting on the basis of (3), one gets (11), but, granting that Philip both knows that Cicero denounced Catiline yet does not know that Tully is Cicero, (11) will be false although (9) and (3) are true.[17] It follows that 'a name may occur referentially in a statement S and yet not occur referentially in a longer statement which is formed by embedding S in the context "is unaware that. . . ." or "believes that. . . ." To sum up the situation in a word, we may speak of (such) contexts . . . as *referentially opaque*'.[18] It is then the case, on Quine's view, that one cannot quantify into referentially opaque contexts unless the values of the variables bound by quantification are intensional objects – which in Frege's cases would be the senses of names. For the further reason (to be canvassed in more detail and in a wider connection later in this chapter and the next chapter) that individuating intensional entities rests upon a notion of analyticity, which Quine rejects outright, he concludes that the Fregean model will not do.

PROPOSITIONS AS MEANINGS CRITICISED FURTHER

A more general criticism of the wisdom of identifying propositions with meanings of sentences is that to say this is to explain the obscure, *viz.*, propositions, by something equally obscure, *viz.*, meanings. The question of meaning is taken up in more detail in later chapters (chapters 7 and 8), so it will suffice at this juncture to put the matter in general and preliminary terms.

What is a 'meaning'? Consider the simpler cases of the putative meanings of names, which on the denotative theory are the objects they denote. In an intuitive sense, one understands very well what it is for the name 'Tom' to pick out some individual person who goes by and answers to that name; but it is by no means clear, other than intuitively, what the denoting relation is or how it works. Consider the simplest case of establishing a denotative word-world link – the ostensive (pointing with a finger) definition of a term like 'table'. Suppose I am teaching a foreign friend English, a language of which he is wholly ignorant; and suppose I point to a table and utter the word 'table'. What settles it for him that I intend him to understand the object taken as whole? Why should he not take me as pointing out to him the colour, or the texture, or the stuff of which the object is made? Imagine my pointing at the table-top and saying 'glossy'. Why should he not understand me as naming the object as a whole, rather than the style of its finish? At what is apparently the simplest level of demonstratively linking a name with the object it is supposed to 'mean', then, there are puzzling difficulties.

The more complex matter of sentence meaning presents added difficulties. Suppose one leaves aside the idea, for the present, that sentences are complex names which denote 'states of affairs' or 'facts' or 'possible facts', and holds to the idea of propositions as 'contents' of sentences. Once again, there is a clear intuitive sense in which one knows what is meant by sentence meaning. Suppose A shows B the sentence

(1) Νοῦς ὁρᾷ καὶ νοῦς ακούει᾿ τ᾿αλλα κωφὰ καὶ τυφλά.

and B asks him what it means; to which A replies that it means

(2) Mens videt, mens audit, cetera surda et coeca,

(which, incidentally, it does mean). If B's linguistic resources also fall short of Latin, he would still not know what is meant. If A then tells him that (1) and (2) mean

(3) The mind sees, the mind hears, all else is deaf and blind,

then B could at last be described as having grasped the meaning which all of (1)-(3) express, and to which, owing to mere nuisance of linguistic limitations, he could only gain access by means of (3). *What* it is he grasps is what all of (1)-(3) express in common with one another – namely, the proposition that 'the mind sees and hears and all else is deaf and blind.'

But has anything informative been said by substituting talk of the proposition which (1)-(3) express for talk of the meaning which (1)-(3) express, or *vice versa*? All that one can infer from the example is that meanings and propositions are somethings which attach to different sentence-tokens and, whether or not they are language-dependent in some sense left open, are none the less not dependent on *particular* languages.

In fact the problem sets in earlier, for it is not clear what is meant by 'expresses' in 'the proposition which the sentence expresses', or 'the meaning which the sentence expresses', for it is to go in a circle to explain 'expresses' by saying 'the proposition which the sentence expresses is that sentence's meaning', or 'the proposition is the "what-is-said" expressed by the sentence', or even '. . . is the "content" of the sentence'; for now we are back with heuristic of the sort appealed to at the beginning of the discussion, when an intuitive grasp of the notion of propositions was being sought.

This criticism comes down to saying that to identify propositions with the meanings of sentences fails on two related counts: first, that the notion of 'meaning' is badly in need of clarification itself, and so can explain nothing about propositions while yet unclarified; and secondly, that in so far as there is any hint here regarding what meaning putatively consists in (namely, denotation), that hint is as full of difficulties as the notion it offers to explain.

Much of the confusion here arises from taking meanings and/or propositions as 'meant entities'. Consider – again to pre-empt, briefly, later discussion – an alternative way of characterising meaning. The later work of Wittgenstein brought into prominence a notion of meaning as *use*. The idea here is that expressions do not (or that the great majority of them do not) simply name or label some extralinguistic item, but instead have a role or function in the language, such that to learn the meaning of an expression is to learn how to use it in these roles. Accordingly, to have a grasp of a term's meaning is to know the rules or conventions governing its deployment in the various linguistic enterprises of stating, asking, commanding, and so on, in which that term appears or can appear. On this view, it is misguided to think that 'meanings' are some sort of timeless entities called 'propositions' (or even just 'meanings' for that matter) occupying a Third Realm; for if the meaning of an expression consists in the rules or conventions governing its use in the language, then meaning is unmysterious and prosaic. I do not wish to suggest in advance of discussing it that this theory is wholly satisfactory; the point, for present purposes, is that seeing how meaning might be handled otherwise than by treating it along the lines of the denotative theory, shows, or goes some way to showing, that acceptance of proposition talk is not forced by considerations of meaning.

If propositions are not to be explained in terms of the meanings of sentences on a denotative theory, for this is what the foregoing criticism disallows, then other options will have to be investigated. One is to take propositions as the meanings of sentences on a 'possible worlds' theory for intensional items; I allude to this in the next chapter. Another option is to avoid talk of denotation by appealing to the idea that propositions are logical constructions out of sets of synonymous sentences; appeal is still being made to certain semantical properties of sentences – in this case synonymy – but the proposal has the virtue that it manageably restricts the abstract objects being invoked. On a strict presentation of such a theory, a proposition can be defined as a class of sentences all having the same meaning as some given sentence, leaving it open that 'meaning' might be independently specified in such a way as to avoid reification. Then the only abstract entity present is the class, and certain nominalists accept classes into their ontologies because they are required by mathematics and science. Nevertheless the problem here will be the notion of synonymity, which would require defending against Quine's attack upon it (see chapter 3); and further, synonymity itself, if successfully defended, would then have to be characterised in a way which did not make prior appeal to propositions (cf. above), for the account would otherwise be circular.

NOMINALISM AND REALISM

Clearly, then, searching out a satisfactory notion of the proposition takes us further afield than the limits of this chapter allow. Nevertheless there is a minimal line to be taken on propositions which allows use of them without the attendant baggage of intensional realism. The desideratum is to reduce appeal to abstract items to the minimum, and it is worth noting why.

The realism-nominalism dispute is a dispute about ontological commitments. It is by no means an idle dispute, particularly in view of the role it plays in contemporary discussions of possible worlds theory (chapter 3, below) and in certain problems arising, as already noted, in the theory of meaning, for example in connection with the motives Russell had for devising the Theory of Descriptions (chapter 4, below). It also arises, in somewhat oblique form but crucially none the less, in the current argument between realists and antirealist over truth-conditional approaches to meaning (chapter 8, below); 'realism' in this context has added complexities and perhaps some differences, and antirealists are not necessarily nominalists.

The problem in modern terms arises from Meinong's realist theory of 'Objects'.[19] Meinong took it that metaphysics deals with everything that both exists and subsists, the distinction being that the totality of existent things is 'infinitely small' in comparison to the totality of the 'Objects' of knowledge, which, when they are non-existent, are at least subsistent in the sense of being things about which there can be thought and talk. Meinong's Objects are thus construable as the accusatives, in general, of thought. Even impossible Objects like the round square subsist, as do the infinities of negative facts such as that 'Aristotle did not have thirty brothers', 'Aristotle did not have thirty-one brothers', 'Aristotle did not have thirty-two brothers'. . . , and so on.[20]

Russell and Quine were chief among those who rejected outright this lavish violation of the principle of Ockham's Razor, a principle which states that one should not posit the existence of more entities than are absolutely necessary for adequate philosophical explantation. This drive to ontological parsimony is the guiding principle of nominalism. In Russell's view, Meinong's postulation of a universe glutted with subsistent entities offends against a 'sense of reality',[21] and Quine castigated Meinong's universe as 'overpopulated', 'rank', a 'slum,' and 'a breeding ground for disorderly elements'.[22] In another memorable tag Quine bracketed unnecessary entities as *entia non grata*, marking a resolution to exclude them from the ontological commitments we make.

There are good theoretical and methodological reasons for thinking the principle of Ockham's Razor a good one. In selecting one from among a number of competing and otherwise adequate hypotheses in any field of enquiry, certain metatheoretical criteria come into play; the hypothesis which is simplest and at the same time most powerful is the obvious one to choose. In the same way, limiting the number of entities invoked by a philosophical theory limits the hostages yielded to fortune from the point of view of the theory's efficacy. The more hostages, the weaker the theory. It is for this reason that Quine's views on ontological commitment[23] have as one of their methodological motives the thought that if two theories give the same conceptual mileage, but one of them involves commitment to the existence of fewer entities, then that is the one to choose. Indeed one should, on both his view and Russell's, actively seek out the most parsimonious theory adequate to the phenomena requiring explanation, and not rest content with overpopulation, however pleasant it makes treating the difficulties in hand; for it is all too easy to misguide oneself by invoking *ad hoc* entities, like entelechies, or subsistent beings, or Forms, as 'explanatory' devices.[24]

One of the chief reasons for Quine's hostility towards abstract entities, including propositions, is that they lack clear *criteria of identity*. A criterion of identity for something is that criterion by means of which we can individuate something, specify which one it is, tell where it begins and another leaves off; in short, by means of which we can pick something out or tell that it is the same one again. The nub of the position taken by Quine is that there is 'no entity without identity'. In Quine's view, criteria of identity for propositions can only be afforded by relations of synonymy between sentences, for example by saying that proposition p is the proposition expressed by the distinct but synonymous sentences x and y. Then, on the grounds that synonymity is an empty notion (cf. chapter 3), Quine takes this to be grounds for rejecting propositions, at least in any but a trivial or reducible nominalist sense – as a *façon de parler* in effect.

Innocuous Propositions

Many of the issues touched upon in this chapter will recur in specific contexts in later chapters. We can leave the question of propositions in this undecided state for the time being by asking, in conclusion, whether it is possible to use the notion of the proposition in later chapters without too great risk. Is there, this is to ask, a satisfactory *façon de parler* sense of 'proposition'?

Thomson suggests that there is.[25] In his view, there would only be a genuinely interesting theory of the proposition if it was claimed that there is only *one* proposition that snow is white, or that Santa Claus exists; for otherwise to say that a proposition is what gets asserted by use of a sentence is to say nothing unobvious or wrong or even interesting. Mackie in similar vein has it that 'the words "statement" and "proposition" are just terms that enable us to speak generally about what is said, what is believed, what is assertable or believable, and so on'.[26] Now in a sense this is certainly right, for it is always an option to employ a notion without commitment to one or another theory arising as a means to unpack that notion fully. But in another sense it is to duck the issues rather than to render unnecessary the task of explaining them; and it frequently happens that one ignores giving details only at the peril of difficulties later on.

Still, the risk has sometimes to be taken. In order to proceed with the following discussions I shall let the matter rest there; the foregoing is a sketch of some of the options, and the difficulties, left undecided by doing so.

NOTES

1. Austin, J. L., 'Performative-Constantive', in Caton, C. E. (ed.), *Philosophy and Ordinary Language,* Urbana, 1963, p.22, *et seq.*
2. Wittgenstein, L., *Philosophical Investigations* cf.§§ 243-315, 348-412.
3. Often philosophers make a three-way distinction, between sentences, statements and propositions. A statement, on the received interpretation, is an actual use of an uttered or inscribed sentence on a particular occasion. Often, however, 'statement' is used as a synonym of 'proposition', and to keep clear of possible confusions I shall restrict attention to the sentence-proposition distinction alone. cf. Aune, B., 'Statements & Propositions' *Nous,* 1967.
4. Henceforth I use 'sentence' for 'declarative sentence', unless otherwise specified.
5. The relativisation of an utterance to a speaker and a time is known as 'indexicality'; thus, a sentence is said to be *indexed* to speakers and times.
6. cf., Plato, *Republic,* 596a 6-7; cf. 507ab.
7. Ryle, G., 'The Theory of Meaning', in Caton, *op. cit.,* p.128, *et seq.* cf. esp. pp.131-45, 148-53. See also Thomson, J. F., 'Truth bearers and the trouble about propositions', *Journal of Philosphy* 66, 1969, p.739.
8. This second motive is related to the first in that the propositions here said to be the meanings of sentences, also do duty as the intentions of propositional attitudes. However the two motives are separable in that commitment to one does not entail commitment to the other.
9. I use here a distinction between sentence 'types' and sentence 'tokens'. The sentence 'John likes Rover' is a particular instance, hence token, of that type. 'Type' is to 'token' what 'species' is to 'individual'.
10. Church A., 'Propositions', *The Encyclopaedia Britannica* (14th ed.) Chicago 1958.
11. Frege G., 'The Thought', in Strawson, P. F. (ed.), *Philosophical Logic,* Oxford, 1967 p. 17, *et seq.*
12. *ibid.,* p.20-1. The expression 'Third Realm' is quoted by Ryle, *ibid* p.149.
13. Frege, G., 'Sense and Reference', in *Frege Translations,* Black, M. and Geach, P., Oxford, 1952, pp.56-78.
14. 'Intension' with an 's', note; not to be confused with the 'intention' with a 't' recently discussed.
15. c.f., Quine, W. V., 'Reference and Modality', *From a Logical Point of View,* New York, 1961, p.139, *et seq.*
16. *Use* of a word and *mention* of it are standardly distinguished by enclosing *mentioned* words in single quotes. The sign of equality, '=', stands for 'is identical with'.
17. Quine, *ibid,* pp.141-2.
18. *ibid.,* p.142.

19. Meinong, A., 'The Theory of Objects', in Chisholm, R. (ed.), *Realism and the Background of Phenomenology,* Glencoe, 1960.
20. *ibid.,* p.79.
21. cf. Russell, B., 'The Philosophy of Logical Atomism in Marsh, R. C. (ed.), *Logic and Knowledge,* London, 1956, p.269, *et seq.*
22. cf., Quine, W. V., 'On What There Is'. *op. cit., n.15.* Meinong here appears as 'Wyman'.
23. *ibid.* I discuss Quine's views on this in chapter 4 below.
24. Closely related issues appear in chapter 3 below. cf. Lycan, W., 'The Trouble With Possible Worlds', in Loux, M. J. (ed.), *The Possible and the Actual,* Cornell, 1979, for a discussion of Meinong's and Quine's views.
25. Thomson, J. F. *op. cit.* p.737, *et seq.*
26. Mackie, J. L., *Truth Probability and Paradox,* Oxford, 1973, pp.20-1.

3 Necessity, Analyticity, and the A Priori

INTRODUCTION

Botanists have found their study a more tractable one since the work of Linnaeus in the eighteenth century, the reason being that Linnaeus pioneered a system of classification for flora which introduced the benefits of organisation and logic into botanical science, and gave it methodical foundations. Classification can be a powerful tool, a fact never lost on philosophers, who, from the time of Aristotle in particular, have made standard use of the technique.[1] Simply put, classification involves making distinctions and comparisons, and sorting things out in terms of them, whether the things in question are plants, as in botany, or notions, as in philosophy. A system of classification is as good as the principles upon which the relevant distinctions are drawn and comparisons made, and no better; so that questions arise not only about how a given topic proceeds on the basis of the use of certain classifications, but whether the principles employed in making those classifications are adequate.

It is a major concern in philosophy to secure an adequate classification of truths, of the propositions expressing truths, and of the ways of coming to know truths. Modifications notwithstanding, there has long been a related group of classifying concepts in use in this connection, which are of fundamental importance in philosophy and upon which a large number of issues turn. The concepts in question are those of necessity, analyticity, and the *a priori*. In this chapter I examine these notions and the connections between them.

I begin by looking at some attempts to define these three notions, and at their relations to each other; and then go on to look in turn at analyticity and necessity in more detail. The discussion of necessity will involve a fairly lengthy detour through the interesting and highly suggestive matter of 'possible worlds', together with some of the attendant debates on transworld identity, essence, and 'unactualised possibilia'. At the close of the chapter, equipped by these discussions, I look at the relations between necessity, analyticity, and the *a priori* again.

CLASSIFICATION OF TRUTHS

Leibniz held that all reasoning is underwritten by two principles — the principle of contradiction and the principle of sufficient reason. It is in virtue of the principle of contradiction that 'we judge *false* that which involves a contradiction, and *true* that which is opposed or contradictory to the false'; and it is in virtue of the principle of sufficient reason that 'we hold that there can be no fact real or existing, no statement true, unless there be a sufficient reason why it should be so and not otherwise, although these reasons cannot usually be known by us'.[2] These two principles are allied to a distinction between two kinds of truths, 'truths of reason' and 'truths of fact'. The former are *necessary* (true, as Leibniz put it, in all possible worlds) and their opposites impossible; the latter are *contingent,* and their opposites possible.[3] In his correspondence with Clark, Leibniz said that the connection between the two principles and the two kinds of truth is shown by the fact that the principle of contradiction is sufficient on its own for a demonstration of the whole of mathematics, but that the principle of sufficient reason is needed in addition in order to pass from mathematics to physics, which deals with a realm of contingent items.[4]

In Leibniz's view, truths of reason, being, as they are, necessary, can be established by analysis, by resolving them into the simple ideas and primary principles out of which they are constituted and which themselves require no proof.[5] The distinction between this kind of truths and the second kind — the contingent truths or truths of fact — foreshadows Hume's division, made in the *Enquiry,* between 'relations of ideas' and 'matters of fact', a division celebrated in the label 'Hume's fork'.[6] (In the *Treatise* Hume had characterised the difference as one holding between 'knowledge' and 'probability', but the terminological variance is insignificant.[7]) Hume claimed that his distinction between relations of ideas and matters of fact exhausts all the truths that can be known. Some truths depend only on relations between ideas in the sense that to deny a statement which is true in virtue of this relation is to fall into contradiction.[8] According to Hume, relations of ideas are discovered either by intuition, as when one simply sees that $5+7=12$, or by demonstration, as when one goes through a deductive argument which validly yields its conclusion. 'Matter of fact' truths, by contrast, are such that to conceive of them as false does not involve contradiction. Their discovery is effected by observation — which for Hume is something we have to assume to be trustworthy — and inference — which for Hume is, in this case, nondemonstrative inference, proceeding by means of the relation of cause and effect.

The distinction both Leibniz and Hume were drawing by these means is the distinction between *necessary* and *contingent* truths. The two other distinctions — the distinction between the *a priori* and the *a posteriori* and the distinction between the *analytic* and the *synthetic* — are closely allied to this one.

The members of the latter pair may be contrasted with one another by saying that analytic statements are those in which the concept of the predicate is already contained in the concept of the subject, so that to see whether it is true or not one need only inspect the terms occurring in the statement; whereas synthetic statements are those in which two different concepts are joined together or 'synthesised', and their truth-value is to be tested by going and looking at the world, to see whether things are as they are claimed to be in the statement.[9] A tautology is a clear example of an analytic statement: 'all married men are married' is a case in point. However, not all analytic statements are tautologies: 'all bodies are spatially extended' is not tautologous, but it is analytic, for its truth-value depends only on the concepts involved, not, as with a synthetic statement like 'snow is white', on the way things happen to be in the world.

The members of the former pair — *a priori-a posteriori* — are usually distinguished by saying that a truth is known *a priori* if it is known independently of any experience of how things are in the world; whereas a truth known *a posteriori* is one which is known only on the basis of empirical investigation; one which is known, and can only be known, as a result of experience. It is accordingly held that truths of arithmetic like $5+7=12$ are known *a priori*, whereas the empirical facts that grass is green and snow is white are known, and can only be known, *a posteriori*.

These three pairs of concepts have been closely linked, and it is obvious why. If a truth is necessary, if it consists in a 'relation of ideas' and is a 'truth of reason', such as 'all bodies are extended', then it seems to be both the case that the statement expressing that truth is analytic — that is, can be judged true merely by inspecting the meaning of the terms involved — and that it is known *a priori* — that is, can be judged true without recourse to empirical investigation. If, on the other hand, a truth is contingent, if it is a 'matter of fact' or 'truth of fact', such as 'some bodies are speckled green', then it seems to be both the case that the statement expressing that truth is synthetic – that is, its truth-value depends on the way things are in the world – and it is known *a posteriori* – that is, its truth-value can be ascertained only by empirical investigation. Such thoughts as these suggest that the relations between the three pairs of notions are quite straightforward and symmetrical.

Kant, however, had other ideas. He took the view that there can be synthetic *a priori* truths, and wrote the first *Critique* largely to prove that this is so. Such a view cuts directly across the apparently ready grouping of the pairs of concepts just given; but this is not as surprising as it seems, for although the three pairs are closely related in the way just shown, there are important differences between them which block a simple characterisation of that relationship, and make it difficult to give an account of any one of the pairs in terms of one or both the others; which appears all the more vexing in view of the fact that it is difficult to get an adequate grasp of any one pair *without* invoking one or both the other pairs in explanation. The differences are, put roughly, that 'necessity' and 'contingency' are metaphysical notions, 'analytic' and 'synthetic' are semantic notions, and '*a priori*' and '*a posteriori*' are epistemological notions. So much is suggested by the way these notions have just been characterised. Accordingly, even if it turns out that the expressions 'analytic', 'necessary' and '*a priori*' had the same extension, that is, coincided in their application – and it is not clear, as Kant's views show, that they do – they nevertheless certainly do not all mean the same.

None of these three sets of notions is unproblematic in its own right, which further complicates the issue of what relationship obtains between them. At first glance the notions of necessity and analyticity appear more opaque than that of the *a priori*, which since Leibniz, and particularly Kant, has had a largely agreed epistemological rendering. The problem with the *a priori* is an acute form of the general problem just noted, that getting a clear idea of the notion depends on invocation of at least one of the others. Leibniz, for example, defined the *a priori* in terms of necessity, as the mode in which necessary truths are apprehended; in his view, to know reality *a priori* is to know it 'by exposing the cause or the possible generation of things',[10] which contrasts with knowing reality *a posteriori*, which is to know, by means of sense-experience, what states of affairs in fact obtain in the world. By 'exposing' Leibniz meant *proving*; therefore because truths of reason are based on 'identical propositions',[11] *a priori* truths can be demonstrated on the grounds of the principle of contradiction, and so Leibniz could talk of 'truths *a priori,* or of reason' as opposed to 'truths *a posteriori,* or of fact'.[12] Accordingly, for Leibniz the *a priori-a posteriori* distinction is one between, respectively, knowledge of necessary truths acquired by reason, and knowledge of contingent truths acquired by sense-experience.

This characterisation will not quite do for Kant's employment of the terms because unlike Leibniz he did not employ a straight distinction between sense-experience and reason, but invoked in addition to these a further faculty, 'understanding'. Nevertheless, his view is essentially similar – the *a priori* is just the 'non-empirical' and the *a posteriori* 'the empirical' in a way directly analogous to Leibniz's usage.[13] For Kant, likewise, *a priori* truths are necessary, and *a posteriori* truths contingent.

What is important, however, is that as these views show, it is not clear how one would explain *a priori* knowledge without appeal either to necessary truth or to the notion of analytic propositions or statements. Conversely, at some point in the explanation of these two latter notions, something like an account of *a priori* knowledge might at least very probably, and very naturally, have to occur. All this reiterates the complexity of the connections at issue.

Evidently getting clear on this cluster of notions demands getting clear on analyticity and necessity in particular. A great deal turns on these notions in contemporary philosophy.

ANALYTICITY

I proceed in this section by reporting Quine's attack on the notion of analyticity, which is central to the contemporary debate, and the notable reply to Quine offered by Grice and Strawson. Thereafter I take up and consider some of the central points at issue.

Analytic judgements were conceived of by Kant as those in which the predicate-concept does not add anything informative to the subject-concept, but merely elucidates, analyses, or 'unpacks' the subject-concept.[14] In synthetic judgements the reverse happens. An alternative way of characterising analyticity is to say that a statement is analytic if its truth-value can be determined merely by inspecting the meanings of the terms involved; this way of putting things owes itself to the Logical Positivists. Ayer, for example, wrote of the contrast in these terms: 'A proposition is analytic when its validity depends solely on the definitions of the symbols it contains, and synthetic when its validity is determined by the facts of experience'.[15]

Analyticity, particularly when employed as the Positivists

employed it, is an important notion. Consider for example what was at stake for the Positivists. They wished to demarcate a class of genuinely significant or meaningful propositions in order to exclude those without cognitive content, for they took the task of philosophy to be the clarification of the language of science, a task therefore of aiding and abetting science in the acquisition of positive knowledge. Metaphysics and theology, together with ethics and aesthetics, seemed to the Positivists cognitively senseless enterprises whose propositions were, at best, distinguishable from jumbles of nonsense syllables only in virtue of having meanings of an emotional, subjective, exhortatory, or prescriptive sort, none of which is useful to science. The principle they adopted for use in discriminating between cognitively senseful and senseless propositions was the celebrated 'verifiability principle', which states, roughly, that the meaning of a statement is the method of its verification, and that all and only those (synthetic) statements which are, at very least in principle, verifiable are cognitively senseful. [16] The parenthetical 'synthetic' is important; for, along lines suggested to the Positivists by Wittgenstein's *Tractatus*, [17] there is a way of coping with certain propositions which are not synthetic but which play a vital role in the sciences – specifically, the propositions of logic and mathematics. This was to view such propositions as analytic, and say that their truth-value depends only on the meanings of the terms occurring in them. Wittgenstein characterised these propositions as tautologies, and therefore empty of content, which accounted for their being propositions whose truth-value can be settled independently of experience. Thus for the Positivists the class of cognitively significant propositions was made up of two kinds, synthetic and analytic; the rest went by the board from the viewpoint of positive knowledge.

Having a grasp of the analytic-synthetic distinction, and what the distinguished notions each consists in, was therefore fundamental for the Positivists just as it had been to Kant; and it remains important in contemporary philosophy because of the concepts to which it is standardly linked and because the need for a classification of truths, their bearers, and our apprehension of them, remains pressing. An attack on the notion hits a vital nerve, and if successful forces choices of certain philosophical options rather than others – always a consequence of moment. In the classic paper 'Two Dogmas of Empiricism', Quine challenged the analytic-synthetic distinction together with an allied 'dogma', reductionism. [18] His arguments are as follows.

In the Positivists' characterisation of analyticity, which in Quine's view captures Kant's intentions also, a presupposed notion of 'meaning' plays a central role, analytic statements being those, in the way noted, whose truth-value is supposed to depend only on the meanings of their constitutive terms. Quine's strategy is first to rid the discussion of any appeal to a concept of meaning, for these reasons. First, as Frege's distinction between sense and reference shows, meaning is not the same as naming.[19] That distinction is made out for singular terms like 'Hesperus' and 'Phosphorus', which, although co-referring, differ in sense. Singular terms purport to name entities, whether concrete or abstract, whereas general terms, like 'creature with a heart', do not name entities, but are said instead to be 'true of' some or other entity, that is, to apply to or be predicable of some or other entity. The class of entities a general term is true of, or to which it applies, is called that term's 'extension'. On analogy with the sense-reference distinction applied to singular terms, two general terms can have the same extension while differing in meaning, as in the case of 'creature with a heart' and 'creature with kidneys'. In fact, the meaning or 'intension' of a general term is explicity contrasted with its extension, a point familiar from the related grammatical distinction between connotation and denotation respectively.

Quine takes the view that once one has the distinction between a theory of meaning and a theory of reference which the above considerations yield, what constitutes a theory of meaning changes character; for a 'conspicuous' question about any (pre-distinction) theory of meaning must be, in Quine's view, 'what sort of things are meanings?'[20] If one dispenses with the notion that there are meant entities, a theory of meaning comes down to a concern with no more than the synonymy of linguistic forms and the analyticity of statements; and 'meanings themselves, as obscure intermediary entities, may well be abandoned'.[21] Getting a grasp of the notion of analyticity has accordingly to be done without appeal to meanings *qua* 'meant entities'.

There are two kinds of statements which are generally reckoned to be analytic, one kind being what Quine calls 'logically true' statements like 'no unmarried man is married', and the other kind being non-tautologous statements like 'no bachelor is married'. In Quine's view, a statement of the former kind is true solely in virtue of the logical particles occurring in it — these being 'no', 'un-', 'if', 'then', 'and' and so on — and remains true under any reinterpretation of its components other than the logical particles. Statements of the latter kind are not logical truths, but can be turned into them by replacing their terms (or one or some of them) by synonyms; thus, the example above can be turned into a logical truth by substituting 'unmarried man' for 'bachelor'. So it turns out that understanding analytic statements of the latter kind depends upon understanding synonymy. The next question, then, is whether we have a clear grasp of synonymy.[22]

Perhaps synonymy can be explained in terms of definition; the thought would be that 'bachelor' and 'unmarried man' *mean the same* because one can be defined in terms of the other. But the notion of definition is problematic, and the question arises, on what are definitions based? One cannot appeal to a dictionary to settle questions of definition, for lexicographers are empirical scientists who find, implicit in standard usage before they write their dictionaries, that there is taken to be a relation of synonymy between certain terms, upon which they therefore report. In consequence, the ground of the synonymy cannot be the fact that lexicographers observe it in linguistic behaviour. Definition rests on synonymy rather than explaining it – with the single exception, allowed by Quine, of the case of explicitly conventional introductions of new notations, where a definiendum has been expressly created as a synonym of its definiens. Otherwise definition does not explain synonymy.[23]

If analyticity is to be explained in terms of synonymy, and if appeal to definition will not explain synonymy, another approach is required. A promising suggestion is that the synonymy of two linguistic forms can be explained by their being intersubstitutable in all contexts *salva veritate*.[24] Leaving aside cases of the failure of intersubstitutivity *salva veritate* of 'unmarried man' for 'bachelor' in ' "bachelor" has eight letters', and concentrating only on 'cognitive' synonymy, the question is whether intersubstitutivity is a strong enough condition for synonymy. Evidently, it will not be strong enough if it turns out that heteronyms (that is, non-synonymous expressions) can be substituted for one another *salva veritate*.

One way of trying to make the notion of intersubstitutivity do the trick is to say that because the statement 'necessarily all and only bachelors are bachelors' is true (construing 'necessarily' to be applicable only to analytic statements), then if 'bachelor' and 'unmarried man' are intersubstitutable *salva veritate*, the statement 'necessarily, all and only bachelors are unmarried men' is also true. To say this is true, in turn, is to say that 'all and only bachelors are unmarried men is analytic' is true; and this, in turn again, says that 'bachelor' and 'unmarried man' are cognitively synonymous. Therefore it looks as though intersubstitutivity is indeed a sufficient condition for cognitive synonymy.[25]

Quine, however, rejects this manoeuvre as 'hocus-pocus'. The problem lies with the modal adverb 'necessarily'. Intersubstitutivity *salva veritate* varies in force according to how rich is the language in hand, and the above argument depends upon possession of a language rich enough to contain 'necessarily', construed as yielding truth only when applied to analytic statements. But 'can we condone a language which contains such an adverb? Does the adverb really make sense? To suppose that it does,' says Quine, 'is to suppose that we have already made satisfactory sense of "analytic".'[26] The reasons why are as follows.

On Quine's view, intersubstitutivity *salva veritate* is meaningful only if relativised to a specified language. Consider a language containing the ordinary trappings of first-order predicate logic, with variables x, y, z . . . and with a stock of one- and many-place predicates, for example F where Fx is 'x is a man' and G where Gxy is 'x loves y'. The atomic wffs of this language truth-functionally concatenate into molecular sentences upon application of the operators 'and', 'if' and so on. There are also the quantifiers. Such a language contains descriptions and standard contexually-defined singular terms, even those naming classes, assuming a two-place predicate of class-membership; and it is a language adequate to classical mathematics and science, except in the case where this latter involves what Quine regards as debatable, if not downright suspicious, devices like counterfactual conditionals and the modal adverbs 'necessarily' and its kind.

Such a language is extensional, in the sense that any two of its predicates which agree in extension can be substituted for one another *salva veritate*. But intersubstitutivity on these lines does not provide the kind of cognitive synonymy needed to ground analyticity. To say that 'bachelor' and 'unmarried man' are intersubstitutable *salva veritate* in an extensional language says no more than that 'all and only bachelors are unmarried men is analytic' is true, which is not to say that the extensional agreement of the terms turns on their meanings rather than on contingent facts, which latter is the case with contingent extensional agreement of heteronyms like 'creature with a heart' and 'creature with kidneys'. To get the required specification of analyticity in terms of cognitive synonymy, this latter would have to be something more than extensional intersubstitutivity; it would have to be such as to equate the synonymy of 'bachelor' and 'unmarried man' with the *analyticity*, not just the *truth*, of 'all and only bachelors are unmarried men is analytic'.[27]

It was noted that if the intensional adverb 'necessarily' is available, then intersubstitutivity does yield cognitive synonymy; but Quine's point is that this can only be so if the notion of analyticity is understood in advance. Quine's opposition to talk of necessity will be canvassed more closely below.

Quine's attack, as it has been reported to this point, is summarised by him thus: 'Analyticity at first seemed most naturally definable by appeal to a realm of meanings. On refinement, the appeal to meanings gave way to an appeal to synonymy or definition. But definition turned out to be a will-o'-the-wisp, and synonymy turned out to be best understood only by dint of prior appeal to analyticity itself. So we are back at the problem of analyticity.'[28] He considers a last attempt to make sense of the notion, one this time turning on the alleged vagueness of ordinary language. Here it is claimed that in a more precise artificial language, call it L_0, the notion of analyticity can be perspicuously set out by reference to 'semantical rules'. Carnap, for example, had suggested how such a move might be made, by offering this sketch: a sentence S is analytic (strictly, L_0-true) in L_0 if and only if S's truth is to be established on the basis of the semantic rules alone, without reference to non-linguistic facts.[29]

Quine is not impressed by this idea. If there is an artificial language L_0 whose rules contain a specification of all its own analytic statements, then we are not helped, for the rules contain the very word – 'analytic' – which we are trying to understand. At best we could construe the rules as conventionally defining a new term, 'analytic-for-L_0'; but this is still unhelpful, for it is not 'analytic-for-L_0' we wish to understand, but 'analytic'. 'Analytic-for-L_0' might less controversially be designated K, and indeed any class of statements K, M, N, etc., could be specified for any purpose whatever; but what does it mean to say that K is, as against M or N, the class of 'analytic' statements in L_0? If a semantical rule was invoked which did not contain 'analytic' but turned solely on what was to count as the truths of L_0 ('L_0-truths'), then perhaps an analytic statement could be derivatively defined as a statement not only true but true just in virtue of the semantical rules of L_0, as Carnap suggested. But even this fails to help, for now appeal is being made, not to the unexplained word 'analytic', but to the unexplained notion of a 'semantical rule'. Quine likens the process to trying to pull oneself up by one's own bootstraps.[30] On this note, and therefore, Quine gives up as hopeless the task of trying to explain analyticity.

Part of the interest in Quine's attack on analyticity lies in what he claims to be the philosophical motivation for employing the notion:

It is obvious that truth in general depends on both language and extralinguistic fact
. . . Thus one is tempted to suppose in general that the truth of a statement is
somehow analysable into a linguistic component and a factual component. Given this
suggestion, it next seems reasonable that in some statements the factual component
should be null; and these are the analytic statements. But, for all its *a priori*
reasonableness, a boundary between analytic and synthetic statements has not been
drawn. That there is such a distinction to be drawn at all is an unempirical dogma of
the empiricists, a metaphysical article of faith.[31]

DEFENDING A DOGMA ·

From the fact that no *boundary* has been drawn between analytic
and synthetic statements, Quine takes it to follow that no *distinction*
has been drawn, and therefore that *no satisfactory sense* has been
made of 'analytic', talk of which should therefore be eschewed. This
conclusion is notably resisted by Grice and Strawson.[32] Their
argument is twofold; it is, first, that difficulties over drawing boundaries do not entail that there is no genuine distinction in the case;
and secondly, that 'satisfactory sense' can indeed be made of
members of the family of notions to which 'analytic' belongs, contrary to Quine's claims. The case is made out in the following way.

A distinction can be criticised for not being sharp enough, for
being confused or ambiguous; but such criticisms do not amount to
a rejection of that distinction, rather they are a prelude to its
clarification. Quine's criticism is not of this sort. Again, a distinction might be criticised for not being useful; but then it is not its
existence but its value which is being put in question, and what
Quine's criticism comes down to is that the distinction simply does
not exist, that to think it does exist is to be a victim of a philosophical
illusion. Accordingly one is justified in asking whether there is no
presumption to the effect that such a distinction exists. Surely, it
does; for, apart from the mere fact of its use by Leibniz, Kant, and
the Positivists among others, it is clear that its use is something on
which philosophers generally agree, in the sense that the terms
'analytic' and 'synthetic' have a largely uniform application in
philosophical usage which conformably extends to new cases, which
is importantly to say that it is not confined to a closed list of cases
which philosphers may have learned outright, but can be creatively
and uniformly applied across fresh ranges of statements.[33]
' "Analytic" and "synthetic" have a more or less established
philosophical *use*,' Grice and Strawson write, 'and this seems to
suggest that it is absurd, even senseless, to say that there is no such
distinction.'[34]

But Quine's complaints run deeper. In the cluster of concepts to which analyticity belongs there is the concept of cognitive synonymy, in terms of which analyticity could be defined if it were itself clear. Quine's view is that it is not clear. Now, to say x and y are cognitively synonymous terms is roughly to say that they 'mean the same' or 'have the same meaning'. If Quine's attack on analyticity goes through, it will follow that no sense can attach to the distinction 'means the same' and 'does not mean the same', in so far as the concept of 'meaning the same' is something different, as applied to predicate expressions, from 'being true of the same objects'. Unlike 'analytic,' 'means the same' is not a philosphical term of art; it is common property. If therefore Quine's views oblige us to say there is no distinction between 'means the same' and 'does not mean the same', which distinction is needed to make sense of the *difference* between ' "Bachelor" means the same as "unmarried man" but "creature with a heart" does not mean the same as "creature with kidneys",' then we are in a paradoxical situation. Not only would we have to give up the notion of predicate synonymy, but of sentence-synonymy too, one of the consequences of which would be that we could not translate between languages.[35] Worse, if talk of synonymy is meaningless, talk of sentence-meaning is also meaningless, for if it makes sense to talk of sentence-meaning we can ask of any sentence 'what does it mean?', which would allow a characterisation of sentence-synonymy of this sort: two sentences are synonymous if and only if any true answer to the question 'what does it mean?', when asked in connection with one of the sentences, is a true answer to the same question asked of the other sentence. Grice and Strawson therefore remark: 'If we are to give up the notion of sentence-synonymy as senseless, we must give up the notion of sentence-significance (of a sentence having meaning) as senseless too. But then perhaps we might as well give up the notion of sense.'[36]

What they pinpoint as going wrong in Quine's argument is that, instead of explaining the use made of the notion of 'meaning the same',he has measured it according to certain standards and found it wanting. Grice and Strawson regard this as a 'typical example' of how philosophers fall into paradox.[37] Quine appears to be seeking some sort of standard of clarifiability which, if we attain it, would entitle us to claim we have made 'satisfactory sense' of the notion under inspection; and he argues that analyticity is not clarified to standard. Grice's and Strawson's response is to say that the standard Quine seeks is inappropriate.

The clarifiability requirements Quine lays down are that, first, an explanation of analyticity must be provided which must not trade upon any concept in the cluster to which the concepts of analyticity and synonymy belong — some other concepts being that of definition and of what counts as logically impossible, self-contradictory, and necessary; and secondly, it must specify some common feature in all cases in which 'analytic' is applied so that we can give an account of the form 'a statement is analytic if and only if. . .'.[38] It would seem, in short, that Quine desires a strict definition. And what makes matters more difficult is that, in addition to requiring a strict definition, Quine takes failure in providing one to entail that the notion has no satisfactory sense.

What it is pertinent to remark in reply to this is that, first, it is unreasonable to assume that a necessary condition of some notion's *having* sense is that we must *make* sense of it along Quine's lines; and secondly, that sense, employing other and less formal means, can indeed be made of a notion from the analyticity cluster. Consider the notion of logical impossibility as an example.

Suppose we are explaining the notion of logical impossibility to someone, and choose to do so by displaying the contrast between natural and logical impossibility, using in particular the notions of the logical impossibility of a three-year-old child's being an adult, and the natural impossibility of a three-year-old child's understanding Russell's Theory of Types. Imagine that Y says, 'my three-year-old child is an adult', and that X says, 'my three-year-old understands the Theory of Types'. Now, one might construe X's remark as inspired by parental fondness and partiality; one answers, 'You mean your child is very bright'. If X insists that the child understands Russell's theory, one might then say, 'That's impossible; I don't believe you'. The child is brought in, expounds the theory, and criticises it; what X said has turned out to be true. Natural impossibilities admit of counter-instances against the odds, however hard to credit; natural impossibilities are not logical impossibilities. In the parallel case of Y's claim, however, nothing whatever *could* make it turn out that Y was right; unless he is using 'adult' in a figurative or jocular sense, what he says *has* no sense — he is not using the word correctly. The matter can be summarised by saying that the appropriate responses to X's and Y's claims are, respectively, disbelief and literal incomprehension.[39]

This is one kind of informal explanation by means of which someone could be given a grasp of 'logically impossible'. It is *one* kind of explanation because other kinds of explanation might be needed for other concepts in the cluster; and it is an *informal* explanation in the obvious sense that it does not amount to formally specifying necessary and sufficient conditions for the concept's application, of the sort 'a statement is — if and only if. . .', where the first blank is filled by 'analytic', or whatever. However, this species of explanation does satisfy Quine's other requirement, in that it breaks out of the cluster of concepts and makes appeal to none of them.[40] That it does so is not to concede, except irenically, that Quine's requirement is one which must invariably be met; Grice and Strawson point out that for many senseful concepts, like those in the cluster 'morally wrong', 'blameworthy', 'breach of moral rules', or in the cluster 'true', 'false', 'statement', 'fact', 'denial', 'assertion', it is not only the case that they are understood and usable concepts despite not being formally defined, but also that grasping any one of them is something we standardly do just in terms of the other concepts in the cluster, which means that such a means of grasping a concept is acceptable and sufficient.

This point is often enough made. Not all circular explanations are vicious; some can be highly informative, even to the extent of yielding genuine semantic insight into the terms in question.[41] Moreover there are additional reasons for agreeing with Grice's and Strawson's view to the effect that Quine's requirements upon a satisfactory account of analyticity are too strong; for they may be so strong indeed that they invite infection by the so-called 'paradox of analysis'. Consider (this argument uses only premises Quine asserts or would find hard to deny) any definition of 'analytic' of the form:

1. Analytic = F

where F is a predicate expression and 1. amounts to a 'satisfactory' definition of 'analytic', meaning by this that 1. entails

2. '(p)(p is analytic if and only Fp)' is analytic.

Here 'p' stands for 'proposition' and '(p)' reads 'for any p'. That 1. entails 2. does not make too great a meal of 'satisfactory'; obviously one would not want to say that 'analytic' and 'F' differ in extension, for if this were so then 1. would not be satisfactory by any standard. On Quine's parenthetical definition of cognitive synonymy[42] as intersubstitutivity *salva analyticitate*, the truth of 2. entails, by way of

3. 'analytic' is cognitively synonymous with 'F'

that 1. itself is cognitively synonymous with

4. 'analytic' = 'analytic'.

Getting 4. as a result makes a nonsense of imposing the kind of requirements which lead directly to it, unless the circularity were not vicious in the sense that something valuable and clarifying had been learned on the way.[43] But then if an explanation is going to have to draw on other members of the concept cluster anyway, why draw the circle like this? Why not concede to Grice's and Strawson's thesis about acceptable explanations directly?

There is a point to be made in connection with Quine's response to Carnap-style efforts at a formal solution to the difficulty. One of Quine's most characteristic doctrines is that 'canonical paraphrase' – which is to say, translation of ordinary talk into the clearer idioms of logic – makes for a better way of dealing with the philosophical questions posed by various ontological considerations and the nature of reference.[44] Accordingly, it is odd that Quine should have had little sympathy with formal attempts to clarify analyticity, dismissing them as he did by means of the bootstrap analogy. One is entitled to take Quine to task for this, on the ground that treatment of analyticity in formal languages is not designed to explain the concept for natural languages, but to improve what pre-canonical understanding we have of it.[45] Given an intuitive grasp of the notion in ordinary usage, of the kind pointed out by Grice and Strawson, consideration of borderline cases gives rise to interest in a sharper characterisation of the notion in a context where rules can be provided explicitly to reduce vague areas of application. Quine argued that 'analytic-for-L_0' tells us nothing about 'analytic'; but this is mistaken, for on these lines 'analytic-for-L_0' is telling us *something* about 'analytic', or is showing in what way an analogy holds between analyticity-in-L_0 and L_0, on the one hand, and analyticity and natural language on the other hand. Moreover, the more closely L_0 models natural language, the more useful will be its specified feature of analyticity in throwing light on the analogous feature in natural language.[46] But so much by way of aside.

'ANALYTIC' AGAIN

Where these discussions of Quine's views and Grice's and Strawson's reply leave us is with the original problem of what analyticity is, which has not yet been explained as such, but merely defended against charges of its being a spurious or illusory notion. Grice and Strawson were concerned to show in a general way, against Quine, that the notion has content and that there are more ways open to giving an account of it than Quine allows. They do not show what content the notion has, nor do they go much beyond gesturing at what an account of it would be like.

From the sketches of analyticity given earlier, and from the targets Quine attacks, it is evident that among the options for an account of analyticity are these: that in some broad sense, an analytic statement is one which, if true, is true in virtue of meaning alone, or − if this is different − that it is in effect a tautology whose predicate does no more than reiterate the subject or part of what is involved in the subject, so that denying an analytically true statement is contradictory; or − if this is different from both or either of the foregoing − that it is a matter of linguistic conventions that certain statements are true if true, which statements are to be characterised as 'analytic'; or finally − and yet again leaving it open whether this is different from any or all of the foregoing − that a statement counts as analytic if it is, or can be reduced to, a logical truth.[47] Quine dismissed the first of these options outright because it trades upon intensions, meanings; Grice and Strawson reassert the option as an option by saying that where there is established use there is meaning. The second option or variant is to be found in Leibniz and Kant, and it immediately suggests an intimate connection between analyticity and necessity. The third, a conventionalist view, is one also often associated with talk of necessity, and it is at least as old as Hobbes. The last is Frege's view and the view of most logicians since. It is also the one which prompts most immediate interest, owing at very least to the fact that Quine himself would allow that it yields a sense of 'analytic' impeachable only on the grounds of otiosity.

Recall that Quine worked from a characterisation of analytic statements which had them falling into two classes, one being logically true statements like 'no unmarried man is married', the other being non-tautologous statements like 'all bodies are extended'. It was the second class he attacked, in effect saying of the first class that, because its members are true in virtue of the logical particles alone, they are unexceptionable. His point then was that none of definition, synonymy, or rules could do the trick of transforming statements of the second class into statements of the first class, so that it is illusory to think that they possess the property, analyticity, whose possession distinguishes them from some other kind of statements (namely, synthetic ones). However, statements of the first class, logically true statements, *are* analytic. The only cavil Quine has here is that to call them analytic is redundant, because uninformative; for we already have a perfectly good label for them − *viz.*, 'logically true'.

If, however, Grice and Strawson are right about the validity of talk of meaning, and therefore of talk of 'sameness of meaning', then we have the seductive prospect of its being possible to transform what we customarily take to be analytic statements into logical truths via synonyms, which, if right, will settle the issue of analyticity once for all. We would in this case have a means of testing for analyticity in cases of non-tautologous analytic statements (more strictly, non-*obviously*-tautologous, where the tautologicality of logical truths is thought of in Wittgenstein's sense), by applying the transformation apparatus derived, thus eliminating the 'non-obvious' qualification. The chief requirement here is that the notion of meaning − granting that meanings are not entities − would have to be made sufficiently precise to be of use here;[48] but it is not obvious in advance that 'meaning', or more narrowly circumscribed talk of definitions or of the conventions governing the use (and hence part, at least, of the meaning) of expressions in a language, will always be too imprecise to allow for a characterisation of analyticity in terms of a logical underlay of the kind in question. If anything, this tack has certain advantages, for it leads directly to a link with another in the crucial family of notions, *viz.*, necessity. For, to deny a logical truth, into which we may find all analytic truths turning, is to contradict oneself; and on at least one construal of necessity, statements are necessary just in case denying them has this consequence. On such a view the classes of necessary and analytic truths may turn out to be coextensive.

Optimism at this juncture is premature, however; for the idea that analyticity could be shown to reduce to logical truth depends upon whether there is a well understood notion of 'logical truth' available. Unhappily, there is not. Quine defined logical truth in terms of the logical particles, understood as those words which have application in any context whatever − 'topic-neutral' words as Ryle called them. But what determines which words are the logical particles? The notion of topic-neutrality is unsatisfactory, for no word is utterly free of dependence on context; even 'if' and 'all' are so, given that the former is applicable only when possibilities are at issue, and the latter only when we are talking of a class of items taken in sum. If 'if' and 'all' are taken to be logical particles nevertheless, there appears to be no reason why 'when', 'above', 'thought', 'body', or any other term, should not likewise be a logical particle.[49]

One way out might be to explain topic-neutrality in terms of 'implicit definition'; whereas 'when' or 'above' requires some kind of ostensive definition, 'if' and 'all' can be introduced by showing how they are used.[50] But it is not clear how this helps, for any word could be implicitly defined by showing how it is used, given a rich enough vocabulary; and given a poor enough one, not even 'if' and 'all' could be so defined.[51]

Making connections between analyticity and necessity is itself far from uncontroversial. Saying this reiterates a point made earlier about this family of notions; whereas certain *differences* between its members are reasonably perspicuous — we recognise that analyticity is a semantic notion, necessity a metaphysical notion, and apriority an epistemological one — the *connections* are much harder to be clear about, because what connections we recognise as holding between them is precisely relative to what philosophical theory we are subscribing to in the background. This point seems to me vital, and its significance will become clearer in due course.

What is already clear is that talk of analyticity will yield little progress in isolation from talk of necessity. There are no guarantees in advance that necessary truths will be thought of either as logical truths or (if these are different) analytic truths merely; indeed, turning now to the question of necessity, it appears that there may be reasons for holding apart the notions of necessity, analyticity, and logical truth.

THE NOTION OF NECESSITY

The characteristics of Leibniz's distinction between necessary and contingent truths were earlier noted to be that the former are such that to deny them involves contradiction, whereas denials of the latter are not contradictory. Another way of putting this is to say that the denial of a necessary truth yields an impossibility, whereas the denial of a contingent truth is as possible as its affirmation. But these remarks are too general; we need to add to them to get a more precise understanding of what necessity consists in. This is to say that although a sketch of the sort we so far have aids recognition of the following as necessary truths:

1. $7+5=12$

and

2. If all humans are featherless and Aristotle is human, then Aristotle is featherless,

and of the following as contingent truths —

3. There are nine planets in the solar system, and

4. Aristotle was born in Macedonia,

none the less all that we have succeeded in doing is to show, by means of an intuitive grasp of the difference in character between denials of 1. and 2. as against denials of 3. and 4., that we have *prima facie* reasons for distinguishing between them. What the distinction turns upon is still imprecise. The reason for this is that to say '1. and 2. are necessary because their denials are impossible or contradictory' is to appeal to notions — the notions of impossibility and contradiction – which are as complex as that of necessity itself.

There is more than one way to skin a cat, however, as the Grice-Strawson considerations in the preceding sections show. Without trying to give an independent specification of one of the concepts in this particular group in terms of which the others are to be defined, one can draw a line around the area of application of these concepts by showing what work they do, and with what concepts they are not to be confounded.[52] More examples will help fix the first of these desiderata. Thus, it appears to be evident that truths of arithmetic and logic like 1. and 2. are necessary, but that necessity is a wider notion than this, for 'Aristotle is not shorter than himself', 'no number is a mammal' and 'everything coloured is extended' are examples of necessary truths which are neither mathematical truths nor, as they stand, logical truths, in at very least the sense in which truths of first-order logic are logical truths. Perhaps therefore one should keep 'necessary truth' and 'logical truth' distinct to show that there are truths of the required stamp outside formal calculi.

Necessity, further, is narrower than merely 'natural necessity' (or 'causal necessity'). A donkey cannot run faster than a jet can fly; and a goldfish cannot swim the Baltic in less than an hour; we say it is 'impossible' for donkeys and goldfish to perform feats of such athleticism, but we do not mean that it is logically impossible that these facts of nature should be other than they are, or that it is contradictory to deny them.

This prompts the thought that what distinguishes necessity from merely natural necessity is that whereas we might be obliged, on being confronted with, say, prodigious donkeys, to give up our belief that it is impossible for donkeys to gallop at speeds of around Mach 4, we cannot give up necessary truths proper. Thus *unrevisibility* might be a focal characteristic of necessary truths, or even defining of them.

The thought that there might be wholly unrevisable truths has been resisted by Quine among others.[53] On Quine's view, our beliefs form a web or system impinging only at its periphery on the world of experience, rather like an inverted bowl resting on its lip. Generally speaking, recalcitrant experiences at the periphery do not make us give up or change the beliefs deeper in the system, but this is not to say that any one such belief is wholly immune to revision; we may, if there are compelling reasons to do so, go so far as to give up logical laws. 'Revision', Quine points out, 'even of the logical law of excluded middle has been proposed as a means of simplifying quantum mechanics';[54] so there is in principle no reason why any belief or law of logic should not be revised if required. Accordingly, if unrevisability is a focal characteristic of necessary truths, then there are no necessary truths, a result which Quine regards with imperturbability.

Quine's views, in turn, have been resisted by defenders of the notion of necessity like Plantinga,[55] in whose view it is not the case that to say a truth is necessary is to say it will never be given up, for the reverse reason that there can be propositions which one might never give up (such as, say, the proposition that Willard is an exceedingly fine fellow) no matter how strong the countervailing evidence, which none the less does not mean 'Willard is an exceedingly fine fellow' is necessarily true. Accordingly, on Plantinga's view, necessity is neither to be defined in terms of unrevisability nor conflated with it. It may still be that necessary truths generally display the characteristics of unrevisability, without unrevisability being essential to necessity; thus the rider, that if for some reason a necessary truth does have to be dropped it is no less necessary for all that, blocks any attempt to identify necessity with unrevisability.[56]

The idea of unrevisability carries with it certain tangentially allied notions which might seem to be characteristic of necessary truths, this time concerning the question of how they are known. These are the epistemological notions of self-evidence and apriority. If one asked, concerning some such necessary truth as 2., or of any instance of *modus ponens* $[(p \rightarrow q) \cdot p] \rightarrow q$, how one knew it to be true, the answer might be that it is just self-evident, we just *see* that it is true. But this will not do, for in order to see that '$z = (a \times 10^3) + (b \times 10^2) + (c \times 10) + d$' is necessarily true, one has to know some mathematics; specifically, that this is an example of the general way of representing intergers using a positional notation in a decimal system, which relatively few people know and therefore relatively few people find self-evident. An easier example would be that the arithmetical proposition '$1233 + 4041 = 5274$' is necessarily true, but not self-evident; one has to work the calculation to see that it is true. Neither is it uncontroversial to say that these truths may be arrived at by a chain of self-evident steps from immediately self-evident propositions, for, say, if Goldbach's Conjecture is true it is necessarily true despite the fact that it is not self-evidently true (it is not known whether it is true or false). In fact there are quite a number of necessary truths which are not self-evident — an example might be 'Kant could not have been a canary' — so that defining necessary truths as self-evident, or self-evidently derivable from self-evident truths, will not on the face of it do.

If necessary truths are not the same thing as self-evident truths, are they *a priori* truths? What this must at least mean is that if they are *a priori* then they are knowable independently of empirical investigation. Both Leibniz and Kant, as remarked, held that necessary truths are so known. Perhaps the question ought only to arise in connection with *known* necessary truths, for in the case of, say, Goldbach's Conjecture, we have a necessary truth or falsehood without its being known which, and so without its being known *a priori*.[57] Restricting attention to known necessary truths, then, the question whether they are known *a priori* becomes either: is every necessary truth known *a priori* to everyone who knows it; or, is every necessary truth a truth knowable *a priori* to at least someone? The answer to the first of these alternatives is that anyone might come to know a necessary truth *a posteriori*, by the simple expedient of learning it second-hand from some source or other. Thus someone might come to learn that twelve is a composite number by being told or by looking it up in a book, having never given the matter any thought beforehand. Experience, of a sort, has played a role here.

The second question is not so easy to answer. It is asked whether necessary truths are truths which are in principle knowable *a priori*. This is not at all the same thing as saying that a truth is necessary if and only if someone or other knows it *a priori*; it is by contrast to say that any known necessary truth would not be necessary unless it *could* be known *a priori* − the distinction here arising from the fact, already noted, that there might be unknown necessary truths. One way of finding out if necessary truths must be knowable *a priori* is to ask the reverse question, whether any necessary truths are discoverable only *a posteriori*, that is, only on the basis of empirical investigation. (This is not the same as the case in the preceding paragraph where a necessary truth was discovered on the basis of investigation; here the question is whether there are necessary truths which could *only* have been so discovered.) It would appear difficult to think offhand of a necessary truth that would fit this bill, but in fact there are some candidates, offered by Kripke, which will be discussed in due course. For the present it suffices to take yet another alternative tack, and to ask whether any *contingent* truths can be known *a priori*, for to say that necessary truths are to be identified with truths knowable only *a priori* would fail if it could be shown that certain contingent truths could be so known. According to Plantinga, there are indeed contingent truths knowable *a priori*. He argues that some such statement as 'I believe that $7+5=12$' is a contingent fact about one of my beliefs, which however I do not have to conduct an empirical investigation to find out I hold; therefore I know a contingent fact *a priori*, and because this is so, the *a priori* cannot be defining of necessity.[58]

DE DICTO AND *DE RE*

So far necessary truths have been characterised by a few examples and by some thoughts suggesting that they are not the same thing as logical truths, being wider than these, nor natural necessities, being narrower than these; nor yet that they are unrevisable or self-evident propositions, or propositions known *a priori*.

The conception of necessity being picked out in these largely negative ways is a conception of necessity as a property attaching to propositions. Necessity in this sense has been called necessity *de dicto* (*dictum* = 'proposition' and *de dicto* = 'about a proposition'), and what this means is that there is a property − called a *modal* property − namely the property of *being necessarily true*, which we are predicating of propositions. The proposition 'Necessarily Aristotle is not shorter than himself' is an assertion of modality *de dicto*, which is to say is a proposition predicting upon the proposition 'Aristotle is not shorter than himself' the property of being necessarily true.

The notion of *de dicto* necessity is invoked to admit of a distinction, important in much traditional philosophy, and once again important in contemporary philosophy, between *de dicto* necessity and *de re* necessity. This latter is a notion of the essential or necessary ownership of a property by an object; accordingly, a proposition in which it is predicted of an object that it possesses some or other property essentially or necessarily, is a proposition expressing *de re* modality. The example often used to make the *de dicto*−*de re* distinction clear is taken from Aquinas, where in the *Summa Contra Gentiles* he considers the problem whether freedom of will is consistent with the foreknowledge of God. Suppose at a time t_1 God sees Aristotle sitting at a later time t_2. Then, given the truth of the proposition 'what is seen to be sitting is necessarily sitting', it would appear that Aristotle could not do anything other than sit at t_2. Here the *de dicto-de re* distinction becomes of use, as Aquinas saw; for if 'what is seen to be sitting is necessarily sitting' is taken *de dicto*, that is as saying 'it is necessarily true that whatever is seen to be sitting is sitting', then it is true; but if it is taken *de re*, that is as saying 'whatever is seen to be sitting has the property of sitting necessarily or essentially', then it is false. An argument to the truth of determinism requires that this latter *de re* reading be true; accordingly, the thesis that determinism follows from God's foreknowledge is false.[59] The distinction between modality *de dicto* and modality *de re* can therefore be summarised like this: A proposition expressing modality *de dicto* is one in which a modality is predicated of some other proposition, whereas a proposition expressing modality *de re* says that a property belongs necessarily or essentially to an object.

Needless to say, the notion of modality *de re* is a highly controversial one. Until lately in contemporary philosophy, the traditional distinction between essential and accidental properties of objects was practically a dead issue. The idea of essence played an important role in Aristotle, whose view was, roughly speaking, that essence is what is expressible as the concept under which something falls if it is to be identified *as* what it is − 'the essence of each thing is that which it is said to be *per se*'.[60] Thus it is essential to a man that he be a rational animal, but not that he be this or that particular height or of this or that coloration.[61] If you 'remove' an essential property from something x, it ceases to be x and becomes either nothing or something y instead. On the other hand, any of x's accidental properties − since x has them contingently, non-essentially − can be removed without x ceasing to be x.

The Aristotelian notion played a central role in Scholastic thought, but, after Locke, ceased to be attractive. Locke made a distinction between *real* and *nominal* essences, the latter being the property or set of properties by means of which we recognise an item and which justifies, on any given occasion, one's application of the item's given name. For example, gold is a metal which is malleable, heavy, and yellow (these properties constituting the nominal essence of the item), and it is in virtue of gold's having these properties that we recognise it as such and can apply 'gold' to it.[62] Locke took the most plausible view of 'real essence' to be that it is the 'real but unknown constitution of [the] insensible parts' of things, 'from which flow those sensible qualities which serve to distinguish them one from another', which latter qualities constitute the nominal essence.[63] This way of putting things seemed to make talk of essences, *qua* 'real' essences, superfluous in the end, for, in line with the increasingly phenomenalist character of empiricism after Berkeley, it was unnecessary (and indeed for many, like Berkeley himself, misguided) to postulate the existence of occult entities lurking behind what there is in the sensible world, like 'matter' or 'substance' or 'essence'. Accordingly, the appeal to essences died out, and it is only in the context of the issues presently under discussion that it has returned.

FORMALISATION AND ESSENCE

The invocation of essences, together with the equally rich notion of possible worlds, possible objects, transworld individuals, and un-actualised individuals – all of which notions I shall comment upon shortly – results from the contemporary effort to give an account of the modalities in rigorous terms. Briefly, formalisations of modal inference were constructed in the earlier part of this century,[64] using standard logical apparatus together with the operators $\square$ and $\triangle$ (sometimes written L and M), respectively standing for 'necessarily' or 'it is necessary that. . .' and 'possibly' or 'it is possible that. . .'. The operators are interdefinable; if $\square$ is taken as primitive then $\triangle$ is definable thus: $\triangle p =$ df.$\sim \square \sim p$. Depending upon choice of axioms, one can get stronger and weaker systems of modal logic. The root system is M, which adds to the truth-functional tautologies the rules of *modus ponens* and necessitation, which latter is a rule to the effect that $\square p$ is a thesis of M if p is; and it has as additional axioms the formulae $\square(p\rightarrow q) \rightarrow (\square p \rightarrow \square q)$ and $\square p \rightarrow p$. Adding axioms adds strength; but it also adds diversity, and for this reason a pressing need was felt for a semantical interpretation of modal calculi to settle the issues which the diversity of uninterpreted mechanisms raised.[65]

Early efforts in this direction, such as Carnap's,[66] made use of an obvious and compelling notion suggested by Leibniz, to the effect that the necessity of a necessary truth resides in the fact that it is a truth not contingent upon how things happen to be, or upon how things might have happened to be if things had turned out otherwise in the world, but upon its being and remaining true in this world and in any possible rearrangement of how things might have been in this or any world. More succinctly, a necessary truth is one which is true in all possible worlds. Carnap's move was to make use of a notion of maximally consistent sets of atomic sentences (such that if S is such a sentence then either it or its negation is a member of the set), which sets he called 'state descriptions'. Then what is meant by saying S is necessarily true is that S is true under every state description.

This theme was taken up and prosecuted vigorously in the following decades, notably by Kripke and Hintikka among others;[67] and a semantics for quantified modal logic was worked out using Leibniz's notion – and terminology – of possible worlds and possible objects.[68] The technical details are such as to provide fruitful extensions to the formalisations of other nonextensional logics like epistemic, deontic, and tense logic. In its wake it brought the metaphysical baggage presently under discussion. With char-

acteristic acuity, Quine early recognised the metaphysical implications of modal formalism, and contested it.[69]

Quine's objections focus precisely on the fact that quantified
modal logic forces a commitment to what he calls 'Aristotelian
essentialism', for these reasons. Modal contexts are, in Quine's
terminology, 'referentially opaque'.[70] The statements (using
Quine's original numbering)

(15) 9 is necessarily greater than 7
(24) the number of planets = 9

are both true, but it would be a misapplication of substitutivity to
exchange 'the number of planets' for '9' in (15) because the resulting
statement

(18) the number of planets is necessarily greater than 7

is false. It is because modal contexts are referentially opaque that
Quine finds them at best obscure and at worst wrongheaded,
particularly in view of the fact that he held it to be philosophically
undesirable to quantify into opaque contexts; the move from (15) to

(30) (x) (x is necessarily greater than 7)

simply does not have a clear sense, *unless* it is taken to be the case
that objects have necessary and contingent properties independently of our ways of specifying them — which is to say, have
their properties in and of themselves, essentially. For Quine such a
commitment is unthinkable, because in his view something's being
'necessarily' this or that way is not a trait it possesses in itself, but
depends on the manner by which we refer to it,[71] a nominalist view
reminiscent of Hume among others. Consider the thing x purports
to refer to in (30); by consulting (15) from which (30) was inferred,
x would appear to refer to 9, which is the number of the planets —
but this conflicts with the fact that (18) is false. The only way out
would appear to be essentialism; 'evidently this reversion to
Aristotelian essentialism is required if quantification into modal
contexts is to be insisted on'[72], from which Quine concludes 'so
much the worse for quantified modal logic'.[73]

Despite the debate generated by these of Quine's views,[74] the
provision of possible-worlds semantics for modal logic rendered his
views less interesting by providing a framework for working with an
openly metaphysical essentialism. (Quine's views antedated the
semantical innovations for modal logic by a decade.) Essentialism,
and certain other of the metaphysical issues to which interest in the
modalities gives rise, accordingly turns on whether or not talk of
'possible worlds' is acceptable. Such talk might be objectionable,
particularly in view of the metaphysical consequences which, on the
face of it, appear too readily to flow from it, together with the fact

that, in the first place, appeal to possible worlds was meant to be purely intuitive or heuristic.[75]

It is at this point that a detour through talk of possible worlds, and the implications of such talk, needs to be taken, if we are to see whether (and if so, how) talk of possible worlds helps us to understand necessity.

POSSIBLE WORLDS

A well-known possibilist *credo*, owing to Lewis, runs like this:

I believe that there are possible worlds other than the one we happen to inhabit. If an argument is wanted, it is this. It is uncontroversially true that things might be otherwise than they are. I believe, and so do you, that things could have been different in countless ways. But what does this mean? Ordinary language permits the paraphrase: there are many ways things could have been besides the way they are. On the face of it this is an existential quantification. It says that there exist many entities of a certain description, to wit 'ways things could have been'. I believe that things could have been different in countless ways; I believe permissible paraphrases of what I believe; taking the paraphrase at face value, I therefore believe in the existence of entities that might be called 'ways things could have been'. I prefer to call them 'possible worlds'.[76]

The questions raised at the end of the last section, concerning the grounds on which this and allied kinds of possible worlds talk might be objectionable, come down to saying this: for one thing, in giving an interpretation of a formal system one is free to choose the interpretative domains and their constituent objects in different ways, consonant with informativeness and consistency; and therefore a logic with the operators $\Box$ and $\triangle$ need not turn on the notion of 'possible worlds' at all. The other thing is that the very idea of possible worlds (together with possible objects, essences, and the rest) conflicts with our common-sense ontology, our rude everyday sense of reality. There is a more or less cavalier rejoinder to this second objection; to the effect that our everyday ontology is altogether too rude to be of service in working out a thorough philosophical account of the world and the thought and talk which range over it. Perhaps unhappily, and for all that it is cavalier, this rejoinder is forceful.[77] The first objection requires a more studied reply.

One thought is that the formalisation of modal inferences starts from the fact that in our ordinary thought and talk we employ the concepts of necessity and possibility, and much of our reasoning involves them. Any interpretation of calculi employing the notions represented by $\Box$ and $\triangle$ must somehow, if they are not to be formalisations of *modal* inference, preserve the senses in which $\Box$

says something about what is the case no matter what else, and △ says something about what can be the case depending on these or those circumstances. By using the notion of possible worlds we succinctly capture these ideas; we can give tight definitions of necessity and possibility without destroying their pre-theoretical flavour, and in terms of the resulting calculus can strictly map the logical relationships obtaining between modified propositions. The test then is to see whether in addition to these virtues, the appeal to possible worlds is fruitful and suggestive in application to further problems. And, indeed, so it is claimed to be.

For example, it is notorious that standard extensional logic cannot adequately deal with counterfactual conditionals, conditionals of the form 'if such and such had been the case, this and that would have been the case'. The antecedent suggests a 'contrary to fact', hence 'counterfactual', state of affairs, and the consequent says or claims how things would have been accordingly different. The problem is that conditional sentences, those of 'if . . . then. . .' form, express propositions which are functions of their constituent propositions, but which − when the conditional sentence is in the subjunctive mood ('if. . . *were* or *had been* . . . then. . .') − are not *truth-functions* of their constituent propositions. How is one to deal with them? The problem has more than one aspect; there is the matter of giving an account of the formal properties of conditionals in general, and there is the matter of solving the difficulty which arises from the fact that even when we have a formal specification of conditionality together with all the facts relevant to a given counterfactual conditional, we may still not be in a position to determine its truth-value. Possible-worlds talk is proposed as a solution to this latter problem.[78] The idea is to construe a counterfactual as stating that in some possible state of affairs in which things are *that* way (that is, other than the way they actually are or have actually turned out), some other thing or things are *this* way.[79] A possible state of affairs is just a possible world.

This approach is inviting because it captures the sense in which we commonly think how things might be or might have gone if . . . or will be if. . . . In particular connection with problems in the philosophy of science, such as the nature of scientific laws and the need to secure an adequate account of causation, possible-worlds analysis of counterfactuals is richly suggestive.[80] Nevertheless, it raises difficulties too, not least among them a commitment, at least potentially, to the somewhat luxurious metaphysical items already mentioned − 'unactualised possibles' and essences.

Another issue, or collection of issues, for which possible-worlds

talk holds out promise concerns meaning and an adequate treatment of properties, relations, and propositions. The special issue of
one component of theory of meaning – namely, theory of reference
– in which advances have been made by means of the idiom of
possible worlds will be canvassed in chapter 7 below. The idea in
general terms is that meaning can be understood by way of an
enriched grasp of the extensions of singular and predicate expressions, enriched in the sense that they are to be said to range over not
only actual objects or n-tuples of them, but also possible objects,
objects in worlds other than the actual world. Employing this
technique, a set-theoretical account of the meaning of a language's
constituents can be given by saying that the meaning of a singular
term is a function from possible worlds to objects, the meaning of a
predicate is a function from worlds to ordered n-tuples of objects,
and the meaning of (declarative) sentences is a function from worlds
to truth-values. In the same way, regarding the abstract objects
properties and *relations*, a property can be defined as a function
from worlds to sets of objects, and a relation likewise as a function
from worlds to ordered n-tuples of objects. A neat circle is then
completed by construing *propositions* as functions from worlds to
truth-values; for on this account it turns out that a proposition is the
meaning of a declarative sentence, *vide* the discussion in chapter 2
above; and because, like the other two classes of abstract objects,
propositions are identified with set-theoretical entities, no difficulty
arises concerning their identity conditions.

These last thoughts make it notable that possible-worlds talk
offers to solve some of the problems which appear most intractable
from an extensionalist point of view. Quine's early hostility to
intensional notions like meaning and necessity sprang precisely
from a desire to operate strictly extensionally; the result was
difficulty over this family of notions. Possible-worlds talk offers
progress with respect to them.

OBJECTIONS TO POSSIBLE-WORLDS DISCOURSE

Nevertheless, talk of possible worlds carries with it a number of
serious difficulties. There is the problem about essentialism; there is
the problem about possible but nonactual entities; and there is a
problem related to these concerning the identity of individuals
across worlds. Each one is potentially vitiating with respect to the
possible-worlds enterprise – or at any rate, if the objections hold,
they seriously weaken its usefulness. I consider them in reverse
order.

The problem of *transworld identity* can be put like this: The possible-worlds theorist wishes to say that a tractable and fruitful way of dealing with the thought that, say, Aristotle might not have been tutor to Alexander the Great, is to say 'there is some possible world in which Aristotle was not Alexander's tutor'. This introduces the idea of Aristotle's existing in more than one world; not only in the actual world, in which he was tutor to Alexander and a pupil of Plato and the son of a Court physician, but in a plurality of possible worlds in which he is variously only some, or only one, or perhaps none of these things, or in which he was all these and more. In the parlance of possible-worlds theory, Aristotle's existence in all these worlds make him a 'transworld individual'. According to the theory, all individuals are transworld individuals, as it happens, because any individual might well have been what it, she, or he is or was *ceteris non paribus*.

The objection to this is that the idea of a transworld individual makes no sense because it violates the principle of the indiscernability of identicals.[81] This principle states that for any objects x and y, if they are identicial then all the properties belonging to one belong to the other and *vice versa*. If some object x is supposed to exist in more than one world, say in the two worlds W_n and W_m, then because W_n and W_m will be *different* worlds only if there is at least one respect in which matters are different in W_n from the way are in W_m − perhaps, let us say, that in W_n Aristotle has a beauty-spot on his cheek. but in W_m he is beauty-spotless − then at very least x-in-W_n will have property (the conjunctive property of 'being x and Aristotle has a beauty-spot') which x-in-W_m fails to have (the cognate property for x-in-W_m is 'being x and Aristotle has no beauty-spot'). But if this is so, x-in-W_n and x-in-W_m are discernible, and hence not identical. There is, therefore, no way one can identify individuals across worlds: in consequence, either one rests content with a notion of 'worldbound individuals', which is to say individuals existing in only one world at a time, which threatens to reduce the interest of possible-worlds talk to vacuity, or, better, one gives up such talk altogether.[82]

Matters are in fact worse for possible-worlds theory than this argument at first suggests. For suppose, in the interests of argument, one concedes the notion of transworld identity; then one can show that it collapses into dilemma. Take two distinct objects x and y, which we grant retain their identities across worlds though suffering changes from one to the next, and a series of world W_1 . . . W_4. Imagine that in W_1 x is a thing large, round, green and soft, and that y is a thing small, square, red and hard, and that these properties are determinate and exhaustive of the identifying properties x and y respectively possess. Further imagine that in moving from W_1 to W_2 x and y exchange their colours; that in moving from W_2 to W_3 they exchange their shapes . . . and so on, such that in W_4 x is both x and small, square, red and hard, which is what y was in W_1; and that y is both y and large, round, green and soft, which is what x was in W_1. Thus x-in-W_4 is indescernible from y-in-W_1, and therefore, according to the principle of indescernibility, identical with it; yet *ex hypothesi* and adhering to the principle of the transitivity of identity, x-in-W_4 is not identical with y-in-W_1 but with x-in-W_1, which is now indescernible from y-in-W_4 . . . and so on. Thus dilemma.[83]

The only way out of this difficulty is to appeal to essences, and say that all entities have contingent properties C and essential properties E such that an entity x has C in some worlds and non-C in others, but has E in every world in which it exists at all; and further, that if there is an entity z which has E in at least one possible world, z and x are identicial. Then in the case of x and y just given, the properties they exchange while passing from one world to the next are C and not E properties, and it is in virtue of the preservation of their E properties that they preserve their identities across worlds.

But will this manoeuvre do? For presumably E properties are not universal properties, but are unique to their bearers because they constitute their bearers' essences, and the problem of how to specify them accordingly arises. What properties are essential to, say, Aristotle? Evidently 'being Plato's pupil' is not essential, for in other worlds he might have been Socrates' pupil, or pupil to no one. How about 'being the greatest philosopher of antiquity to hail from Macedonia'? But then in some worlds he might have hailed from Athens or Miletus, or not been a philosopher at all. And so on for all Aristotle's properties. In short, it appears to be insurmountably difficult to settle which subset of Aristotle's properties are his E properties. If Aristotle's E properties cannot be picked out, how do we know that in moving from W_n to W_m we have not left one or more of the E properties behind, and with them Aristotle?[84]

The upshot of such considerations would seem to be that talk of possible worlds is either incoherent because the concept of transworld identity is incoherent, or at best is of limited value because we can only employ a notion of worldbound individuals. In view of the fact that such a notion leads to the seemingly counterintuitive result that Aristotle can only be Aristotle if he was as he was and that things could not have gone otherwise with him — that is, that all the properties he in fact possessed were essential to him — this entire way of talking would appear to be misguided.

Possible-worlds theorists counter these objections with some ingenuity. Lewis, for example, has a theory designed specifically to steer a middle course between the problematic notions of trans-world identity and worldbound individuals. It is called 'counterpart theory.' The idea is that individuals are indeed worldbound; are, indeed, bound to the actual world; but have counterparts in other worlds, which resemble their actual-world counterparts 'more closely than do other things in their worlds', and in such a way that for anything x in the actual world W, its counterpart x-in-W_n just is what x-in-W would have been, had things been different in the way things are different as between W and W_n.[86] Using these notions, we can express the idea that Aristotle might not have tutored Alexander by saying that Aristotle has a counterpart in some world W_n which resembles him in all respects save that counterpart-Aristotle did not tutor counterpart-Alexander.

The most damaging criticisms of counterpart theory are offered by other possible-worlds theorists, notable Kripke and Plantinga.[87] Consider the case of counterfactuals: 'if Alexander had paid attention to Aristotle's tutoring, he might not have died from drink'. Aristotle might, we say, have felt personal regret (or, for that matter, relief) at not having been a more vigorous tutor in view of Alexander's early demise due to excessive potation. On Kripke's view, we can make no sense of Aristotle's regret or relief; for the persons referred to in the counterfactual are not Aristotle and Alexander, but their counterparts. Plantinga's complaint is a variant of this; it is that counterpart theory does nothing to avoid the worldboundedness problem, for to make sense of the idea of some-thing's being different or going otherwise for a given individual or entity x, we must be able to say that x's being F in one dispensation of things W_n, and being G in some other dispensation W_m, is such that in W_n the properties F and x's-being-self-identical are coexem-plified, and in W_m the properties G and x's-being-self-identical are coexemplified. If however we say that x-in-W_n and x-in-W_m are counterparts, then we have failed to account for our intuitions to the effect that x might have been G rather than F. To say, in other words, that Aristotle might not have tutored Alexander is to say that Aristotle might have been Aristotle yet not have tutored Alexander, which is surely what we want to say; but if Alexander's-tutor-Aristotle and not-Alexander's-tutor-Aristotle are mere counterparts of one another and not the self-same Aristotle, then we have lost the sense in which things might have gone differently for that one and the self-same man Aristotle.

The line preferred by possible-worlds theorists who reject counterpart theory is to tackle the question of identity directly, chiefly by providing an enriched characterisation of the notion of identity itself. The key lies in the fact that the arguments sketched above threaten damage to identity across time as well as across worlds; for evidently the infant Aristotle and the aged Aristotle will have very few identifyingly manifest properties in common – infant Aristotle might, so to say, be small, pink, round and soft, and adult Aristotle large, brown, square and hard – while yet being the self-same Aristotle. In changing over time, an item loses some and gains other properties; and our insistence on regarding the item as self-identical throughout shows that the principle of identity we are working with is more complex than the objections suggest. Thus, the possession by an item of a property ought perhaps to be temporally indexed – x has F *at a time t* – and accordingly a statement of the principle of identity ought to carry a temporal quantifier, thus: for any objects x and y, if they are identical then for any property F and time t, x has F at t if and only if y has F at t. Then a statement of identity in worlds parlance would carry quantification over both worlds and times to yield: for any x and y, if x = y then for any W,F, and t, x has F and W at t iff y likewise.[88]

A summary solution to the difficulties posed by transworld identity is offered by Kripke. In his view it is a pseudo-problem, which arises from taking 'the metaphor of possible worlds much too seriously in some way. It is as if a "possible world" were like a foreign country, or distant planet way out there. It is as if we see dimly through a telescope various actors on this distant planet'[89] Kripke rejects the metaphor. In doing so he is taking a position directly opposite to Lewis' possiblist realism.

UNACTUALISED POSSIBILIA

The foregoing discussion of identity marks a point in the debate on the matter, not a resolution of it. It is evident that possible-worlds theorists have, however, a reasonably robust account to give of themselves in that arena. Considerably more vexed an issue is the question of what further and more focal ontological commitments are demanded by the appeal to possible worlds; specifically, the question is – what sense can be made of talk about possibilia, that is possible but non-actual worlds and the objects they contain?

There are, broadly speaking, two strategies which have been adopted by defenders of possible-worlds talk in this connection. One is an extreme possibilism of the kind favoured by Lewis; the other consists in a set of variant theories taking it that there is only one actual world, namely this world, and defining possible worlds and their contents in terms of one or more such intensional items as properties, propositions, or states of affairs, together with certain modal notions like 'instantiability' (a *de re* notion) or 'possible truth) (a *de dicto* notion) employed as primitives.

The problem is, simply, that the idea of nonexistent items like possible worlds and possible objects is flatly contradictory. The reply offered by Lewis is that there is merely an appearance of contradiction here owing to the fact that assertions of existence are being taken univocally; to paraphrase 'there is something x which is nonactual' by means of the starkly contradictory formula $(\exists x) \sim (\exists y)(x=y)$ is to fail to capture the possibilist's intentions. One has to distinguish between an unrestricted form of the existential quantifier and a restricted form which indexes the existence-assertion to a particular world. Then to say that x is an unactualised possibilium is to say $(\exists x)$ $(\exists^{\omega} y)$ $(x=y)$, where $(\exists^{\omega} . .)$ is a restricted quantifier asserting actuality in the world in which the utterance is made. The formula reads, 'there is something x which does not exist in W_n', W_n being understood as *this* world, the actual world, from which the legitimacy of saying x is *existent but not actual* follows.[90] The analogy is to time; present time is only one time among others, which we call 'present' because we inhabit it; inhabitants of other times use that same indexical expression to refer to their own presents.[91] The term 'actual' functions indexically as does 'present', such that use of it does not confer special ontological status on any world in which it is indexically used, but merely picks out which world it is in which the relevant utterance is issued.

Lewis is completely in earnest about taking it that possible worlds exist just as our own world does. 'When I profess realism about possible worlds, I mean to be taken literally . . . Our actual world is only one among others. We call it alone actual not because it differs in kind from all the rest but because it is the world we inhabit.'[92] This, one notes in passing, explains why Lewis is committed to counterpart theory; for if all possible worlds are equally real, an individual can exist in one of them only, rather as a thing can only be in one place at a time.

Most of Lewis' critics find these views simply unintelligible,[93] although in view of the fact that they have something of a precedent in Meinong and are consistent, they are eminently discussable.[94] Nevertheless, practically all other possible worlds theorists are fastidious enough to shy away from the disagreeable nature of what

Haack, taking a cue from Quine, calls 'Lewis's ontological slum',[95] for the reason that there are, at least potentially, strategies available for handling these difficulties without resort to a crowded universe.

Briefly, the strategies in question turn on admitting only one actual world, our own, and giving an account of possible worlds in terms of modal constructions from it. Any view of this general kind is called 'actualism'. One variant turns upon a distinction between existence and instantiation applied to intensional items like states of affairs, relations, properties, and so on. Stalnaker, for example, argues that a possible world is to be identified with existent but uninstantiated properties, and that the actual world is the world whose properties are in fact instantiated.[96] Plantinga's views resemble this; possible worlds are obtainable states of affairs, the actual world is the world in which the constituent states of affairs actually obtain.[97] The notions of 'instantiability' and 'obtainability' are *de re* modal notions. There are important differences of detail between the two views, affecting among other things what account is to be given of properties, propositions, and states of affairs, all which are closely related — for example, having the concept of some state of affairs, like that of Aristotle's being Alexander's tutor, is to know the corresponding proposition 'that Aristotle is Alexander's tutor'.[98]

The closeness of this connection gives rise to a third alternative view, owing to Adams who originated the label 'actualism'. In his view a possible world is a set S (a 'world-story') of propositions such that, both, for every proposition either it or its contradictory is a member of S, and it is possible for there to be a true conjunction of all members of S. The first condition is a 'maximalisation' condition; the actual world is that maximal set of propositions the conjunction of whose members is in fact true. Adams' theory is a *de dicto* actualism because the modality invoked is a property of propositions; from which it is evident that the existence of propositions is not dependent upon their truth.[99] This view resembles Carnap's use of the notion of state descriptions.

Adams' theory invites two considerable difficulties. Unless it contains a mechanism for resolving semantic paradoxes, such as the case of a proposition asserting of itself that it is false,[100] then because a possible world is a maximally consistent set of propositions, there can be no possible worlds.[101] The second difficulty arises from set-theoretical considerations and suggests that the notion of a maximal set of propositions is incoherent. The reason is that for any putatively maximal set S of propositions, its power set will have a greater cardinality than S. Each member of the power set will be a proposition and the set itself consistent, and the new set will have a greater cardinality than the old; the power set of their union, again, will have a greater cardinality . . . and so on. [102]

EXISTENCE AND ACTUALITY: SOME PROBLEMS

There are yet further strategies for making out a difference between existence and actuality to allow for the coherence of possible-worlds talk. [103] Diversity of opinion is frequently a good measure of the difficulty which making out a satisfactory account involves, and this case is exemplary. Apart from the problems which beset the detail of the various proposals, there are certain general cavils which an opponent of the programme will stress. Among them is the problem whether 'exists' is a predicate, that is, whether existence is a property, a question which arises prior to the question whether there can in some sense be some things having and other things lacking that property. (See chapter 4 below.) On the face of it, common parlance suggests we do make use of the notion of existence in this way; but at the cost, as it turns out on analysis, of commitment to a Meinongian or at any rate quasi-Meinongian universe. Now, the reasons offered by possible-worlds theorists for dispensing with Ockham's Razor have to be very good ones; it may be that what possible-worlds discourse promises and delivers, in the way of dealing with a broad range of philosophical problems, itself constitutes such reasons, but on the whole one is inclined to think that it is the *detail* of specific proposals which will have to carry the weight of persuasion to the effect that existence and actuality are properties, and moreover properties which are distinct from one another. Such a view seems to me more likely to be mistaken than not. Among the difficulties of the enterprise is that, as the foregoing sketches show, the concept of properties itself acquires content on the basis of possible-worlds talk, defined as functions from worlds to objects; accordingly it would be circular to explain possible worlds in terms of them (or, say, in terms of propositions) unless they are taken to be primitives or are given some independent specification.

The root difficulty with possibilia is that they are unintuitive in a quite serious way. Intuitively, there seem to be good reasons for understanding the concepts of existence and actuality univocally, as having the force of qualifying what there is, of stating what it is that can be encountered in the universe. The idea of a possible item, one which might be encountered if things were this or that way different, certainly occurs in our discourse and thought; but the big question is whether it occurs as an idea of something that exists, so that we can comfortably grasp the idea that *there is* x, but that x is (somehow) not *actual*, is not to be encountered in *this* world. Alternatively put, the question is whether the fact that we can grasp the idea that things might be otherwise or might have developed otherwise, commits us to believing that these alternatives, in order to be thinkable, must *be*. Put thus baldly, the claim that they must or do exist seems misguided. Arguably this feeling is appropriate only to possibilist realism of extreme kinds, such as Lewis' views consist in. It is not so clear that the views of Plantinga, Stalnaker, and Adams are as unacceptable. Here, it could be argued, the ontological bullet one is asked to bite is not nearly so tooth-shattering; there is no quantification over non-actual objects, at least, and given a soundly drawn distinction between existence on the one hand and instantiation or obtainability on the other, possible worlds can be constructed out of actually existing items − or, alternatively, sense can be made of them by using the notions, surely not too exotic, of propositions and possible truth, as is done by Adams. Any plausability will lie in these or cognate directions.

Whether this appearance of plausibility is more than appearance will depend, again, largely on details; but there are some thoughts about the general notion of nonactual items of which, to be adeqiate, detailed theories will need to give an account. These thoughts are *not* those offered by Quine, whose attack on possibilia is, predictably, that they lack identity criteria.[104] (He savages them by saying, 'Take the possible fat man in that doorway; and again, the possible bald man in that doorway. Are they the same possible man, or two possible men? How do we decide? . . . What sense can be found in talking of entities which cannot meaningfully be said to be identical with themselves and distinct from one another?'[105] Possibilists might reply that two possible objects are identical when their defining descriptions are equivalent; which is one way of saying, when they have all and only the same essential properties in common.) Rather, the thoughts are that, outside extreme realism, it might be correct to say that possibilia are essentially dependent on conception. Whereas we can talk sensefully of the existence of thoughts of possibilia, we cannot (without being extreme realists) talk in the same way at least of the existence of the possibilities we think of;[106] and then difficulties arise, because in order for possibilia to be useful items, their dependence on thought must not be such that they have in fact to be conceived of by someone in order to exist, but that they be, generically, conceivable; for there are infinities of them, and they have to be objective in the sense that they are available to any conceptualiser, rather than being subjective to some particular conceptualiser at some particular time.[107] Thus a concept of objectivity is required which either satisfactorily denies, or accords with, the mind-dependence of possibilia, a concept which will form one of a perspicuously understood family of concepts including 'real', 'exists', and 'actual'.[108] So far, the situation in this region is anarchic.

ESSENTIALISM

Throughout these discussions there has been talk of essences. Minimally, any essentialist thesis is one which recognises a twofold distinction between the properties something x possesses; namely, a distinction between *essential properties* and *accidental properties*. The former are those properties x possesses necessarily, that is, which x could not lack; the latter are those properties x possesses contingently, that is, which x might equally well have or not, either way still being x. Some of the motives for commitment to some or other form of essentialism have been displayed in preceding sections. The question now is: is commitment to some form of essentialism defensible?

Critics of essentialism have aimed to show that the notion of essence is either trivial (and therefore uninteresting), or unintelligible. On the first count, it is pointed out that in giving examples, essentialists cite as paradigms such cases as that everything whatever is essentially self-identical, and that everything is essentially not what it is not; but these cases, critics say, are philosophically uninteresting.[109] Other candidates for essential properties lose their triviality only at the expense of controversy; it is when controversy arises that critics argue that the notion is unintelligible. One way of sorting through these issues is as follows.

There are various formulations of essentialism, but most standardly have it that some subset of the properties of a thing x are essential to it, the rest being accidental. The essential properties are not sufficient to pick out x from other individuals, but they are severally necessary for the task. It is this that gives rise to the appearance, at least, of difficulties over transworld identity; if an individual *a* exists in more than one possible world and differs only accidentally from world to world, how does one pick out *a* in any given world? The readiest way round this is to take Kripke's line; we stipulate that some world contains *a* with these and those accidental differences as against *a* in the actual world.[110] This manoeuvre explicitly presupposes a clear distinction between essence and accident, for what is *not* stipulative on this view are *a*'s essential properties. This view in turn invites the rejoinder, discussed shortly, that what properties count as essential and accidental to *a* are in fact always stipulative; Quine's paradox of the mathematical cyclist (see below) is intended to show that essence is always relative to interest, and does not lie out there in the world – which is to argue, in other words, that there are no *de re* necessities.

On the view that essential properties are a subset of x's properties, one way of discriminating between them and x's accidental properties is to say that x's essential properties in some sense 'make x the particular individual it is'. This is not at all a clear formulation as it stands, but it has certain similarities to Locke's suggestion, that essence is the invisible underlay – perhaps structure or internal constitution – of x, which is such as to give rise to x's manifest nature. What do 'makes' and 'give rise to' mean in these formulations? An obvious suggestion is that they mean 'cause'. This creates certain difficulties; in empiricist orthodoxy, causal nexuses obtain between events, not between properties of objects and their being the objects they are. Nevertheless, it is intuitively quite clear that there is a determinate relation between x's having the essential properties it does have and its being the thing it is; that the relation is somehow causal can be suggestively argued.[111] It is no worse saying this than being content with saying that what x is 'follows from' its essential nature.

However such a roughly Lockean notion is to be made out on this score, it will evidently not do as it otherwise stands; for it to be useful, there must be a restriction on what effects follow from or are given rise to by x having the essence it does. If there were no such restrictions it would turn out that, say, Averroes' authorship of a commentary on Aristotle is given rise to by Aristotle's essential properties, and it is surely counterintuitive to claim that what Averroes wrote is a part of feature of Aristotle's being who he was – which would be to say that Averroes having written this or that is, in effect, a property of Aristotle. But what sort of restriction would do the trick? If appeal were made to just those features of x which engage our interest in x, then our specification of x's essential properties will be open to attack on conventionalist lines of Quine's kind (see below). If, alternatively, x's essential properties are taken to be those which are somehow crucial to x's being that individual x, then we are moving in an unexplanatory circle.

Such considerations make a roughly Aristotelian notion of essence a more attractive alternative.[112] Here one moves away from trying to explain what makes x the *individual* it is to what makes x the *kind of thing* it is. Thus, talk of essential properties is talk of those properties which make x a member of a kind K; if x is a man, then x's essential properties are those which make him a member of the kind *man*. Not only does this strategy avoid the difficulties encountered, it also has certain virtues or apparent virtues in addition. For one thing, there is a short way of proving an important essentialist claim to the effect that if x is a K then x is necessarily a K, provided one allows that 'x has all the properties of a K' entails 'x is a K'. Then if x is a K, the properties which make it a K are, by the Aristotelian notion stated, essential properties of x; therefore, it is necessary that x is a K.[113]

QUINE'S PARADOX OF THE MATHEMATICAL CYCLIST

A serious problem arises at this juncture, however, concerning what are to count as the essential and what the accidental properties of an x. According to Quine, our decisions on this are always relative to our interests; this view is known as 'conventionalism'. It is forcefully displayed in this passage:

Mathematicians may conceivably be said to be necessarily rational and not necessarily two-legged, and cyclists necessarily two-legged and not necessarily rational. But what of an individual who counts among his eccentricities both mathematics and cycling? Is this concrete individual necessarily rational and contingently two-legged, or *vice versa*? Just in so far as we are talking referentially of the object, with no special bias towards a background grouping of mathematicians as against cyclists or *vice versa*, there is no semblance of sense in rating some of his attributes as necessary and others as contingent.[114]

Commitment to essentialism, in other words, appears to result in paradox, for the reason that, relative to certain interests, certain properties will be essential, while, relative to others, they will be accidental; and so a given individual will be both essentially and accidentally so-and-so.

It has been pointed out that Quine's observations will not do as a refutation of essentialism, for the reason that ambiguity infects the sentences 'mathematicians are necessarily rational and not necessarily two-legged' and 'cyclists are necessarily two-legged and not necessarily rational'.[115] On a *de dicto* reading they assert that 'mathematicians are rational' and 'cyclists are two-legged' are necessary truths, whereas 'mathematicians are two-legged' and 'cyclists are rational' are not necessary truths. This entails that every mathematical cyclist is both rational and bipedal. On a *de re* reading they assert that every mathematician is necessarily rational and not necessarily bipedal, and conversely for the cyclist. But there is no reason to suppose that the essentialist is committed to both propositions.[116] However, it was not so much Quine's concern directly to refute essentialism by means of this argument, as to display its unintelligibility; for it points up the dilemma we are in if we regard our classifications of things as being governed by anything other than our interests. Presented with a mathematical cyclist, how *would* it be decided that he is necessarily or not necessarily rational?

An essentialist reply appears to be available if one adheres to the idiom of kinds. Essentialists claim that the only relevant question is: what K is x, where K is strictly 'what kind of thing'? Thus suppose x is a dog; then it is legitimate to ask 'what kind of thing is x?' to get the answer 'an animal', and 'what kind of animal? to get the answer 'a dog'; but hereafter, for such questions as 'what kind of dog?' inviting answers like 'a vicious dog' or 'a large dog', the point is being missed: 'large dogs' and 'vicious dogs' do not denote kinds.[117] This restriction turns on a thesis about kinds, a feature of which will be that any x is of at least some one K, and if it is a K_1 as well, it is such only if K_1 comprehends or is comprehended by K.

There are however some uncomfortable cases for the Aristotelian notion as thus enriched to avoid Quine's criticism. A good example is provided by the histories of bacteria. Bacteriologists use the immunological properties of bacterial strains as criteria of identity for them; but bacteria undergo mutations, often violent and extreme, in response to antisera, and so belong to different groups of strains at different times. Essentialists are apt to deny either that the groups in question are kinds, or, if they are, that bacteria preserve their identity across groups; but neither strategy is of any help to empirical scientists, who in this connection prefer to be conventionalists in order to make sense of the task in hand. Here essence is relative to interest, because kinds are relative to interest and essence depends on kinds.[118] In this case, further, the kinds to which bacteria belong at different times do not comprehend one another as the essentialist modification, in response to Quine, demands. The result appears to be that the essentialist claim, or at any rate this version of it, is of doubtful value.

Critics of essentialism arrive at this conclusion by insisting on the fact that impediments to understanding modalities *de re* arise from the fact that, as Quine's observations show, the modal status of a statement about a given object depends upon the choice of designation for the object in question. Thus '9 is greater than 7' is necessarily true, but 'the number of the planets is greater than 7' is not. A reply might be that the impediments are illusory. Consider cases where we can effect 'transparent' readings of opaque constructions, as when Philip believes that Cicero denounced Catiline but, because he does not know that Cicero is Tully, does not believe that Tully denounced Catiline. In such a case we perfectly well understand that there is a person, namely Cicero, of whom Philip believes it to be true that he denounced Catiline. Why then can we not understand the notion of 9's being essentially greater than 7? The necessary truth of '9 is greater than 7' says something about a property 9 necessarily possesses; and the fact that 'the number of planets is greater than 7' is contingent does nothing to alter our grasp of the independent fact about 9. Alternatively put, if the contingency attaching to what the number of the planets is somehow casts doubt on 9's being necessarily greater than 7, then how it 'somehow' does so is not clear. There is, after all, a perspicuous remedy at hand for the difficulty: the truths (and the relations between them) 'the number of planets is in fact 9; 9 is necessarily greater than 7; the number in fact of the planets is necessarily greater than 7' are all consistent with its being contingent that there are nine planets.

ESSENCE, ORIGIN AND STRUCTURE

It is still unclear, however, how to specify which properties of a thing are essential and which accidental. Two suggestions for providing a solution to this difficulty are to be found in Kripke.[119] One is that the origin of an individual, or the material of which it is made, are essential to that individual; another is that the essence of a kind of individuals consists in the internal structure of all individuals of that kind, such that membership of that kind essentially depends upon having the appropriate internal structure. Neither suggestion is uncontroversial.

Kripke's origin argument has it that if a given table is made of wood, then that table essentially originates from wood, even if it later turned into some other substance – say, silver.[120] Slote has offered a counter-argument to this.[121] Suppose that a table t came from a block of wood w which, before being made into t, had changed into a block of silver and then back again into wood, 'steadily and lawfully' both ways. Then surely it is possible that t might have been made from w during its silver stage, and later, as t, have changed into wood. If so, then t only accidentally originates from wood, and in general it follows that at least some things might accidentally be of the material out of which they are in fact originally composed.

It seems more intuitive to argue the Kripkean point about origin for the case of persons. McGinn has offered an initially compelling argument on this head, to the effect that the necessity of personal origin arises from the fact that a person is necessarily identical with the zygote from which he grew, and that there is a necessary link between the zygote and the pair of gametes supplied by his parents.[122] On the first point, it is taken by McGinn to be evident that adults are identical with the children they used to be, children with infants, infants with foetuses, and these with zygotes. On the second point, the zygote cannot be identical with the pair of gametes since they are two and the zygote one, so McGinn appeals to intuition: consider a world in which McGinn comes from Nixon's gametes, with its being the case that the actual gametes from which McGinn came are also present in that world. Which individual has the stronger title to be McGinn? He suggests the latter.[123]

The plausibility of this argument has been contested.[124] It happens that one's intuitions do not invariably run the way McGinn suggests they do;[125] and because this is so, it can further be shown – contrary to McGinn's first point – that biological (or, more generally, scientifically-grounded) continuity does not always settle identity. The argument is as follows. Imagine, using Johnson's example,[126] a world in which gametes develop into a person whose every stage of life is indistinguishable from the corresponding stages in Hitler's actual life; and suppose Hitler's gametes in that same world to develop indistinguishably from Nixon's actual development. Which has the greater title to be Hitler? Our intuitions suggest the former; which runs counter to McGinn's example despite having the same form.

These thoughts suggest that if there were two possible people, a and b, whose life histories were such that from birth to a time t a's history is indistinguishable from that of some third person c but differs thereafter, and b's history is different from c's history until t but indistinguishable thereafter, then it is not clear that only a, who has the right origin, has a title to be identical with c; for b can also plausibly be identified with c. Often used in this connection is Sprigge's example of Queen Elizabeth;[127] suppose that c is Queen Elizabeth, and that a and b are two women. Then a and Queen Elizabeth have indistinguishable histories of birth and childhood to t, and b and Queen Elizabeth have indistinguishable histories thereafter. What makes it plausible to say that b has as much title as a to be Queen Elizabeth would be some such occurrence as constitutes the subject of Mark Twain's story *The Prince and the Pauper*.

What is at issue here is whether a biological or scientifically-grounded claim is sufficient to uphold a claim about the necessity of origin; and the argument is that it is not. [128] Consider a related case: if a and b are in different worlds, they are both easily identified with Queen Elizabeth. This is because the worlds in question may reflect in their constitution quite different emphases on contextual features, a familiar way of (and reason for) discriminating between worlds. In such a case, Queen Elizabeth may quite well not develop from Queen Elizabeth's actual zygote, and if so would, literally, not be identical with it. [129]

The other suggestion made by Kripke concerns kinds. His view is that it is necessary that a thing has a certain internal structure if it does indeed have that structure; if cats are animals (have a certain internal structure which identifies them as animals) then any cat-like creature which fails to have the appropriate internal structure is not a cat. [130] Varying his choice of example, Kripke says 'tigers . . . cannot be defined simply in terms of their appearance; it is possible that there should have been a different species with all the external appearances of tigers but which had a different internal structure and therefore was not the species of tigers'. [131]

Does the notion of internal structure (IS) as essence make sense? There are various difficulties. Suppose that ISs are nested. Tigers are composed of a certain arrangement of internal organs and other physiological structures, which in turn have an IS of cells, which in turn have an IS of molecules . . . atoms . . . subatomic particles . . . and so on perhaps, to quanta of energy and beyond. Which level of IS is *the* level constituting the essence? Suppose two tigers have the same IS at all levels IS_1 . . . IS_n but differ thereafter. Which is the tiger? It might be replied that any level of IS entails that all other levels are uniformly correspondent, so that specifying similarities at one level is sufficient; but if levels of structure are uniformly correspondent, then there is every reason to suppose that the correspondence runs up to and includes external structure, such that − a point Kripke denies − external structure (which is to say, appearance) is enough to settle that something is a thing of a certain kind. Moreover, if differences of IS mark differences of kind, then a counter-intuitive result appears to follow, to the effect that each individual is its own kind. For, every individual is unique − this tiger has longer hairs on its left ear than that one − and such differences result from differences in IS. This unpalatable result can be blocked by saying that it is a logical sum of the internal properties which count, namely the logical sum of inclusive disjunction. However, this notion is one which Kripke contests in connection with external appearance; yet here the appeal to a logical sum of properties arises in connection with internal structure, which is, epistemologically, a far less appetising situation than relying upon a logical sum of appearances for kind differentiation.

Internal structure is invoked principally because it seems precise and unequivocal to give the essence of, say, gold or water, by saying that all and only the stuff of atomic number 79 in any world is gold, and water is all and only the stuff of molecular structure H_2O in any world. At first blush elements and compounds like these may seem to require an alternative analysis, given their simplicity as against the complexity of biological kinds like tigers; but the same arguments – and criticisms – go through. H_2O is a molecular structure with an 'internal' structure of atoms which in turn have an internal structure . . . and so on. It is logically possible that ISs be infinitely nested;[132] because this is so, essentialists cannot say that *whatever* the internal structure something x may have (that is, even if we do not know what it is), it is a K in virtue of it – for if we could not in principle know what made x a K, we could not recognise some further thing y as a K owing to its having the same IS as x. At one point Kripke indeed relies on this '*whatever* it is' strategy for ISs, which on this argument will not do.

What these sketches show is that the notion of essence is not a wholly perspicuous one. If it is not clear what essences are, it cannot be clear how they are to be recognised. Like that other crucial ingredient of possible worlds talk, namely the concept of unactualised possibles, the concept of essence plays an important role, and to the extent that it is itself problematic, it casts doubt on the value of appeal to possible-worlds notions wherever these latter involve commitments to essentialism. This is not to deny essentialism or certain kinds of possible worlds talk outright; secure formulations of the notions may yet be forthcoming.

NECESSITY AGAIN, ANALYTICITY, AND THE *A PRIORI*

The foregoing sections constitute a lengthy excursus into talk of possible worlds, together with a number of attendant consequences and commitments of possible-worlds talk; the idea being that if necessary truth is to be explained as truth in all possible worlds, necessary falsehood as truth in none, and contingency as truth in at least one, then the concept of possible worlds must itself survive scrutiny. What the discussion shows is that the concept is controversial and complex. In its defence it is often argued that in so far as possible worlds are stipulative devices, to be construed as sets of sentences having certain features such as maximal consistency and the like, no particular dangers are invited. Nevertheless it seems to me worth remarking that it is altogether too easy, as the foregoing sketches show, to slip into talk of possibilia and essences without having a precise way of containing these notions; to this extent it is well to be wary about worlds, the idea of which is highly metaphysically seductive. Kripke himself commented: 'the apparatus of possible worlds has (I hope) been very useful as far as the set-theoretical model-theory of modal logic is concerned, but has encouraged pseudo-problems and misleading pictures'.[133]

If one employs the idea of necessary truth as truth in all possible worlds, however, one is equipped with a useful *point de prise* for the family of notions – necessity, analyticity, and the *a priori* – at issue in this chapter. Moreover, certain rather interesting consequences appear to follow for the relations between them.

Necessity on this construal becomes the limiting case for truth; it is truth in all possible states and arrangements of the ways things can be. Thus, no matter how things are, $2+2=4$ is necessarily true, and so is Goldbach's Conjecture if it is true. In Kripke's view, our grasp on the notion of necessity arises from our understanding answers to the question whether something might have been true or false. If something might have been false, then it is not necessary; if it is true, and if it is not possible that the world might have been otherwise in relevant respects, then it is necessarily true.[134] In a way this makes necessity a rather simple notion, echoing Quinton's view, representative of a certain tradition in this matter, that the distinction between necessary and contingent statements is a 'commonplace' one: 'A necessary truth is one that is true in itself, true, in Lewis' phrase, "no matter what', must be true and cannot be false. A contingent truth, as etymology suggests, is one that is true dependently on or because of something else, something outside itself. As depending on this something else it does not have to be true. The necessary and the contingent make an exclusive and exhaustive division of the realm of truths.'[135] Quinton's characterisation of necessity, like Kripke's, echoes Leibniz's characterisation of the notion, which was employed without discussion by Kant as well. This general way of saying what necessity is fits well with the possible-worlds model for necessity, because, of course, the latter was designed specifically to capture the informal intuitions embodied in the former. The community of agreement evident here is extensive. Writing more recently, Swinburne gives alternative characterisations of necessity as depending centrally either on the idea that denials of necessary propositions are incoherent, or on the idea that necessity is non-contingency (with the notion of con-

tingency being taken as antecedently well established).[136]
Evidently, then, there is some consensus at least at this level of
discussion.

However, the consensus is superficial, for disagreements arise
directly more detail is called for. Quinton argued that all necessary *a
priori* truths are analytic in all four at once of the senses of 'analytic'
noted on p.57-8 above. On this view, the identification of necessity
with analyticity arises from an argument for necessity's being conventional: 'a statement is a necessary truth because of the meaning
of the words of which it is composed. The meaning that worlds have
is assigned to them by convention. Therefore it is linguistic convention that makes a form of words express a necessary truth,' which ill
accords with the idea that there are *de re* necessities, necessities
'objectively discoverable in the nature of things'.[137] Kripke's views
are in agreement to the extent at least that, if only by stipulation,
analytic truths can be regarded as truths which are *both a priori* and
necessary: 'Let's just make the stipulation that an analytic statement is, in some sense, true by virtue of its meaning, and true in all
possible worlds by virtue of its meaning'.[138] But not all necessary
truths are *a priori* for Kripke; and this is where the big difference
lies.

It had been crucial to Kant that there should be a class of synthetic
a priori truths, but on the conventionalist line shared by Quinton,
because all necessary truths are analytic and only these can be
known *a priori,* there can be no such class. Kripke's novel departure
against Quinton and conventionalism lies in his introduction of the
startling idea that there can be necessary *a posteriori* truths, and
even contingent *a priori* truths. This results from the application of
his views to the problem of reference.[139]

It is essential to recall Kripke's observation that the notions of
necessity, apriority, and analyticity (and their converses) are respectively metaphysical, epistemological, and semantic notions.[140]
Accordingly, one may *discover* certain *necessities,* for example that
Hesperus and Phosphorus are one and the same entity; thus, the
identity statement 'Hesperus = phosphorus' is *a posteriori* necessary
because the entity referred to by the names 'Hesperus' and 'Phosphorus' is necessarily self-identical; the names themselves, given
that they *do* refer to that entity, are 'rigid designators' (which
means, by Kripke's definition, that they refer to the same object in
every possible world in which that object exists); and it was an
empirical, that is, an *a posteriori*, discovery that Hesperus and
Phosphorus are one and the same object.

Again, in Kripke's view there may be *a priori* contingent truths, such as the one that there is a certain stick S in Paris which is the standard for the metre.[141] If 'S is one metre long (at a time t)' fixes the reference of 'one metre', and is not an abbreviative or synonymous definition of 'one metre', then one knows that S is one metre long *a priori*; yet its being the case that S is one metre long is not a necessary but a contingent matter, for the stick selected as the standard unit of length may have been any length — it may have been two centimetres longer or shorter, say, or whatever.

The result of inspecting Kripke's line on these issues and contrasting them with Kant's views is instructive. Let us go through the combinations. For Kant, propositions divide into two classes, the analytic and the synthetic. All the former are necessary and *a priori*, some of the latter are known *a priori*, the rest *a posteriori*. Those synthetic truths known *a priori* are fundamental to Kant's philosophical theory. In virtue of being *a priori*, they are necessary, for all truths known *a priori* are necessary for Kant. Kripke has nothing to say about the synthetic *a priori*, which is not surprising owing to the fact that his concern is with a nonintensional theory of naming, in which names are not synonymous with descriptions, but have reference only (see chapter 7 below). Because analyticity and syntheticity are intensional notions, the question whether 'Hesperus=Phosphorus' is either analytic or synthetic, as well as being necessary and *a posteriori*, does not arise.

It follows from Kant's view that all *a priori* truths are necessary, but only some are analytic. Kripke simply stipulates that any statement which is both necessary and *a priori* is analytic, but because not all necessary truths are *a priori*, the question whether some of them are *either* analytic *or* synthetic does not, as just noted, arise. Thus whereas some synthetic truths will be necessary for Kant, there will be no categories of synthetic necessary and synthetic *a priori* truths for Kripke. Instead he has categories of *a posteriori* necessary and *a priori* contingent truths, neither of which Kant has.

Kant, perhaps Kripke, and most of if not all other philosophers, would agree that all contingent-truths are synthetic and not *vice versa*, except for Kripke's special case of the contingent *a priori* where this classification does not arise at all. Almost everyone would be inclined to agree that any propositon which is *a posteriori* is synthetic, but, again, not *vice versa*; except, yet again, for the Kripkean case where the classification does not arise.

For Kant, all necessary truths are *a priori*; for Kripke the two classes do not always coincide, for he admits a class of *a posteriori* necessities. Finally, Kripke thinks there can be contingent *a priori* truths, which is a novel idea and would be denied by Kant; and at least many philosophers (bearing in mind Kripke's contingent *a priori*) would hold that contingent truths will be discoverable *a posteriori*, although not all *a posteriori* discoveries are discoveries of contingent truths if Kripke is right about there being a category of *a posteriori* necessary truths.

Thus the various combinations as Kant and Kripke would have them. What does one say about the differences apparent here? They bristle with complexities, and disentangling the two sets of classifications would require a detailed discussion of the background theories which give rise to them. And precisely here lies the clue to what is remarkable about the issue: I noted earlier that *how* one construes necessity, analyticity, and the *a priori*, and the connections between them, is precisely relative to the philosophical theory (of knowledge and/or language) lying in the background. Background theory generates the view to be taken on these categories and their connections, rather than being determined by them; so that the choices we make in this area will not in the end depend upon the analyses we try to give of them in their own right, but on the commitments we make regarding the nature of our conceptual scheme and (if this is different, which I doubt) our language.

CONCLUDING REMARK

After travelling fairly far afield in an effort to pin down what analyticity, necessity and the *a priori* consist in and what relationships obtain between them, it may seem a little disappointing to conclude that one can fix an answer only on the basis of choices made in our more general epistemological and metaphysical theories. In fact this is quite a substantial result; it reveals the role that notions of this kind play in the structure of philosophical thought, and the degree of indeterminacy they possess until located in the context of a more inclusive theory. There is a core of agreement at a certain level concerning what is to be understood by the terms 'analytic', '*a priori*', 'necessary' and their opposites, and frequently it is possible to employ the concepts attaching to them on the basis only of that surface consensus. Nevertheless, they are crucial concepts; in a detailed spelling out of a particular theory, a detailed account of the work they do is demanded.

A great deal of what has been discussed in this chapter is relevant to the discussion in chapter 7 below, and I shall there assume the apparatus of possible worlds, and Kripke's views on necessity, as presented here.

NOTES

1. Plato's method of 'dialectic' involves the earliest systematic approach of this kind; cf. the *Phaedrus*.
2. Leibniz, G. W., *The Monadology*, (trans. Latta, R.), Oxford, 1898, §§ 31-2.
3. ibid., § 33.
4. cf., ibid., n.54, pp.236-7.
5. ibid., §§ 33-5.
6. Hume, D., *Enquiry Concerning Human Understanding* § IV, pt. 1.
7. Hume, D., *Treatise of Human Nature*, BK. I, § Pt. III.
8. ibid.
9. This (rather imprecise) way of putting things owes itself to Kant. cf. Kant, I., *Critique of Pure Reason*, A7/B10-11; cf. B4.
10. Leibniz, *New Essays Concerning Human Understanding*, (trans. Langley, A. G.), Chicago, 1916, III.3.
11. Leibniz, *Monadology*, § 34.
12. Leibniz, *New Essays*, IV.9.
13. Kant, *Critique of Pure Reason*.
14. ibid.
15. Ayer, A. J. *Language Truth and Logic*, 2nd ed., London, 1946, p.78. and cf. chapter 4 *passim*.
16. cf chapter 17 below, where the verification theory is discussed at more length.
17. Wittgenstein, L., *Tractatus Logico-Philosophicus* (trans. Ogden, C. K.), London, 1922.
18. Quine, W. V., 'Two Dogmas of Empiricism', *From A Logical Point Of View*, 2nd ed., Harvard, 1961, and often reprinted; as in Feigl, H., *et al.* (eds), *Readings in Philosophical Analysis*, New York, 1972, pp.81-94.
19. cf. chapter 2 above.
20. Quine, *op. cit.*, p.82.
21. ibid.
22. ibid., pp.82-3.
23. ibid., pp.83-5.
24. cf. chapter 2 above.
25. Quine, ibid., p.80.
26. ibid.
27. ibid., pp.86-7.
28. ibid., p.87.
29. Carnap, R. *Meaning and Necessity*, Chicago, 1947, p.10.
30. Quine, ibid., pp.87-8.
31. ibid., p.89.
32. Grice, H. P. and Strawson, P. F., 'In Defense of a Dogma', *Philosophical Review*, 1956 pp.141-58; reprinted in Feigl *et al.*, *op. cit.*, pp.126-36, to which the following references are made.
33. ibid., pp.126-7.
34. ibid., p.127.
35. In fact, Quine believes that translation will in any case be indeterminate; for his thesis regarding the indeterminacy of translation cf. chapter 9 below.
36. Grice and Strawson, *op. cit.*, p.129.
37. It has to be pointed out that in the 1950s, under the influence of Wittgenstein and Austin, and in a way perfectly characteristic of that decade's briefly-flourishing school of 'Ordinary Language Philosophy', the sharpest needle in the philosophical work-basket was the 'look at the use' one (cf. chapter 7 below).

Philosophical *faux pas* was thought to arise chiefly from failure to do so. Still, this does not invalidate Grice's and Strawson's point here: they are remarking that where there is agreed use for a notion, it is appropriate to take it that the notion has content — a sometimes controvertible point, as reflection on the notion of, say, witchcraft will show. However this does not affect the substance of their argument to follow.

38. Grice and Strawson, *op. cit.* p.130.
39. ibid., p.131.
40. ibid., p.132.
41. cf. Mates, B., 'Analytic Sentences', *Philosophical Review,* 1951, pp.525-34; reprinted in Feigl, *et all., op. cit.,* pp.147-52, to which the following references are made.
42. cf. Quine, *op. cit.,* p.87, where in an aside he talks of reversing the attempt to define 'analytic' in terms of 'cognitive synonymy', defining the latter in terms of the former instead — 'cognitive synonymy' is thus to be defined in terms of intersubstitutivity *salva analyticitate.*
43. Mates, *op. cit.,* p.140.
44. cf. Quine, *Word and Object,* MIT, 1960, esp. chapter 2, *passim.*
45. cf. Mates, ibid.
46. cf. ibid., p.142. Also see the papers by Carnap, and Quine's response, in Feigl *et al., op. cit.,* where the issue of the artificial treatment of analyticity is discussed. Also cf. chapter 1 above where this kind of point was made about the use of formalities in philosophy.
47. cf. Quinton. A. M., 'The *A Priori* and the Analytic', *Proceedings of the Aristotlean Society.* 64, 1963-4, pp.31, *et seq.* Reprinted in Strawson, *Philosophical Logic op. cit.*
48. cf. Chapters 7 and 8 below, which are devoted to discussion of meaning.
49. Swinburne, R. G., 'Analyticity, Necessity, and Apriority', *Mind* 84, 1975, p.226.
50. cf. Quinton, *op. cit.,* p.49.
51. Swinburne, *op. cit.,* p.227.
52. A useful if biased guide is to be found in Plantinga, A., *The Nature of Necessity,* Oxford, 1971, chapters 1 and 2, pp.1-26.
53. Quine, 'Two Dogmas', *op. cit.,* p.93.
54. ibid.
55. Plantinga, *op. cit.,* pp.3-4.
56. ibid., p.4.
57. cf. Kitch, P., 'Apriority and Necessity', *Australasian Journal of Philosophy,* vol.58, No.2, June 1980, p.89, *et seq.*
58. Plantinga, *op. cit.,* p.8.
59. ibid., pp.10-11.
60. Aristotle, *Metaphysics,* Z 1029 b 14; cf. 1028 a 10-1032 a 11.
61. cf., ibid., 1031 a 15 ff.
62. This kind of view is hotly contested by some contemporary reference theorists; cf. chapter 7 below.
63. Locke, J., *Essay Concerning Human Understanding,* III.3.17.
64. cf., e.g., Lewis, C. I. and Langford C., *Symbolic Logic,* 2nd ed., New York, 1951.
65. If one adds to M the axiom $p \rightarrow \Box \Diamond p$ one gets the Brouwer system; if instead of this one adds $\Box p \rightarrow \Box \Box p$ one gets the system S-4, in which are derivable the formulae $\Box p \equiv \Box \Box p$ and $\Diamond p \equiv \Diamond \Diamond p$, showing that a string of iterated operators can have substituted for it the last operator in the string alone. The system S-5 has M and the Brouwer and S-4 axioms; more briefly, one can add to

M the axiom $\Diamond p \to \Box \Diamond p$, and show by the derivations $\Diamond p \equiv \Box \Diamond p$ and $\Box p$ $\equiv \Diamond \Box p$ that the final operator in a mixed string can be substituted for the string. There are yet other modal systems. See Kripke, n.67 below; and Hughes, G. E. and Cresswell, M. J., *An Introduction To Modal Logic*, London, 1968.

66. cf. Carnap, *Meaning and Necessity, op. cit.*

67. cf. Kripke, S., 'Semantical Considerations on Modal Logic', reprinted in Linsky, L. (ed.), *Reference and Modality*, (Oxford, 1971; Hintikka, J., 'Models of Modality', reprinted in Loux, M. J. (ed.), *The Possible and the Actual*, Cornell, 1979.

68. Kripke's semantics for quantified modal logic may be illustrated briefly thus: We use a model structure $<G,K,R>$ where $K = \{G,H\}$, $G \neq H$, and $R = K^2$. The model is quantificational when we define $\psi (G) = \{a\}$, $\psi (H) = \{a,b\}$, $a \neq b$. For a monadic predicate letter '*P*' we define a model ϕ such that $\phi (P,G) = \{a\}$, $\phi (P,H) = \{a\}$. Now: $\Box Px$ is true in G when x is assigned a. Since a is the only element of $\psi (g)$, $(x)\Box(Px)$ is also true in G. When x is assigned b, $\phi (Px,H) = F$, from which it follows that $(x)(Px)$ is false in H and $\Box(x)(Px)$ is false in G. The connection with possible worlds arises thus: we notice $\Box Px$ is true in G when x is assigned a, because then Px is true in both G and H. Intuitively this is to say a falls under the extension of P in H and in G, that is, in all possible worlds. As Kripke puts the intuitive unpacking of the ordered triple G,K,R'K is the set of all possible worlds, $G \,\epsilon\, kR$ is a reflexive relation on K (such that H_1RH_2 means that H_2 is 'possible relative' to H_1, i.e., that every proposition *true* in H_2 is *possible* in H_1, and G is the 'real world', *op. cit.*, p.64.

69. Quine, 'Reference and Modality', *From A Logical Point Of View*, to which the following references are made. Reprinted in Linsky, *op. cit.*

70. cf., chapter 2 above, where identity is discussed.

71. Quine, ibid., p.148.

72. ibid., p.155.

73. ibid., p.156.

74. The papers in the Linsky volume (*op. cit.*), particularly those by Marcus, Smullyan, Føllesdal and Kaplan represent the core of the debate over Quine's objections. The net result of their replies to Quine is that his attitude to quantifying into modal contexts is over-anxious.

75. Kripke, *op. cit.*

76. Lewis, D., *Counterfactuals*, Harvard, 1973, pp.84-5.

77. A point often damagingly made against philosophers of G. E. Moore's persuasion. I shall revert to this and allied points in later chapters.

78. cf. Stalnaker, R. C., 'A Theory of Conditionals', in Rescher, N., *Studies in Logical Theory*, APQ Monograph, Oxford, 1968, pp.165-79, reprinted in Sosa, E. (ed.), *Causation and Conditionals*, Oxford, 1975. cf. also the contributions by Sellars, Chisholm, Rescher and Kim, in Sosa.

79. cf., Lewis, *op. cit.*, p.1, and *passim*.

80. cf., E.G., Lewis, 'Causation', in Sosa, *op. cit.*, pp. 180-91.

81. Which is the converse of Leibniz's principle of the identity of indiscernibles, which states that if x and y are indiscernible, in the sense of all x's properties being the same as y's properties and *vice versa*, then x is identical with y.

82. cf. Chisholm, 'Identity Through Possible Worlds', in Loux, *op. cit.*, pp.80-2.

83. This is a modified version of Chisholm's Adam and Noah example, ibid., pp.82-4.

84. ibid., pp.85-6.

85. Lewis, D., 'Counterpart Theory and Quantified Modal Logic,' in Loux, *op. cit.*, pp.110-28.

86. ibid., p.112.

87. cf. Kripke, 'Identity and Necessity', in Munitiz, M., *Identity and Individuation*, New York, 1971; and Schwartz, S. P., *Naming, Necessity, and Natural Kinds*, Cornell, 1977, p.66ff., to which the following references are made; and Plantinga, A., 'Transworld Identity or Worldbound Individuals?', in Loux, *op. cit.*, pp.146-65; and *The Nature of Necessity*, chapter VI, *passim*.

88. cf. Plantinga, 'World and Essence', *Philosophical Review* 79, 1970, pp.461-92; and *The Nature of Necessity*, pp.94-5.

89. Kripke, 'Identity and Necessity', in Schwartz, *op. cit.*, pp.80.

90. Lewis, *Counterfactuals*, pp.84-91; reprinted as excerpt in Loux, *op cit.*, p.182ff; cf. p.185.

91. ibid., p.184.

92. ibid., pp.183-4.

93. cf. in particular Lycan, W., 'The Trouble With Possible Worlds', in Loux, *op. cit.*, p.274ff.; Haack, S., 'Lewis' Ontological Slum', *Review of Metaphysics* 33, 1977, p.415ff.; and Richards, T., 'The Worlds of David Lewis', *Australasian Journal of Philosophy* 53, 1975, p.105ff.

94. cf. Lycan's discussion ibid., for the Meinongian dimension. At p.297 Lycan says 'I do not believe that it is possible to refute Lewis' position', which suggests reasons for its discussability.

95. Haack, ibid.

96. Stalnaker '*Possible Worlds*', in Loux *op. cit.*, cf. P.228

97. Plantinga, 'Actualism and Possible Worlds', in Loux, *op. cit.*, pp.237-52.

98. cf. Plantinga's discussion of his differences with Stalnaker, ibid.

99. Adams, R. M., 'Theories of Actuality', in Loux, *op. cit.*, p.190ff., esp. p.204ff.

100. cf. the discussion of Tarski in chapter 6 below.

101. cf. Adams, ibid., pp.207-8.

102. A power set is the set of all subsets of a given set including the null set.

103. cf. Lycan *op. cit.*, in Loux *op. cit.*, for a survey of these, esp. p.302 *et seq.*; and Loux's own 'Introduction', which is to some extent based on Lycan's paper.

104. Quine, 'On What There Is', *From A Logical Point of View, op. cit.*, p.1, *et seq.*

105. ibid., p.4.

106. Rescher, 'The Ontology of the Possible', in Loux, *op. cit.*, p.166, *et seq.*, surveys the options; cf. esp. p.169.

107. ibid., pp.73-4.

108. cf. Mondadori, F. and Morton, A., 'Modal Realism; The Poisoned Pawn', in Loux, *op. cit.*, p.235, *et seq.*

109. cf. Slote, M., *Metaphysics and Essence,* Oxford, 1974, pp.6-7.

110. Kripke, *Naming and Necessity,* Oxford, 1980, p.42.

111. cf. Enc., B., 'Necessary Properties and Linnaean Essentialism', *Canadian Journal of Philosophy*, vol. V. No.1, 1975.pp.85-7, and refs. p.86.

112. I say a 'roughly' Aristotelean notion because Aristotle's theory of essence is a matter of live and lively scholarly discussion still, and I can do no more than employ a concept of essence which is approximately central to the tradition, and which is shared by some contemporary essentialists.

113. cf., Enc, *op. cit.,* p.88.

114. Quine, *Word and Object,* p.199.

115. cf., Cartwright, R. L., 'Some Remarks on Essentialism', *Journal of Philosophy*, vol.LXV, No. 20, 1968, p.619.

116. ibid.

117. cf. Enc, *op.cit.,* p.89.

118. ibid., p.90.

119. cf. Kripke, *Naming and Necessity*; and 'Identity and Necessity', in Schwartz, *op.cit.,* particular page references follow.

120. *Naming and Necessity*, p.113.
121. Slote, *op.cit.*, p.8.
122. McGinn, C., 'On the Necessity of Origin', *Journal of Philosophy* 73, 1976.
123. ibid., p.132.
124. Johnson P., 'Origin and Necessity', *Philosophical Studies* 32 1977, pp.413 *et seq.*
125. Dummett argues that just such appeals to intuition often fail at crucial points in setting up possible-worlds talk and its ramifications. Lectures in Oxford Hilary 1981.
126. Johnson, *op.cit.*, p.414.
127. Sprigge, 'Internal and External Properties', *Mind* 71, 1962, pp.202-3.
128. Johnson, *op. cit.*, p.416.
129. ibid.
130. cf., Kripke, *Naming and Necessity*, p.126, *et seq.*
131. ibid., p.156 For the argument against Kripke which follows, see my 'Internal Structure and Essence' *Analysis* June 1982.
132. The theory of essence at issue is realist, and is therefore infected by a notion of logical possibility of this scepticism-inviting kind. cf. chapter 8 below.
133. Kripke, *Naming and Necessity*, p.48n.
134. ibid., pp.35-6.
135. Quinton, *op. cit.*, p.109.
136. Swinburne, *op. cit.*, pp.232-8.
137. Quinton, *op. cit.*, pp.115-16.
138. Kripke, *op. cit.*, p.39.
139. Kripke's theory of reference is discussed in chapter 7 below.
140. Kripke, ibid., p.34, *et seq.*
141. ibid., pp.55-7.

4 Existence, Presuppositions and Descriptions

INTRODUCTION

A central concern in philosophy is the problem of what exists, of what there is in the universe.[1] Some of the difficulties which present themselves have been touched upon in each of the preceding chapters. It seems clear that there are tables and trees, people and planets; but are there subsistent entities in Meinong's sense? Are there unactualised objects, propositions, numbers, classes, minds, God? And if there are any of these things, do they exist in the same way as do tables and planets, or in some other way — and if so, what way is that? Attempting answers demands a different approach to each of these disputed items or categories of items; showing that there are numbers, for example, would do little or nothing to show that there are, say, minds, or even how one might go about showing that there are minds. On the whole, any particular argument for the existence or nonexistence of some particular candidate for either state has to be geared specifically to that candidate. Nevertheless, there are general features of existence or existence talk which enter into all ontological discussions; and it is with these more general issues that this chaper is concerned.

In the first chapter it was pointed out that philosophical interest in language arises chiefly from the fact that investigating language gives access to thought and the world, in the sense that understanding the former goes a long way towards providing an understanding of the two latter. In the present case, the first step towards clarifying ontological issues is to investigate two related matters: a) the way we talk about existence; and b) the existential implications and assumptions of the way we talk.

Problem a) has to do with assertions of existence. How does one make sense of predications of existence as in 'Socrates exists' and 'Pegasus does not exist'? Is 'exists' a predicate at all? The first half of the chapter deals with this and related questions.

Problem b) has to do with the underlying ontological assumptions of assertions, particularly in connection with the use, truth-conditions, and/or meaning of sentences. If there is no King of France, is the sentence 'the King of France is bald' a false sentence or a meaningless one? Or does the question of its truth-value not arise at all? The expression 'the King of France' is a definite description. Russell's celebrated theory of descriptions, discussed in the second half of this chapter, constitutes a proposed analysis of these, and in so doing draws together questions of existence and language use.

IS 'EXISTS' A PREDICATE?

In the fifth *Meditation* Descartes gives a verson of the Ontological Argument for the existence of God, commenting 'I clearly see that existence can no more be separated from the essence of God than can its having three angles equal to two right angles be separated from the essence of a triangle'.[2] The idea is that the notion of the nonexistence of God is a contradiction; for God is perfect and existence is a perfection, so God exists. Kant objected to the Ontological Argument, with Descartes' formulation of it in mind, and one of his reasons for objecting to it was that, in his view, existence is not a property – that is, that 'exists' is not a genuine predicate. His view lays bare the essentials of the problem concerning 'exists'.[3]

Kant's reasons for denying that 'exists' is a predicate are that whereas *grammatically* 'exists' is indeed a predicate, *logically* it does not function as one at all. Consider genuine predicates like '. . .is red', '. . .is square', '. . .is a tame tiger'. If I inform you that x is red, is round, or is a tame tiger, then I am furnishing you with facts about x. But if I say x exists, I am not giving you any information about x, or offering a further description of it. It would seem odd to say that all three of the following are important facts about x – that it is a tiger, that it is tame, and that it exists. As Kant put it: ' "Being" is obviously not a real predicate; that is, it is not a concept of something which could be added to the concept of a thing'.[4] The way this works in Kant's rejection of Descartes' version of the Ontological Argument is that since existence is not a property, it cannot be a perfection; hence if (which is independently debatable) perfection is a necessary property of God – that is, is essential to God – it still does not follow that there is God.

In short, then, the problem of 'exists' centres on the view that, since to say of some x that it exists adds nothing to the concept of x, 'exists' is not a predicate; for however we understand predicates, at least what happens in predication is that something is *said about* x,

and on this view of 'exists', saying 'x exists' says nothing about —
adds nothing to the concept of — x.[5]

What has been said so far is somewhat inexact and vague. For, in
a sense, to say of tigers that they exist *does* add something; it says
that the concept of a tiger has instances in reality — that is, that *there
are* tigers to be met with in the world. Clearly, although it might
seem peculiar in normal circumstances to iterate that tigers exist
with this purpose in view, a difference can be made by doing so.
Kant himself conceded that a hundred pounds which exist make a
difference to my bank balance which a hundred nonexistent
pounds cannot make. So indeed might an existent tiger make a
difference; I can imagine circumstances in which someone might say
— 'What would you do if there were a tiger in the room?' and (as a
surrogate for 'Well, there *is* a tiger in the room') then add 'that tiger
exists'. It would be a relief if the tiger were tame to boot.

Moreover, as Pears points out, it is not true to say that in saying
'tigers exist' one is saying nothing about tigers; for if anyone were to
ask 'what are you talking about?' the appropriate answer is 'tigers'.[6]
The same holds good if someone said 'tigers do not exist' or 'winged
horses do not exist'; he is talking about tigers and winged horses.
Consequently it is incorrect to hold that nothing is being *said about*
whatever is asserted to exist or not exist. The view, therefore, that
'exists' is not a predicate because a) it adds nothing to the concept,
and b) it says nothing about the concept, needs refinement.

Part of the peculiarity which attaches to uses of 'exists' arises from
the difference between saying 'tigers exist' and 'tigers are striped'.
According to Pears, the peculiarity of the assertion 'tigers exist'
arises from the fact that the expression is *referentially tautologous*.
Consider the case of one's saying 'this room exists'. The expression
'this room' implies that there is a room, namely this one; and it
implies this in virtue of having been used to make reference to this
room. To add 'exists' is to assert the existence of the room all over
again; it is as if one were saying 'this room (which exists) exists' —
hence the tautology. If one says 'this room does not exist' then the
existence of the room is implied by reference having been made to
it, after which the speaker implicitly contradicts himself by saying,
in effect, 'this room (which exists) does not exist'. Pears calls this
referential contradiction. These notions of referential tautology and
contradiction consititute a refinement of the Kantian thesis in this
way: they assert that 'exists' is not a genuine predicate because a') it
adds nothing *new* to the concept, and b') it says nothing that has not
been said *implicitly* already. Contrast a') and b') with a) and b)
above.

Pears calls a') the 'minimal thesis'. It needs qualification in three ways. First, the subject term of a singular existential statement might refer to something or somebody in the world of fiction, for example David Copperfield, and thus imply existence in that world but not in the real world. If one says of David Copperfield that he existed in real life, the subject term of the statement, *viz.*, 'David Copperfield', would imply existence only in the fictional world created by Dickens, and so one's saying of David Copperfield that he existed in the real world would indeed be adding something new. Accordingly one would not be guilty of referential tautology. The reason is clear – the statement has application to two worlds, the fictional and the real. It *implies* existence in the fictional world but *asserts* it in the real world; and it is certainly novel to claim that David Copperfield was a genuine historical figure. For the same reasons, if one denied that David Copperfield existed in real life, one would be guiltless of referential contradiction.

Secondly, someone might say 'the Euston Arch no longer exists', and accordingly appear to be guilty of referential contradiction, because existence has been both implied and denied in the real world. But since the Euston Arch's existence has been implied for one time and denied for a later time, referential contradiction is avoided. And *mutatis mutandis* for affirmative cases.

Thirdly, suppose someone hallucinates, like Macbeth, a dagger before him, and says to himself 'that dagger doesn't exist'. Here matters are more complicated, but Pears offers a way round. Referential contradiction is escaped if it is held that there are two senses in which the dagger might be considered to exist: as a visually experienced dagger, so that the expression 'that dagger' refers to it at least at that level; and as a dagger in space, that is, a real dagger independent of any visual experience of it. Then one's saying 'that dagger (*qua* visually-experienced dagger) does not exist (*qua* dagger in space)' does not involve a referential contradiction, for what is being implied at one is being denied at another level – rather on analogy with the time case.

So, with the following cases excepted, namely that implication and assertion are about different worlds, or different times, or different 'levels', we have Pears' thesis as follows: if the subject term of a singular existential statement implies existence, then, if the verb asserts existence, the resulting statement will be a referential tautology; and if the statement denies existence, it is referentially contradictory.

An idea being exployed by Pears in this account is that of a 'presuppositional implication', which owes itself to Strawson.[7] Pre-

supposition, according to Strawson, is a relation between two statements A and B, such that A is said to presuppose B if and only if A is
neither true nor false unless B is true. The statement 'the man in
the garden is whistling' can only possess a truth-value if the presupposed statement 'there is a man in the garden' is true. The
presupposition relation must be distinguished from the relation of
entailment. In cases where A entails B, the conjunction of A with
the denial of B is a contradiction; that is, it is contradictory to affirm
A and at the same time to deny B, because the truth of B is a
necessary condition for the truth of A. But where A presupposes B,
the truth of B is a necessary condition for the truth *or* the falsity of
A; which is to say, B's truth is a necessary condition for A's possessing a truth-value at all. As Strawson put it, it would constitute a
'different kind of absurdity' to conjoin the affirmation of A with the
denial of B. Pears is appealing to just such a notion of presupposition in saying that subject terms, in referring, imply (that is,
presuppositionally imply) the existence of that to which they refer.[8]

Pears himself specifies the major weakness of his thesis; which is
that it turns upon but leaves unanalysed a notion of reference. This
question arises again here and will be discussed in a later chapter, so
I shall leave it aside for the present.

The suggestions in Pears' paper are developments of ideas put
forward earlier by Moore, whose thoughts were as follows.[9]
Consider the expressions

1. tame tigers growl
1'. some tame tigers growl
2. tame tigers exist
2'. some tame tigers exist.

Whereas 1. admits of the more explicit variant formulations 'all
tame tigers growl', 'most tame tigers growl', and 'some tame tigers
growl', 2. does not; one cannot say 'all tame tigers exist' or 'most
tame tigers exist', although one can say 2'., that is 'some tame tigers
exist'.[10] In 1., the truth of the 'all' and 'most' formulations depends
on the truth of the 'some' formulation; in 2., this latter formulation
is the only possible one. The sentences 'all tame tigers exist' and
'most tame tigers exist' are in Moore's view 'queer and puzzling
expressions'; they have 'no clear meaning'.[11]

The difference between the two cases can be made out by
contrasting

3. some tame tigers don't growl
and
4. some tame tigers don't exist.

Both 3. and its contrary 1'. have 'perfectly clear' meanings, but 4.

does not, despite the fact that 2′. does; 2′. after all just means 'there are some tame tigers'.[12] In Moore's view 'exist' must have different meanings in 2′. and 4., because a sense can indeed be attached to the latter case, as when someone says 'some tame tigers are not real tigers' or '. . .are imaginary'.[13] But if the sense of 'exist' were univocal and 'exist' means only what it does in 2., then 4. would be meaningless, and 2′. would be as meaningless as 4., which is not the case.

On the basis of these thoughts Moore says that he can see why some philosophers have held that existence is not a property as redness or (so to say) growlingness are. Another reason is that 1′. and 2′. differ in the fact that whereas the former asserts that some values of the propositional function 'x is a tame tiger *and growls*' are true, the latter asserts only that some values of 'x is a tame tiger' are true; 2′. asserts only what it does because it is not used to say 'this is a tame tiger *and exists*'. As Moore puts it, 'by pointing and saying "this exists" we . . . express *no proposition at all*'. whereas by pointing and saying 'this growls' we do express a proposition.[14]

Although these constitute reasons for saying that 'exists' does not function predicatively in the way that 'growls' does, and, accordingly, that existence is not a property, Moore was uncomfortable about the analysis because it is at odds with certain other considerations. One is that it can be said of something 'this might not have existed', which, if it is significant, permits one to say the converse, 'this exists', with propriety.[15] Moore suggested that perhaps it is the case that 'this exists' is part of what is meant by asserting, say, 'this is a book' or 'this is red'; and further, perhaps part of what it means to say that such predicates as 'is a book' or 'is red' stand for properties, 'is that *part but not the whole* of what is asserted by any value of "x is a book", "x is red" etc., is "this exists",' in which case 'exists' would not stand for a property 'solely because the whole of what it asserts, and not merely a part, is "this exists".'[16]

Pears' notion of referential tautology derives from the later points made here; the earlier idea, to the effect that the status of the predicate depends upon what quantifiers its subject takes, is used by Strawson in a more recent discussion, commented on below.

LOGICAL PREDICATES AND ONTOLOGICAL COMMITMENT

The topic to which Moore specifically addressed himself was whether 'exists' functions as a *logical* predicate. What it means to distinguish logical from grammatical predicates, and why 'exists' may not count as the former, can be set out in the following way.[17]

It is manifest that the verb 'exists' is a grammatical predicate, for one would parse the sentence 'this room is warm' and 'this room exists' in exactly the same way. The argument against 'exists' does not consist in a denial of this, but, as noted, in a denial of its being a logical predicate; and in fact it is precisely because it is the former that logicians are so anxious to point out that it is not the latter. For its being the former sometimes induces people to assume it is the latter as well, which gives rise to confusions. The question therefore is: what is meant by saying that 'exists' is not a logical predicate?

By a 'logical predicate' is meant something that would count as a predicate in an interpretation of first-order predicate logic. In this logic, familiarly, there are the individual constants a,b,c. . ., variables x,y,z. . ., predicate letters F,G,H. . ., quantifiers (∃ x), (x), and truth-functional operators →, v,~, ·. Among the well-formed formulae constructed from these primitive materials there are, for example, Fa (John is happy), Gab (John loves Catherine), (∃x)(Gxa) (someone loves John), and so on. The idea of a logical predicate is just the ordinary idea of a grammatical predicate, but in a special language. So when it is said that 'exists' is not a logical predicate what is meant is that it is not treated as one in first-order logic. Any serious statement one wished to make containing the word 'exists' has a translation in the language of logic which serves the same purpose but does not contain 'exists'; hence 'exists' is dispensible. Although people habitually utter sentences containing 'exists' as a (grammatical) predicate, there is no need to do so; for example, instead of saying 'the round square does not exist' one can say 'no square is round' or 'for any figure, that figure will not be both square and round': $(x)(Sx \rightarrow \sim Rx)$ or $\sim(\exists x)$ $(Sx \cdot Rx)$. This interpretation is a qualified Russellian one — a point which will become clear by the end of the chapter. It points out that we may be misled as to the logical form of facts by the grammatical form of sentences stating them; which point Russell regarded as a fundamental insight.

Still, the apparent ease of dealing with 'exists' in this way might itself be misleading. One can translate existence statements into regimented form with impunity so long as one's interpretation of the quantifiers $(x),(\exists x)$ is *objectual* or *referential*, in the sense that the variables bound by the quanitifiers are taken to refer to objects in the given domain of discourse. Some philosophers of logic are discontented with objectual readings of the quantifiers, and argue for alternatives — the chief of which is the proposed *substitutional* reading, in which the values of the variables are names, not objects.[18] Consider the case of

1. Pegasus is a flying horse.

This would seem to entail directly

2. There is a flying horse.

Now, 1. is true; but if 2. is to be given a regimented translation as

3. $(\exists x)(x$ is a flying horse),

then 2. is false. How is this difficulty to be overcome? One solution is to interpret 2. as

4. There is a term x such as 'x is a flying horse' is true,

which makes 2. true and allows 3. to be inferred from 1. What has changed is the interpretation of the quantifiers and variables in 3.; $(\exists x)$ no longer reads 'there is an object. . .' but 'there is a term. . .' with according changes throughout. The choice of a substitutional in preference to an objectual reading in consequence yields an apparently more intuitive result.

On second thoughts, however, it is not so clear that the result is intuitive.[19] Whatever the logical form of 1. may be, it is not a sentence composed of a denoting singular term and a monadic predicate. The difference between 1 and

1′. Arkle is a horse.

is that in 1′. 'Arkle' is a denoting singular term whereas in 1. 'Pegasus' is not. This is a difference which makes a difference. What then is 'Pegasus'? In Russell's view — to be discussed shortly — 'Pegasus' is to be thought of as a *description*, and analysed accordingly. The fact that 'Pegasus' is, like 'Arkle', syntactically a name, may in other words be misleading as to the analysis which ought properly to be given of sentences containing it. One thing that the substitutional reinterpretation of 1. does is to render 3., like 1., *not* an existential claim after all, whereas intuitively 3. seems to consist in the very paradigm of an existential claim, thus suggesting a treatment of 1. which makes clear that the syntactical role of 'Pegasus' in it cannot alone determine what treatment 1. as a whole should receive.

These issues, and their importance, become clear if we look at them in connection with an influential theory advanced by Quine.

Taking the view that talk about existence is properly to be effected in the idiom of quanitificational logic has significant results for ontology. Quine's view of the matter is that what we are committed to counting into our ontology are all and only the values of the bound variables of (objectually construed) quantification, a view summarised in the slogan 'to be is to be the value of a variable'.[20] On Quine's view, ontological commitments are relative to theory, including our 'immemorial' theory of the everyday world, and they are revealed by the use to which we put quantification. 'The ontology to which an [interpreted] theory is committed comprises all and only the objects over which the bound variables of the theory have to be construed as ranging in order that the statements affirmed in the theory be true'.[21] More explicitly as to the role of the quantifiers, Quine holds that recasting our talk into the canonical notation of quanitificational logic reveals that

the objects we are to be understood to admit are precisely the objects which we reckon to the universe of values over which the bound variables of quantification are to be considered to range. Such is simply the intended sense of the quantifiers'(x)' and '($\exists$ x)': 'every object x is such that' and 'there is an object x such that'. The quantifiers are encapsulations of these specially selected, unequivocally referential idioms of ordinary language. To paraphrase a sentence into the canonical notation of quantification is, first and foremost, to make its ontic content explicit, quantification being a device for talking in general of objects.[22]

Quine's theory has it that if we are prepared to infer from some such sentences as 'Arkle is a horse' the existential generalisation ($\exists$ x)(x is a horse), then we are committed to horses in our ontology. But this view invites a difficulty for cases where the name or singular term is empty, such as the Pegasus case. For from the true sentence 'Pegasus is a flying horse' it ought to be inferrable by existential generalisation ($\exists$ x)(x is a flying horse), but this as we saw is false. Quine's solution is to argue for the eliminability of singular terms — of which names are a subset — in two steps; the first of which involves paraphrasing them into definite descriptions. Thus 'Pegasus' becomes 'the unique object which has the property of being Pegasus', or, more succinctly, 'the unique object which pegasises' where 'pegasises' is a predicate expression doing duty for the predicate 'has the property of being Pegasus'. The second step is then to eliminate the description by giving it a Russellian analysis, on which analysis quantifiers and variables do all the work. The sentence 'Pegasus is a flying horse' becomes:

($\exists$x) (x pegasises· [(y) (y pegasises $\rightarrow$ y=x)]· x is a flying horse.
Because there is nothing in the domain of discourse which is a flying horse — which is to say, since no object in the domain satisfies the predicate 'is a flying horse' — the whole sentence is false.[23]

Ascending from ordinary ways of talking, where we say 'Pegasus is a flying horse', to the regimented forms of first-order logic, where we say ($\exists$ x)(x pegasises. . .) as above, is not to indulge in translation, for the two expressions are not synonymous. In Quine's opinion, the ascent from ordinary to formal discourse constitutes a clarifying paraphrase of the former by the latter; all that is philosophically essential is preserved, and what is misleading is eliminated.[24]

It is now clear why the proposed substitutional reading of the quantifiers is important, for anyone who takes this alternative view is thereby contesting Quine's results, which, if right, are obviously significant for our treatment of ontological issues. Accordingly, let us look at the substitutional reading again.

The power of the substitutional reading reveals itself in the handling of certain difficulties which affect the regimented forms of opaque sentences like

1. John believes that Helen = Helen.

The existential generalisation of 1. is

2. (∃ x)(John believes Helen = x)

which on an objectual reading yields

3. There is an x such that John believes Helen = x.

If there were no Helen, 3. would be false even though 1. is true. But if 2. is read substitutionally it yields

4. For some instance x it is true that John believes Helen = x,

and the happy result is that 4. is true if 1. is, which is as it should be.[26]

A substitutional reading does not, then, offer an alternative analysis of the ontological features of language, but places the emphasis elsewhere; specifically, on the truth-conditions of particular substitutions. The main issue is which of the two readings is to be preferred. Part of the reasons dictating which reading should be chosen will involve more general ontological considerations; for one example, it seems odd to accept the objectual reading for (∃ x)(Fx v ~Fx), because on such a reading it appears to be the case that the fact that anything exists at all is a matter of logic.[27] The virtue of the substitutional reading is that in general it does not force ontological commitments every time we wish to clarify what we say by means of canonical paraphrase. This, together with the fact that we are able, without ontic absurdity, to retain names and singular expressions in analyses, and to quantify into opaque contexts as in the above example, constitutes a strong recommendation of the strategy. Nevertheless, the issue is an open one.

There are other criticisms of other aspects of Quine's views in this connection. Strawson, for example, raises doubts about whether singular terms can be dispensed with, as Quine's theory requires, owing to the fundamental role they play in identifying the topic of a particular assertion or discourse, a function which is to be distinguished from, and not assimilated to, that of asserting there is one and only one thing which is thus-and-so.[28] This point comes out strongly in Strawson's criticism of Russell, discussed below; Quine's views derive in part from those of Russell. In any case Quine himself set up the class of unfamiliar predicates like 'pegasises' − required for substantiating his views − by saying that they could be thought of as meaning '. . .is identical with a' where 'a' is a name, like 'Pegasus'; so that '. . .pegasises' is to be explained as meaning '. . .is identical with Pegasus'. Although this manoeuvre was intended by Quine as no more than a purely heuristic comment on the new style of predicates, the question remains whether Quine could indeed dispense with appeal to singular terms, or whether, at some point, essential reference would have to be made of them in a presentation of his account. And there is a problem in the opposite direction: whether or not singular terms can be treated as Quine desires, it turns out that quantifiers and variables are themselves eliminable, if use is made of the combinatory logic devised by Curry and Schönfinkel.[29] But these technicalities need not detain; it is enough to note for the present that Quine's proposals invite controversy.

EXISTENCE AND PRESUPPOSED CLASSES

Trying to handle existence talk by means of the quantificational apparatus of logic carries one away from the use of 'exists' in ordinary discourse. A more recent attempt to give an account of 'exists' as a logically unexceptionable predicate, without at the same time assimilating it to the quantificational apparatus itself, is offered by Strawson.[30] They key idea in his suggestions derives in part from some points made by Moore, and in part from Strawson's own notion of presupposition. The proposal is as follows.

'Exists' is a logical predicate when it satisfies the condition which, whenever satisfied, makes any grammatical predicate a logical predicate. (The force of 'logical' here is 'genuine'.) The condition is this: if the grammatical subject of a sentence admits of commencing with all of the quantifying adjectives 'all', 'most', 'many', 'some', 'a few', 'none', 'at least one', and so on, then it is a logical subject; and the predicate of a logical subject is a logical predicate. Accordingly, if 'exists' is the grammatical predicate of a subject which admits of commencing with all of the quantifying adjectives, then it is a logical, that is a genuine, predicate.[31] The subject of existence-asserting statements will still carry an existential presupposition; but an account of this can be given.

Strawson devises the notion of 'presupposed class' and explains it by means of the example of a classical dictionary. Consider the fact that of the characters listed in a classical dictionary, some are mythical and some are genuine historical figures. On Strawson's view, one can talk in this connection of a class of characters whose existence is presupposed in virtue of their being the topic of discourse in a given situation — as when someone says of the characters in the dictionary 'some of those listed are mythical but most of them existed'.[32] This class is however 'ontologically heterogeneous', since it contains a subclass of genuine historical characters and a subclass of mythical characters.

Consider now the sentences 'King Alfred existed' and 'King Arthur did not exist'. In Strawson's view, 'we have only to see the names as serving to identify, within the heterogeneous class of kingly characters being talked about — a class which comprises both actual and legendary kings — a particular member of that class in each case; and then see the predicate as serving to assign that particular member to the appropriate subclass. Thus "exists" appears as a predicate, and not as a predicate of a concept; but as a predicate of some, and not of other, members of the heterogeneous class'.[33]

An heuristic device employed by Strawson to make the point clearer is the idea of a graphic representation of property-ascription. Suppose one draws a circle to represent a class of items. Then saying of some of these items that they have a certain property is to shade part of the circle; saying all of them have a certain property is to shade the whole circle; and by shading parts of the circle more and less one can capture the sense of any of the quantifying adjectives we standardly use. In the case of saying something exists, there is no circle to begin with; saying 'at least one x exists' is to be represented by drawing the smallest circle possible, saying 'some xs exist' is to draw a somewhat larger circle — and so on.[34] But in the case of the use of 'exists' to assign an item to a subclass as above, what one is doing is much more closely akin to the former than the latter enterprise. Hence the use of 'exists' in such a case is predicative.

The first thing to be noted about this proposal is that the concept of presupposition has been widened in an unusual way, from one having to do with the presupposed existence of the referent of a subject expression, to one having to do with the classes whose existence is presupposed, not by the use of a singular expression, but by *contexts of discussion*. This creates a difficulty. In this widened sense of presupposition, what is presupposed, namely the class of things being talked about, requires a way of being demarcated. It is not easy to see for all, or even most, imaginable cases of presupposed classes how one would determine their extension.

More importantly, it is left open how we are to know when to affix 'exists' to a subject expression by way of assigning its referent to the appropriate subclass; for, if anything, it would seem that the question whether an item merits membership of one rather than another subclass has to be decided in advance of its election to such membership; and this would mean that we know when to predicate 'exists' legitimately already — that is, without prior appeal to a context and the class presupposed to it.

Much the same criticism can be arrived at from another angle. By asking how the use of 'exists' marks off the subclass of real or existent entities, the question can be raised whether this subclass is to be determined extensionally or intensionally. If the former, then the subclass would be composed of an indefinite collection of singular statements 'x exists', 'y exists', and so on; and this seems to resurrect, with a vengeance, the problem of how to understand the logic of statements of the form 'x exists' without getting involved in regress. If the latter, then the problem is even less tractable, since one would now be faced with pondering whether 'exists' is to be a primitive or undefined concept, or whether it is to be defined. Yet whichever is the case, what will come to be understood by 'exists' in application to subclasses will be the same as what is understood by 'exists' in application to their individual members; which would be wholly unenlightening as to the predicative use of the term.

On either an extensional or an intensional reading, then, what the appeal to a presupposed class seems in effect to do is to postpone rather than clarify the problems of determing how 'exists' is used as a logical predicate, of determining when it is so used, if ever, and determining what effect follows for the 'absurdity' problem which Strawson had himself identified in earlier writings. In these earlier writings Strawson argued that 'x exists' statements were not subject-predicate in form, for to say a subject expression x in 'x exists' presupposes the existence of x is patently absurd, because it carries as a presupposition what the statement, of which it is a part, as a whole asserts. Hence x can have no particular-referring role, and that is why 'x exists' is not subject-predicate in form. At this point Strawson had felt that the 'x exists' form is better dealt with in the quantificational idiom after the fashion of Quine's proposals. He put the same argument alternatively like this: if one attempted to assimilate 'x exists' to any of the four traditional types of categorical propositions, 'or to regard them as subject-predicate statements at all, we should be faced with the absurd result that the question of whether they were true or false could only arise if they were true; or that, if they were false, the question of whether they were true or false could not arise.'[35]

Strawson's solution in terms of presupposed classes is erected on the basis of a premiss to the effect that every singular statement of subject-predicate form is such that its subject, if it has or looks to have a particular-referring role at least, carries a presupposition concerning the existence of its referent. One suggestion is that the entire debate could be undercut by refusing to accept this premiss for cases where a statement explicitly asserts the existence of its subject's referent. We could say that in cases where 'exists' occupies predicate position, it effects an estoppal of presupposition, so that we would have a rule to the effect that all subject-predicate statements, with the exception of those asserting existence, involve a presupposition concerning the existence of the subject's referent. Then one could proceed to attempt an account of existential claims unencumbered by anxieties of absurdity.[36]

So much is the merest sketch of a programme, but it suggests two virtues: it would avoid the cumbrous business of appealing to heterogeneous classes of entities presupposed by contexts of discourse, and it would run closer to pretheoretical intuitions to the effect that there is point and substance in saying of some things – like Arkle – that they exist, and of other things – like Pegasus – that they do not exist. This is not to deny the value of the notion of presupposition; it is just to say that we sometimes put up our ontological interests for debate, and need an account of the forms of talk used in doing so.

THE THEORY OF DESCRIPTIONS

I turn now to give an account of Russell's theory of definite descriptions. Its relevance to the foregoing has already been made apparent by the fact that discussions of 'exists' proceed with Russell's theory lying somewhere close in the background, whether the view in question trades upon or controverts Russell's approach. The theory is best appreciated when seen in the context of certain more general philosophical issues, and these I sketch, together with the theory's epistemological corollaries.

Russell's distinction between two species of knowledge, 'knowledge by acquaintance' and 'knowledge by description', was mentioned in chapter 1 above. The distinction is drawn as follows. The former is a dyadic relation between a knowing subject and an object of direct awareness. 'I say that I am *acquainted* with an object when I have a direct cognitive relation to that object, i.e., when I am directly aware of the object itself'.[37] By 'directly aware' Russell meant 'without the intermediary of any process of inference or any knowledge of truths'.[38] The kinds of thing we may be acquainted with – that is, the objects of acquaintance – are particulars, like sense-data, memories, and our own awareness of objects; and universals, like redness and roundness, the awareness of which Russell calls 'conceiving', and which he calls 'concepts' for those cases in which anyone is in fact aware of them. Russell regarded relations too as being objects of acquaintance under this heading.[39] Particulars and universals exhaust the domain of our epistemological acquaintances.

Physical objects and other minds are not, as the foregoing makes apparent, among the objects of acquaintance. On the contrary, these are known by *description*. By 'description' Russell meant any phrase of the forms 'a so-and-so' and 'the so-and-so'. The first, 'a so-and-so', Russell called an ambiguous description.[40] The second form, 'the so-and-so', are definite descriptions in the singular, and these constitute the object of attention for Russell because 'the', the definite article, appears to make the description a referential device of an ontologically committal kind. 'We shall say that an object is "known by description" when we know that it is "the so-and-so," i.e. when we know there is one object, and no more, having a certain property; and it will be generally implied that we do not have knowledge by acquaintance of the same object.'[41] For Russell 'common nouns, even proper names' are descriptions, owing to the fact that 'the thought in the mind of the person using a proper name correctly can generally only be expressed *explicitly* if we replace the proper name by a description'.[42]

Underlying Russell's enterprise in articulating the theory of descriptions was a view of the nature of philosophy. This is that philosophy is concerned with analysing the language by means of which we describe the world. A proper or correct analysis will expose what language is really about. Analysis is necessary for the reason that ordinary language is ontologically misleading, not because people have insufficiently good grounds for what they say, but because it is frequently the case that the grammatical and logical forms of language are incongruent. It is the logical rather than the grammatical structure of language which reveals what there is. If care is not taken over the points where logic and grammar diverge, there is a danger of assimilating grammatical to logical, and thence to ontological, categories – often with disastrous results, as for example finding that it has become necessary to postulate the existence of subsistent entities.

It was Russell's rejection of Meinong's position in this respect, which, together with his rejection of Idealism and his early work in logic, was the immediate source of the theory of descriptions.

Russell shared with Meinong and others a belief in the denotative theory of meaning. In terms of this theory it constitutes a serious problem that propositions like 'the present King of France is wise' are palpably meaningful despite having nothing for the subject-expression to denote. It was to solve this problem that Meinong was led to accept a notion of subsistence. Russell, who at one time accepted Meinong's view, soon found it intolerable, because it offended his 'vivid sense of reality'. The theory of descriptions was devised to avoid making do with Meinong's result while at the same time preserving intact the denotative theory of meaning, which seemed to Russell correct. His solution was, as noted, to say that most common nouns and proper names are in fact concealed descriptions, and not 'logically proper' names at all — which latter are alone suitable for occupying the subject place in genuine subject-predicate propositions; and, further, to offer a method of analysing descriptions in order to make explicit their logical form.

What Russell therefore did was to say that it is only logically proper names which directly and unambiguously correspond to, that is denote, something in the world. To hold that descriptions function as names would be to fall into the Meinongian trap of having to accept that, since each constituent of a proposition is tied to something in the world, a proposition like 'the unicorn does not exist' obliges one to assert that there have in some sense to be unicorns in order for one meaningfully to deny that unicorns exist. Russell's theory accordingly involves a transmutation of descriptions into 'incomplete symbols', which acquire meaning only in context and have no significance on their own account, and which can be seen on analysis to make nondescriptive claims about the existence (and uniqueness) of the entities the original description purported to describe; in this way securing their meaningfulness (in context) without blunting Ockham's Razor. 'In the true analysis of the proposition, the description is broken up and disappears';[43] thus descriptions cease to have the unpalatable implications which a denotative theory seems to carry with it essentially.

Russell gave the following as examples of sentences containing definite descriptions:

1. Scott is the author of *Waverley*.
2. The present King of France is wise.
3. The $\sqrt{-1}$ is half the $\sqrt{-4}$.

The descriptive phrases here are respectively, 'the author of *Waverley*', 'the present King of France', 'the $\sqrt{-1}$', and 'the

$\sqrt{}$ -4'. What is the correct analysis of sentences containing them? The most obvious (and naïve) response is to say that descriptive phrases are complex names and function as such; but for the reasons just given, taking this view will not do. Moreover it can be demonstrated that it will not do. Consider the identity statement 'Scott is the author of *Waverley*'. (I shall symbolise this for convenience as 'a is D' where 'D' stands for the description.') If D is another name for Scott then 'a is D' = 'Scott is Scott', which is a tautology. If, on the other hand, one tries to substitute a name other than 'Scott' for D, for example 'Keats', the resulting assertion is false. Therefore under any substitution of a name for D, the sentence 'a is D' is either tautologous or false. Since 'a is D' is neither, D is not a name.

Secondly, names are arbitrary, so if D is taken to be synonymous with 'Scott' then the identity of Scott with the author of *Waverley* is a nomenclatural decision; but you cannot, as Russell observed, settle by choice of nomenclature whether or not Scott is the author of *Waverley*.[44]

Descriptions therefore cannot be names. The correct analysis of sentences in which descriptive phrases occur, then, Russell held to be as follows. Sentences containing descriptions are to be analysed into an equivalent set of statements in which no descriptive phrases occur and which make explicit the logical structure of what is being asserted. In the case of 2. above, the analysis yields:

2a.　There is a King of France,
2b.　there is not more than one King of France, and
2c.　anything which is King of France is wise;
or, more accurately,
　　$(\exists x)(Fx \cdot [(y)(Fy \rightarrow y=x)] \cdot Gx)$.
Because 2a. is false, 2. is false.

Sentence 2a. is captured by the existential generalisation; 2b. is the uniqueness condition encapsulated by 'the', the definite article, in common parlance; and 2c. asserts that the unique existent x has a certain property − in this case wisdom. The formal symbolism into which sentences containing descriptions are to be cast is itself, rather than the set of English sentences into which description-embedding sentences are to be translated, alone totally unambiguous; it is the perfect language.

This is what Russell meant by saying that the surface forms of language are misleading; for in 2. the description appears to have a denoting role, whereas in the formal paraphrase of the entire sentence there occur no singular terms, but only variables bound by quantifiers, predicates, and identity. This eliminates the difficulty created by vacuous descriptions, descriptions to which nothing answers, by showing that they are not logically proper names, that is names which denote and are therefore entitled to serve as the logical subjects of predication.

The point was naturally an important one for Russell, because it seemed to him that any meaningful sentences has a truth-value, is determinately either true or false. Thus, if 'the present King of France' were a logical as well as a grammatical subject expression, either it would have to denote something – a subsistent entity, say – or sentences in which it occurred would be meaningless. Neither option was attractive to Russell for the reasons given. Accordingly the theory of descriptions provided what is, given the terms in which Russell set the problem for himself, a masterly way out, by saying that sentences with descriptions in subject place are not logical subject-predicate sentences, and that descriptions, far from being representable as singular terms in a formal language, are in fact concealed existence and uniqueness assertions. When these latter are false, as shown above, the original sentence is as a whole false.

Quine, it is worth noting, derives his view of ontological commitment directly from Russell's strategy, but without espousing either of Russell's doctrines concerning logically proper names or the correlative epistemological notions of acquaintance and description. On this score, Russell held that the only logically proper names there are, are 'this' and 'that' – that is, demonstratives picking out objects of direct acquaintance. Quine's epistemological outlook, which is holistic, is quite opposite in character to this thoroughgoing atomism, an outlook in large part forced by Russell's view of logical form.

STRAWSON ON DESCRIPTIONS

Strawson's criticism of the theory of descriptions consists in a rejection of the theory of meaning underlying it, so laying an axe to its root. The criticism is, centrally, that no words or expressions have as their meaning some designated object. In Strawson's view, meaning resides in the activities of language users. If meaning is not denotation, then there cannot be 'logically proper names', nor descriptions in Russell's sense, for in Strawson's view no one uttering such a sentence as 'the present King of France is wise' is asserting that there is a King of France. Russell, as Strawson saw it, had failed to distinguish between a) the use of an expression to make a unique reference, and b) asserting that there is one and no more than one individual possessing certain characteristics.[45]

Russell's objective in devising the theory of descriptions was identified by Strawson as an attempt to escape the consequences of arguments like the following: 1) The phrase 'the King of France' is the subject of the sentence S. If S is a significant or meaningful sentence, then S is *about* the King of France. But if the King of France does not exist, then S is not about anything, and hence not about the King of France. But it *is* about the King of France, and it *is* meaningful; therefore there must in some sense be (exist, or subsist) the King of France. Or 2) if the sentence S is significant or meaningful, it is either true or false. It is true if the King of France is wise, and false if he is not wise. But 'the King of France is wise' and 'the King of France is not wise' have the truth-values they do only if there is, in some sense, something which is King of France; therefore in some sense there must be (exist, or subsist) the King of France.

Strawson commended Russell's desire to avoid the consequences of these arguments, which are bad arguments; but he argued that in formulating his theory as a means of doing so, Russell had accepted the spurious assumptions upon which the arguments are themselves based. These are that meaning is denotation, and that if the subject of a subject-predicate sentence is a logically proper subject – that is, not merely a grammatical subject – and the sentence is meaningful, then there is something to which its subject-term refers. Strawson pointed out that Russell recognised only two ways in which sentences, which seem in virtue of their grammatical form to be about some particular person, object, or event, can be significant; one is that if their grammatical and logical forms are incongruent, then they should be analysable as an existential sentence of a special sort, and the other is that the meaning of the grammatical subject of such a sentence should be the individual thing it designates, that is that it should be a logically proper name.

To make out his case Strawson drew a three-way distinction among a sentence, a use of a sentence, and an utterance of a sentence.[46] One can imagine the sentence 'the King of France is wise', call it K, being uttered in successive reigns of French kings, and it is natural to speak of K as being the same sentence each time. Evidently, however, there are differences between the *occasions of use* each time; users of K would be talking about different kings, and, depending on the nature of the kings in question, would sometimes be saying something true and sometimes something false. These are different *uses* of K. Similarly if two people used K during the same reign, then their use of K would be the same.

On Strawson's view, it follows from these distinctions that it is not the *sentence* which is true or false, but, instead, that what is true or false is the assertion or proposition which the sentence is used to make.

Analogously, a three-way distinction can be drawn among an expression, a use of an expression, and an utterance of an expression. The expression at issue is the description 'the King of France', call it D. As for K, it cannot be said that D refers to or mentions the King of France, but that it can be *used* to mention or refer on a particular occasion of utterance. ' "Mentioning" or "referring", is not something an expression does; it is something one can use an expression to do . . . [it] is a characteristic of *a use* of an expression, just as "being about something", and truth-or-falsity, are characteristic of *a use* of a sentence.'[47]

Strawson is not saying that there are sentences and descriptions *and* uses of them *and* utterances of them, as there are ships *and* shoes *and* sealing-wax; he is saying we cannot say *the same things* about these linguistic forms *and* their uses *and* utterances of them. But Russell thought we could do this; and this is where he went wrong, in Strawson's opinion, for

to give the meaning of an expression . . . is to give *general directions* for its use to refer . . . [and] to give the meaning of a sentence is to give *general directions* for its use in making true or false assertions . . . the meaning of an expression cannot be identified with the object it is used, on a particular occasion, to refer to. The meaning of a sentence cannot be identified with the assertion it is used, on a particular occasion, to make.[48]

whereas Russell thought that referring, if it occurred at all, was meaning; he confused the description, on the one hand, with its *use in a particular context* on the other hand. 'The important point,' Strawson wrote, 'is that the question whether the sentence is significant or not is quite independent of the question that can be raised about a particular use of it, *viz*. the question whether it is a genuine or spurious use.'[49]

Russell has said two true things and two false things about K, in Strawson's view. The two true things are that K is significant, and that K would be true only if there exists one and no more than one King of France who is wise. The two false things are that anyone now uttering K would be making an assertion which is either true or false, and that part of what K would be asserting is that there is one and only one King of France.

The two false things are false for the following reasons. If someone uttered K seriously now, we would not reply – 'That's false'. We would point out that there is no King of France at present, so the question of whether K as a whole is true or false does not arise; K is truth-valueless. And secondly: there is an obvious difference between a uniquely existential sentence, of the form 'there is only one such-and-such', and a sentence containing an expression, like D, which on particular occasions can be used to mention or refer to a particular person or thing. When someone uses K he neither *asserts* that there is someone who is uniquely King of France, nor does his use of the expression *entail* that there is someone who is uniquely King of France (even although, if his use of K is serious, he *presupposes* that there is such a person.) 'When we begin a sentence with "the such-and-such" the use of "the" shows, but does not state that we are, or intend to be, referring to one particular . . . "such-and-such".'[50] Russell conflated sentences which can be used to make particular reference with uniquely existential sentences; and did so because of the theory of meaning which is assumed by his view as a whole.

An important feature of Strawson's proposed alternative analysis is the distinction he insists upon between statements and sentences. The former are actual uses of the latter on some particular occasion, as noted. A sentence has meaning, but it is not a sentence, or some or other constituent of it, which refers; rather, reference happens when a given sentence is used on a given occasion to make a statement. The expression 'the King of France' is therefore meaningful, but when actually used, fails to refer to anything. The statement in question is truth-valueless − that is, is neither true nor false. Thus Strawson admits 'truth-value gaps' for statements in those cases where reference fails.

There are certain points in this account which need clarification. It is not clear whether Strawson's view is that use of the kind of sentence in question does not make a statement, or whether it does make a statement but one which is truth-valueless.[51] The solution to this is connected with the solution to a further doubt, concerning whether in Strawson's view the presupposition that there is a King of France is something entertained by the utterer of the sentence, or whether it is a relation obtaining between the statement and a further, suppressed, existential statement asserting that there is a King of France. Strawson's intention was that presupposition should not be construed as an epistemological relation of the first sort, but as a logical relation of the second sort, as his later papers show;[52] accordingly, in line with the sketch given above, presupposition is a relation such that a given statement A has truth-value if and only if a presupposed statement B is true. This then solves the first ambiguity: the use of a sentence makes a statement, but in the case of uses of sentences like K, the statement made is truth-valueless.

Truth-valuelessness is a controversial notion. Among the critics of Strawson's view number those who are anxious to preserve bivalence – that is, the principle that all statements are determinately either true or false. Retaining the principle of bivalence is essential for taking an extensionalist approach to philosophical issues, as Quine does and as do 'realists' in the philosophy of language. The thesis of extensionality is the thesis that the truth-values of statements are functions of the truth-values of their constituents; thus 'p·q' is true if and only if 'p' is true and 'q' is true, and 'pvq' is true if and only if at least one of 'p' and 'q' is true, and so on. Abandoning bivalence amounts to abandoning truth-functionality, in this familiar sense at least. It may also involve abandoning the Law of Excluded Middle, which states that 'everything is either A or not A'. This 'Law', one of Aristotle's three 'Laws of Thought' (the other two being the principles of Identity and Non-contradiction, respectively 'A is A' and 'not both A and not A'), appears to be unshakeably self-evident. But in quantum logic and in antirealist critiques of realist theory of meaning, bivalence is attacked.[53] In short, admitting truth-value gaps is to admit at least a third truth-value; and with the abandonment of bivalence come significant results for one's approach to other central philosophical concerns.

Strawson's views echo those of Frege. Frege, unlike Russell, did not recognise a class of logically proper names. Nevertheless, by means of the sense-reference distinction he was able to allow that sentences containing expressions which fail to denote can have sense; which is, for Frege, to say that they express propositions. Now, in Frege's view references of sentences – namely, truth-values[54] – depend upon the references of their constituent parts, so it follows that if one constituent of a given sentence has no reference, the sentence as whole has none – that is, it is truth-valueless. This is accordingly a presuppositional account not too dissimilar to the one adopted by Strawson, for a sentence will have a truth-value only if there is something to which the constituent singular terms refer.

Owing to his view that singular terms which fail to denote constitute one of the dispensable nuisances of natural language, Frege suggested that in the perfect language – the language of logic – all singular terms should be guaranteed denotations, even artificial ones if necessary. He suggested that the number O could be taken as the object referred to by expressions whose referents are difficult to locate. A systematic effort to work out these ideas was offered by Carnap.[55]

A minor reservation about Strawson's position is worth noting at this juncture. The theory of meaning he prefers to Russell's has it that to give the meaning of an expression is to give 'general directions' for its use to refer or mention; and to give the meaning of a sentence is to give 'general directions' for its use in making true or false assertions. However as this stands, this sketch of a theory of meaning is by no means self-evident. What does 'giving directions' amount to? Giving directions may include giving information – perhaps even ostensive information – of a sort which makes the theory covertly very similar to the denotative theory it purports to displace; for if the directions are *too* general, and cover any mentioning or referring expression, then they will be equally applicable to 'the pig in the sty' and 'the King of France'. But if they apply equally to both expressions in this way, they do not explain the differences between the two expressions. Directions for using words to refer might, then, actually include explanation of their meanings so like denotation that it is hardly worth arguing about.

REFERENTIAL AND ATTRIBUTIVE USES OF DESCRIPTIONS

The preceding discussion concerns what form an analysis of descriptions should take, given that descriptions may sometimes be vacuous. According to Donnellan, the analyses offered by both Russell and Strawson are unsatisfactory, chiefly because they fail to recognise that descriptions have two possible functions, and that a given description may have either function depending on the use made of the sentence in which it occurs.[56]

Donnellan calls the two uses to which descriptions can be put the 'referential' and the 'attributive' use respectively. When using a description attributively, a speaker is asserting something about whoever or whatever is 'the so-and-so'; the description occurs essentially, because the speaker is attributing something to whoever or whatever fits the description. The attribute of being the so-and-so is all-important in this case. By contrast, when a speaker uses a description referentially, he is doing so to enable his audience to pick out or identify whoever or whatever he is talking about; the description here is merely a tool for effecting reference, and the job might equally well be done by any other referential device, such as a name or some other description.[57]

Illustrations make the distinction clearer. Consider the sentence 'Smith's murderer is insane', which we might utter in the case of an endearing man called Smith who has been horribly killed. If I do not know who the murderer is, I can none the less attribute insanity to him. If however some particular person, say Jones, has been arraigned for the crime, then in my uttering this sentence I clearly use the description referentially, to pick out Jones. The contrast is yet clearer in the case where, say, Smith was not murdered at all but (unbeknownst to us) had an accident. Then by using the description 'Smith's murderer' we presuppose or imply[58] that there is a murderer, with different results according as to which use the description is being put. If attributively, the predicate '. . .is insane' applies to nobody, for there is nobody to whom insanity could be correctly attributed. If referentially, however, we may succeed in picking someone out (the wrongfully accused Jones, say) even although the description 'Smith's murderer' does not fit him or anyone else. And even if someone in the audience knew or believed Jones to be innocent, he would still know who was being referred to by use of the description.[59]

To vary the example: using a description referentially, one can successfully pick out a man as 'the man drinking Champagne' even if the description does not fit, say because it is water and not Champagne in the glass. But if the chairman of the Teetotaler's Union has been told there is someone at the party drinking Champagne, and asks 'which is the man drinking Champagne?', thus using the description attributively, then if there is no one who fits the description, no one can be picked out as the person of whom the question has been asked.[60]

One of the important results flowing from Donnellan's distinction is the difference made to the issue of the existential presupposition or implication carried by descriptions. In general, there is a presupposition that a person using a description referentially believes that there is a whoever or whatever, and that the description fits it. Misdescriptions usually mislead an audience; nevertheless, even if nothing in fact fits a referentially-used description, it can still successfully serve to pick out whatever it was that the speaker intended to pick out for his audience.

By contrast, there is not the same possibility of misdescription in the attributive case. 'Smith's murderer' attributively used cannot misdescribe because it is not being used to pick out Jones or some one or other particular person, but *anyone* who happens to fit the description, even if it is not known whom. Rather, the presupposition or implication is carried by the attributively-used description because, if nothing answered to the description, the purpose of the speech-act in which it figured would be thwarted. Thus the description might figure in a statement, or a command, or a question; if it failed to fit anyone or anything, then the speaker would have failed to make a statement, or to command anyone to do something, or to ask a question.[61]

This shows in what respect both Russell and Strawson have gone wrong in Donnellan's view. Russell held that 'the ϕ is ψ' entails 'there exists one and only one ϕ'; but whereas this might be so in the attributive case, it does not appear to be so in the referential case. Here there is a presumption based on what is normally true of the referential use of descriptions, namely that there is something which is the ϕ; but this does not amount to an *entailment* of an existence and uniqueness assertion by the sentence containing the description. Russell's analysis, in consequence, straightforwardly fits only the attributive case.

The definition of denoting given by Russell was that a term denotes if there is an entity which it picks out. This fits both uses of descriptions; and accordingly, on Donnellan's view, shows that denoting (which both kinds of descriptions do) and referring (which only one kind of description does) are different things. Russell recognises only the former. Donnellan argues that a denoting-referring distinction is fruitful, for it provides a way of dealing with such cases as the following. One naturally does not know in advance who will be the prime minister in 2000 AD, but suppose one says 'the prime minister in 2000 AD will be a Social Democrat'. Suppose it in fact turns out that a Social Democrat called Shirley Williams is indeed Prime Minister in that year. The description denotes Williams; but one used the description attributively and did not — because one could not — *refer* to Williams. The denoting-referring distinction makes clear what is and what is not going on in uses of descriptions in this way.[62]

Donnellan's criticism of Strawson is that Strawson's theory goes too far in the direction of making descriptions referential, thus obscuring their attributive function. On Donnellan's view Strawson's theory consists in the following propositions:

1. If someone asserts that the ϕ is ψ he has not made a true or false statement if there is no ϕ.
2. If there is no ϕ then the speaker has failed to refer to anything.
3. The reason he has said nothing true or false is that he has failed to refer.[63]

The first proposition may be true in the attributive case; for if

Smith had no murderer then 'Smith's murderer is insane' says nothing true. However if the description was used referentially to pick out Jones, then even if Jones is innocent he may none the less be insane, and so something true has been said.[64] For this same reason, proposition 2. is simply false; there may be no ϕ , that is no 'Smith's murderer', yet Jones has been successfully referred to.[65]

Matters are more complicated with regard to proposition 3. Strawson took it that 3. ties together 1. and 2. But 3. does not work, for the attributive case at least, as an account of the truth-valueless-ness of statements when their presuppositions are false. For the reason given is that reference has failed; and this does not explain why a speaker making an attributive use of a description fails to state anything true or false when nothing fits the description.[66] In the referential case, it would seem that a speaker fails to refer only in rather extreme cases of perceptual or, more generally, epistemic error, as when someone, deluded by a trick of the light, say, says 'is that man with the handkerchief the Waynflete Professor of Metaphysics?' when there is in fact no one at all, so that it cannot be said to whom or what it was that the speaker intended to refer.

Donnellan concludes that 'neither Russell's nor Strawson's theory represents a correct account of the use of definite descriptions — Russell's because it ignores altogether the referential use, Strawson's because it ignores altogether the distinction between the referential and attributive and mixes together truths about each (together with some things that are false)'.[67]

There are difficulties in Donnellan's account, arising chiefly from independent problems about the notion of reference and a distinction which may be drawn between speaker's reference and semantic reference. Grice, for example, proposed that we should distinguish between a) what a speaker's *words* mean, and b) what the *speaker* means by using those words on that occasion, as when someone says 'The cops have arrived' meaning 'Let's get out of here'. The speaker means the latter by using the former, and the words constituting the former do not at all mean in their own right what the speaker used them to mean.[68]

Kripke adopts this notion to challenge Donnellan's account.[69] In Kripke's view, the *semantic* referent of a designating expression is given by the speaker's *general* intention to refer to a certain object on a specific occasion. If the speaker believes that an object he wishes to talk about satisfies the conditions for being the semantic referent of the term he uses, then he believes that there is no conflict between his general and specific intentions. It is in the light of this that Kripke thinks Donnellan's views should be considered, because there are two ways in which the speaker's belief in the coincidence of his general and specific intentions arise. One – the 'simple' case – is when the speaker's specific intention just is his general semantic intention, as when he uses 'Jones' as a name of Jones; the other – the 'complex' case – is when he has a specific intention distinct from his general intention, both which he believes to be coincident in fact, as when he wishes to refer to 'the man over there' believing that that man *is* Jones.[70]

Kripke's argument is that Donnellan's attributive use of descriptions is nothing but the 'simple' case, and the referential use the 'complex' case; and that accordingly it was wrong for Donnellan to assimilate the referential use of descriptions to the referential use of proper names; for the simple-complex distinction applies just as much to proper names as descriptions.[71] The argument is made out by means of a test involving languages with more and less specific forms than the one (in this case English) for which Donnellan's case is made out; with a view to seeing whether the referential-attributive ambiguity postulated by Donnellan holds for English. Kripke concludes that it does not necessarily hold for English, since in more specific variants of English the ambiguity vanishes; and that therefore Russell's unitary account of descriptions is preferable.[72] The details of this argument turn on considerations specific to the nature of reference, and since I deal with these in a later chapter I shall leave the matter aside for the present.

Suffice it to say at this juncture that if Kripke's views are right, they go some way to explaining the interest and vitality of Russell's insights into the issue of existence claims and assumptions. That interest is evidenced by the use made by Quine of Russell's insights, and by the fact that Pears ended his paper by saying that if his proposals have to be abandoned, the option is 'to treat existence in the way Russell treated it', and similarly Thomson ended his paper by saying 'It is, of course, Russell's theory that I have, with many qualifications, been explaining'.

NOTES

1. This branch of philosophy is called *ontology*, 'theory of being'.
2. Descartes, R., *Meditations* (trans. Anscombe, G. E. M. and Geach, P. T.). *The Philosophical Writings*, London, 1970, pp.59-124.
3. Kant, *Critique of Pure Reason,* cf. A590/B618, *et seq.*
4. ibid., A598/B626.
5. Aristotle concluded much the same: 'that there is such a thing is not what anything is . . . being is not a genus', *Analytica Posteriora* II,7, 92 b 13.

6. Pears, D. F., 'Is Existence a Predicate?', in Strawson (ed.) *Philosophical Logic*, Oxford, 1967, pp.79-102. For some reason it has become traditional to put the question this way; more accurately, one should ask whether '*exists*' is a *predicate* or whether *existence* is a *property*. The word 'exists' cannot be a property of anything, and existence is not a linguistic entity.

7. cf. Strawson, *Introduction To Logical Theory,* Oxford, 1952, pp.175, *et seq.*

8. The notion of presuppositional implication is not without its problems. See below; and cf. Nerlich, G., 'Presupposition and Entailment', *American Philosophical Quarterly* 2, 1969; and 'Presupposition and Classical Logical Relations', *Analysis,* XXVII, 1967. cf. also Munitz, M. K., *Existence and Logic,* New York, 1974. and Dummett M. A. E., *Truth and other Enigmas* Duckworth 1978.

9. Moore, G. E., 'Is Existence a Predicate?' *Proceedings of the Aristotelian Society* Supplementary Volume 1936, pp.175-88. Moore was replying to a paper on the same topic by Kneale. W. M., *op. cit.*

10. ibid., pp.177-8.

11. ibid., pp.178-9.

12. ibid., p.179.

13. ibid., p.180.

14. ibid, p.185, Moore's italics.

15. ibid., p.186.

16. ibid., p.187, Moore's italics.

17. Thomson, J., 'Is Existence A predicate?', in Strawson, *Philosophical Logic, passim.*

18. cf. Orenstein. A., *Existence and the Particular Quantifier*, Philadelphia, 1978, *passim.*

19. Lipton, M. R., Review of Orenstein, *op. cit.,* in *Philosophical Review,* July 1980, p.487, *et seq.*

20. Quine, W. V., 'Designation and Existence,' *Journal of Philosophy,* XXXVI, 1939, pp.707-8; reprinted in Feigl and Sellars, *Readings in Philosophical Analysis,* New York, 1949.

21. Quine, 'Ontology and Ideology', *Philosophical Studies* II, 1951, p.11; reprinted in Feigl, *et al., New Readings in Philosophical Analysis,* New York, 1972.

22. Quine, *Word and Object,* MIT, 1960, p.242.

23. cf. below, this chapter, for Russell's treatment of descriptions, and cf. chapter 6 below for a discussion of the notion of 'satisfaction' in the sections on Tarski.

24. Quine, ibid., pp.258-9.

25. Orenstein, A., 'On explicating Existence in Terms of Quantification', in Munitz, M. K. (ed.), *Logic and Ontology,* New York, 1973, p.73.

26. cf. ibid; the example is drawn from Hintikka and shows that the substitutional reading has advantages over the objectual for quantification in opaque contexts.

27. Haack, S., *Philosophy of Logics,* p.50; and pp.50-5 for a discussion of which choice to make. Haack is fond of diagrams and provides some useful ones in her text.

28. Strawson, 'Singular Terms and Predication', in Strawson *op. cit.,* pp.69-88; cf. esp. p.77.

29. cf. Haack, *op. cit.,* p.47, *et seq.*

30. Strawson, 'Is Existence Never A Predicate?', *Freedom and Resentment,* London, 1974.

31. ibid., pp.193-4.

32. ibid., p.196.

33. ibid., pp.196-7.

34. ibid., p.194.

35. Strawson, *Introduction to Logical Theory*, p.191.
36. cf. Munitz, 'Existence and Presupposition,' in Munitz, *op. cit.*, p.85 *et seq.*
37. Russell, B., *Mysticism and Logic*, London 1917, p.209.
38. Russell, *The Problems of Philosophy*, London, 1912, p.25.
39. Russell, *Mysticism and Logic*, pp.212-13.
40. Russell discussed these in Marsh, R. C. (ed.), 'Lectures on Logical Atomism 5' *Logic and Knowledge*, London, 1956.
41. Russell, *Problems of Philosophy*, p.29.
42. ibid.
43. *Logic and Knowledge*, pp.247-8.
44. ibid., p.245.
45. Strawson, 'On Referring', *Mind* 1950, pp.320-44; reprinted in Feigl *et al.*, *op. cit.* pp.35-50.
46. ibid., p.38.
47. ibid., p.39.
48. ibid., pp.34-40
49. ibid., p.41.
50. ibid., p.42.
51. cf. Nerlich., *op. cit.*
52. cf. Strawson, 'A Reply To Mr. Sellars', *Philosophical Review*, 1954, reprinted in Feigl, *et al. op. cit.*, pp.51-4; and 'Identifying Reference and Truth-Values', *Theoria* 30, 1964; reprinted in *Logico-Linguistic Papers*.
53. Matters are more complex than I have just sketched them here; cf. chapter 8 below, where the discussion is more extended. Note that Dummett attacks the notion of presupposition and the principle of bivalence. cf. *op. cit.*
54. cf. chapter 2 above.
55. cf. Carnap, R., *Introduction To Semantics and Formalisation of Logic*, Havard, 1942.
56. Donnellan, K. S., 'Reference and Definite Descriptions', *Philosophical Review*, LXX-V, 1966, pp.281-304; reprinted in Schwarz, S. P. (ed.), *Naming, Necessity, and Natural Kinds*, Cornell, 1977, pp.42-65. References are to this edition. 'Description' means 'definite description' here as thoughout this chapter.
57. ibid., p.46.
58. Use of this disjunction leaves open the issue between Russell and Strawson as to whether the description presupposes or implies that there is a murderer.
59. ibid., pp.47-8.
60. ibid., p.48.
61. ibid., pp.52-3.
62. ibid., pp.54-5.
63. ibid., pp.55-6.
64. ibid., p.56.
65. ibid.
66. ibid., pp.56-7.
67. ibid., p.58.
68. Grice, H. P., 'Speaker's Meaning, Sentence-Meaning, and Word-Meaning', *Foundations of Language* 4, 1968, pp.225-42.
69. Kripke, S., 'Speaker's Reference and Semantic Reference', in French, *et al.*, *Contemporary Perspectives in the Philosophy of Language*, Minnesota 1977.
70. ibid., p.15.
71. ibid.
72. ibid., pp.16-18.

5   Truth: The Pragmatic and Coherence Theories

INTRODUCTION

It is a philosophical commonplace that there can be no progress in understanding a concept unless one's enquiry begins with the right questions. The *wrong* question to ask about truth is 'what is truth?' for these reasons.

Consider the difference between the questions 'what is kelp?' and 'what is rationality?' It is relatively easy to answer the first; an appropriate reply would be 'it is a kind of seaweed'. The second poses more difficulties, and accordingly demands a more studied reply. What is being asked for is an account of a complex concept, and it would seem to make good sense to begin by investigating in what one's possession of the concept consists, which is in part at least to ask how and when one uses that concept. Thus it would appear to be better to reply in this second case in a way which, although more circuitous, is in the end more informative, by recasting the question into 'what is it for someone to make a rational decision or choice?', the idea being that gaining clarity on this issue is the first step to understanding the concept of rationality in general.

Questions about truth are, for the same reasons, best approached in this way. The question 'what is truth?' has the character of a sheer cliff, which it is quite perplexing to know how to begin climbing. As it stands, the question looks like a request to know what truth ('Truth') is in some ultimate, inclusive, perhaps mystical sense; but it is evident that even if there were Truth in this sense, it would be necessary to begin with more modest aims. The task, accordingly, is made easier by asking 'what is it for a proposition (statement, sentence, or belief) to be true?' It is the purpose of this chapter and the next to investigate the major theories framed in reply.

The pragmatic, coherence, correspondence, redundancy, and semantic theories of truth are the major theories in question. A rough preliminary characterisation of each would go as follows: The *pragmatic* theory is that true beliefs are those which are fruitful, which have as it were 'cash-value' in terms of experience. The *coherence* theory has it that truth consists in a relation of coherence between beliefs or propositions in a set, such that a belief is false when it fails to fit with other mutually coherent members of a set. The *correspondence* theory has it that a proposition is true when it corresponds to the facts; the relation here is between propositions and the way things are in the world. The *redundancy* theory has it that because 'p is true' and 'p' mean the same, ' . . . is true' is redundant. In the *semantic* theory, finally, truth is made out as a property of sentences in terms of a recursive notion of satisfaction as a relation between sentences of a given language and a domain. There are variants and sophistications of each of these theories, and some overlaps between some of them. These features will emerge as the discussion proceeds.

The chief point of the discussion about propositions in chapter 2 above was to make out clearly the distinction between propositions and sentences. The usefulness of the distinction now becomes manifest. It is, for example, crucial to traditional versions of the correspondence theory that the correspondence relation holds between propositions (not sentences) and states of affairs in the world; whereas in the semantic theory, truth is viewed as a property of sentences. Similarly it would involve unnecessary and perhaps insuperable difficulties to render the coherence and pragmatic theories as being about, respectively, coherence between sentences, or the utility of committing oneself epistemologically to certain grammatically well-formed strings of uttered or inscribed (and therefore spatio-temporal) sounds or marks. So much will, however become clearer as the sequel unfolds.

Problems concerning truth have been taken to revolve upon two principal issues: the first concerns the meaning of the word 'true', while the second concerns the criterion or criteria by means of which truth or falsity is to be recognised as attaching to whatever is the truth-bearer.[1] One reason why it is important to take note of the distinction is that it may turn out that whereas one of the truth theories gives a definition of the meaning of 'true', another gives the criterion or test of what truth-value a truth-bearer has. For example, it might be held that, in meaning, 'true' is an evaluative term, like 'good' whereas the criterion of truth is utility — such a view was held by the pragmatist Schiller. Bradley seemed to think that in meaning 'true' has a correspondence flavour — 'truth to be truth must be true of something' — whereas coherence furnishes the criterion or test of truth.[2] Most pragmatists identified the definition and the criterion of truth by saying that one gives the meaning of 'true' by supplying criteria for the term's application — a view which has affinities with Wittgenstein's later thought and 'use' theories of meaning in general.[3] Some coherence theorists like Blanshard similarly held that the definition and the criterion run together, in this case because of the fact that truth *is* coherence, and so the notion supplies at once a test for truth and a definition of 'true'.[4]

THE PRAGMATIC THEORY OF TRUTH

The currently least favoured theory of truth is the pragmatic theory. Articulation of its main original variants owes itself to three of the leading figures in American philosophy of the late nineteenth and early twentieth centuries — Peirce, James and Dewey. Owing to the common ground in their philosophical outlooks they are grouped as 'pragmatists'; hence the label for their theory — or, more accurately, roughly similar variants on a theory — of truth. Their influence remains in the work of Quine and to some extent in the later views of Wittgenstein; Dummett also manifests certain pragmatist tendencies in his work.[5]

In the pragmatists' view, a concept's meaning is given by reference to the practical or experimental (hence 'pragmatic') con-sequences of its application. As James had it 'there can *be* no difference that *makes* no difference',[6] which directly echoes Peirce's less aphoristic dictum 'there is no distinction of meaning so fine as to consists in anything but a possible difference of practice'.[7] This comes down to saying that the right approach to truth is to enquire what *difference* is made by a belief's being true.

Peirce held that truth is that opinion upon which scientists (in the broad sense of 'those who use the scientific method') will, if they go on long enough, eventually agree; and he held this in consequence of a prior view about what is, in effect, the psychology of enquiry. For Peirce, beliefs consist in dipositions to action, and doubts are the negative effects on such dispositions which result from unruly experiences, experiences which subvert our theories or fail to fit some general pattern which our views of the world take. Such doubts, said Peirce, prompt enquiry because they induce an un-pleasant state in us, which we try to overcome by acquiring fixed and stable beliefs. Scientific method enables us to acquire such beliefs, because alone among belief-acquiring methods it is constrained by the way things actually are — that is, by reality — and since the way things are is independent of anyone's beliefs, that constraint will bring about a convergence of opinions to some eventual consensus. This eventual consensus will be the truth. Not only will the truth be wholly satisfying to believe, since it is immune from the disturbances of doubt, but it will also consist in correspondence with reality. In this way Peirce's version of the pragmatist theory contains elements of a correspondence theory.

James' version in some ways elaborates upon, and in some ways differs from, Peirce's view. James argued that the value of having true beliefs consists in their immunity from unruly experiences; and true beliefs are those which are confirmed by experience in the long run, that is, which are verifiable. James believed that we accommodate awkward experiences by adjusting our system of beliefs in such a way as best to preserve its overall internal consistency, while finding a place for recalcitrant experiential results within it. This foreshadows the 'web of beliefs' view mooted by Quine,[8] and has a coherence flavour to it.

Whereas Peirce was something of a realist, however, James had nominalist instincts; and accordingly he was troubled by the fact that the verifiability notion committed him to there being truths which no one has yet verified – that is, to the existence of possible, but not yet realised, verifications. This result was embarrassing for one with nominalist scruples, and consequently James sometimes wrote as if wishing to be understood as holding that truths are *manufactured* by the verification of beliefs. This feature of his views was adopted by Schiller, and a similar view is held by certain contemporary philosophers, notably the extreme relativist Feyerabend.[9] The idea that truths are created by enquiry is, however, inconsistent with the view that beliefs converge to truth by verification processes; so there is tension in James' theory in this respect.

Another feature of James' view which invited criticism was his propensity to speak of truth as that which it is 'good', 'useful', or 'expedient' to believe. He wrote, for example, that 'the true is only the expedient in the way of our thinking, just as the right is only the expedient in our way of behaving'.[10] Russell and Moore took James to task for this on the grounds that he was making the crude, and also morally objectionable, point that truth is the same as congenial belief. But defenders of James argue that James was trying to show that the superiority of true over false beliefs consists in their immunity to falsification, and that since empirical evidence is by itself frequently unable to help us adjudicate between competing theories, considerations of utility can and should be invoked to aid decision.[11]

Dewey accepted Peirce's definition of truth as 'absolute fixity of belief'. Together with Peirce he believed that making sense of our ideas demands that we examine them at work, in their contexts of use.[12] When particular ideas are seen to work successfully and to provide solutions to doubts or problems, that is, to be confirmed in practice, then we are warranted in asserting those ideas – which is to say, warranted in committing ourselves to them as true. Thus Dewey preferred to speak of truth as a property attaching to ideas which we are warranted in asserting.

This amounts to saying that truth is a property of beliefs which they come to possess by being verified in practice; and this has counter-intuitive results. Suppose White murders Brown on Tuesday, and a detective verifies White's guilt on Thursday. Then it would seem that the proposition 'White murdered Brown' *became true* on Thursday, and was not true beforehand. But surely 'White murdered Brown' was true the instant of White's murdering Brown; if Dewey's views are correct, we might not be able to convict White at all, owing to the fact that for a period after Brown's murder it was *not* true 'that White murdered Brown'. This shows that there may be an important difference between the notions of confirmation and truth, for whereas confirmation appears to be a datable occurrence (the detective confirmed White's guilt on Thursday), truth is standarly taken to be such that a proposition does not become true upon being verified or apprehended, but simply is or is not true – even, on some views, whether anyone knows it to be true or not.

This last thought suggests a criticism on upholder of the principle of bivalence might make. This is that to define 'true' as 'confirmed' violates the principle; for if 'true' means 'confirmed' then, since the principle requires that for every proposition either it or its negation, but not both, be true, it would follow that every proposition or its negation is confirmed. But this is simply false; for although it is either true that 'it snowed in Oxfordshire in 10,000 BC', or true that 'it did not snow in Oxfordshire in 10,000 BC,' as the principle demands, it is certainly not the case that either proposition is confirmed.

It has been fashionable, since the attacks on pragmatism mounted by Russell, Moore and Carnap, to regard the pragmatic theory as outdated and wrong-headed. One finds it mentioned only to be dismissed, and from this cursory attitude a rather crude misunderstanding of the theory results. This is that the theory consists in defining 'true' simply as 'what works', and that this is wholly mistaken since it is quite obvious that many falsehoods 'work' (only consider Plato's view that the general population should be encouraged in religious beliefs, since although these beliefs are false, they will promote good conduct) whereas many truths, for example that 'Aristotle's father was a physician', do no real 'work' at all (as has been said, they 'bake no bread'.) But it will be clear, even from the foregoing sketches, that the pragmatic theory is rather more subtle than the imputed equation 'true = what works' suggests.

JAMES' DEFENCE

Consider, in a little more detail, James' view of the matter. He did most among the pragmatists to contest misunderstanding of the pragmatic theory, and wrote upon it often.[13] There is no better statement of his view than one provided by himself, which is worth quoting at length because it is so infrequently read:

Truth is a property of certain of our ideas. It means their agreement, as falsity means their disagreement, with reality . . . Pragmatism asks its usual question. 'Grant an idea or belief to be true,' it says, 'what concrete difference will its being true make in anyone's actual life? What experiences [may] be different from those which would obtain if the belief were false? What, in short, is the truth's cash-value in experiential terms?' The moment pragmatism asks this question, it sees the answer: *True ideas are those we can assimilate, validate, corroborate, and verify. False ideas are those that we cannot.* That is the practical difference it makes to us to have true ideas; that therefore is the meaning of truth, for it is all that truth is known as.

　　The truth of an idea is not a stagnant property inherent in it. Truth *happens* to an idea. It *becomes* true, is *made* true by events. Its verity *is* in fact an event, a process, the process namely of its verifying itself, its *verification* . . . Any idea that helps us to deal, whether practically or intellectually, with reality, that doesn't entangle our progress in frustrations, that *fits*, in fact, and adapts our life to the reality's whole setting, will agree sufficiently to meet the requirement. It will be true of that reality. *The true,* to put it very briefly, *is only the expedient in our way of thinking, just as the right is only the expedient in the way of our behaving.* Expedient in almost any fashion, and expedient in the long run and on the whole, of course; for what meets expediently all the experience in sight won't necessarily meet all further experience equally satisfactorily. Experience, as we know, has ways of *boiling over*, and making us correct our present formulas.[14]

Moore and Russell, as noted, took this view to come down simply to an equation between truth and utility, and rejected it on the grounds that some falsehoods are useful, some truths inexpedient – 'Is it not clear,' Moore asked, 'that we do actually sometimes have true ideas, at times when they are not useful, but positively in the way?'[15] The objection misses the point, however, for James intended to be understood as saying that truth is satisfactory or useful belief in the sense that it is belief which is secure 'in the long run', safe – given a theory of how we assimilate subsequent experiences to our scheme of things – from overthrow.[16] If the Moore-Russell criticism touches a nerve at all, it does so in connection with James' opinion that religious beliefs are expedient (in more or less the standard sense of that term) because they maximise the coherence of one's experience and one's values together.[17]

It is, accordingly, when the connection is seen between, on the one hand, expediency or utility in James' main sense, and on the other hand the notion of maximising coherence across the totality of experience, that the relation between utility and verifiability becomes clear. Moore and Russell did not see this connection; but they objected as strongly to the assimilation of truth to verification as they did to the assimilation of truth to utility. Their grounds for doing so were similar; namely, that just as there may be inexpedient truths which nevertheless are truths, so there may be truths which have never been verified but which are nevertheless truths. If James had identified truth with verification there would be point to this objection, but in fact he made the subtler identification of truth with *verifiability*, so leaving it open that there can be as yet unverified truths which are none the less truths because they are verifiable.[18] However this manoeuvre created the tension in James' views, noted above, between truths as an accreting corpus of individual beliefs, each becoming a member upon being verified, and truths as something which were always true before being verified owing to the fact that they were, antecedent to verification, verifiable. This tension James did not resolve.

The pragmatist theory of truth is heavily epistemological, and owing to the vital connection between epistemological and onto-logical considerations, which are equally both important and vulnerable to dispute, the theory stands or falls according to how well these latter issues are dealt with by the pragmatists. Peirce in the end adopted a fallibilist realism about the objects of perception, but James' nominalism left him with certain difficulties, having elected to dispense with a notion of 'trans-empirical' reality, that is an independent but epistemologically inaccessible reality; for it was precisely this that made it difficult for him to resolve the verifiability problem just sketched.[19]

Saying this does not substantiate another of the common criticisms of the pragmatist theory, however; the criticism this time being that the theory is subjectivist in the sense that it makes truth depend on the knowing subject's outlook. Although, in order to secure a workable notion of objectivity, the pragmatists were under an obligation to give an account of what reality consists in, and although they did not do this to satisfaction, they were nevertheless firm in holding, in their several ways, that part of what it is for a belief to be true is that it corresponds to reality. 'The only *real* guarantee we have,' James wrote, 'against licentious thinking is the circumpressure of reality itself, which gets us sick of concrete error, whether there be a trans-empirical reality or not.'[20] The point, thus, is not that beliefs are true because they suit the believer in some epistemologically hedonistic way, but because they accord with experience and help the believer to deal with it; it is then a further, although related, matter, that there is a need for James to supply an account of the reality over which that experience ranges. But at any rate it cannot do to reject the pragmatic conception of truth outright on the grounds, as Moore and Russell seem to have done, of a suppressed assumption about the nature of reality − in particular where that supressed view is a 'realist' one in the sense to be discussed in a later chapter; for realism has an inbuilt slant on truth quite opposed, as the very labels suggest, to antirealist theories such as James'.

The foregoing is far from being a vindication of the pragmatist theory of truth, nor is it even a partial defence of it, for evidently there are difficulties in the view which it would require a great deal of reworking to eliminate. Rather, it is in part a defence of the claim that the theory should be taken more seriously than it has been in the past. And part of the reason for this, in turn, is the fact that contemporary antirealism, discussed below, has some important features in common with certain elements of the pragmatist view.

THE COHERENCE THEORY OF TRUTH

The coherence and correspondence theories are generally regarded as the two chief traditional doctrines of truth. In point of antiquity the correspondence theory takes all laurels; it is discussed by Plato in the *Sophist*. The coherence theory, as a recognisable theory, comes considerably later, dating in the main from Kant's critique of the notion of *adaequatio intellectus et rei,* that is, the adequacy or correspondence of thought to things. In Kant's view, because noumenal reality − the *Ding an sich*, which James called 'trans-empirical reality' − is inaccessible to human intuition, it must follow that the idea of a correspondence between, on the one hand, the mind's apprehension of things, and on the other hand things themselves, is questionable.[21]

The domicile of the coherence theory of truth is, speaking generally, rationalist thought, like that of Leibniz and Spinoza in the seventeenth century, and Hegel and Bradley at the beginning and end of the nineteenth century respectively. However, a coherence theory was also held by some of this century's logical positivists, in particular Neurath and Hempel, and from oddly similar motives as will be seen. Very recently the theory has been defended by Rescher at length.[22]

The basic idea of the coherence theory is a simple one. It is that a proposition is true if it coheres with other propositions in a system, and false otherwise. This is sometimes alternatively put as: truth consists in a relation of coherence among the members of a set of beliefs.

The theory is best explained in context of the metaphysical or epistemological views it has been invoked to serve. Bradley, for example, was concerned to argue that reality is a unified and coherent whole, which he called the Absolute, and nothing short of the whole taken *as* a whole is a fully real, from which it follows that anything said of *parts* of the whole can be at best only *partly* true. If we consider only a part or aspect of the whole, we may attain to a degree of truth; but since in any case we apprehend parts of the whole by means of *appearances,* which unlike reality (the Absolute) are riddled with contradiction, this partial grasp of the truth is irreducibly unsatisfactory. It is important to note that if Bradley is right in holding that appearances are at least partially deceiving because contradictory, then knowledge (and hence truth) has no incorrigible basis in the judgements of perception. This is what makes Bradley something of a rationalist as to method; if one denies that sense-experience furnishes the basis for knowledge, and holds instead that excogitation − rational inference − alone carries us to the truth about reality (as did, in their fashion, all of Plato, Leibniz, Spinoza, Hegel, and Bradley himself), then a coherence theory of truth is an essential ingredient in one's epistemology. For the only test there can be, for the truth of a proposition stating a belief in context of a rationally-deduced system of beliefs, is whether it coheres with that system of beliefs. No reference to discrete parcels of fact over against our thought is permissable on the assumption of a rationalist epistemology, and hence no correspondence relation can be invoked to secure a notion of truth for propositions on a blow-by-blow basis.

The theoretical basis of the coherence theory lies in the notion of a system. Bradley epitomised the connection between coherence and system by saying 'truth is an ideal expression of the Universe, at once coherent and comprehensive. It must not conflict with itself and there must be no suggestion which fails to fall inside it. Perfect truth, in short, must realise the idea of a systematic whole'.[23] The suggestion is that coherence consists in consistency and interdependence; thus, for a set of beliefs to be a coherent set, its constituent beliefs must be consistent with respect to each other and, in some way to be specified, dependent upon other beliefs in the set.

COHERENCE AS DEPENDENCE

Consistency is a minimum requirement, and relatively unproblematic. The major difficulty is to specify what relation of dependence holds between the set's member beliefs or the judgements expressing them. One suggestion is that any judgement must entail and be entailed by every other judgement; this is what Blanshard held, and he cited geometry as the nearest to a paradigm of a system in which this is the case.[24] '[In] a completely satisfactory system,' he wrote, ' . . . no proposition would be arbitrary, every prosposition would be entailed by the others jointly and even singly, no proposition would stand outside the system.'[25] But this will not do; the proposed relation is far too strong, and makes the coherence theory a theory of assertive redundancy, with the effect that in a coherent system of judgements each judgement says exactly the same as all the rest.[26] It would then be the case not only that the true statement 'Alexander was King of Macedon' entails and is entailed by, say, 'my next-door neighbour is wearing a white vest today', but, worse, that the two statements are in fact somehow equivalent. In the preferred idiom of the Absolute idealists, in which all statements are diguised predications on the Absolute, 'the Absolute is Alexander-King-of-Macedonly' and 'the Absolute is neighbour-white-vestly' would thus be repetitions of one another, a view by any standards hard to swallow.

A more promising line is taken by Ewing, who suggests that coherence is to be understood as a more diffuse relationship of logic between propositions in a set; specifically, that 'any one proposition in the set follows with logical necessity if all the other propositions in the set are true' and 'no set of propositions within the whole set is logically independent of all propositions in the remainder of the set.'[27] This preserves the idea of the interrelatedness of the truth of all the propositions in the set without knitting them too tightly together along Blanshard's lines. As it stands, however, the characterisation is vague, and would seem to demand that it be understood as turning on a requirement that the set of propositions be complete. But then any proposition added to the set will make it incoherent; and these include the logical consequences of the set's member propositions themselves, an unsatisfactory consequence. Moreover, there is the equally important fact that it is unclear how we could know when a set of propositions is complete − this is in particular so regarding the set, if the idea of a 'set' makes sense here, of propositions about the universe; a sharply-restricted formal system may be different.

THE CHARACTER OF COHERENCE

In general, however, the coherence notion has the following overall character. Because truth is to be determined by means of a test of 'coherence' somehow specified, the question of a proposition's value turns on its relations with other propositions in a set, and accordingly the notion of a context or system plays a vital role in the account we are to give of truth. The notion of a system, in turn, is to be made out in terms of consistency, connectedness, and completeness, and it is these ideas which need to be specified precisely if the theory is to recommend itself. Even in advancing of doing so, however, we can see in what direction the theory takes us in our efforts to understand truth.

One line of objection which might be followed regarding the coherence theory is that we need not discuss it at all because it arises in connection with a certain type of metaphysical theory, or at any rate with a certain epistemological style – namely, rationalism – both which are independently objectionable. This is to question the very motives for discussing the coherence theory, and was at one time in the recent past a fashionable reason for ignoring it. Such a strategy is of course altogether too cavalier in what it assumes about the virtues of the metaphysical and epistemological doctrines at issue, which have more to recommend them than at first appears; and in any case it overlooks the fact that some of the logical positivists also were persuaded to adopt a coherence theory, for reasons much more familiar and contemporary. Before discussing particular objections to coherence theories, then, it is worth looking at why some of the positivists chose to espouse one.

POSITIVIST COHERENTISM

To do so one needs to recall a debate which split the positivists after they came under the influence of Wittgenstein's *Tractatus*. The positivists adopted the correspondence theory implicit in the *Tractatus*, but for the reason that they were largely motivated by epistemological considerations, about which the *Tractatus* had practically nothing to say because its aims lay elsewhere, they needed to work out the theory in more concrete detail.

They did this by saying that statements reporting immediate

perceptual experience (basic or 'protocol' statements) are incorrigible and certain because they directly correspond to the facts; and that the truth of other (nonprotocol) statements can be determined by means of their logical relations to the basic statements. Carnap, in an influential paper, argued that scientific knowledge rests upon protocol sentences, which consist in incorrigible reports of observations and therefore require no further verification.[28] Schlick likewise argued that there are protocol sentences and that they constitute 'the unshakable point of contact between knowledge and reality', and he further held that 'we come to know these absolutely fixed points of contact, the confirmations, in their individuality; they are the only synthetic statements that are not hypotheses.'[29]

This way of viewing matters marked a departure from what would broadly be thought of as a classical correspondence theory, for it has it that only a certain class of propositions earns truth by corresponding to facts, while the remaining bulk of propositions does so in virtue of relations with other propositions – a coherence-flavoured doctrine. It was, accordingly, a fairly short step for some of the positivists, notably Neurath, from this view to a full-blown coherence theory. Neurath decided that protocol statements could not be incorrigible, chiefly for the reason that, at best, it can only be a conventional matter which propositions are regarded as somehow 'basic'; and accordingly a direct verifying check on correspondence between protocol statements and 'the facts' is impossible.[30] He therefore settled for a test of truth as consisting in the relations between propositions themselves, and in so doing departed from the orthodox fold of the positivists under Schlick, with whom he engaged in considerable controversy over the matter.

Neurath's view was that no statement is immune to revision because all statements are 'subject to verification, that is to say . . . may be discarded.'[31] 'There is no way,' he wrote, 'of taking conclusively established pure protocol sentences as the starting point of the sciences. No *tabula rasa* exists. We are like sailors who must rebuild their ship on the open sea',[32] meaning by this that we do not begin our investigations of nature with a clean slate, but have an apparatus of theories and assumptions which constitute the very conditions of our enquiries, so that we have to refine or change them bit by bit as we proceed. Accordingly, because the object is to construct a consistent system of observational and theoretical – that is, protocol and nonprotocol – sentences, the only test available for new sentences offered as candidates for membership of the system is to 'compare it with the system . . . and determine whether or not it conflicts with that system. If the sentence does conflict with the system, we may discard it as useless (or false) . . . One may, on the other hand, accept the sentence and so change the system that it remains consistent . . . the sentence would then be called "true" "[33] This is undisguisedly a coherence theory.

For Neurath as for the rationalist metaphysicians earlier, the primary motive for adopting a coherence theory is the apparent impossibility of getting outside thought or language to reality, in some way which is not conditioned by our thought or language itself. The view is that we cannot step aside to some point of judicial privilege which allows us to compare our judgements with the reality they are judgements about; and since there is no word-world relation which can serve as the foundation for truth, truth must consist in a relation of coherence between propositions themselves, viewed as constituting a system or belief set, as a whole satisfying the criteria – identified above – of consistency, connectedness and completeness.

CRITERIA FOR COHERENCE

This last point about the criteria of a coherent system is, as already noted, of paramount importance, because only by making out these criteria clearly is it possible to dispel the vagueness of the notion of 'coherence' itself. A recent effort to make sense of these crucial ideas owes itself to Rescher.[34]

In Rescher's view, what is needed is a way of choosing the set of beliefs which one is warranted in holding true, from out of the array of data available to us. Since there are more than one consistent set (or rather, subset) of beliefs in the data available, and since no external criteria can be invoked to help choose between them, Rescher suggested that a 'plausibility filter' be used to reduce the number of maximally consistent subsets which are eligible. By a 'plausibility filter' Rescher meant no more than a procedure for discriminating which data are *prima facie* plausible, and which are not. And since even this proceeding may be insufficient to pick out a unique subset of maximally consistent beliefs, Rescher suggested that we constitute our belief system out of the disjunction of all those subsets let through by the plausibility filter.

The need to use some such 'filter' notion arises from a ready criticism which opponents of the coherence theory can level. This is that since it is logically possible for there to be any number of internally coherent systems of beliefs, and since there are no external criteria for choosing among them, it cannot be known which is the 'right' one. (Russell had put this criticism by saying that the coherence theory cannot distinguish the truth from a consistent fairy-tale.[35]) Positivist coherentists had replied that 'the belief-system accepted by the scientists of our culture circle' is the right one; but this answer is wholly unsatisfactory, for in appealing to an external criterion (to a fact *about* the belief system which can only be determined true from without), it breaches contract with the coherence theory itself.

DIFFICULTIES AND OBJECTIONS

Despite Rescher's attempts to defend a coherence view, difficulties remain. It is by no means fortuitous that those who have adopted this theory have in general been those whose philosophical outlook is shaped by admiration for mathematics. Seventeenth-century rationalists, and Plato long before them, were sceptical of the power of sense-experience to deliver truths about the world, and correspondingly impressed by the power of formal deduction, as in mathematics and geometry, to generate an entire corpus of solid knowledge from a limited base of self-evident assumptions. Spinoza's major work, the *Ethics,* has as its full Latin title *Ethica Ordine Geometrico Demonstrata,* which makes explicit the rationale of his own and this general kind of methodological approach.

It may indeed be the case that in formal systems like mathematics and logic, coherence *is* the criterion of truth. To say of some proposition that it is 'true within a system' is just to say that it is a theorem of that system, that is, that it is provable in the sense that it can be deduced from that system's axioms by means of the specified transformation rules. But this way of speaking is apt to be misleading, especially if generalised to serve as an unpacking of the notion of truth *tout court.* For, as noted earlier, in the wider case 'coherence' would have to be explained either in a negative way as the mere absence of inconsistency between propositions in a set, or in a positive way as the presence of supporting relations between propositions in a set. If 'coherence' is understood negatively, it is unhelpful to the point of vacuity; whereas if it is understood positively, as a criterion it still lacks precision enough to serve as a sufficient condition for truth, owing at very least to the fact that however consistent a set of propositions may be, it is logically possible that it yet fails to describe the world correctly – especially if, as we can, we deny that comprehensiveness can ever be claimed for any set of propositions; for what grounds could we have for saying that any current stock of available propositions says all there is to say about the world, or even some portion of it? It could indeed be argued that comprehensiveness is in principle an impossible characteristic to claim for any set; and if this is so, consistency alone can furnish no guarantees.

Moreover, it is worth noting that whereas a negative construal of coherence indeed states a necessary (but not a sufficient) condition for truth, the positive construal does not do so much. Apart from serious difficulties about the notion of 'support' between propositions which the positive account demands – entailment is far too strong; what are the other candidates? – it remains that it is by no means unnatural to talk of the truth of a proposition whose logical, or even merely aesthetic, relations to some (still less all) members of a relevant set are opaque to us; how this can be so is left worse than unexplained by the coherence theory.

Some critics put this objection to coherentism in this way: they see the fault of the theory as lying in the fact that whereas coherence *does* furnish a test for truth in respect of *a priori* propositions, only the (incorrect) view that all propositions about the world are *a priori* could motivate one to see coherence as the test for truth in general. Since some rationalist metaphysicians thought that all propositions are, like mathematical ones, *a priori,* they naturally took this view of truth. An assumption of this version of the criticism is that there are *a posteriori* propositions which are not only individually about bits of the world, or episodes of experience, but are individually testable against those bits or experiences – that, in other words, correspondence determines truth here. Such as assumption falls foul, however, of Neurath's criticism as to whether there can be a class of protocol sentences; so one finds oneself pushed back into the arena of epistemology.

Among the other criticisms of the coherence theory, however, is the thought that coherence cannot serve as a characterisation of truth because any understanding of its constituent notions of consistency and the interdependence of judgements or propositions rests on logic, and therefore, circularly, on an antecedent grasp of truth.[36] One reply available to coherentists is to say that logic is regulative, that it consists not in theses construed as truths but in rules or principles of inference; and that these in turn are to be judged on the basis of considerations not involving appeal to truth but, say, to pragmatics.[37]

More plausibly, perhaps, a coherentist might say that coherence provides a test of truth for matters of fact and value outside logic, for which truth is otherwise determined, and which forms part of the foundation of the coherence theory itself. Certainly this has the virtue of providing a more substantial basis for the coherence theory, but it does so at the cost of rendering the theory less than global, and no longer fundamental, and leaves open the problem of what is to be said about truth in the new fundamental sense now required.

In any case, one of the things these considerations appear to do is to contradict the idea expressed two paragraphs ago, that coherence naturally attaches to sets of *a priori* propositions; for it now appears that coherence is to be regarded primarily as a test of empirical truth, that is of *a posteriori* propositions. If this is so, then the objection sketched earlier, to the effect that there might be a plurality of equally coherent but distinct and perhaps mutually contradictory sets of beliefs or propositions, becomes more especially embarrassing to the coherentist.

Finally, a criticism worth mentioning again concerns the vagueness of the notion of coherence, but this time in another direction. The question can be asked, 'coherence *with what?*'[38] It would be absurd to hold that a proposition is true only if it coheres with *all* other propositions whatever, because the class of all meaningful propositions necessarily contains inconsistency, owing to the fact that at least most of these have equally meaningful denials. Thus the class of all meaningful propositions contains both 'it is rational to believe that there is a deity' and 'it is irrational to believe that there is a deity'. On the other hand, to say that a proposition must cohere with *some* other propositions to be true is to say far too little. Any proposition whatever coheres with some others; on this view, astrology is a body of truths, and so is *Lord of the Rings*. And of course it would not at all do to say that a proposition is true if it coheres with other truths, for this is to beg the very question at issue.

The coherentist's only manoeuvre in reply to the criticism implicit here is to specify an actual 'target domain' of propositions, as Rescher calls it, in the context of which coherence as a test of truth applies.[39] The chief candidate for such a domain is the set of propositions describing or reporting our experience; this suggestion emerges with equal clarity from both idealist and positivist uses of the notion. Yet again, however, the difficulty arises that there can be more than one coherent set of propositions describing our experience, a point on which Quine in particular has often insisted; and it is still not clear from the perspective of the coherence theory itself how one is to select the 'right' one − which, if there is to be *truth* in anything more than a relative sense, would need to be done.

One reason for the vagueness of the notion of coherence may be that it is not a logical notion at all, but, in a sense, a strategic one. Thus perhaps the vagueness of 'coherent' does not stem from its indeterminate place somewhere between entailment, which is far too strong, and absence of inconsistency, which is far too weak, but from the fact that what a given philosopher regards as a coherent system is just what he regards as a *rational* system (on analogy with the slogan of Hegelianism, 'the real is the rational'). If this is so, then since what counts as a rational system of beliefs depends entirely on the assumptions and objectives which any such system is concerned to connect, 'coherent' will be, so to speak, the servant rather than the determinant of the propositions domiciled in the system as true. This is by no means an implausible thought; for by any minimally accepted standards in the ethics of rationality, the conjoining of a proposition with some set of propositions with which it is inconsistent is straightforwardly impermissable. To see the coherence theory, in particular in the context of rationalist metaphysics, as a major extension of this strategy, has considerable explanatory possibilities. It does not, however, resolve the doubts which the coherence theory is fertile in suggesting even to a sympathetic investigator.

NOTES

1. cf. Russell, B., 'James' Conception of Truth', *Philosophical Essays,* London, 1910, and Mackie, J. L., *Truth Probability and Paradox*, Oxford, 1973.
2. Bradley, F. H., *Essays on Truth and Reality*, Oxford, 1914, p.325.
3. cf. chapter 7 below.
4. Blanshard, B., *The Nature of Thought,* London, 1939, p.268.
5. cf. the diagram and accompanying text in Haack, *Philosophy of Logics,* p.87.
6. James, W., *Pragmatism*, New York. 1970, esp. Lect. VI, p.197, *et seq.*
7. Peirce, C. S., 'How To Make Our Ideas Clear', *Collected Papers* Hartshorne *et. al.*, (eds.) Harvard, 1930-58.
8. cf. Quine, 'Two Dogmas of Empiricism', in Feigl, *et al., op. cit.*
9. cf, Feyerabend, P., *Against method*, London, 1975.
10. James, *Pragamatism*, p.222.
11. cf. Haack, S., 'The Pragmatist Theory of Truth', *The British Journal for the Philosophy of Science,* 27, 1976, pp.234-5.
12. Dewey: cf. 'A Short Catechism Concerning Truth', in *The Influence of Darwin on Philosophy.* New York 1901; and cf. also *Experience and Nature*, Dover 1958.
13. cf. James, *op. cit.,* which collects his papers on truth.
14. ibid., pp.v-vii.
15. Moore. G. E., 'Professor James' Pragmatism,' *Proceedings of the Aristotelian Society*, 1908, p.110.
16. Haack, *op. cit.*, p.234.
17. cf. James, 'The Will To Believe,' in *Selected Papers In Philosophy,* London 1917, *passim.*

18. James, 'Pragmatism's Conception of Truth', *Pragmatism*, pp. 197, *et seq*.
19. cf., Haack, *op. cit.*, pp.242-4.
20. James 'Humanism and Truth', *The Meaning of Truth*; and *Pragmatism*, Lect. VII, p.239, *et seq*.
21. cf. Moore, G. E., *'Truth'*, in Baldwin's *Dictionary*.
22. Rescher, N., *The Coherence Theory of Truth*, Oxford, 1973.
23 Bradley, *op. cit.*, p.223.
24. Blanshard, *op. cit.*, p.264. cf. also Joachim, H. H., *Logical Studies*, Oxford, 1948, as another coherentist of this strong type.
25. Blanshard, ibid., pp.265-6.
26. Rescher *op. cit.*, p.35.
27. Ewing, A. C., *Idealism: A Critical Survey*, London, 1934, pp.229-30.
28. Carnap, R. *The Unity of Science*, London, 1934, cf. p.47ff.
29. Schlick, M., 'The Foundations of Knowledge', in Ayer, A. J., *Logical Positivism*, Glencoe, 1954, pp.209-27.
30. Neurath, O., 'Protocol Sentences', (trans. Schlick), in Ayer, *ibid.*, pp.201-4.
31. ibid.
32. ibid.
33. ibid. Carnap was eventually won over to Neurath's view, and Quine is an obvious adherent of this line. There are echoes of pragmatism here too. For a discussion of the positivists' debate on these issues see Hempel, G. C., 'On the Logical Positivists', *Theory of Truth Analysis* 2, 1935, pp.49-59,; and Scheffler, I., *Science and Subjectivity*, New York, 1967 esp. chapter 5, *passim*.
34. Rescher, *op. cit.*, esp. Chapter IV S3, p.78ff.
35. Russell, *The Problems of Philosophy*, p.190.
36. cf. Ewing, *op. cit.*, pp.237, 241.
37. cf. Rescher, *op. cit.*, p.45.
38. cf. ibid., p.49.
39. ibid., p.50.

6 Truth: The Correspondence, Redundancy and Semantic Theories

THE CORRESPONDENCE THEORY OF TRUTH

It has already been noted how venerable, and therefore how enduring, the correspondence theory is: after Plato's discussion of it in the *Sophist* one finds Aristotle defining truth as the saying 'of what is that it is, or of what is not that it is not'.[1] How close his view of truth stands to modern versions of the correspondence theory can be seen from a passage in the *Categories*: 'The fact of the being of a man carries with it the truth of the proposition that he is . . . for if a man is, the proposition wherein we allege that he is, is true . . . the fact of the man's being does seem somehow to be the cause of the truth of the proposition, for the truth or falsity of the proposition depend on the fact of the man's being or not being'.[2] This comes down to saying what is basic to the correspondence theory overall, namely that truth consists in a relation of correspondence between propositions and the way things are in the world. A proposition which says that the facts are thus-and-so when the facts are indeed thus-and-so, is true; and a proposition successfully says the facts are thus-and-so when it corresponds to those facts.

The theory is intuitively compelling in a way that the other theories are not. It seems quite obviously right that a proposition is true if, simply, it states what is the case, 'tells it like it is' in the once popular phrase. But that initial plausibility melts away directly one considers how problematic are all three crucial notions in terms of which the theory is articulated. The crucial notions are 'proposition', 'correspondence', and 'facts' (or their cognates). Earlier I canvassed the difficulties which hedge an understanding of the proposition. 'Correspondence' and 'facts' are no less controversial. What is this relation of 'correspondence' which marries propositions to facts? What are 'facts'?

CORRESPONDENCE AND ATOMISM

One takes fuel on board for a discussion of these questions by looking at some attempts — on the part of Locke, Wittgenstein and Russell to begin with — to state and employ a correspondence theory. Evidently the empirical foundation of the theory is significant particularly for philosophers like Locke and Russell; for it is natural to see truth as consisting in a relation of correspondence between what we say and what it is we are talking about, if the source of our knowledge of the world is sense-experience. Sense-experience is privileged in that it is somehow immediate; we are in touch with the world, and can check our reports on it by seeing whether they fit what we sense. The level of generality at which this characterisation moves is mirrored by Locke's dictum that 'truth seems to me, in the proper import of the word, to signify but the joining or separating of the signs, as the things signified by them do agree or disagree with one another'.[3] Locke is saying that words and ideas signify 'things', and are combined together in propositions which if true correspond to the way the relevant things are combined together in the world. On all counts there are problems with the way Locke states his view. Do words 'mean' by being 'signs', that is, by denoting? What is it for them to be 'joined' together into propositions such that, if true, these propositions are 'as' the 'agreeing' of the 'things' their constituent words 'signify'? This way of putting things is muddling owing to the large number of questionable assumptions and unclarities which bristle about it. A more systematic account of these issues is given by Wittgenstein and Russell in their Logical Atomist period.

In the *Tractatus* Wittgenstein held that propositions are complexes truth-functionally compounded out of elementary propositions, which in turn are constituted by arrangements of names. This structure mirrors the way the world is arranged; there are facts built out of states-of-affairs, which in turn are constituted out of objects in certain arrangements. Names directly refer to objects; and because elementary propositions are constituted of names arranged in the way that objects are arranged in states-of-affairs, elementary propositions 'picture' those states-of-affairs. Thus the propositions compounded out of elementary propositions correspond to the facts built out of the states-of-affairs. Graphically, the situation is this, in order of logical decomposition:

$$
\begin{array}{ccc}
\text{proposition} & \rightarrow & \text{facts} \\
\downarrow & & \downarrow \\
\text{elementary proposition} & \rightarrow & \text{states-of-affairs} \\
\downarrow & & \downarrow \\
\text{names} & \rightarrow & \text{objects}
\end{array}
$$

Wittgenstein's aims in the *Tractatus* were to elucidate the structure of language (as just sketched) and its function (which he held to be to describe the world); epistemological concerns did not come into it, so he was untroubled by being unable to give examples of names and objects, or even elementary propositions and states-of-affairs. Russell developed his atomist views independently of Wittgenstein's views after a short period of contact between them before the First World War, and he gave m re prominence to epistemological considerations, and so is more in rmative about this version of the correspondence theory.

For Russell, the logical aton or simples (his version of the 'objects' of the *Tractatus*) are sense-data — for example, colour-patches in the visual field. These are the objects of direct acquaintance. The names out of which propositions are built refer to the simple objects of acquaint ice: propositions accrue their meaningfulness from the relation of their constituents to the atomic simples with which we are directly acquainted in perception. Descriptive knowledge is inferred from, or can be justifyingly referred back to, episodes of acquaintance, where a simple proposition — 'this green' for example, or 'this green now' — directly links to the state-of-affairs presented in the episode.

What is central to both Russell's and Wittgenstein's views is that correspondence is a relation of *structural isomorphism* between propositions and facts. They therefore provide a more detailed account of the structure of both terms of the relation, and of the relation itself, than does Locke; but one would now see how a sympathetic investigation of Locke's intentions would proceed, for evidently he was trying to state much the same kind of view.

Nevertheless, crucial difficulties remain. The notion of correspondence is made no clearer by interpreting it as a 'structural isomorphism', since neither the idea of 'structure' in propositions and facts, nor the idea of a putative 'isomorphism' between them, is very clear; not least because isomorphism is itself a concept to be understood in terms of structure and correspondence; one would naturally define the concept of isomorphism as 'an information-preserving similarity or correspondence of structure holding for and relating two or more items', and this raises the spectre of circularity.

Consider the well-worn example of the proposition 'the cat is on the mat'. This proposition has at least three elements — the cat, the mat, and the relation 'on'; whereas the fact out there in the world has only two — the cat and the mat. Actually it is absurdly difficult to say how many constituents a proposition has, since it is possible that in some language other than English there is a proposition expressible in a single word which says the same as 'the cat is on the mat'. How would the 'constituents' of such a proposition correspond to the constituents of that state-of-affairs in which the cat is on the mat? What price 'structural isomorphism' in such a case? This difficulty is bad enough; worse is the difficulty of specifying a structural isomorphism between propositions like 'the weather is bad' and 'the political situation is complicated' and their relevant states-of-affairs.

AUSTIN AND CONVENTIONS

Correspondence as isomorphism between the structures of propositions and facts in the world is heavily conditioned by the atomistic metaphysics, and the thrust towards an ideally per-spicuous language, which characterises Wittgenstein's Tractarian views and the phase in Russell's thought influenced by Wittgen-stein. An attempt to spell out a correspondence theory free of such a metaphysics and such an aim for language was made by Austin.[4] Austin sought to explain correspondence in terms of purely con-ventional relations between words and the world, which he held to be correlated in two ways: a) by means of 'descriptive' conventions correlating words (=sentences) with *types* of situations to be found in the world, and b) 'demonstrative conventions' correlating words (= statements; that is, actually issued sentences) with actual situations, situations in fact found in the world on particular occasions.

How this works is as follows. Suppose someone s says at a time t 'I am eating'. Then the descriptive conventions correlate the words with situations in which people eat, and the demonstrative con-ventions correlate the words with the actual activity of s at t. What s says at t will be *true* if the actual situation, correlated with the words s utters by the demonstrative conventions, is of the type correlated with those words by the descriptive conventions. Austin's use of 'conventions' was seriously intended; any arbitrary words could be correlated with any situation whatever so long as the correlations are sufficiently consistent for communication to take place success-fully; and this shows that the correlations in no way covertly substitute for, or in any way resemble, something like a relation of isomorphism.

One immediate problem with Austin's view is that, as it stands, it appears to work only for indexical statements, that is statements tied to a particular utterer and time of utterance. For they are statements which, in virtue of not being explicitly referential like general or indefinite statements, cannot be employed in different situations, so that the demonstrative conventions would have no part to play in the determination of their truth; and Austin's account essentially depends on both species of correlation. Of course, a defender of Austin might argue that the truth of these statements, although not to be determined in the two-conventions way described, nonetheless might depend on the truth of other, more basic, statements whose truth *is* so determined. One would have to see this suggestion fully spelled out to judge whether it is plausible.

There is in any case a more serious objection, or at any rate one that was thought to be more serious, to the effect that Austin's account implies that in pronouncing a statement true one is (as Ayer put it) 'engaging in a semantic disquisition about the conditions of its being meaningful'.[5] Certainly for a statement to be true in the way Austin describes, it is necessary that it should possess the meaning it does; but this does not come to the same thing as our 'profiting by the occasion to give semantic rules' − Strawson's words[6] − when we say a certain statement is true; nor does it come down to saying that the utterer of the statement has used his words correctly in making that statement. So whereas we do 'use the word "true" when the semantic conditions described by Austin are fullfilled . . . we do not, using the word, *state* that they are fulfilled'.[7] And if what Ayer called the 'semantic accretions' of Austin's theory are removed, what is left − namely the bare point that a statement is true if what it states is the case − hardly constitutes a defence, still less a challenging new formulation, of the correspondence theory.

This criticism, proffered chiefly by Strawson, has it that Austin was guilty of a fundamental confusion between 1) the semantic conditions which must be satisfied for the truth of a statement S_1 which states of some other statement S_2 that S_2 is true, and 2) what is asserted when S_2 is stated to be true. For, if Austin is right in holding that to say a statement is true is to say that the relevant demonstrative and descriptive conditions are satisfied, then it follows that in saying of some statement that it is true we are either talking about the meanings of the words used by the speaker, or we are saying that the speaker used the words properly. Yet, in Strawson's view, 'it is patently *false* that we are doing either of these things',[8] for we are not talking about the words used at all, but confirming or agreeing with what was said.[9] 'The damage is done,' Strawson wrote, 'by asking the question: *When* do we use the word "true"? instead of the question: *How* do we use the word "true"?'[10]

CORRELATION AND CONGRUITY

Thus armed, we can leave particular attempts at formulating a correspondence theory, and revert to what is crucial about the generally received core of any such theory — the notion of 'correspondence' itself. In his introduction to *Truth* Pitcher usefully sets out and discusses two possible interpretations of the notion of correspondence, and I shall borrow some of his approach here.

The competing interpretations are of correspondence as *correlation*, which is a 'weak' relation, and *congruity*, which is a 'richer' one. Correlation may be exemplified by considering the pairing-off of items on a one-to-one basis. Suppose we put the series of integers into one-to-one correspondence with the series of even integers thus:

Integers:	1	2	3	4	5	6	. . .	n
	↓	↓	↓	↓	↓	↓		↓
Even integers:	2	4	6	8	10	12	. . .	2n.

Then 1 in the series of integers corresponds to 2 in the series of even integers, 4 in the series of integers corresponds to 8 in the series of even integers, and so on. It is evident that we have to specify a rule or principle for the correspondences, since in the absence of a context and specified rules, saying '5 corresponds to 10' would be, because it comes out of the blue, puzzling and pointless.

Congruity, on the other hand, may best be understood in terms of fit' or 'match', as when we say that the rejoined edges of a torn piece of paper 'fit together' or 'match' exactly. That 'correlation' and 'congruity' pick out quite different sense of 'correspondence' is evidenced by the fact that whereas we can say of the bits of torn paper that they fit together (correspond) *exactly* or *perfectly* on being rejoined, we cannot say of 3 in the series of integers that it exactly or perfectly corresponds to 6, nor indeed that it *im*perfectly corresponds to 6; such qualifications are wholly misplaced.

White puts the contrast as one obtaining between 'correspondence *with*' and 'correspondence *to*'; the former is correspondence as congruity, and the latter correspondence as correlation.[11] Thus 'a key may correspond *with* its key-hole and one half of a stamp *with* the other half, while an entry in a ledger may correspond *to* a sale, and one rank in the army *to* another in the navy'.[12]

The question then arises as to which of these two interpretations of correspondence has most generally served as the requisite relation in the correspondence tradition. The answer is that it is 'correspondence *with*', that is, *congruity*, which has so served. In

the views of Wittgenstein and Russell, for example, the correspondence between the constituents of facts and propositions is a correspondence of 'fit', demonstrated by Wittgenstein's talk of the
'pitcturing' relation which holds between elementary propositions
and states-of-affairs in virtue of the sameness of arrangement in the
names and objects which respectively constitute them. But the
difficulties on this construal of the correspondence relation are
formidable.

To begin with, as already noted, there is the difficulty of determining how many constituents a proposition has; and even if there
were a rule for doing so, it is by no means clear that every proposition
has the same number of constituents as the fact to which it
corresponds. In the case of 'the cat is on the mat' there appear to be
at least three propositional constituents as against the fact's two; in
the case of 'the car is blue' there appear to be two propositional
constituents as against the fact's one. But an added difficulty arises
from the discomfiture we ought to feel in talking about the 'constituents of facts' too. For someone might argue that in the case of
the cat on the mat, there are indeed three constituents; the cat, the
mat, and over and above them the actual spatial arrangement in
which they stand to one another. To say this is to reify relations –
that is, to make them actual constituents of the world in the way cats
and mats are; and this constitues a metaphysical thesis which
demands some arguing.

The situation looks still less promising when one notes that the
congruity interpretation depends upon a denotative theory of
meaning. That the congruity interpretation appears to demand such
a theory is plain, for if the constituents 'cat' and 'mat' in the
proposition are to 'fit' the constituents cat and mat in the fact, then
'cat' denotes the cat and 'mat' denotes the mat. So far so good; but
what of the putative third element, the relation in which the cat and
the mat stand to one another? Is 'on' the *name* of this relation?

Another aspect of the difficulty here is illustrated by an example
like 'the car is blue'. On the congruity interpretation, for there to be
constituents of the fact to 'fit' both 'the car' and 'blue' we should
have to commit ourselves to the view that properties such as
blueness exist independently of blue things – that is, that properties
exist in the Platonist sense. We may then also be led to commit
ourselves to the view that particulars like the object in question –
the car – are something over and above the cluster of properties by
means of which we know them to be there; and if so we are
committed to a doctrine of *substance*, which is, traditionally, that
invisible and intangible *quid* which underlies the properties
inhering in it and which somehow keeps them glued together in a

determinate spatio-temporal slot. In short, talk of 'facts' takes the
lid off a series of barely tractable metaphysical problems, which are
altogether too important to be glossed over; and in the face of such
difficulties any attempt to 'constitualise' facts so that propositions –
leaving aside the problem of constitualising *them* – can fit them, is
bound to be excessively controversial.

Moreover, these objections are directed at the least complex case,
that of the relation in which fairly straightforward propositions like
'the cat is on the mat' and 'the car is blue' are supposed to stand with
respect to the facts that the cat is on the mat and the car is blue.
Difficulties multiply more rapidly and decisively still if one asks how
there can be a correspondence as congruity relation between true
negative, conditional, or disjunctive statements, and whatever it is
that makes them true. In other words, to what does 'if the cat is on
the mat, then he is warm' correspond? Or to what does 'the cat is not
on the mat' correspond?[13]

The problems which therefore bedevil a congruity interpretation
of correspondence concern, first, our alleged ability to 'constitualise' propositions; secondly, the problem of the nature of 'facts';
and thirdly, the suspect denotative theory of meaning which underlies the enterprise.

The failure of the congruity interpretation leads one to resort to
the weaker correlation interpretation This strategy has been
favourably regarded by a number of writers.[14] In White's view it
preserves the 'basic and indisputable principle that p is true if and
only if p'; for when, in his view, there is talk of a particular statement *saying that* this is how things are, what is meant is no more or
less than that what is said corresponds to how things are, with no
further explanation necessary.[15] It appears from White's characterisation that matters are after all quite simple; but in fact he
leaves wholly unexplained what it is that serves to fix, mediate, and
maintain the relation between 'what is said' on the one hand, and
'things' on the other hand; and without explanation, the relation of
correspondence construed as correlation is no more convincing
than its alternative.

One persuasive suggestion arises from what has already been
noted in connection with correlating the series of integers and even
integers. This is that words and sentences can be paired off with
situations in the world according to a rule, which is to use the insight
that expressions are correlated with (bits of) the world by conventional means. Austin's view is thus a view of correspondence as
correlation by a rule. A virtue of this way of viewing the matter is
that it captures something which seems to be true of word-world

relations; namely that they are arbitrary in at least this sense, that any sign or mark can be agreed upon to stand for something in the world, which fact is exemplified by coinings of new words. Naturally this feature of the conventionality of language has to do only with words which are tied to bits of the world; for although it is surely also a conventional matter that, for example, syncategorematic words ('on', 'if', 'but', 'and', and so on, which always and only have a role in sentences of the language, and are otherwise incomplete in themselves) are employed in the particular way they are, the conventions governing them are a different story again.

There is however a difficult issue here; for despite the conventionality of nouns like 'cat' and 'mat', language itself, in terms of its function and structure overall, is not wholly conventional. To put the matter very crudely, it is not wholly fortuitous that the chief grammatical categories like nouns, adjectives, and verbs, somehow 'pick out' what could be described as the chief categories in our pre-theoretical ontology; namely, things, their qualities, and events involving them. There is a view to this effect in Lotze.[16] Thus Robert Louis Stevenson's dictum, that language came after the world and was constructed on different principles is, though probably true in respect of its first conjunct, not wholly true in respect of its second.

MEANING AND TRUTH

But the question which is at issue here is whether interpreting correspondence in terms of correlation provides a satisfactory version of the correspondence theory. The problem is that making sense of correspondence in these terms turns upon – crucially and centrally turns upon – the nature of the correlative rules. What this in turn means is that truth is to be explained by explaining language – and the enterprise therefore is identical with the large matter of giving an account of how language functions as the device people employ to communicate and comment upon features of the world and their experience of it. Giving such an account is exceedingly complex, and the whole of the philosophy of language is devoted to it. The expectation that truth will be explained, or, more accurately, that an explanation of truth will naturally materialise during the construction of a theory of how language works, seems very plausible in prospect; but a complicating factor is that a strong tendency among philosophers of language has been to take it – with good reason – that the proper logical direction in this area is, in fact, exactly the other way round – that it is, in short, truth which will explain meaning and not *vice versa*. This is the line taken by Davidson and contemporary realists, who are by no means the first to opt for such a strategy. How and why this is so will be discussed at some length in chapter 8 below.

If the concept of truth is the key to understanding meaning, it cannot be the case that a portmanteau appeal to semantic rules will explain truth. This suggests that Austin's theory, as a prime example of an attempt to make out truth in terms of semantics, is altogether too facile. This is not to be dismissive of his attempt; rather, it is to point out that what truth is said to consist in on his account is so complex that, as a little reflection shows, it in fact explains nothing at all. For there are, submerged in Austin's notion of the two correlating conventions, epistemological and semantic issues which have long occasioned, and still occasion, the liveliest philosophical dispute.

On the other hand, it is possible to see Austin's proposal, and by extension the correlation construal as a whole, as pointing in a certain direction, or as showing that there is a certain kind of special relation between the concept of truth and the semantics of natural language. This point as it stands is neutral between the partisans of the opposed views that truth explains, or will be explained by, language; one can imagine that a line slightly different from Austin's might consist in an argument for truth as a supervenient feature of meaning-rules without ignoring the latter's complexity. Possibly a verificationist theory, in some variant, would be like this (see chapters 7,8 and 9 below). At any rate the insight is a valuable one, despite being so general. And because it is hard to see how the question of truth can be divorced from the question of how language functions, it seems that the appropriate place to begin one's enquiry is the conceptual region where the connections between truth and meaning lie.

An important first step in this programme is provided by Tarski's semantic theory of truth, to which I shortly turn. First, however, it is necessary to canvass, fairly briefly, a related but differently orientated view about the relation of truth and meaning; a view which has it that the concept of truth has no place because meaning, so to speak, does all the required work by itself.

THE REDUNDANCY THEORY OF TRUTH

In his criticism of Austin, Strawson put forward an alternative view of truth, which was that to say a statement is true is effectively no different from agreeing with it, or saying 'yes', or merely nodding –

a view sometimes therefore called the 'performative' theory of truth. This emerged above in the quotation in which Strawson identified the 'right' question to ask about truth to be '*how* is "true" used?' This view has affinities with the 'redundancy' theory put forward by Ramsay in 1927.[17]

In the course of a discussion of judgement, Ramsay made some remarks about truth 'in order to show that there is really no separate problem of truth but merely a linguistic muddle'.[18] In his view, truth and falsity are primarily ascribed to propositions, and propositions can either be explicitly given or described. In the case of an explictly given proposition such as 'Caesar was murdered', it is evident, in Ramsay's view, that 'it is true that Caesar was murdered' means precisely the same as 'Caesar was murdered', and 'it is false that Caesar was murdered' means precisely the same as 'Caesar was not murdered'. Accordingly, the ascriptions of truth and falsity in these cases are redundant; at best they add emphasis, or mark the place the proposition has in the argument, or are placed there for stylistic reasons.[19] One could equally well say 'it is a fact that Caesar was murdered' or 'that Caesar was murdered is contrary to fact'. Yet appeal to 'facts' is as redundant as appeal to truth and falsity.

Similarly, 'is true' and 'is false' are redundant in the case of described propositions, although matters are somewhat more complex here. If I say 'he is always right', I mean that 'the propositions he asserts are always true', and on the face of it there seems no way to dispense with the word 'true' in expressing the point. However Ramsay suggests an analysis to eliminate 'true'; the first step is to recast 'the propositions he asserts are always true' as 'for all p, if he asserts p, p is true', and then we see that the propositional function 'p is true' is simply the same as p, just as in the Caesar case above; 'for all p, if he asserts p, then p'.[20]

Ramsay suggested that we add 'is true' in English to give the sentence a verb, forgetting that 'p' already contains one. The point is clearer if one considers, say, the relational form of the proposition, aRb; then 'he is always right' can be put as 'for all a,R,b, if he asserts aRb, then aRb'. Adding 'is true' would be obviously superfluous.

In general, Ramsay took it that our real interest in this connection does not conern the nature of truth and falsity, but the nature of judgement or assertion; for the problem in the foregoing example is how to analyse 'He asserts aRb'.

The redundancy view comes down, then, to saying that 'true' and 'false' are predicates which can be dropped without semantic loss, having only a stylistic or otherwise pragmatic role. There are certain virtues attaching to this view; for one thing, it avoids all the difficulties of a correspondence theory, for no question arises about any of the three correspondence terms – the relata of facts and propositions and the relation of correspondence itself. 'It is a fact that' is redundant like 'it is true that', which does away with facts; and because 'is true' is an eliminable predicate, it does not introduce a genuine property to be attached to whatever is asserted, and so there is no pressing need to invoke propositions as truth-bearers, for if there is no truth to be borne, no bearers of truth are required. And then, if neither facts nor propositions occur in the picture essentially, there is no need to specify a relation between them. Thus every difficulty encountered by the correspondence theory appears not to arise at all.

Nevertheless Ramsay's propoposal has, beneath its surface simplicity, certain profound difficulties. Specifically, his account demands a suitable handling of second-order quantification for the case where propositions are described – that is, where what is asserted is not explicitly given but introduced obliquely. Ramsay's offering was 'for all p, if he asserts p, p' as an analysis of such cases, containing no use of 'true'. But now the question arises: is the universal quantifier 'for all . . . ' to be understood objectually or substitutionally?[21]

If objectually, then for one thing it looks as though propositions may have to be retained after all as the objects quantified over; and anyway if the bound variables, 'p's, are to have the syntactic function of singular terms, as on this interpretation would be the case, then the final 'p' in 'for all p, if he asserts p, then p' will have to be regarded as an ellipsis of 'p is true' in order for it to be sufficiently sentence-like to stand on the right-hand-side of 'then'. But if this is so, 'is true' turns out not to be redundant after all.

If the quantifier is interpreted substitutionally, on the other hand, then 'for all p, if he asserts p, then p' turns into 'all substitution instances of "if he asserts p, then p" *are true*'; and so 'true' remains firmly entrenched in the analysis and will not disappear.

PROFORMS AND REDUNDANCY

Because 'true' refuses to be redundant on either of these standard interpretations of the quantifiers, another tack will have to be taken. An ingenious idea to this end was proposed by Grover.[22] It has often been remarked that there are words and expressions which behave, in respect of other grammatical categories, in the same useful portmanteau fashion as do pronouns ('he', 'it', and so on) for nouns and descriptions. Thus the verb 'do' will work in place of most verbs, and 'such' is a portmanteau adjective. On analogy with pronouns, such words can be called pro-verbs and pro-adjectives respectively. Grover specifies a general category of *proforms* to collect pronouns, proverbs, proadjectives, and the like, and this category has the feature that all of its members must be capable of anaphoric use – that is, can be cross-referentially used in the way pronouns are as in '*Tom* wanted to buy it, but *he* didn't have enough money', or 'if a *bomb* falls, get out of *its* way'.

The proform Grover is chiefly concerned to introduce is a *prosentence,* 'thatt', which can be used anaphorically for any sentence. The proposal is that 'for all p, if he asserts that p, then p' is to be recast as 'for all propositions, if he asserts that thatt, then thatt'. The idea is that the difficulty encountered by Ramsay's view arises only because there are no words or phrases which can stand for sentences as pronouns stand for nouns, thus blocking the required richer reading of the quantifiers. Supplying prosentences removes the difficulty. One striking virtue of the suggestion is that, from the purely formal point of view, this reading is compatible with both the objectual and substitutional interpretations of the quantifiers.

Two difficulties infect Grover's manoeuvre. One is that there have to be very strong reasons for adding to English in this way, or, at least, it must be the case that there is room, made available by the analogical similarity of prosentences to other anaphoric devices already available in the language, which as it were invites just this kind of proform to fill it. The room does not *naturally* exist (English gets along without prosentences), and so the question becomes, does anything oblige us to make that room? Now, the chief motive for inventing the prosentence is to free us from having to make essential use of 'is true' and 'is false'. But is it clear we have to be free in this way? Ramsay's argument itself does not, at least as it stands, show that the notions of truth and falsity are genuinely redundant, still less (as he claimed) misleading. Why then accept the neologism 'thatt' in the first place, if its purpose is merely to force a reading of the quantifiers which will conform to Ramsay's view?

The answer lies in the fact, as Grover and before her Prior noted,[23] that without suitable expressions for second-order quantifiers, we appear to be bound to use noun-like idioms such as 'every*thing*' and 'some*thing*' with all the objectual implications of so doing. Prior himself suggested using '-whether' as the appropriate reading, so that (∃p) would be 'somewhether' and (p) 'anywhether', and thus a string like '(p)(p → p)' would be read 'if anywhether, then thether'.[24] Grover's proposal is a refinement along the same lines. The thought is, in other words, that Ramsay had groped after a way of expressing the point that if one could only make out a proper account of second-order quantification, predications of 'true' and 'false' would be seen as otiose in just the way we glimpse when we see that 'it is true that Caesar was murdered' says no more than 'Caesar was murdered'; and the innovations provided by Prior and Grover supply materials for the right kind of account.

Still, there is the second difficulty, and it is much more of a difficulty. Grover and others[25] applied the prosentence idea to the redundancy theory by proposing that 'that is true' is itself to be regarded as a prosentence. Use of 'it is true' as an atomic prosentence eliminates the need for ascriptions of truth; 'true' itself remains only residually as a non-separable part of the prosentence. But will this do? Haack, for one, thinks not: ' "True", one is told, is eliminable; not from English, to be sure, but from English + "thatt". But how are we to understand "thatt"? Well, there's nothing *exactly* like it in English, but it works like "that's true", except for being atomic rather than compound'.[26] – and so 'true' remains.

In an extended reformulating defence of Ramsay's theory, Loar suggests that no controversial new interpretations of the quantifiers are needed at all, but instead that a proper working out of Ramsay's theory of belief will provide a powerful foundation for the theory of meaning and truth.[27] Loar sketches a theory in which truth is predicated of beliefs, the account of beliefs being such that whatever is true or false has that property in virtue of contingently satisfying whatever conditions make it a *belief* that such-and-such.[28] The detail of Loar's argument reveals that Tarski-style considerations are essential to its presentation, and because I turn to Tarski's views next I shall not discuss the matter here. The point of interest is that it is not, if Loar is right, crucial to making sense of Ramsay's views that the quantification issues be settled.

In general, however, the redundancy view seems less than plausible. Ramsay cited examples in which 'is true' was used corroboratively, and it is certainly the case that there are more ways of agreeing with or corroborating what is said, than by saying 'that's true' or affixing 'is true' to a repetition of what is said. One feels, for example, that the issue of truth arises earlier, in this sense: suppose Tom tells Dick something of central importance to Dick's life, liberty or estate. Dick may urgently wish to know whether what Tom said is as Tom said, and accordingly checks with Harry. If

Harry says 'what Tom said is true', what is of crucial interest to Dick is that Harry means 'things are actually as Tom says they are', for it would be very much less interesting to Tom if all that Harry meant was 'I go along with what Tom said, leaving aside any question of whether or not matters are as Tom said they are'. It is in other words the fact that there is a difference between saying 'that *is* the case' and 'hear, hear' that makes for the interest — and puzzle — in truth; and in any case the very notion of corroboration or agreement must turn in part on an account of 'taking to be true' and hence again of 'true'. It may indeed be that there is 'no separate problem of truth' in the sense that truth may turn out to be satisfactorily accounted for by our investigation of certain epistemological or semantic considerations, but it is not immediately clear that this kind of result would entail a redundancy theory. Moreover, it turns out that some important contemporary philosophical theories, far from issuing in a redundancy theory of truth, in fact — as noted above — turn upon a use of the notion of truth itself.

THE SEMANTIC THEORY OF TRUTH

Tarski's semantic theory of truth is highly influential and widely discussed in contemporary philosophy,[29] not least because of the use made of it in truth-conditional approaches to meaning, particularly of Davidson's variety.[30]

The objective Tarski set himself was to find a satisfactory definition of truth, one which is both *materially adequate* and *formally correct*,[31] and which does justice to the intuition expressed in what he calls the 'classical Aristotelian conception of truth',[32] namely 'to say what is that it is not, or of what is not that it is, is false, while to say of what is that it is, or of what is not that it is not, is true'.[33] In modern terminology this might be expressed as 'the truth of a sentence consists in agreement with (or correspondence to) reality.' But Tarski regarded both formulations as too imprecise, and liable therefore to create misunderstandings.[34] Accordingly his aim was to provide a 'more precise expression' of these intuitions.

A useful way of setting out Tarski's proposals is to view them as arising from a solution to a form of the Liar Paradox.[35] The solution proceeds by means of a distinction between what is said in a sentence of a language and what it is said about this sentence in a 'metalanguage', that is, a language of higher order than the language which it takes as its 'object language' and in which this latter is discussed. Consider this version of the Liar Paradox:

> What is written in the box on this page is false.

Tarski considered that the source of paradox here – if what is written in the box is false, then it is true; and if it is true, then it is false – lies in the *self-reference* of the sentence. Strictly speaking, Tarski's view was that the fault lies in the fact that the sentence belongs to a 'semantically closed' language – that is, a language containing not only its expected stock of expressions, but the names of these expressions, and semantic terms like 'true' referring to its sentences; and moreover, the tacit assumption is that all sentences which determine the use of 'true' can be asserted in that language itself.[36] The problem is, however, more readily characterisable in terms of the self-reference of the boxed sentence, which is just what its being a sentence of a semantically closed language effectively amounts to.

Tarski accordingly drew the object language-metalanguage distinction to prohibit self-reference of this sort, and held that ascriptions of truth or falsity to sentences are metalinguistic: thus ' "New York is a large city" is true' is a metalinguistic assertion about the sentence 'New York is a large city'. Truth is in this way construed as a predicate of a metalanguage applicable to sentences of its object language. Truth is thus a semantic property of object language sentences. A sentence bears the property 'true' if it designates what is in fact the case.

Tarski's reason for this view was that sentences can only be true or false as parts of a given language. There might be a language, say Anglish, in which 'snow is black' means the same as is meant by our English expression 'snow is white', for the reason that in Anglish 'black' designates what 'white' standardly designates in English; hence 'snow is black' would be true in Anglish, because its extension is identical to 'white' in English, and because snow is white. So to say a sentence S is true is to say it is true in some language L. But then to say 'S is true in L' cannot be a sentence of L itself (at risk of paradox), but is a sentence of a metalanguage which takes L as its object language, and in which the sentences of L are not *used* but only *mentioned* and discussed.

Tarski's purpose was to provide a definition of the expression 'true sentence' for a given language L in the metalanguage M of L, such that it will entail all sentences of M of the form 'S is a true sentence of L if and only if p', where 'S' is the name, or a structural description, of a sentence in L, and 'p' is the translation of that sentence into M.[37] Since M may include L as part of itself, such sentences of L are their own translation into M. The requirement that the definition entails sentences of this form constitutes a criterion of material adequacy for any satisfactory definition of truth, and it is called 'Convention(T)'.

What is meant by saying that Convention (T) furnishes a criterion of adequacy for truth definitions is, to reiterate, just this: any acceptable definition of truth should have as consequence all instances of the schema –

(T) S is true in L if and only if p.

An example of an instance of this schema is –

'Snow is white' is true in English iff snow is white.

Here 'snow is white' on the left-hand-side is the 'name' of the sentence on the right-hand-side. Note particularly that Convention (T) is not a definition of truth, but a *material adequacy condition,* such that all its instances must be entailed by any definition of truth which is materially adequate. Thus the (T) schema determines not the *intension* (that is, the meaning) of the term 'true', but its *extension* – its proper range, so to say.

In order to provide a definition of truth, something has to be added to the adequacy condition – namely, proof of formal correctness in respect of both the structure of the language in which truth is defined, and the concepts employed in the definition. Definitions of truth are given in an L's metalanguage M, and this is why L must be included in or translated into M. Because all equivalences of the form (T) must be implied by a definition of truth owing to the adequacy condition, not only must M contain L or translations into itself of all L-sentences, but also the equipment to refer to L-sentences; for (T) instances have L-sentences and expressions referring to them on the right- and left-hand-sides respectively. Moreover, Tarski required that both M and L should be 'formally specifiable'; we must be able to specify the well-formed formulae (the 'wffs') of L in order to define truth-in-L, since these are the items which the predicate 'true-in-L' qualifies. Since no natural language (for example English, French, Swahili) is formally specifiable, Tarski regarded this requirement as practically ruling out the possibility of defining 'true' for natural languages. This makes for one of the controversial issues surrounding Tarski's theory, owing to the fact that certain philosophers believe that the extension to natural language *can* indeed be made. I shall return to this point.

Tarski's actual definition of truth proceeds by way of the definition of the concept of 'satisfaction'. Satisfaction is a relation between objects, on one hand, and expressions called 'sentential functions', like 'x is white' or 'x is greater than y', on the other hand. These expressions are sentential *functions* rather than sentences because they contain free variables marking gaps into which, to form a sentence proper, suitable terms or expressions have to be substituted. The definition of a sentential function involves the notion of a 'recursive procedure'. First the simplest sentential functions are described, and then it is shown what operations can be performed to construct compound functions out of them. An example of one such operation would be the formation of the logical disjunction or conjunction of any two functions; they are combined by means of the words 'or' and 'and' respectively.

A sentence, accordingly, can be defined straightforwardly as a sentential function containing no free variables. To explain satisfaction heuristically, one could say: a given object satisfies a given function if the function can be turned into a true sentence by replacing the free variable occurring in it by the name of the given object. Thus, for example, snow (not the name 'snow' but the actual stuff) satisfies 'x is white' because the sentence 'snow is white' is true. However this is a *merely* heuristic way of explaining satisfaction, for 'true' is being *used* here; and because we wish to define 'true', we must seek for an account not involving 'true'.

This is done, again recursively, by first indicating which objects satisfy the simplest sentential functions, and then by stating under what conditions given objects satisfy compound functions constructed out of those simple functions. For example, we say of certain numbers that they satisfy the disjunction 'x is greater than y or x is equal to y' if they satisfy either the function 'x is greater than y' or the function 'x is equal to y'.

The notion of satisfaction thus defined applies automatically to sentential functions containing no free variables – that is, to sentences. On investigation of the formal details it turns out that only two cases are possible for a sentence: it is either satisfied by all objects, or by no objects. The sentence is true in the first case and false in the second.[38]

This is a very informal presentation of the key concepts by means of which Tarski defined truth. I now give a condensed formal account of the same points, which those who have no taste for technicality may ignore.[39]

A FORMAL SKETCH

Open sentences like Fx do not have truth-values, but are satisfied (or not satisfied) by sequences of objects – which is to say, by pairs of objects, or triples of objects – in general, by any ordered *n*-tuple of objects. Thus 'x is a man' is satisfied by Socrates; 'x is the teacher of y' is satisfied by <Socrates, Plato> (though not the other way round; hence the importance of the *ordering* of *n*-tuples); and 'x taught y who taught z' is satisfied by <Socrates, Plato, Aristotle>. Thus satisfaction is a *relation* between open sentences and ordered *n*-tuples of objects.

Since *n* could be any number whatever, Tarski defined satisfaction as the relation between open sentences and *infinite* sequences under a certain convention, *viz.*, that $F(x_1, x_2, \ldots x_n)$ is to be satisfied by the sequence '$<O_1, O_2 \ldots O_{n+1}, \ldots >$' (where 'O' is any object) in those cases where it is satisfied by the first *n* numbers of the sequence; the rest of the sequence is ignored. The negation of an open sentence S_1 will be satisfied by all sequences which do not satisfy S_1; the conjunction of S_1 and S_2 will be satisfied by those sequences which satisfy both S_1 and S_2; and the existential quantification of an open sentence will be satisfied by a sequence of objects in those cases where there is another sequence, differing from the first sequence in at most the *i*th place, where the *i*th is the variable bound by the quantifier, which satisfies the sentence opened by dropping the quantifier. For example, ($\exists$x)(x is a country between y and z) is satisfied by the sequence (a) <London, Holland, Spain> because for example the sentence (b) <France, Holland, Spain> satisfies 'x is a country between y and z'. Here the difference in the sequences ('London' in (a) and 'France' in (b)) occur at no more than the place of the bound variable x; and sequence (b) satisfies the open sentence which results from dropping the existential quantifier in point of 'x is a country between y and z'.

Sentences with no free variables, that is, sentences in which all the variables are bound by quantifiers, are 'closed' sentences, and closed sentences are in effect special cases of open sentences – they are open sentences with no places (they are O-place open sentences). Now, the first and all subsequent members of a sequence are irrelevant to whether or not that sequence satisfies a O-place open sentence. Accordingly Tarski defined a sentence as true in those cases where it is satisfied by all sequences whatever, and false when it is satisfied by none. For example, the open sentence with two places 'x is the teacher of y' is satisfied by all sequences, for example <Socrates, Plato, . . .>, no matter what their third, fourth, and subsequent members. The one-place open sentence 'x is a teacher' is satisfied by all sequences, for example <Socrates, . . .>, irrespective of their second and subsequent members. And the O-place open sentence – that is, closed sentence – ($\exists$x)(x is a teacher) is satisfied by all sequences < . . ., . . ., . . .> no matter what their first and subsequent members – for there is a sequence, for example <Socrates, . . .>, which is different from any other sequence you like in at most the first place, and which satisfies the sentence (formed by dropping the quantifier) 'x is a teacher'. Closed sentences cannot be satisfied by just these and not some other sequences; they are satisfied by all sequences or by none.

So Tarski's view is that 'true =df. satisfied by all sequences' and 'false=df. satisfied by no sequences'. To see why, consider the closed sentence ($\exists$ x)(x is a teacher) again, and let there be a sequence of objects A. As stated, this sentence is satisfied by any sequence of objects if and only if there is some other sequence B, different from A in at most the first place, which satisfies the sentence 'x is a teacher' formed by dropping the quantifier. This sentence will be satisfied by an object O where O is a teacher; so there is such a sequence if there is some object which is a teacher. Accordingly ($\exists$ x)(x is a teacher) is satisfied by all sequences if something is a teacher.

One can give the formal definition as follows. Tarski defined truth for a class calculus using a formalised metalanguage. Following Quine and Haack, however, it is simpler to demonstrate the procedure for a sparse version of standard first-order predicate calculus.[40] We have the usual variables and predicate letters; just two sentence-forming operators, $\sim$ and $\cdot$; the existential quantifier; and brackets. That completes the syntax. The atomic sentences are strings consisting of n-place predicates followed by n variables. Nothing is a wff other than atomic sentences A,B. . . , and whatever can be well-formed from them by applying $\sim$, $\cdot$, and ($\exists$ . . .); thus $\sim$A is a wff, (A·B) is a wff, ($\exists$ x)A is a wff.

The recursive or inductive definition is then as follows. Let A and B range over sentences of our sparse first-order language, and let the expressions X and Y range over sequences of objects, with the expression 'Xi' denoting the ith member of any sequence X. Satisfaction is then defined for atomic sentences thus:

I.i. For all i and X:
    X satisfies 'Fxi' if and only if Xi is F.
This provides a clause for one-place predicates.

I.ii. For all i and X:
X satisfies '$Gxixj$' if and only if Xi and Xj stand in the relation G.
This provides a clause for two-place predicates. And so on for all predicates. We then turn to negation, conjunction and quantification in similar fashion.

2. For all X and A:
    X satisfies '$\sim$A' if and only if X does not satisfy 'A'.
3. For all X, A, and B:

X satisfies 'A·B' if and only if X satisfies A and X satisfies B.

4. For all X, A, and i:

X satisfies ($\exists x_i$)A if and only if there is a sequence Y such that $X_i = Y_j$ for all $j \neq i$, and Y satisfies A.

A closed sentence, that is a wff with no free variables, will be satisfied by all sequences or none. 'True' accordingly is defined thus: a closed sentence of this sparse first-order language is true if and only if it is satisfied by all sequences. That, in essentials, is the manner of Tarski's definition of 'true'.

TARSKI, NATURAL LANGUAGE AND NEUTRALITY

Tarski held that his formal correctness conditions rule out the possibility of an adequate definition of truth for any language which is semantically closed, that is, which itself contains semantic terms like 'true', 'refers', and so on, and which is not formally specifiable; hence there can be no adequate definition of truth for natural languages, because it is only formal languages which have the required characteristics of semantic openness and formal specifiability.

Natural languages, in short, contain their own metalanguages, and in Tarski's view this is the source of paradox in them. Moreover they are living things, constantly in a state of change and development, riddled with such features as vagueness, indexicality, and ambiguity, all of which considerations made Tarski very pessimistic about the possibility of a truth-definition for them.[41] He also believed that since his theory was specific to formal contexts, it was neutral with respect to traditional epistemological and metaphysical controversies; we could, in his view, accept the semantic theory of truth and remain in whatever philosophical camp to which we had been antecedently committed.[42]

However, Tarski's own assessment of the implications and applications of his theory has not been accepted; it is claimed that philosphical consequences of great moment follow from it, and that it rests on philosophically significant assumptions. An inspection of Tarski's 'polemical' remarks on the theory[43] will show, I think, that although he was an incisive and innovative logician, his specifically philosophical interests were minimal, and so accordingly was his level of philosophical sensitivity.[44] Accordingly, these claims on behalf of his theory have to be examined. It turns out they are not without foundation.

Consider first the facts that a) Tarski's account makes use of an objectional reading of the quantifiers − (∃ x)Fx is true if there is an object which is F; b) that the objects ranged over by the variables are located in the world, and not in a model domain or possible world − 'x is white', in his own example, is satisfied by snow (the stuff, not the name 'snow'); and c) that the material adequacy condition rules out all nonbivalent truth theories, as is demonstrated by the fact that if 'p' in ' "p" is true if and only if p' is truth-valueless, then ' "p" is true' is false, with the result that ' "p" is true if and only if p' as a whole must be, if not false, then at least not true. The net result of considerations a)-c) is that Tarski's theory strongly appears both to assume and to promote a particular metaphysical view, namely a realist materialism or 'physicalism'.[45]

This point is well made by Field.[46] Tarski's intentions are revealed by his saying that truth must be defined without appeal to semantic primitives, because such an appeal produces unclarity and makes it 'difficult to bring this method into harmony with the postulates of the unity of science and of physicalism'.[47] Tarski wished to make semantics a respectable enquiry from the point of view of science,[48] and since it is an assumption of the notion of unified science − that is, of 'physicalism' in Tarski's sense − that all phenomena can be so reduced that they admit of subsumption by physical laws, it follows that Tarski took himself to be providing a characterisation of truth of an appropriate physicalist kind.

Having identified Tarski's non-neutral objectives in this way, Field argues that Tarski failed to realise them. That is, Tarski did not succeed in providing an account of semantic primitives in acceptable physicalist terms, for his definition turns out in fact to rest on them. (Himself a physicalist and keen to see Tarski's aims fulfilled, Field accordingly offers a reworking of Tarski's theory to that end, turning chiefly on the claim that extensional equivalence is not enough for a successful semantic-term to physical-term reduction, but that something stronger is required.[49]) The point of main interest here, however, is that Tarski's theory, whether successful or not in its physicalist aims, none the less involves them; the theory is not neutral as he claimed.

IS TARSKI'S THEORY A CORRESPONDENCE THEORY?

Another point of importance is in what respect if any the semantic theory is, or at least particularly supports, or in some way preserves the essential intuitions of, the correspondence theory of truth. Popper's grateful reception of Tarski's theory, as at last providing what had hitherto been lacking in correspondence theories – namely a proper characterisation of the correspondence relation – suggests the first possibility;[50] but Tarski's own comments at very most suggest the third.[51] Popper's claim is a very strong one; it is that Tarski has 'rehabilitated the correspondence theory of absolute or objective truth' and 'vindicated the free use of the intuitive idea of truth as correspondence to the facts'.[52] Evidently this matter merits investigation.

One way of looking at instances of the (T) schema like ' "snow is white" is true if and only if snow is white' is to take it that the left-hand-side refers to a linguistic item – a sentence – and that the right-hand-side refers to an extralinguistic item – a fact or state-of-affairs. It then looks as if the (T) schema itself – that is, ' "p" is true if and only if p' states a recipe for correspondence between linguistic and extralinguistic items. But this in fact will not do; for the (T) schema, constituting as it does no more than a proposed condition of adequacy for any truth theory, does not specify the correspondence theory as uniquely correct, but is in fact consonant with other truth theories too. For example, it shows that a redundancy theory – in the form '(p)(p is true if and only if p)' – is materially adequate; and it is even compatible with fanciful theories of the sort we would get if ' "p" is true' were defined as, say, ' "p" is asserted by a philosopher', for ' "snow is white" is asserted by a philosopher if and only if snow is white' is an instance of the (T) schema in just the requisite sense that anyone who accepted this definition of ' "p" is true' would accept or reject the left-hand-side just in case he accepted or rejected, respectively, the right-hand-side.[53]

Matters are slightly more promising if, instead, one looks at Tarski's definition of truth itself. The definition contains material for supporting a correspondence construal in this sense, that it is made out in terms of a definition of satisfaction, and satisfaction is a relation between sentences and sequences of objects; so it is somewhat analogous to Wittgenstein's picturing notion, in which the structure of names in elementary propositions mirrors the structure of objects in states-of-affairs. But the difficulty with this putative analogy is that Tarski's definition has it that true and false sentences are respectively satisfied by all sequences and none, with no appeal being made to *specific* sequences.[54] Moreover, as Haack points out, 'it is symptomatic that analytic as well as synthetic truth is embraced by Tarski's theory; yet it is surely less plausible to suppose that analytic truth consists in "correspondence to the facts" than that synthetic truth does so'.[55]

Part of the problem here is that because there are no fully

satisfactory correspondence theories, it is hard to see what features Tarski's theory must display in order to count as one. There are, for instance, considerable differences between Austin's account of correspondence and Tarski's theory, yet Austin's account was offered as an alternative to Wittgenstein's and Russell's Atomistic views, improving on all those respects in which their views had failed. Thus in Austin's account indexical statements (not sentences) occupy centre-stage, whereas Tarski ignores indexicality altogether and takes sentences (not statements) to be the truth-bearers. Tarski selects sentences as the truth-bearers because crucial use has to be made of their syntactic structure in order to define truth by means of satisfaction. Austin on the other hand held that the descriptive conventions – that is, the conventions correlating expressions to types of situations in the world – are *purely* conventional; any words would do, let structure fall where it may.[56]

If therefore Austin's theory is at least a good example of a good attempt at a correspondence theory, then Tarski's theory is after all unlike a correspondence theory. If Tarski's theory is to be considered a correspondence theory because it has analogies to Wittgenstein's theory, then for one thing the analogy is to an arguably not very helpful attempt at a correspondence theory, and for another thing the analogy, turning on the importance of a notion of 'structure' in both Tarski's and Wittgenstein's views, turns out to be a rather poor one anyway.

The question I asked about Tarski's theory was 'is it, or does it particularly support, or does it at least preserve the intuitions of, a correspondence theory?', and I am tempted to reply that it does neither of the first two things at all, and if it does the third thing, then because it is also compatible with other truth-theories (which must be at least to say that it does not impugn the intuitions *they* embody), it does not do so in any specially significant way. Thus far, one element of Tarski's own claim that his definition is neutral is vindicated, at the cost of contradicting his other claim that the theory makes precise the intuitions of the correspondence notion.

This result makes claims about the *objectivity* of Tarski's theory problematic. On the face of it, it would seem inappropriate to characterise Tarski's view of truth as absolute and objective if only because it makes truth essentially language-relative; the definition is not of 'true' *simpliciter* but 'true-in-L'. 'The extension of the concept to be defined', Tarski wrote, 'depends in an essential way on the particular language under consideration. The same expression can, in one language, be a true statement, in another a false or meaningless expression. There will be no question at all here of giving a single general definition of the term'.[57] There are two very good reasons, from Tarski's point of view, why this must be so; the definition relies essentially on syntactic structure, and language-relativity is required for avoidance of the paradoxes.

One of the critics answered by Tarski had complained that the semantic theory involves itself in an 'uncritical realism', because a sentence like 'snow is white' is true if and only 'if snow is *in fact white*'.[58] Tarski objected to the 'in fact', replying that the definition of 'true' implies nothing whatever as to the conditions under which 'snow is white' can be asserted; instead it only implies that whenever we do assert or reject 'snow is white' we must be ready to assert or reject the correlated sentence 'the sentence "snow is white" is true'.[59] And Tarski goes on immediately to remark 'Thus, we may accept the semantic conception of truth without giving up any epistemological attitude we may have had; we may remain naîve realists, critical realists or idealists, empiricists or metaphysicians — whatever we were before. The semantic conception is completely neutral towards all these issues.'[60]

Because Tarski's definition is compatible with rival views of truth — rival in both senses of supplying different definitions of truth and different critieria or tests for ascription of truth — then what Tarski says about the semantic theory's independence from particular philosophical commitments derives some credibility. But then this conflicts with what was identified earlier as the physicalist character of Tarski's views. Could it be that the objectivity claim has some basis after all, despite Tarski's own pronouncements?

Two suggestions appear to offer support to this possibility. One is to deny that, in the end, there are different languages. If this is so, then Tarski's theory ceases to be genuinely relative, but applies across the board — that is, absolutely. Davidson has argued, for example, that no sense attaches to the idea of genuinely different — in the sense of mutually unintelligible or inaccessible — languages, for the very criterion of languagehood is 'translatability into a familiar idiom'.[61] A similar idea underlies Popper's view that if p is a true sentence of L and there is a translation p_1 of p in another language L_1, then p and p_1 will have the same truth-values.[62] However, even if this is right, it only goes as far as supporting the contention that Tarski's theory is absolute — that is, universally applicable — for it is a further matter to show how, or even perhaps that, this entails its also being objective. There are enormous difficulties here: 'objectivity' is a complex notion, and on the face of it the most that appears to be readily claimable is that a theory of truth's being absolute is a necessary condition for its being obective

– which is to say that it is not immediately apparent that its being absolute is sufficient for its also being objective (in an intuitively suitable sense of 'objective'). Taking this tack with Tarski's theory therefore involves settling a number of vexed, delicate, and difficult issues first, and no guarantee can be available in advance that all the results will be just those required to back Popper's 'absolute and objective' claim for Tarski's view.

The other suggestion turns on the fact that Tarski's view countenances only bivalent theories of truth. It is a key feature of Dummett's arguments that bivalent truth-theories carry commitments to realism, for the reason that if sentences are to be regarded as determinately either true or false, then there must be something in virtue of which they are true or false. I discuss this at some length in chapter 8 below and thefore will not go into the matter here, save to say that it is not *prima facie* clear that Tarski (rightly or wrongly) would accept this, given his remark, quoted earlier, that his theory does not involve any notion of conditions under which a given sentence is assertible. Dummett, for reasons I shall discuss, would regard it as an error to believe that one can unpack the concept of truth without appealing to assertibility conditions, and so there is a fundamental theoretical conflict here. Suffice it to say that if Dummett is right, Tarski is committed to realism, even if only at a remove; if wrong, then it remains unclear whether Tarski's theory is or is not 'objective.'

A final thought might be, however, that if an *objective* theory of truth is any theory which does not identify truth with what people believe (and such a view would very appropriately merit the label 'subjectivist'), then Tarski's theory is of course objective. Still, this does very little to help; excluding a particularly obvious and even rather crude subjectivist line does not explain objectivity. Popper's claim for Tarski suggests that Tarski's theory delivers something fairly solid in the way of showing truth to be a relation between language and the world in just the way philosophers are urgent to specify; but on the strength of the foregoing discussion, it would appear that Popper's estimation was, at least, over-enthusiastic.

CONCLUDING REMARKS

These considerations, together with Tarski's own pessimism about natural language, make it very far from clear whether the semantic theory provides us with a way of understanding 'true' in intuitive ordinary-language situations where, upon someone's stating that such-and-such is the case, we wish to employ a satisfactory notion of truth to capture what is being said and done. This is not a difficulty which is to be solved by the enormously complex task of so rational- ising ordinary language that it fits a formal analysis of itself in order for it to be possible to plug in and switch on a Tarski-style theory; for in such cases the truth of what someone says is relativised to the speaker, the time, and the context of utterance − that is, is heavily indexed, in a way which makes the mere *sentence* uttered appear too thin a plank to bear truth's load, and the whole indexed complex *too* complex to be explained simply in terms of entailment via Conven- tion (T). In this respect, then, Tarski's own pessimism about exten- ding his theory to natural languages seems to be justified. And this consideration touches only on indexicality; the situation is in fact very much more complex owing to the presence in natural language of ambiguity, vagueness, ellipsis, irony, and other such features.

To say that a definition of truth Tarski-style cannot be given for natural languages does not amount to saying that truth in natural languages cannot be explained at all − still less that there are no truths expressed or expressible in natural languages. What it may mean is that truth Tarski-style is, since it is specific to formal contexts, not truth at all, but truth-in-formal-contexts, which could well be a quite different matter and thefore irrelevant to truth *simpliciter*. Tarski himself was prepared to acknowledge as much, offering to call his truth 'fruth' if necessary, so that his definition would be a definition of 'frue' where this means, roughly, 'truth-in- formal-contexts'. This way of putting things is unhelpful, though, since we still do not have a theory of 'true' of which 'frue' can be the formal analogue.

Moreover it may well be, as Strawson argued, that even if a Tarski-style truth notion could be extended to natural language in some way, it would not really explain the meaning of 'true', but, at best, of 'true if and only if'; because equivalences like ' "New York is a large city" is true iff New York is a large city' could be construed as degenerate cases of equivalences in which we could read 'means that' for 'true iff', as for example in ' "New York est une grande cité" is true iff New York is a large city'. Of course it needs to be said, however, that someone like Davidson might take this criticism to be no criticism at all, but the specification of a virtue (again, see chapter 8).

More generally still, there is another early Strawson criticism − a variant of which he uses against Austin as discussed earlier − to the effect that the semantic theory, or for that matter any theory which identifies truth with a language-world relation, gets questions of meaning mixed up with questions of truth, and in consequence is committed to an inadequate theory of meaning. This criticism has considerable justice in respect of all those areas of language which consist in imperatives, questions, and so on, where it is not easy to see how a direct truth-conditional approach to meaning might be of use. But this once again raises the lid on truth-conditional theories of meaning, which argues, as against such views as Strawson then held, that the meaning-truth connection is close and important.[63]

Evidently, then, the general (as opposed to merely formal) relevance and, if it is relevant, importance of Tarski's theory of truth is something which can only be determined by looking at an attempt like Davidson's to make it work in the context of natural language. It is plain that Tarski's work has great merit and significance in at least the formal arena; truth-conditional semantic theory will, if it is successful, extend that merit to philosophy in general.

NOTES

1. Aristotle, *Metaphysics,* 1011 b 26.
2. Aristotle, *Categories,* 14 b 14-21.
3. Locke, J., *Essay Concerning Human Understanding*, IV.V., § 2.
4. Austin, J. L., 'Truth', in Pitcher, G., *Truth,* New Jersey, 1964, p.18, *et seq.*
5. Ayer, A. J., *The Concept of a Person,* London, 1963, p.184.
6. Strawson, P. F., 'Truth', in Pitcher, *op. cit.,* p.44.
7. ibid.
8. ibid., pp.43-4.
9. ibid., pp.47-8, and cf. Warnock, G. J., 'A Problem About Truth', in Pitcher, *op. cit.,* p.55 *et seq.*
10. Strawson, ibid.
11. White, A. R., *Truth,* London, 1970, p.105.
12. ibid.
13. ibid., pp.106-7.
14. cf. e.g., Moore, G. E., *Some Main Problems of Philosophy,* London, 1953, ch. 14, *passim*; and White *op. cit.,* pp.108-9.
15. White, ibid., p.108.
16. cf. Lotze, *Logic* (trans. and ed. Bosanquet B.), Oxford 1884.
17. Ramsay, F. P., 'Facts and Propositions', Proceedings of the Aristotelian Society, supp. vol., 1927; reprinted as excerpt in Pitcher, *op. cit.,* pp.16-17.
18. ibid., p.16.
19. ibid.
20. ibid., p.17.
21. cf. chapter 4 above.
22. cf. Grover, D. L., 'Propositional Quantifiers' *Journal of Philosophical Logic* 1, 1973.
23. Prior, A. N., *The Objects of Thought,* Oxford, 1971. cf. p.37., *et seq.*
24. ibid., p.37.
25. Grover, D. L., Camp J. and Belnap N. D., 'A Prosentential Theory of Truth', *Philosophical Studies* 27, 1973.
26. Haack, *Philosophy of Logics,* p.133.

27. Loar, B., 'Ramsay's Theory of Belief and Truth', in Mellor, A. H., *Prospects for Pragmatism,* Cambridge, 1980, pp.49, *et seq.*
28. cf. ibid., pp.62-5.
29. Tarski, A., 'The Concept of Truth in Formalized Languages', in (trans. Woodger J. H.), *Logic, Semantics, Metamathematics,* Oxford, 1956, pp.152-278; and (a very good introduction) Tarski, A., 'The Semantic Conception of Truth', in Feigl, H. and Sellars, W., *Readings in Philosophical Analysis,* New York, 1949, pp.52-84. I shall call these 1 and 2 respectively in references to follow.
30. cf. Davidson, D., 'Truth and Meaning', *Synthese* 17, 1967.
31. Tarski, 2 p.52.
32. ibid., 2 p.53-4; 1 p.155
33. Aristotle, *Metaphysics* 1011 b 26; a better translation than the one given earlier.
34. Tarski, 2 p.54; cf. 1 p.155.
35. ibid., 1 pp.157-65; 2 pp.58-9.
36. cf. ibid., 2 p.59.
37. ibid., 2 p.60; 1 pp.162-5.
38. This informal presentation has closely followed Tarski's own in 2 p.63.
39. A clear formal account of the notions of satisfaction by sequences and recursion is given by Quine, *Philosophy of Logic,* New Jersey, 1970, ch. 3, *passim,* esp. pp.35-40, which precedes a discussion of Tarski pp.40 *et seq.*; see also Haack *op. cit.,* pp. 106-8. My presentation follows hers.
40. Quine, *op. cit.,* pp.40-2, Haack *op. cit.,* pp.108-9. Again I follow Haack.
41. cf., Tarski, 1 p.153; 2 p.54.
42. ibid., 2 pp.70-4.
43. ibid 2 pp.65-79.
44. This is a polite way of saying Tarski was a better logician than a philosopher. The contrast with, say, Russell and Quine is striking.
45. 'Physicalism' was used by Tarski to mean materialism, i.e., the doctrine that the world contains nothing but physical objects and their properties. 'Physicalism' standardly designates, in contemporary philosophy, a thesis about mind-brain identity. The two construals are obviously very closely linked. Matters are kept clear if, with McDowell, one thinks of physicalism as the thesis that '1. all events are physical events, i.e., have physical descriptions, and 2. under their physical descriptions, all agents are susceptible to total explanation, of the kind paradigmatically afforded by physics, in terms of physical laws'. McDowell J., 'Physicalism and Denotation in Field on Tarski', in Platts, M. (ed.), *Reference, Truth, and Reality,* London, 1980, p.128.
46. Field, H., 'Tarski's Theory of Truth', *Journal of Philosophy* LXIX, No. 13, 1972, reprinted in Platts, *op. cit.,* pp.83-110; cf. esp. SIII, pp.91-4.
47. Tarski, 1 p.406.
48. ibid., and cf. 2 pp.56-7.
49. Field, *op. cit.* See esp. pp.84-90, 94-103; and McDowell's reply *op. cit.*
50. Popper, K., *Conjectures and Refutations,* London, 1960, p.223. See also Popper's *Objective Knowledge,* London, 1973, p.320.
51. Tarski, 1 p.155, 2 pp.53-4.
52. Popper, *ibid.,* p.224.
53. Haack, S., 'Is It True What They Say About Tarski?' *Philosophy* 51, 1976, p.325.
54. ibid. See also Haack's *Philosophy of Logics,* p.113.
55. ibid.
56. ibid., pp.326-7.
57. Tarski, 1 p.153.
58. Tarski, 2 p.71. The critic was Gonseth, writing in the *Review Thomiste* XLIV, 1938.

59. ibid.
60. ibid.
61. Davidson, D., 'On The Very Idea of a Conceptual Scheme' *Proceedings of the American Philosophical Association* 1974.
62. Popper, *Objective Knowledge,* p.45.
63. Strawson now appears to believe the reverse of what he then believed; cf. 'Scruton and Wright on Anti-Realism,' Proceedings of the Aristotelian Society. 1976-7.

7 Meaning, Reference, Verification and Use

INTRODUCTION

In this and the following chapter I look at theories of meaning. Meaning is one of the chief philosophical preoccupations of our time, and much ingenuity and effort have been, and continue to be, lavished upon it, the reason being that questions of meaning ramify into every conceivable branch of philosophy, and have a significant effect upon them. This in turn results from the fact, noted more than once earlier, that a philosophical understanding of language provides a route to understanding thought and the world; which is why questions of meaning have arisen in one form or another in all the preceding chapters, where it can be seen that substantial philosophical doctrines variously assume, turn upon, or arise from this or that view of language.

It is important to be clear about the question of the nature of *philosophical* interest in language, by discriminating between it and two other kinds of interest in language. One of these is not philosophical at all, although it often enough gives rise to matters of philosophical interest. The other, although certainly philosophical, is philosophical in a sectarian rather than in a general sense. The first kind of interest in language is represented by linguistics, the second by Wittgenstein's and the 'ordinary language' school's theory of the nature of philosophy.

First consider linguistics. Language is interesting in its own right, and as a subject for empirical investigation presents numerous and suble difficulties. The goal of linguistics is to examine and describe language, giving an account of its structure and how it functions. Linguistic theory can give rise to philosophically interesting issues; certain ideas owing to the generative grammarian Chomsky, for one example, provoke reconsideration of a controversy which engaged Locke, Leibniz and the Cambridge Platonists of the seventeenth century, concerning 'innate ideas'. Chomsky pointed out that children evidence mastery of the deep structure of language in their early years, and do so upon exposure to fragmentary and degenerate examples of language – so fragmentary and degenerate, indeed, that they could not possibly have inferred the deep structure of language from it; from which he concluded that linguistic capacity must be innate. Put any infant into any linguistic community and it will rapidly learn the language in question – Chinese, Swahili, Greek, or Swedish – so not only must the infant's linguistic capacity be innate, but all languages must share a common stock of universals arising from that innate human capability.[1] This view, if right, raises a number of obvious philosophical questions.

Moreover, some philosophers approach semantics specifically from the viewpoint of theoretical linguistics; Katz and Fodor are prime examples.[2] Other philosophers, although not themselves engaged in semantics of this kind, none the less believe it to be the right way to investigate language.[3]

However, philosophical interest in language is not one that can be satisfied by linguistics. Descriptive treatment of the structure, functioning, and history of language will not by itself answer the metaphysical and epistemological questions which it is the philosopher's concern to investigate. Rather, it is the nature of thought, and – in the most general terms – the contents and disposition of the universe, which exercise philosophers; accordingly their interest lies with semantics – that is, with meaning, with the philosophical assumptions and consequences of viewing language in this or that light, with *logical* structure and relations, with truth. The philosopher is not concerned with phonetics and morphology, and his interest in syntax and grammar lies well beyond syntax and grammar itself.[4] Accordingly, linguistics and philosophy are quite distinct enterprises.

The second thing which philosophical interest in language is not, is a view to the effect that philosophical problems are to be solved – or, as Wittgenstein and the 'ordinary language' school put it, 'dissolved' – by attention to the currencies of ordinary discourse. Wittgenstein took the view that philosophical problems arise from misuse of language, from seeing false analogies between different uses to which language can be put, or from assimilating disparate kinds of expressions to one another. We dissolve philosophical problems, on this view, not because we are reforming language, or finding perspicuous paraphrases of it in an ideal philosophical idiom, but simply because we are seeing how language really works in all its variety. (I shall have more to say about Wittgenstein's attitude in a later section of this chapter.) This view is in effect a view about philosophical method; the view being that there *is* no method, only 'therapy' for disentangling muddled uses of language and showing how these create the illusion of philosophical difficulty.[5] For a brief period after the Second World War this 'therapeutic' conception of philosophy was adopted and practised with great fervour.

Looking at the way language is used, with a view to noting where and when misuse of a philosophically treacherous sort arises, is a salutary and pointful thing to do, and philosophers have employed the technique since Plato. But it is quite obviously not the whole story. Philosophical interest in language does not, therefore, arise for the reasons insisted upon by Wittgenstein, but, to reiterate, because it furnishes some of the best evidence for the way we think about the world and our experience of it, and therefore − in turn − for what we are to make of the nature of the world. A philosophical investigation of language accordingly holds out promise of supplying information on these heads, and is not an end in itself; it is certainly far from being a way of dispelling philosophical problems in the sense of obviating the necessity of thinking about them, but, rather, it is a way of better understanding and dealing with them.

In preceding chapters the discussion centred upon particular problems, and questions of meaning arose at natural junctures during the course of those discussions. Here and in the following chapter I look at questions of meaning themselves, adopting the following procedure.

In this chapter I range fairly widely over questions of meaning as these have been treated in 'traditional' theories, together with some contemporary extensions of them. Thus I look at the denotative theory again, and move from there to the issue of reference as it is currently treated on possible-worlds lines. Then I revert to another traditional theory − the 'ideational' theory as Alston calls it − and follow that with the discussion of behaviourist views of meaning in both the earlier and the Quine varieties. I then look at the verificationists' views, and after that at the 'use' theory associated chiefly with Wittgenstein. This provides a survey of all but one of the main theories of meaning together with some of their developments, and constitutes a background review for the chapters to follow.

In the next chapter I concentrate on the remaining major theory of meaning, one which has attracted considerable recent attention owing to its importance: truth-conditional semantics. This enterprise raises a number of philosophical issues of wider import than the issue of meaning itself, and these I discuss, both there and in chapter 9.

It is well to begin with a preliminary view of what it is we are looking for in trying to give an account of meaning. Consider the following dictationary definition:

1. *xyster* n. a surgical bone-scraper.

and contrast it with these sentences:

2. He means to be a millionaire one day.
3. The arrival of the cuckoo means summer is at hand.
4. The French word *plume* means 'pen'.

This is not an exhaustive list of the various ways 'means' enters naturally into our talk, nor are the senses of 'means' in 2-4 wholly independent of one another. But the sense of 'means' we are directly after is that sense in 4. which we would regard as approximate in some expansion of the dictionary definition in 1., for example ' "xyster" means "a surgical bone-scraper" '. How meaning is to be understood, in this sense of 'meaning', is the problem at hand. Naturally enough one is also concerned with intentions ('means' in 2. has the sense of 'intends') and the nature of signs and their relation to the things they signify ('means' in 3. has the sense of 'is a sign of'); not only for their own sake but also because they have a good deal to do with meaning in the 1. and 4. senses. But the 2. and 3. senses of 'means' are comprehended in the larger problem of meaning in the focal cases exemplified by 1. and 4. There are, as noted, a number of other senses of 'means', many of which, like 2. and 3., also contribute to the overall problem. However, this provides enough of a grasp of where the problem lies to make a start.

In canvassing theories of meaning I shall employ a classification of their 'traditional' forms due to Alston,[6] who labelled them the 'referential', 'ideational', and 'behavioural' theories respectively. I shall however call the first of these the 'denotative' theory for reasons which will become apparent.

THE DENOTATIVE THEORY OF MEANING

This theory has been met with frequently in earlier chapters. Ryle unlovingly dubbed it 'the "Fido"-fido' theory in exemplification of its basic tenet. It is, on the face of it, the simplest and most immediately plausible of all the theories. It starts from the paradigm of the proper name − for example, 'Dick' − which is simply a label, a word that stands for something in the world. On the one hand there is the name 'Dick', and on the other hand, the man who goes by and answers to that name. From there one moves to the more general view that words mean by denoting items in the world. One recalls what Russell's theory of descriptions was invented to do; it was invented to show that apparently denoting singular descriptive phrases could be analysed-out in order to show that they are 'incomplete', after the fashion of syncategorematic words like 'and', 'if', 'but' and the like, so that subsistent entities do no need to be postulated as the denotations of these phrases in order for them to be meaningful. Russell's choice was to hold to the denotative theory and elaborate the theory of descriptions as a way of dealing with its unpalatable consequences. The unpalatable consequences in question have among them the fact that, on this view, only if a word like 'unicorn' denotes something is it even meaningful to deny of unicorns that they exist, which appears absurd. Russell none the less felt that the denotative theory recommended itself too strongly to be abandoned: 'all words have meaning, in the simple sense that they are symbols that stand for something other than themselves'.[6]

Denotative theorists did not, of course, make the trite mistake of thinking that *all* words mean by denoting an object; the syncategorematic words, for example, get meaning 'in context', for quite obviously there are no ifs and buts in the world (as there are tables and trees), for the words 'if' and 'but' to name.

The idea that the meaning of a word is, straightforwardly, its referent or denotation is shown to be false by two considerations, already noted in earlier chapters. One is Wittgenstein's point about ostension, the other is Frege's sense-reference distinction. The first consideration shows that owing to the difficulties which infect ostensive definition, it is problematic at the outset to know how, for most words, even a simple labelling correlation is to be set up without recourse to more extensive and non-ostensive conventions governing the use of expressions. For, apart from the ambiguity which attaches to ostension (how does the learner of English know that I mean the object rather than its uses, colour, texture, or whatever, when I point and say 'table'?), there is this problem: 'table' is used on particular occasions to pick out a particular table, but the word itself does not denote this or that particular table, but rather the class of all tables. But what does it mean to say that the word 'table' picks out the class of all tables? I shall revert to this shortly.

The second consideration is decisive. Frege's distinction between sense and reference shows that two words or phrases might refer to the same thing but have different senses, as 'the morning star' and 'the evening star' exemplify. Accordingly, it is out of the question to make a simple identification of the meaning of a word with its referent. This demonstrates that what has been so far characterised is naïve or crude version of the theory.

One of the most swingeing attacks on the denotative theory in this form occurs in Strawson's discussion of Russell's theory of descriptions. In Strawson's view, Russell's belief that the meaning of a term is the object it denotes would, if true, permit one to produce the meaning of the word 'handkerchief' from one's pocket; but this is nonsense, and so too is the idea that the meaning of 'handkerchief' is all the handkerchiefs there are, were, and will be.[7] Because Russell held the denotative theory,

he thought that if there were expressions having a uniquely referring use, which were about what they seemed (i.e., logical subjects) and not something else in disguise, their meaning must *be* the particular object which they were used to refer to. Hence the troublesome mythology of the logically proper name. But if someone asks me the meaning of the expression "this" − once Russell's favourite candidate for this status − I do not hand him the object I have just used the expression to refer to, adding at the same time that the meaning of the word changes every time it is used. Nor do I hand him all the objects it has ever been, or might be, used to refer to.[8]

Accordingly it is a straightforward mistake to conflate the meaning and the denotation of a term.

Defenders of the denotative theory, faced with these criticisms, have however a somewhat more sophisticated option to fall back upon. This is to identify the meaning of a term with the *relation* between it and its referent; thus, meaning is the referring or denoting relation between a term and the object it picks out. 'When we ask what constitutes meaning,' Russell later wrote, 'we are asking, not who is the individual meant, but what is the relation of the word to the individual which makes the one mean the other.'[9]

What is this relation? It is first necessary to draw a distinction. One suggestion is that it is not words that refer, but the people who use words. Thus in talking of my pen, it is not the word 'pen' which refers to my pen, but my use of the words 'my pen' which effects reference to my pen. A possible way out for defenders of the denotative theory is thus to insist on a distinction between referring and denoting, such that it can be left to people to refer, while denoting is reserved to words. On this view, 'pen' denotes my pen, while I refer to my pen by using the word which denotes it.

This seems to suggest a rather interesting emphasis in the basic idea. If reference is what occurs when a speaker uses a denoting expression, and if the meaning of the word is to be specified in terms of the relation between it and the relevant object − that relation being denotation − then the theory is specifically a denotative theory of meaning rather than a referential theory of meaning. (That is why I did not follow Alston in calling this a 'referential' theory.) There is then a way of handling the problem arising from the fact that 'table' is a general term. 'Table' does not, strictly speaking, *refer* to the class of tables, it *denotes* that class; and this says no more than that the class of tables is that class to whose members the word 'table' can be correctly applied.[10] There are other reasons why a reference-denotation distinction is valuable; some of these became apparent in the discussion of Donnellan in chapter 4 above.

But is the move just characterised satisfactory? Certainly the 'refers'–'denotes' distinction appears soundly drawn and useful, but it does not solve the problem for defenders of the denotative theory, for we cannot get away with saying simply that a person refers, in this sense, when he uses a 'denoting expression' yet to be explained, perhaps by appealing, as we should have to give an account of what it is for someone to refer to something by means of a denoting expression, in some sense of 'denoting expression' yet to be explained, perhaps by appealing, as Strawson does in a related connection, to speakers' intentions, hearers' identifying knowledge, and so on.[11]

There is no need to spell out theories of reference and denotation tailored to salvaging the theory in this form, however, for certain general considerations render it implausible. These are that many classes of terms, like connectives, prepositions, articles, modal auxiliaries and the like, do not have denotations but *functions*, and therefore because they make essential contributions to the meaning of expressions in which they occur, the meaning of such expressions could never be wholly reduced to the denotations of certain of their principle parts. Indeed, because the class of terms which appears to be paradigmatically denotative – that is, nouns – contain very many members which do not denote (or at least, do not denote as un-equivocally as concrete nouns like 'table' do; leaving aside names of non-existent objects like 'unicorn', what do abstract nouns like 'hope', 'idea', or 'history' denote?), it is not clear that the meaning of at least many expressions can be explained by appeal to denota-tion, because none of their parts, principal or otherwise, may denote in a straightforward sense at all.

It is a notable feature of the denotative theory that it leads its adherents into some awkward philosophical spots. One is the con-sequence that if, as the theory demands, every meaningful expres-sion is such in virtue of having a denotation, then whole sentences which are meaningful must have denotations too; and this is un-intuitive. Whereas it may be natural to think of picking something out by means of a sentence, it is not natural to think of the sentence as a whole being a denoting or (in Frege's case) referring device. Espousal of the theory, or some of its features, leads however to a demand that this be done; and accordingly one finds talk of 'facts' or propositions as the referents of sentences, or even, on some views, the whole of reality (Bradley) or truth-values (Frege). Such proposals are uncomfortable, and lead one to think that if the denotative theory, or some of its features, is one of the motivations behind such proposals, it must be mistaken. In any case, these thoughts point to an important consideration, to the effect that the basic unit of meaning is not the word, as the denotative theory has it, but the sentence; Austin in particular mounted a lively attack on the idea that word-meaning is basic, regarding the phrase 'the meaning of a word' as 'in general . . . a dangerous nonsense-phrase'.[12] I discuss this later.

What the foregoing remarks show, I think, is that it is a mistake to hope that the concept of denotation will serve as the key to an explication of meaning. Nevertheless, the original intuition regarding the way proper names function, and the fact that reference is an integral part of language and linguistic activity, raises certain important issues. There are classes of words which do, or can be used to, refer to items in the world; how does this work? What is it that reference consists in?

REFERENCE AND THE CAUSAL THEORY

The idea that it is not words but people who refer is one among a number of proposals designed to furnish an account of how certain classes of terms − referring terms − apply or are used to apply to items in the world. In general it has been taken as unexceptionable to view terms which have a referring use as being themselves referring devices, so that investigation of them can proceed in terms which do not involve essential reference to speakers' and audience's intentions and knowledge, leaving a specific treatment of these factors for a more inclusive or an alternative account. In the following sketch of some considerations about reference, accordingly, I adopt the idiom of referential terms.[13]

A common feature of many theories of meaning, in particular the more traditional ones like the denotative theory, is their reliance on a distinction between the intension (sense) and extension (reference) of general terms and names. The idea is that the intension − the concept or meaning − of a term determines the collection of things − the extension − to which the term applies. This distinction was discussed in chapter 2. Traditional theories trade on the idea that names and general terms refer to those things which fit the properties which those names and general terms 'mean'. Thus the *reference* of a name or general term is determined by its *sense*; and since the intension of a term is 'given' by descriptions which consist in a setting-out of the concept or meaning of the term, it is descriptions – on this view – which determine reference.

This way of looking at the issue has been challenged recently in the work of Donnellan, Kripke and Putnam among others.[14] The chief of their views is that names, and by extension certain other terms – in particular, natural kind terms, that is, terms which designate naturally occurring stuffs like gold and water – have no intension as understood by traditional theorists, and accordingly do not have their references fixed by the concepts or descriptions associated with them; but that reference is effected by a causal chain (or something like it) linking such terms and their referents together. This view, which I shall call the 'causal theory' of reference, constitutes an important challenge to traditional ways of thinking, and in addition has some important implications for debates elsewhere in philosophy.

Consider the work which, on the traditional view, an intension-extension distinction does. The intension of a term is given by specifying a list of properties. To use Putnam's example,[15] the meaning of 'lemon' is given by setting out a conjunction of properties $P_1 \ldots P_n$, such that to say 'anything with properties $P_1 \ldots P_n$ is a lemon' is analytic, as is 'lemons have the property P_1. The idea is then that the conjunction of properties which constitutes the meaning or intension of 'lemon' determines the extension of the term; all and only those things with properties $P_1 \ldots P_n$ are lemons.

This species of view, in one or another variant, was held by Locke, Berkeley, Hume, Mill, Wittgenstein, and others. The initial task of proposers of the causal theory is to refute it. Donnellan does so by showing, in connection first with proper names, that reference is effected independently of descriptions; which he does by drawing the distinction, discussed in chapter 4 above, between the referential and attributive uses of descriptions.[16]

A recapitulation of that distinction will be useful. Attributive use is made of a description when, it will be recalled, a speaker means to be saying something about whoever or whatever fits the description, even if he has no idea who or what *does* fit the description. Suppose, to use the same example as before, the agreeable Smith has been foully murdered. We might say – 'Smith's murderer is insane', without having the faintest idea who Smith's murderer is. Contrasted with this is the referential use. Here the speaker has someone or something definite in mind. Suppose Jones has been indicted for Smith's murder, and has behaved in an unbalanced way during the trial. If we say 'Smith's murderer is insane', referring to Jones, then we have used the description 'Smith's murderer' referentially. If it turns out that Jones is not Smith's murderer, say because Brown comes along and confesses, reference has still been effected by the description even although Jones in fact failed to fit it.

From this it can be seen that reference does not always or only occur via descriptions, but it can and does occur independently of them. The point is well driven home by consideration of a case like this: Thales is the philosopher who held that the *arche* or principle of the universe is water. Now suppose that in fact Thales was a well-digger and not a philosopher at all. Does the fact that he fails to fit the description 'the philosopher who held that the *arche* is water' mean that we are not talking about Thales? On the contrary. It only makes sense to say that a description fits or fails to fit someone or something if we can refer independently of descriptions; otherwise we should be obliged to say that if Thales does not fit the descriptions of him, he would not have existed.

Much the same point is made by Kripke.[17] In Kripke's view, names are 'rigid designators', that is, terms which refer to the same individual in every possible world in which that individual exists. Because individuals will have different properties in different possible worlds – their being *different* possible worlds will turn in some cases just on the hypothesis that some selected individual answers to different descriptions in those worlds – it cannot be the case that the name of that individual is synonymous with some set of descriptions. In other possible dispensations of things Aristotle may have been a hoplite, a physician, or whatever; but his name still rigidly designates him in all the worlds in which he exists. He will only possess in *all* possible worlds such properties as are essential to his being Aristotle. This allows what is surely true, that we can discover of individuals that certain descriptions fail to fit them. For example, suppose it is confirmed that Bacon did indeed write *Othello, Hamlet,* and the rest; nevertheless the name 'Shakespeare' will not cease to refer because the description 'the author of *Hamlet*' ceases to apply to that individual. For if we irreversibly *identify* whoever is designated by 'Shakespeare' with 'the author of *Hamlet*', it would be impossible to discover that he did not write *Hamlet*.

This then is the first important feature of the causal theory, that ordinary proper names are rigid designators and not abbreviations for clusters of descriptions. An interesting consequence of this relates to identity statements.[18] It is commonly held that identity statements like 'Hesperus is Phosphorus' are contingent, because the fact that the two are one is something that had to be established *a posteriori.* But Kripke argues that if 'Hesperus is Phosphorus' is true, then since both names are rigid designators and refer to the same entity in all possible worlds in which that entity exists, the identity statement is *necessarily* true. Philosophers had supposed this identity statement to be only contingently true because 'Hesperus is Phosphorus' is not analytic; but a failure to distinguish the metaphysical notion of necessity both from the epistemological notion of apriority and the semantic notion of analyticity makes for the muddle here. On Kripke's view, 'necessarily true' means 'true in all possible worlds';[19] so although 'Hesperus is Phosphorus' is *a posteriori*, it is necessary — and if this is right, it establishes the existence of necessary *a posteriori* truths, an exciting result.

Another important feature of the casual theory is its implications for our understanding of 'natural kind' terms.[20] These are terms which designate naturally occurring stuffs like gold and water, as opposed to artificial categories of things like spinsters, professors, and bicycles. Kripke holds that natural kind terms work like names in being rigid designators, which means that 'gold' always refers to the same stuff whatever its overt phenomenal characteristics might be.[21] Suppose it to be the essence of gold that it is the element of atomic number 79. Then whether or not it is yellow and malleable, if it is the element of atomic number 79 it is gold. Traditionally it had been held that it is a defining characteristic of gold that it is yellow and malleable; but since it is perfectly possible that we could find stuff composed of atomic number 79 which has neither of those characteristics, then 'gold is yellow' and gold is malleable' cannot be analytic.

This reinforces the point that descriptions commonly associated with something are not decisive in fixing whether a term applies to it or not. Iron pyrites look like gold, but are not gold; here is a case in point. The descriptions might be useful as a general guide to identifying something, but they do not settle what it is for a thing to be a thing of that kind; what settles whether something is or is not gold is its atomic structure. In just the same way, water is water only if it has the right kind of chemical structure, *viz.* H_2O; something is not water merely in virtue of being a colourless, odourless and tasteless liquid. (Stinking black brackish water is still, after all, water — precisely because it is H_2O.) The point is to be put more precisely by saying — there is no possible world in which something could be H_2O but not water.

The question now arises: if reference is not effected by descriptions, how is it effected? Matters are a little less clear here. The suggestion is that reference works via a causal chain of some sort, historically linking present uses of a term to the occasion on which the referent of the term was fixed. In much the same way as 'Tom' refers to Tom because he was so christened and the name has continued to pick him out ever since, so, on this view, objects were 'baptised' and their names have been handed on from speaker to speaker. So long as later speakers in the chain intend to refer, by means of the name, to what it was originally intended to refer to, the causal chain is the right kind of chain. Certain sophistications of this view have been offered; Donnellan talks not of 'causal chains' but of an 'historical explanation theory' which allows that not all links in the chain are causal;[22] while Evans attempts to establish that the causal link is not one between a referent and a current use of a term, but between the referent and the current body of knowledge concerning it.[23] Sophistications of this sort – in particular Donnellan's sort – are required to deal with terms which fail to refer, like 'Pegasus' and 'unicorn'; just such terms, indeed, had prompted Russell's view that they must be concealed descriptions, but on the causal theory if it is not the case that there is a set of descriptions constituting the sense of a term and therefore the 'route to the referent', still less is any such term itself a disguised description and amenable to Russellian analysis.[24]

An apparent fault with the causal theory is that it appears to leave a question-mark over the one respect in which theories relying on a descriptive route for reference succeed in accounting for our intuitions about the use of names. This is that non-accidental success in applying a name would seem to demand that the user of the name has relevant identifying knowledge to the effect that *this* name picks out *that* referent, and that such knowledge is by its nature descriptive. The knowledge in question may be derivative, in the sense that it is not necessary for every user of the name to have a determinate way of identifying the referent so long as *someone* does;[25] and it may also be that what the user of the name knows is only some or even one contingent fact about the referent. But we would expect a user of a name to have some justification for his claim to be making a genuine use of the name; for if he did not, the comment 'he doesn't know who/what he's talking about' would be literally true.

But this does not in fact constitute a serious difficulty for the causal theory. Kripke acknowledges that we may fix the reference of a term by giving descriptions, but that this is not the same thing as giving the meaning. This is to reiterate the central point at issue, that names and natural kind terms have references but no senses; to ask for the *meaning* of either kind of term is accordingly misguided.

The theory is, in a way, an updated and extended version of Mill's view that proper names have denotations but no connotations; a name, for Mill, is not bestowed on a variety of individuals 'to indicate any qualities, or anything which belongs to them in common; and cannot be said to be affirmed of them in any *sense* at all'.[26]

There are two related questions which need to be asked about the causal theory, however; what exactly constitutes the reference of a rigid designator? and, what of other referring terms, for example those which pick out non-natural kinds? A rigid designator is defined as a term which designates the same item in every world in which that item exists. But what is the item? It cannot be the extension of the term, because the very idea of a possible world is premissed on the fact that extensions can vary across worlds. For example, if there is a possible world in which Aristotle is not a teacher, the extension of 'teacher' is different in that world from its extension in the world in which Aristotle teaches. ('Teacher' is not a natural kind term, but it is open as yet whether it designates rigidly or not.) It is indeed possible that there are two worlds in which the extensions of a given term are entirely disjoint. Accordingly the extension of a term cannot be what the term designates.

The option is to say that a rigid designator designates the kind or species itself. This is more plausible, but it has the drawback that it confers rigidity on terms like 'teacher' and 'spinster', designating non-natural kinds, so that 'teacher' would pick out, from world to world, all and only those individuals·who imparted information to, demonstrated to, or instructed others in a certain characteristically educational way. Putnam takes the view that practically all kind terms are rigid.[27] But the problem is that in the case of non-natural kind terms we do not standardly have a *kind* of thing in mind; it is rather the case that we employ certain general specifications such that if anything fits a minimum sufficiency of them, we apply the label. We can first name a natural kind and then proceed to find out what it is, as with elements or animals; by contrast, naming a non-natural kind just *is* saying what it is. The descriptive theory appears therefore to apply here, for non-natural kinds lack biological or atomic essences, and appear to have what Locke called 'nominal' essences only.

If different accounts have to be given of natural and non-natural kind terms respectively, then it will inevitably happen that there will arise disputes as to whether something is a thing of one or the other kind, perhaps in particularly difficult cases like mental events and sensations.[28] Is a pain, for example, to be differentiated with respect to the essential nature of the system of which it is an expression, or is it arbitrary from nature's viewpoint and differentiated by reason of the classifications we make for our own social convenience?

These last thoughts, touching as they do on the issue of essentialism, draw attention to the fact that if there are problems about the notion of possible worlds, and particularly about the notion of essence which plays a pivotal role in some possible-worlds theories, then these problems are also problems – and very significant ones – for the causal theory of reference, which stands or falls by them. I have sketched some of the relevant difficulties in chapter 3 above and shall not repeat them here.

THE IDEATIONAL THEORY OF MEANING

This theory has it that the meaning of an expression is the idea it stands for. Locke gave an excellent statement of it: 'The use . . . of words is to be sensible marks of ideas; and the ideas they stand for are their proper and immediate signification'.[29] The theory underpinning this view is that language is an instrument for reporting thought, and thought consists of successions of ideas in consciousness. Ideas are private; only I have access to my own thoughts. Therefore to communicate our ideas to each other we need a system of intersubjectively available sounds and marks, so connected to ideas that the proper use of them by one person will arouse the appropriate ideas in another person's mind. Accordingly what a word means is the idea with which it is regularly connected.

Preliminary difficulties with this view concern the fact that it is arguable whether thought and language are independent of one another. How could thought above a rudimentary level be possible without language? This is not an easy issue to unravel, but certain observations would appear to be pertinent. For one thing, it is somewhat implausible to think that prelinguistic man may have enjoyed a fairly rich thought-life, and invented language to report and communicate it only when the social demand for language became pressing. Philosophical speculation either way on this matter would constitute *a priori* anthropology at its worst, of course, but it seems clear that anything like systematic thought requires linguistic ability to make it possible. A caveman's ability to mull over features of his environment and his experience of it, in some way which was fruitful of his having opinions about it, seems incredible unless a means of thinking 'articulately' is imputed to him. The net effect of the 'private language' debate, instigated by some of Wittgenstein's remarks in the *Philosophical Investigations*, strongly suggests that language (this 'articulateness') could not be an enterprise wholly private to some individual, but must be, and therefore must have started out as, a shared and public enterprise.[30]

Moreover, it appears on reflection plausible to say that the richer the language, the greater the possibility its users have for thinking discriminatively about the world. An heuristic set of considerations in support of this thought might go as follows. Consider two men walking through a wood, one of whom is an expert botanist with the name of every tree and shrub at his fingertips, and a command of much floral knowledge. The other man, by contrast, enjoys as much ignorance of botany as his companion enjoys knowledge, so that his experience of the wood is, on the whole, one of a barely differentiated mass of wood and leaf. Plainly, possession of the botanical language, and all that went into learning it, makes the first man's experience of the wood a great deal richer, more finely differentiated, and significant, *qua* experience of the wood as a wood, than is the second man's experience of it. Of course the second man, despite his botanical ignorance, might have poetic, or, more generally, aesthetic experiences arising from his woodland walk, which leave the first man's scientific experience in, as we say, the shade; but the point at issue here is the relevance of their relative commands of the language specific to making their experience of the wood *qua* wood more and less finely discriminative respectively.

So much is merely speculative. It does however show that the question whether language and thought are independent is more likely to merit a negative than an affirmative answer, in whatever way one is to spell out the reasons for giving the negative answer.

All this aside, there are more strictly philosophical problems with the ideational theory. What is it for a word to be (in Locke's terminology) a 'mark' of an idea? And what indeed is an 'idea'?

The word 'idea' entered into ordinary English usage only a few centuries ago, until which time it had been strictly a philosophical term of art. Plato's use of 'Idea', usually translated as 'Form', is one of the very earliest; but since his employment of it as designating a real, perfect, and immutable entity in the realm of Being, it has undergone as many changes and chances as there have been philosophers to use it. Consequently there is no clear philosophical consensus as to what 'idea' signifies. Generally speaking, the various interpretations have these kinds of construals to give of 'idea' — as what is before the mind in thought or experience, for example sense-data, or feelings; as the objects of introspection, memory, and imagination; as the residue or impression on the mind of experiences; as abstractions into generality from particular experiences or reflections; as a concept, rather like a definition, attaching to words; as subjective associations aroused by words (as *opposed* to their meanings – this is Frege's use); as a representation in one's mind of things in the world that is, an image; and so on. The British Empiricists (Locke, Berkeley, and Hume), who were excessively fond of the notion of ideas, classified them into simple and complex ideas of sense and reflection, and specified their relations (for example, a complex idea of sense is composed of simple ideas of sense); but since they had no clear and univocal idea of 'idea', their classifications did not help to fix a workable philosophical sense for the term.

Now, Locke was too sophisticated a thinker to construe 'idea' merely as 'image' (that is, a picture in the mind), nor did he hold that the meanings of all words are the ideas they 'signify', for he quite appreciated that words like 'if' and 'but' have functions rather than meanings – the function being, for the class of such words as a whole, to join words and sentences and 'signify the connection that the mind gives to ideas or propositions, one with another'.[31] But Locke's use of 'ideas' as the meanings of words is none the less unclear. The most plausible construal, for Locke's or any ideational theory of meaning, is of 'idea' as *concept,* that is, some sort of specification of definition. On this view my 'idea' of a dog would be the concept of a certain kind of four-footed mammal of a certain general shape, size, behaviour-pattern, and domicile. By this I do not mean that my concept of a dog is some odd image of a rather indeterminate dog with no specific shape, colour, or size, for as Berkeley pointed out, any image of a dog one might call to mind would be of a dog with *particular* characteristics. Rather I mean this: suppose, a bit implausibly, that the word 'dog' has slipped my mind for a moment, and yet I am trying to say something about dogs. I might say – 'You know, those four-legged animals which people keep as pets or for herding sheep; they bark, and have tails which they wag when they are pleased', and so on. What I would be doing here is giving a *specification* of sorts; I would be unpacking my *concept* of 'dog'. But now the problem becomes – what is a 'concept'? Is there any way to define 'idea' in terms of 'concept' such that the definition of 'concept' itself does not covertly rely on our pre-theoretical grasp of 'idea'?

Nor indeed will it do to appeal to 'definition' as was done in the preceding paragraph, for definitions are simply not constitutive of what we would ordinarily classify as ideas or concepts. To begin with, the zoologist's definition of 'dog' will be far more detailed and precise than is mine, and mine will be far more precise and detailed than a baby's; yet both I and the baby will have ideas about dogs. Moreover — to speak circularly and to beg the questions we are dealing with for the sake of heuristics — a definition is a word or, more usually, a series of words, which make explicit the meaning, use, and/or limits of application of, some other word; whereas a concept is (to continue moving in the circle) an idea of something taken as a whole, or perhaps one's own understanding of that idea taken as a whole (that is, with as many of its features and implications as are known to one).

An example might help here. The word 'lexicographer' means (is defined as) 'a writer of dictionaries'. The celebrated Dr. Johnson was a lexicographer; and in his dictionary he defined 'lexicographer' as 'a harmless drudge'. Lexicographers may indeed tend to be harmless drudges, but of course the being a harmless drudge is not of the essence of lexicographers; for all one knows, some of them may be dangerous firebrands and yet still be lexicographers. Johnson may have *conceived* (had a concept of) lexicographers as harmless drudges; but his *definition* of them as such is no more than a wry joke at his own expense. Thus the distinction, even though it has had to be drawn by circular appeal to the very notions which are up for explanation.

The net result of trying to clarify the idea of 'idea' in this way is to reveal that it is no more informative a notion than the notion of 'meaning' itself. So to say that the meaning of the word is the idea it stands for is to explain the obscure by appeal to the equally obscure. There are no advances to be made on that front. But suppose, now, that one leaves 'idea' rather vague, taking it to signify whatever it is before one's mind that one is conscious of thinking about. Is there no way it can be said: words mean by pointing to, or evoking, or in some way being 'translations into public marks' of these things?'

To raise the question in this form is to suggest that language *encodes* thought, that what one is doing in expressing one's ideas is putting them into a code — *viz.* language — by means of which to transmit them to someone else. But what is the *relation* between ideas and language in which this encoding procedure might consist?

An analogy with translation from one language into another — from a foreign language into one's own language, say — might be thought to help. Translation here can proceed by means of a translation-mutual which maps words of the foreign tongue into words of the language we already understand; having mastery of a translation-mutual explains having mastery of the other language. And it must be possible, in principle at least, to translate one language into another without going via 'meanings'. In this way we know what it is to associate words in two different languages with one another.

But is it clear that we know what it is to associate an idea and a word? For one thing, it seems implausible to say that ideas have representations which mediate between them and words; for if they *do* have such representations, then we are embroiled in a problem of regress, because the question now arises as to what mediates between the idea and its representation, let alone between the idea's representation and the word. How an idea and a word can be related in the 'encoding' way, therefore, is a major problem.

An allied consideration is that whereas it appears natural and intelligible to talk of a word or idea 'coming into the mind' or 'occurring to one', to talk of a *meaning* 'coming into the mind' is not. If ideas are the meanings of words, then we are bound to say that meanings occur to one, or pop into one's mind. This ungainliness suggests that it is mistaken to hold words and meanings apart, and to identify the latter with ideas; there is little sense to the notion of a meaning occurring to one independently of the word whose meaning it is. Ideas or concepts, as constituents of thoughts which, implicitly, have an articulation in language, then come to be seen more appropriately as complexes which, far from being *prior* to words, are what the use of words manifest.

In this way one abandons the notion that words and ideas (language and thought) are separate, with the latter being presupposed to the former, and there having to be some relation obtaining between them. The problem of a relation of this kind vanishes; on the view of thought and language being substituted here for the transmitter-code notion, language is a *vehicle* for thought, in the sense that use of a word by an utterer constitutes sufficient grounds for ascribing possession of the concept or idea to the utterer.

On the code conception, by contrast, we must suppose that there can be possession of ideas prior to, or independently of, language. Such a view might seem, at first blush, to do justice to dogs and other intelligent creatures, to whom we frequently ascribe ideas – 'he knows his master is at the door', we say. But, at most, appeal to these facts shows that there can be rudimentary thought without language; on the whole, language possession is a condition for having thoughts above such a level. A dog cannot be said to have, say, the idea of oneness, because (as Frege pointed out) although it can discriminate between being attacked by one dog and many dogs, it cannot see what is common to being attacked by one dog and chasing one cat. Wittgenstein similarly pointed out that although we can say of a dog that it expects its master home, we cannot say that it expects its master home next week. Here is the difference.

An ideationalist might attempt to preserve some honour for his theory by pointing out that at least in the case of words closely connected to sensory images (or ideas construed as images), ideas are the meanings of words. But this will not work either. Any image you care to think of could well arise in connection with a number of different words, and conversely a particular word might evoke as many images in people's minds as hear or read it. For an example of the first possibility, I might imagine a cat on the mat before the fire, and the words 'sleep', 'hearth', 'tabby', 'comfort', 'warmth', and a host of others, could associate themselves. And regarding the second possibility: the word 'gun' might evoke images of pistols, or rifles, or English gentlemen on the moors, or cowboys, or artillery – the associable images are legion. The psychoanalyst's practice of encouraging patients to 'free-associate' ideas is premissed in part on the sheer variety of image-and-word nexuses of which humans are capable; which fact sharply reduces the credibility of this version of the ideationalist theory.

It does not look as though the ideationalist theory will pass muster. One feature of it which is worth noting is that, like the crudest version of the denotative theory, it identifies the meaning of a word with an entity; both theories regard meaning as being somehow like *labelling*. That neither theory carries conviction might perhaps be taken to indicate that the covert notion of labelling is somehow misguided, and that any theory which depends upon it is accordingly at risk.

THE BEHAVIOURAL THEORY OF MEANING

The application of empirical as opposed to speculative techniques in those areas of philosophy concerned with the nature of the physical world gave rise, in the seventeenth century and after, to the natural sciences – physics, chemistry, biology, and the rest. The success of natural science prompted practitioners of the social sciences, in particular psychology, to attempt to make their subjects more rigorous by applying quantitative (as opposed to 'qualitative') techniques to them in imitation of methodology in natural science. One result has been a schism between – in the case of psychology at any rate – 'experimental' and 'social' branches of the discipline.

This sketch is a little hasty. Because the phenomena studied by natural scientists are repeatable and public, they are amenable to quantitive investigation; they can be observed and measured. The phenomena studied by social scientists are often unique and private, as in the case of the sentiments and intentions of individuals; or they are historically parochial, mutable, subtle, and complex, as in the case of social institutions. Some philosophers of social science consequently hold that there is a methodology of social science properly distinct from that of natural science. Dilthey, Weber and others — the hermeneutic theorists — claimed that *verstehen* theory provides the basis for this methodology.[32] This is not a matter that can be gone into here. Suffice it to say that not all social scientists agree with the *verstehen* theorists that their disciplines are to be held apart from natural science; these claim that the proper approach is quantitive empirical investigation of public phenomena. Experimental psychologists and behaviourists figure on this, the most influential, side of the dispute.

A well-known early example of experimental psychology is furnished by the work of Pavlov, who conditioned dogs in such a way that their salivatory relfexes could be prompted by the ringing of a bell. Inspired by work of this general nature,[33] many psychologists became behaviourists — that is, exponents of the view, called the 'behavioural theory', that the mental life of men and animals can be explained solely in terms of their overt behaviour, construed on stimulus-response lines; and that appeal to inner, secret, mental goings-on ('intentions') in people's heads is old-fashioned and unscientific nonsense. Those who hold that there is a ghost-world of mental entities, over and above the firings of cells in a person's central nervous system, are bracketed as 'mentalists' — a derogatory term in the behaviourists' lexicon. One of the founders of behaviourism took the view that thought consists of 'tiny laryngeal spasms' — that is, sub-vocal, self-addressed speech; which view well illustrates the early behaviourist outlook. On a behaviourist view, to say of someone that he is happy is not to attribute to him a certain state of mind, but to say that he is acting, or is disposed to act, in a certain way — smiling, walking with a spring, being generally sunny and good humoured.[34]

This kind of analysis is extended to the concept of meaning by behaviourist-inclined philosophers. Since speech and writing — in general, communication — is a developed form of behaviour, behaviourists believe that, like all other kinds of behaviour, it can be explained in terms of the stimulus-response model. Their view is as follows.[35]

In any communicating situation there are, broadly speaking, three elements: the *cause* of the communication (the utterance or script) whose meaning we are here concerned to explain; the *context* of the communication; and the *effect* on the communication's audience. This last seemed to the behaviourists to be the most promising place to look for an account of meaning; especially because the purpose of communication lies in its audience-directedness. We communicate with others in order to inform them, modify their behaviour, prevent or impel them, and so on.

Accordingly, early forms of the behavioural theory had it that the *meaning* of an utterance or piece of script is the *response* it evokes from its audience in a particular situation. This is best illustrated by recalling Pavlov's dogs: the bell 'meant' food to them, and that is why they responded to a rung bell by salivating. The theory accordingly has it that the constituents of language mean by virtue of the response which people are conditioned to make to them.

This is the simplest version of the theory; as an account of meaning it is woefully inadequate. Suppose I am with two people, one of them an arachnophobe, and the other an arachnophile. Suppose I say – 'there's a spider on the wall'. The responses of the two will be widely different. How can the meaning of what I say consist in the two widely divergent effects caused by my utterance? How indeed could my two hearers respond in the way they do unless they first understood the sentence?

Further, suppose my nervous friend dislikes mice as well as spiders. Because his response – anxiety and 'avoiding-action' – will be the same whether I say: 'there's a mouse' or 'there's a spider', his response cannot be constitutive of the meanings of these sentences, for his response is the same to both sentences and yet they manifestly differ in meaning. In fact, if the response to an utterance determines its meaning, then any number of such state-ments, as, for example, 'grass is green', 'yellow is a colour', 'people eat food', 'most dogs have four legs', and so forth – all of which are dull and trivial things to assert and would cause one's audience (at worst) infinite boredom or (at best) mildly irritated puzzlement if one trotted them out in sequence – would have the same 'meaning' – *viz.*, that constituted by the audience's bored reaction.

It is in fact much more natural, and much more plausible – although perhaps no more clear – to say that part at least of the determinant of an utterance's meaning is indeed the utterance's *intended effect* on the hearer – but that the effect consists in an evoking of certain concepts in the hearer, the association-for-him of which will determine his response. But this, in harking back to the ideational theory, also reintroduces mentalistic notions; and that is anathema to the behaviourist. But in so far as the behaviourist is right about communication having effects on its audience, some such account − involving appeal to the intentional concepts as it does − seems, even if only *prima facie,* to do more justice to meaning than the pure behavourist theory, in its simple form at least.[36]

A slight sophistication of the simple behaviourist theory adds, to the audience's response, the context of utterance as a factor in meaning. But this is no real advance. The infinite variety of situations in which a particular term or sentence can be uttered while meaning the same, contains nothing that we could possibly identify as that common contextual element which, together with hearers' responses in all those situations, constitutes the expression's meaning.

There are, however, versions of the behavioural theory a good deal more sophisticated than either of the preceding versions; and these trade on the notions of 'implicit responses' (especially to cover cases where, upon hearing something, an audience does nothing at all but, for example, continues to sit impassively) or, more subtly still, 'dispositions'. The way these elaborate construals of the behaviourist theory work is as follows.[37]

On the 'implicit responses' view, an utterance will evoke in a person certain 'fractional' responses − thus, the word 'telephone' might cause certain of the hearer's muscles to twitch, glands to secrete, and an ear-lobe to engorge minutely with blood; but these responses will constitute only a 'fraction' of the gross overt behavioural responses which would accompany a real telephone call by the hearer. Hence the response is 'implicit'. On the 'dispositions' view, an utterance will not go so far as to issue in these subcutaneous twitchings and secretions, but will dispose the hearer's organism in such a way that if certain other conditions were to be fulfilled, or inhibitions withdrawn, these physiological responses would occur, and, in full and in sum, would cause an actual telephone call.

In all these variants of the behavioural theory, from the crude to the subtle, a basic premiss is that language functions as a system of signs, different only in degree of complexity (to match the far greater neural complexity of humans) from the twittering of birds and foot-thumping of rabbits. Bird-song has, in part, territorial significance; rabbits thump their feet as a danger signal, and self-respecting rabbits disappear down their holes when they hear the signal, as a matter of self-preservatory neutral reflex. Now, the question to be asked in connection with the more sophisticated versions of the behavioural theory is whether human language is just a vastly more intricate system of signals than the rabbits' danger-signal or the birds' dawn chorus. (It offends human feelings of superiority to think that this might be so, but feeling offended is no argument against the view. It has to be borne in mind that behavioural techniques in clinical psychology have been very effective in overcoming certain people's purely physiological phobia responses to quite harmless situations; which is something in favour of a behavioural construal of humanity.)

The first element in favour of a negative answer to this question is the fact that the behavioural theory construes language as a system of *signs*. This is a major difficulty. Only a relatively small proportion of a language's constituent items could, with any plausibility, be construed as such; and for these something analogous to the problems which beset the denotative theory would most certainly arise. Secondly, neither the notion of 'implicit responses' nor that of 'dispositions' is very helpful. How could one begin to unpack the meaning of 'house', say, if in order to do so one had to specify some common set of minute physiological reflexes which all speakers of English over the age of approximately two years displayed – *per impossibile,* to some super neurosurgeon – upon hearing that word? To put the cavil another way: the entities, *viz.*, the secretions and twitches, which are jointly the meaning of 'house', are incredibly difficult to identify; they do no at all 'distribute' properly to serve as the word's meaning. If appeal is made instead to 'dispositions' the problem is similar; the notion is unhelpful because to specify the meaning of a word in terms of the dispositions which it summons up would involve us in the infinite task of specifying all the possible modifying conditions which prevent the disposition from realisation if it remains unrealised, or all the conditions which are uniquely satisfied for a given hearer in a given context if the disposition successfully wells up through implicit to explicit or overt response. This is an impossible task; and accordingly as it stands, a useless way to give an account of meaning.

QUINE, BEHAVIOUR AND LANGUAGE

There is however a contemporary behavioural theory of language-acquisition, advanced by Quine, which merits consideration. Quine is not interested in questions of meaning as such, for the reason that he thinks extensional concepts like reference are more tractable, and hence more fruitful to investigation, than intensional concepts like meaning. He had early divided semantic notions into two groups, the first consisting in theories of reference (extensional theories turning on such notions as 'designates' and 'satisfies'), and the second consisting in theories of meaning (intensional theories turning on notions like synonymy). Theories of reference in his view are more philosophically promising, and in 'better shape', than theories of meaning, which are badly infected by obscurities.[38] Nevertheless, an assumption of his views is that making philosophical sense of language is to be achieved by investigating the sources of language-mastery. (Dummett – independently, for different reasons, and with different results – effectively and explicitly utilises a similar view; he takes it that understanding the conditions of language-mastery provides the basis for a theory of meaning.[39])

Quine's position may be summarised as follows.[40] He shuns mentalism, particularly of the kind given currency by classical empiricism, which turns centrally, as shown earlier, on appeal to 'ideas'. In Quine's view the bankruptcy of the 'way of ideas' is evidenced by the fact that it issued variously in Humean scepticism, Berkeleyan idealism, and a laborious Lockean realism, or cognates of these; none of which is tenable. Accordingly standard epistemology is to be rejected and a fresh – and more down to earth – approach taken. This involves accepting the deliverances of modern science. Taking science for granted, the question to be addressed is, how did we achieve scientific knowledge? Because language is fundamental to the acquisition of such knowledge, and because reference is fundamental to language, the task finally reduces to an enquiry into 'the roots of reference'.

In Quine's view, taking science for granted involves seeing knowledge in terms of the behavioural output which is the response to environmental impingements on human exteriors. There is to be no speculation about inner goings-on in minds; the only evidence is to be utterances of words 'out where we can see and hear them' and thus 'accessible to human science'.[41] Simply, language is learned by conditioning; the teacher conditions the child to respond thus-and-so in the appropriate observable situations. Language-learning 'falls within the standard range of animal training', consisting as it does in the bringing about of internal modifications which result in further selective responses to stimuli.

A crucial step in the psychogenetic development from learning simple terms to learning science is the attainment of objective reference, which Quine regards as occurring when the learner has mastered predication by way of quantification. The referential apparatus of natural language is less tidy than that of logic, where it is effected by the quantifiers $(\exists x)$ and (x) and the variables they bind; nevertheless, once the learner has learned predication, he has advanced far enough beyond the primitive level of 'occasion sentences' and 'observation terms' to be properly on the road to science.[42]

The route to predication and reference passes through several stages of prepredicative language use. Observation terms fall into three classes, examples of which are

1. red, sugar, snow, water, white;
2. Fido, mama;
3. dog, buckle, apple, woman.

To begin with, all three classes are alike to the learner, in that it is the recurrence of some recognisable circumstance which prompts utterance of the terms as one-word occasion sentences. But the three classes are significantly different. Items of class 1. can occur in simultaneous scattered chunks, whereas with items of class 2. shape is important; mama is not scattered, she is a body. Nevertheless 1. and 2. terms have a certain semantic simplicity in comparison to 3., for class 3. terms have individuation built into them, which is to say that principles of individuation have to be grasped by the learner in order for him to master terms of that class. Noting this fact constitutes a piece of sophisticated retrospection; so far the learner himself does not distinguish between the classes in this way, for he has not attained to the quantification level. Accordingly these terms are protogeneral and protosingular terms merely, not yet general and singular terms proper.

Class 3. terms come close to being referential because individuation attaches to them; but for the reason that the learner at this stage uses the terms as one-word occasion-sentences, they still involve no predication. This remains so even when the learner develops the ability to formulate 'observation compounds' out of them, as when, from one-word sentences like 'yellow' and 'paper', the learner forms 'yellow paper'. This does not involve predication because assent to 'yellow paper' at this stage still requires the presence of the relevant stimuli, and so is occasion-dependent.

The next step — the transition to predication and reference proper — involves crossing a gulf, Quine says; a gulf bridged by a different mechanism of learning.[43] Whereas observation-sentences are occasion-dependent, 'standing sentences' (Quine sometimes calls them 'eternal sentences') are no so dependent. The step across the gulf to predicative use of language is somewhat mysterious, in Quine's view, but he suggests that it involves the following essential feature: there is a 'transfer' from *observational* stimuli to *verbal* stimuli, such that, for example, the presence of the *word* 'snow' will be sufficient to induce assent to the word 'white' irrespective of the presence or absence of snow. The transfer is a transfer of conditioning, a transfer of response from thing to word. Thus the learner learns to respond to eternal sentences like 'snow is white', 'Fido is a dog'.

The picture Quine draws is one in which predication and objective reference belong to eternal sentences, with a gulf lying between these and occasion-sentences. An initial plausibility attaches to this picture; it particularly recommends itself by being dressed in the colours of science. Nevertheless there are good reasons for thinking it to be misguided from the outset.

For one thing, as Quine's account develops from early learning to the more sophisticated conceptual levels where the acquisition of scientific knowledge becomes possible, appeal to physiological mechanisms recedes into the background. Quine simply says – perhaps one day that part of the story will be filled in. But this optimism is presumptive. It appears among other things to rest on a debatable choice in the dispute over the mind-brain identity thesis in the philosophy of mind; the choice being that mental events are identical with brain-events, so that all intentional concepts can be analysed in terms of physical concepts, allowing psychology to be exhaustively reduced to physics.[44] This thesis is a very strong one, arguing more than that the truth-values of statements about mental events are dependent on the truth-values in a reductive class of physical statements; for this latter could be the case without its being true that mental statements can be *translated* into physical statements without remainder. A strong identity thesis consists in the claim that just such a translation is possible. If one holds that it is possible that a physiological account can, and one day will, exhaustively explain language acquisition, one is thereby committing oneself to a strong identity thesis.

The identity thesis is widely opposed on the grounds that the required reduction is *in principle*, not merely empirically, impossible, for the reason that mental and physical descriptions are incommensurable, which is in part to say that predicates in the two discourses radically fail to match in extension. An example will illustrate this idea: suppose a physicist and a sociologist are watching a certain event. The physicist describes it in terms of bodies of a certain mass, volume, and velocity, emitting noises and reflecting light at certain frequencies, and so forth. The sociologist describes it as a football match, and explains it in terms of two teams with certain aims, strategies, and hopes, governed by the requirement to observe certain rules and procedures. The two descriptions are of the same historical event, but cannot be reduced to one another because there is nothing in the language of physics by means of which one can explain concepts like 'team', 'aim', 'strategy', 'penalty', and the like, and nothing in the language of sociology to explain the concepts of 'mass' and 'velocity'. Accordingly these are irreducibly distinct descriptions of recognisably the same events, each being consistent and complete relative to their given theoretical purposes.

The suggestion then is that the language of brain physiology and our intentional or phychological discourse are irreducibly distinct in the same way. Nevertheless, the physicist and sociologist have the means to 'locate' the set of events they are each describing *as* one and the same set of events; in just the same way, the physiologist and psychologist can agree on certain correlations which establish that at least for some of the time they are both attending to the intersection (in the set-theoretical sense) of sets of related phenomena. I cannot argue the case for this view here; suffice it to say that these considerations show that one of Quine's initial assumptions is too questionable and controversial to be permitted to stand unchallenged.

One of the first steps in Quine's argument is to make use of the apparently innocuous picture of language being learned in a publicly observable situation. But how does the theorist know what kind of situation counts as a language-learning situation? It makes sense to characterise a situation in this way only if the learner in it can be credited with a considerable conceptual load. Suppose the learner is in process of mastering the term 'red'. Then he must recognise what is pointed out to him *as* the feature of the environment which is the correct stimulus for 'red'; and he must also grasp, or antecedently have a grasp of the fact, that what he sees he is seeing *as* red – and so on. Wittgenstein's comments about the poverty of ostension apply here in full. Similarly, the teacher also has to be credited with a conceptual load – indeed, a greater one; for he is consciously selecting simple sensible qualities instead of, say, function, or origin, or artistic category, as the feature he wants to name. But then how is one to provide a characterisation of learning-situations without appeal to intentional concepts in the way just done? Evidently the theorist cannot get going at all without appeal to some sort of mentalistic apparatus.

Strawson challenges Quine on the ordering of primitiveness between the classes of terms 2. and 3., that is, singular and general terms respectively.[45] In Quine's view singular terms like 'Fido' and 'mama' are more primitive than class 3. terms because the latter require grasp of principles of individuation for their mastery, and such a grasp consists in being able to make similarity comparisons and the relevant semantic generalisations from them. However, Quine acknowledges that in coming to master 'Fido' as a proto-singular term, the learner must rule out a plurality of Fidos, for otherwise 'Fido' would be semantically indistinguishable from 'dog'. Strawson fastens onto this admission, and points out that if Fido is the one-and-only Fido, 'Fido' is *more* complex than 'dog', because it involves *both* individuation and uniqueness. Accordingly the ordering of primitiveness between 2. and 3., if it is to be insisted that there is one, has to be reversed.

From there Strawson moves to remark that even if Quine is right in holding that the learner has not acquired the *whole* quantification apparatus by the time he has mastered terms of classes 1.-3. and can use them as occasion-sentences, it does not follow that he has failed to master *some* of it. For in Strawson's view, even a one-word occasion-sentence has a certain duality which strongly prefigures predication; for such sentences would not be capable of truth-value unless, in addition to the uttered one-word sentence itself, there was an implicit 'here-now' component. Thus when the learner says 'dog' he is in effect saying 'dog here now' — that is, he is effectively expressing an observational *judgement* about a salience in his perceptual environment, a judgement capable of being assented to or denied by his interlocutors. In this way occasion-sentences have at least a proto-predicative quality, which closes, or goes a long way to closing, the mysterious gulf hanging between Quine's pre-predicative and predicative levels of language mastery.

These considerations are enough to dispel the initial plausibility of Quine's behavioural account, and to call it into question. One is strongly tempted to conclude that behaviourism's failure to persuade is a sign of the fact that appeal to intentional concepts may be unavoidable if any progress is to be made, not only in the theory of meaning and reference, but in other philosophical pursuits besides. It is not obvious that this is an unfortunate result; accepting the irreducibility of appeal to intentional concepts appears rather to do justice to the richness and complexity of thought. But this, in turn, is not the same as saying that a crude mentalism will suffice; the behaviourists' insistence on at least the relevance of public criteria for the application of the concepts we employ is healthful.

THE VERIFICATION THEORY OF MEANING

Views about meaning which involve the notion of 'verification' fall into two categories, one of which merits the label 'the verification theory of meaning' because it purports to specify the *nature of meaning*, while the other, which sets out to furnish a *criterion of meaningfulness* for sentences, is better described by the more familiar label, 'the verification principle'. The former view is summed up in Schlick's slogan 'the meaning of a propositions is its method of verification',[46] the latter is summed up in Ayer's dictum to the effect that 'a sentence is factually significant to a given person if, and only if, he knows how to verify the proposition which it purports to express'.[47] In both cases 'verification' means checking by observation; which is to say, a proposition is verifiable if and only if there are empirical means by which its truth-value may be determined. It is important to note that if the verification theory of meaning is correct, then the verification principle is true; but not *vice versa*, for even if it is true that a proposition acquires factual significance for me only if I can verify it, it does not follow from this alone that the *method* of verifying the proposition constitutes its meaning.

The Logical Positivists selected verification as the key concept for a theory of meaning because they wished to have a means of distinguishing genuinely significant propositions from those which are not genuinely significant.[48] Ayer quotes Hume as giving 'an excellent statement of the positivists's position',[49] thus: 'When we run over libraries, persuaded of these principles, what havoc must we make? If we take in our hand any volume; of divinity or school metaphysics, for instance; let us ask, *Does it contain an abstract reasoning concerning quantity or number?* No. *Does it contain any experimental reasoning concerning matter of fact and existence?* No. Commit it then to the flames, for it can contain nothing but sophistry and illusion'.[50] On similar grounds the positivists regarded significant propositions as falling into two classes: formal propositions, such as those of logic and pure mathematics, which they followed Wittgenstein of the *Tractatus* in regarding as tautological;[51] and factual propositions, which were required to be empirically verifiable. The detail of their views is as follows.

The verification principle involves a distinction between sentences and propositions, drawn for the kinds of reasons discussed in chapter 2. A *sentence* is said to be 'factually significant' only if the *proposition* it purports to express is verifiable. Thus a sentence which does not express a verifiable proposition expresses no proposition at all; it is nonsensical in the literal acceptation of this term. This indicates that the meaning of a sentence is, on this view, the proposition it expresses. Consider the two sentences

1. God is in his Heaven

and

2. The dove is in his cote.

Since there are means of verifying whether the dove is in the cote (one can go and look), 2. expresses a proposition, and is therefore meaningful; but there is no way of verifying whether what 1. says is either true or false, so it expresses no proposition, and is therefore meaningless − or, more correctly, 'factually insignificant', for the verificationists allowed that 1. might well have emotive meaning as expressing a particular non-cognitive attitude to the world. (This is how verificationists explained all moral, aesthetic, and religious utterances: according to the verification principle, such utterances are 'factually insignificant' because nothing could count as a method of verification for determining their truth-value; but they do have *emotive* meaning for those who utter them.)

So far the verification principle has been given in a restricted form, as stating that a sentence is factually meaningless if for a given person there is no means of verifying what the sentence states. But the principle can be generalised: if what a sentence says cannot be verified by anyone, then the sentence is straightforwardly and without any qualifications factually insignificant or meaningless. In this form the principle itself requires a qualification; sentences which are factually meaningless in this way are those for which there is no means of verification *in principle*. If one did not qualify the principle like this, then a particular sentence might be meaningless only in virtue of the contingent fact that no one had as yet verified what it said, but would become meaningful once someone had done so. The qualification avoids the difficulty that the pragmatic theory of truth (chapter 5) runs into in one of its variants.

The view is, then, that a sentence is meaningful if and only if what it says is verifiable in principle. There are problems with this view, which fact proponents of the theory themselves saw.[52] For one thing, the general laws of science turn out not to be, even in principle, verifiable, if 'verifying' means furnishing *proof* of their truth. Another victim is history: in what way can the truth of assertions about the past be verified by present or future observations? Yet both science and history are bodies of factually significant sentences. Worse still is the consideration that not even an assertion about some currently observed physical object can be conclusively verified, owing to the fact that the number of observations relevant to its verification may be infinite, and hence in principle incompletable; and while there remains the possibility of one future observation refuting what one states to be the case concerning the object, that statement is not and cannot be counted as verified.

The move made by verificationists in response to these difficulties was to suggest a liberalisation of the principle, so that it admitted of cases where all that is possible is evidence *relevant* to the truth of a statement; a sentence is on this view factually significant if empirical procedures are relevant to determining its truth-value.[53] This preserves the distinction between 1. and 2. while overcoming the difficulties just sketched. But this merely causes the problem to reappear in another quarter − specifically, to do with the nature of 'relevance'.

One way of illustrating this difficulty is as follows. What is 'relevant' evidence for or against an assertion about empirical matters of fact is, in the sense discussed in connection with Neurath's views in chapter 5 above, to a large extent a matter of policy; what counts as relevant evidence may therefore vary widely according to the conceptual strategy of observers, but only on a very extreme relativist view (such as Feyerabend's view[54]) would the meaning of terms vary with the relevant verifying context. To illustrate this: suppose that in some remote country during a drought it was made to rain. According to Western scientists involved in the rain-making episode, the immediate cause of rain was CO_2 seeding of the clouds, effected from an aeroplane based at a nearby scientific establishment. According to the local native community, however, it was the village witch-doctor who, by performing a rain-dance and shaking the bones, succeeded in causing rainfall. Each school of thought will have quite different views as to what counts as relevant evidence in verifying what is said by the sentences 'silver iodide seeding caused the rainfall' and 'the witch-doctor caused the rainfall'.

This is an extreme example; but just this sort of dispute over relevance can and does arise within a particular framework. Consider the astrophysicist's dispute over the question whether quasars are at cosmological distances, or whether, instead, they are 'local' phenomena. If the first, then the redshift displayed by quasars is Newtonian and is evidence of enormous speeds and distances; but then the energy they discharge is so great that revisions in our present understanding of physics are required to explain them. If the latter, then some account of non-Newtonian redshift is needed, which is also not available in terms of current theory. Thus the evidence so far available is, to some extent, relevant to both hypotheses, but is not yet sufficiently strong to license a choice between them. Both hypotheses are none the less factually significant.

More sophisticated attempts to substantiate the verification principle as a criterion of meaningfulness have turned on the idea that a sentence is verifiable if it *entails* observation statements in certain specified ways. But a strong objection to any such attempt is to point out that the truth of a sentence stating something about some physical state of affairs is quite consistent with the falsity of any observational report associated with it. Waismann gives this example:[55] suppose someone says 'Jones is on the other side of the street', and I look across the street but fail to see Jones – perhaps because he has just gone into a shop or has been obscured by a passing lorry. My failing to see Jones – that is, the truth of the statement 'I do not see Jones on the other side of the street' – is consistent with the truth of 'Jones is on the other side of the street'; it would be absurd to take it that the failure of the observation cancels the latter statement's truth. If what a sentence says is true and the observation statement it is supposed to entail false, we would have a contradiction on our hands; but there is nothing contradictory implicit in the example.

An objection that opponents of verificationism were quick to make is that the principle itself falls into neither of the categories of significant propositions which it is used to demarcate. It is not a tautology, nor is it empirically verifiable. What status, its critics asked, is it supposed to have? Ayer suggests that the positivists adopted the principle as a *convention*, in the sense that they were propounding a definition of meaning which accords with the conditions that are in fact satisfied by empirically informative propositions.[56] This, together with their account of the *a priori* propositions of logic and mathematics, amounted to a *description* of the classes of significant propositions. They then added a *prescriptive* element by saying that only statements of these classes should be regarded as having truth-value, and only statements having truth-value should be regarded as literally meaningful.[57]

The difficulty with these manoeuvres is twofold: the prescriptive element is challangeable as being no more than a piece of arbitrary legislation; and the most that the descriptive element does is to show that the statements of metaphysics, ethics, aesthetics and theology do not fall into the classes of statements preferred by the positivists, from which it does not follow that they lack truth-value or fail to be meaningful. At most, therefore, the descriptive element of the principle affirms what is already recognised, that an account of the meaning and – if the notion is applicable – truth-value of statements, or extremely general statements about the nature of the world or human experience, requires a treatment different both from that which accounts for assertions about observable phenomena, and that which characterises formal languages. This of itself gives no grounds for excluding metaphysics, or any of the other enquiries, in sole favour of what can be of use to natural science.

If the verification principle as a *criterion* of meaningfulness encounters so many difficulties, perhaps the verification theory of meaning constitutes a more promising alternative. The theory – 'the meaning of a proposition is the method of its verification' – has as a virtue the fact that it does not presuppose a view of 'meaning' as some sort of entity. Instead it construes meaning as a method. 'Stating the meaning of a sentence,' Schlick wrote, 'amounts to stating the rules according to which the sentence is to be used, and this is the same as stating the way in which it can be verified (or falsified).'[58]

This requires explanation, best furnished by considering a rather analogous view, 'operationalism', in the philosophy of science. Consider Bridgman's example of the word 'length'.[59] If we can determine the length of an object, then we know what 'length' means. Determining the length of an object involves the performance of certain physical operations, and it is the set of these length-determining operations which can be viewed as constituting the *meaning* of 'length'. In verificationist terms, we would put this by saying that the meaning of 'length' is the method of verifying sentences which say 'the length of such-and-such is x units'.

This has a certain plausibility, because it does indeed seem to be the case that the meaning of 'such-and-such is x units long' is constituted by its method of verification, *viz.,* the process of measuring the such-and-such. But its plausibility does not extend to other cases, and so is misleading. A sentence like 'the space-shuttle landed at an air-base in California' does not mean the way we go about checking whether this is true; it means that a space-shuttle landed at an air-base in California. One is tempted to say – surely the business of setting out to verify the statement (that is, determine whether the statement is true or not) would be impossible unless we already knew its meaning.

Schlick believed, against Neurath, that there are protocol sentences which, as observational reports, are directly verified in experience; and that the observational terms occurring in protocol sentences are ostensively defined. He wrote 'there is no way of understanding any meaning without ultimate reference to ostensive definition, and this means, in an obvious sense, reference to "experience" or "possibility of verification" '.[60] The equation of 'experience' with 'possibility of verification' is interesting; having the experience which protocol sentences report is just to realise the possibility of verification − that is, to make verification actual. It is in this sense that the procedure of looking or testing constitutes the meaning of empirical statements, for the possibility of there being this procedure for ostensively linking terms of protocol sentences to what is observed, is precisely what constitutes the sense of those terms.

Two evident weaknesses in Schlick's account arise from its dependence on the theory of protocol sentences − attacked by Neurath − and ostension − attacked by Wittgenstein. I earlier gave reasons for thinking that both attacks are successful, and if this is right it creates serious difficulties for Schlick's position. Dispensing with the notions of protocol sentences and ostension makes room for a theory of Quine's sort[61] to the effect that observation is theory-laden; the idea being that our observations are largely conducted in terms of our antecedent theories, which in a sense therefore determine what we observe. Thus recalcitrant observations are as likely to be ignored, or dismissed as aberrant, or put down to observational error, as they are to oblige us to make changes throughout our web of theory to accommodate them. But if theory is carried *to* observation, then the 'meaning' of observation terms, and the very idea of observational confirmation of theory itself, is established in advance − logically speaking − of observation. That may have a faintly paradoxical air; the concept, however, plays a major role in discussions in the philosophy of science.

Nevertheless, an important idea is suggested by Schlick's somewhat instrumentalist notion of meaning, and it was an idea of this stamp which came into vogue in association with the later work of Wittgenstein. For to say that a word means the method of its verification, where this is construed on something like operationalist lines, is to say that its meaning has connections with its use; which thought leads one to consider theories based on this general insight.

THE USE THEORY OF MEANING: THE LATER WITTGENSTEIN AND METHOD

The slogan of the use theory is 'don't look for the meaning, look for the use', and Wittgenstein's dictum was 'look at the sentence as an instrument, and at is sense as its employment'.[62] An immediately apparent strength of the programme which these encapsulations of the use theory offer, is that it transfers attention away from the view that language has a single function by reference to which meaning can be explained – a view to which Wittgenstein himself earlier fell prey in the *Tractatus* – and focuses it instead on the fact that language has a variety of uses, so that meaning is something which has to be understood in the context of the multi-variant 'language games', as Wittgenstein called them, playable within the broad setting of natural language.

Some of the theories of meaning considered earlier traded on the notion that meaning consists in what expressions stand for, represent, or evoke. One consequence of this kind of view, if right, would be that 'giving the meaning' of an expression can be done by matching the expression itself with whatever extralinguistic item or event is supposed to give it its content. The use theory denies that expressions have meaning in isolation in this way, by arguing that it is an expression's role in the language which determines sense;[63] so to 'give the meaning' of an expression is to show how that expression enters into the language games in the context of which it variously functions as it does. There is therefore no 'giving the meaning' without essential reference to language in general (or tracts of it) and the many and various uses to which language, or these and those tracts of it, can be put.

It is useful to look at the detail of these proposals in connection with Wittgenstein's views. In the opening sections of the *Philosophical Investigations* Wittgenstein attacked the general principle of a denotative model for meaning, and urged instead that we see 'the multiplicity of kinds of words and sentences' there are.[64] Failure to grasp the variety in language use results in our assimilating different kinds of expressions to the denotative model alone, which model we are all too liable to regard as basic because we think of someone's 'learning the meaning of a word' in situations like this: the learner, already possessed of a large measure of language-mastery, has a word explained to him by means of definition or ostension – the teacher says '——means. . .' where the second blank is filled by a synonyom or translation of what fills the first blank, or by 'this' together with ostension of an object.[65] But this method of learning depends, in Wittgenstein's view, upon the learner's already having a command of stretches of the language, and constitutes a developed language-game in its own right. The meaning of expressions is not to be looked for in correlations with matched extralinguistic items, then, but in the use to which they are put in the various language-games there are. The key notions here are those of 'use' and 'language-game'.

There is nothing sacrosanct about 'use'; Wittgenstein talks

variously of the *functions* of words and sentences,[66] of their *aims* and *purposes*[67] and even their *offices*,[68] and of their *roles* and *employments*.[69] It does not appear that Wittgenstein saw any difference between these different locutions, although arguably there may be some. The main point however is that Wittgenstein intended to fix on a general notion of the *part expressions play in language* as the key notion, the idea being that mastery of a language consists in being able to employ its expressions in different contexts − in stating, describing, asking, commanding, promising, evaluating, denying and so on. Each of these activities constitutes a language-game. What Wittgenstein meant by appealing to the concept of a *game* can be seen in this passage:

Consider . . . the proceedings which we call 'games'. I mean board-games, card-games, ball games, Olympic games and so on. What is common to them all? − Don't say: 'there must be something common or they would not be called "games",' but *look and see* whether there is anything common to *all*, − for if you look at them you will not see something that is in common to all, but similarities, relationships, and a whole series of them at that . . . And the result of this examination is: we see a complicated network of similarities overlapping and criss-crossing . . . I can think of no better expression to characterise these similarities than 'family resemblances'; for the various resemblances between members of a family: build, features, colour of eyes, gait, temperament, etc. etc., overlap and criss-cross in the same way. − And I shall say: 'games' form a family.[70]

To 'give the meaning' of an expression is accordingly to show how it is used in the different but related 'games' of stating, commanding, and so on.

There is something beguiling in the idea that meaning is use, and the notion quickly came to command widespread assent.[71] However, 'use' as a key to meaning is not a particularly clear notion as it stands, and it is, accordingly, difficult to be very precise about what is meant by it. Its imprecision does not worry everybody; Quinton wrote 'the identification of meaning with the way a word is used is vague, but this is inevitable, for words are used in many different ways and have many different sorts of meaning'.[72] Strawson took the view that 'It is not a complaint to say that this central notion is not immediately and wholly clear,' for 'the general aim is clear enough: to get us away from our fascination with the dubious relation of naming . . . and to make us look at . . . language as one human activity among others, interacting with others'.[73] Nevertheless it is worth trying to see what is at issue here.[74]

Talk of use is itself various, and not all talk of use will be the required sort for explaining meaning. Consider how one might talk of the uses of objects or stuffs, like hammers or olive oil. One can talk about *how* the hammer is used ('grasp the handle. . .'), and with what purpose (to drive nails . . . as a paperweight . . . as a weapon); one can talk about what olive oil is used *in* (salads, dressings), and *for* (frying).[75] Explanations of the uses of such items – the how, the what in, and what for, and so on – explains, or goes a long way to explaining, the nature of the item in question. One can talk of the uses of words in an analogous way; one can explain how a word is used, when its use is appropriate, and what kind of linguistic job it can be used to do. But not all explanations of how, when, and what-for will be explanations of meaning. For example, 'he used the term frequently/effectively/insolently' tells one how the speaker used the term, but without any relevance to its meaning.[76] Similarly, saying that it is sometimes appropriate to use 'Help!', 'Let's run!', 'Look!', 'Shoot!', and so on, in the presence of tigers, does not by itself explain what these expressions mean; although, given a longer story, they can exemplify uses of those terms in a way which contributes towards an explanation of their place in the relevant language-games. Again, to point out that a word – a swear-word, say – can be used to insult or irritate another, or to relieve one's own feelings, does not give the meaning of that word, despite telling us something of what it can be used to do.

These remarks on use none the less point in the general direction intended by Wittgenstein and other use theorists. When language is taught, *what* is taught is the relevance and effects of the employment of expressions in these and those contexts, and this is precisely what 'giving the meaning' or 'explaining the meaning' comes down to on this view; the thought is that one does not show when, how, and with what purpose an expression is to be used, and *then* go on to explain the meaning as though 'meaning' were something additional.

For Wittgenstein, in particular, the notion of use as thus construed was essentially linked to the way in which people behave. A language-game was in his view a 'form of life'.[77] The uses of expressions are linked to the things people do, and accordingly to master a language is to master a scheme of intentions and beliefs and to enter into a shared world-view. This explains Wittgenstein's gnomic remark 'If a lion could talk, we could not understand him';[78] for the lion's world-view would be so radically different from our own that we simply could not comprehend what he meant even if he produced a grammatically well-formed English sentence.[79] Not everyone would agree with the relativism such a view consists in; but its point is clear – the language-games within which expressions alone have meaning consists of 'language and the actions into which it is woven',[80] for 'an expression has meaning only in the stream of life'.[81]

It is helpful to remember, in looking at what is compelling and attractive about the use theory, that Wittgenstein and other use theorists had a certain view of philosophical method – or perhaps it is more accurate to say, a view about the aims of philosophy – which is closely allied to the use idea and throws light upon it. This view is that philosophical puzzles arise from *misuse* of language, or from misunderstandings about the nature of language. If we have an incorrect model of language-functioning we shall be prone to confusions; for example, we shall assimilate the use of one kind of expression to that of a quite disparate kind, or – which is perhaps the same thing – we shall try to understand a piece of language in isolation from the context in which it normally does its work, and so fall into error. 'The confusions which occupy us,' Wittgenstein wrote, 'arise when language is like an engine idling, not when it is doing work.'[82] 'Philosophical problems arise when language *goes on holiday*'.[83] To remedy this situation one must look at how language *actually* works; as Wittgenstein put it, '[Philosophical problems] are, of course, not empirical problems; they are solved, rather, by looking into the workings of our language, and that in such a way as to make us recognise those workings: *in despite of* an urge to misunderstand them'.[84]

Properly considered, then, philosophical problems will vanish, on this view, when we see that they arise only because we mishandle and misunderstand the workings of language. Until such a remedy is applied, philosophers are like flies trapped in a bottle, buzzing hopelessly around with no way out; Wittgenstein remarked, 'What is your aim in philosophy? – To shew the fly the way out of the fly-bottle'.[85] In Wittgenstein's view we must therefore grasp the difference between what he called 'surface grammar' and 'depth grammar', for it is concentration *solely* upon the former which misleads philosophers: 'In the use of words one might distinguish "surface grammar" from "depth grammar" . . . compare the depth grammar, say, of the word "to mean", with what its surface grammar would lead us to suspect. No wonder we find it difficult to know our way about'.[86] Wittgenstein accordingly called his enquiry into the proper workings of language a 'grammatical' enquiry: 'Our investigation is therefore a grammatical one. Such an investigation sheds light on our problem by clearing misunderstandings away'.[87]

Wittgenstein applied his method in the *Philosophical Investigations* to 'dissolving' difficulties not only about meaning but also, for example, the problem about the existence of other minds.[88] Examples of the appeal to use in other philosophers are afforded by Strawson in his attack on Russell,[89] and Austin in his attack on the phenomenalism of Ayer;[90] there are many others. In the latter case, which is in many respects paradigmatic of the use model in action, Austin sought to show that the *problem* to which Ayer addressed himself resulted from misperceptions about language in the first place, so that there is no need to discuss the *solutions* phenomenalists proposed, for these are accordingly otiose. The problems in question arise from misunderstanding the proper workings of terms like 'illusion', 'seeing', and the like.

The question now to be considered is whether the use theory will do. A difficulty which affects making an evaluation of the theory arises from what a number of critics in fact regard as its worst fault; namely, that the use made of 'use' in the theory is very general and vague. The appeal to use is highly programmatic, and offers nothing in the way of specific guidance for specific cases. Nor does it come anywhere near to showing in detail just how it is that meaning consists in, or is to be explained by, use; for, on the theory's own terms, there are multiplicities of uses to which expressions can be put, and consequently there are − or so the suggestion seems to be − multiplicities of (kinds of?) of meanings. Accordingly no univocal account of meaning is to be expected beyond the general observation that the only way to give an account of meaning demands essential invocation of the concept of use. Strawson and Quinton held that this, in the nature of things, is only to be expected; critics of the use theory argue that the theory's generality and vagueness are too great to make it of any value.

What is to be said of this? Well, for one thing, it is without question a mistake to *identify* meaning and use as Wittgenstein appears to do. One can know the meaning of a word without knowing its use, and one can know the use of a word without knowing its meaning. For example, someone may know, because he has been reliably informed, that the meaning of the Latin word *jejunus* is 'hungry', without knowing how to use it in a Latin sentence; conversely, many people know how to use the expressions 'amen' and 'QED' without having the faintest idea what they mean.[91] Names − or most of them − have uses without having meanings, and so do prepositions, conjunctions, and the like. Clearly therefore it is wrong to say that meaning *is* use. This is not to deny that in at least many cases there is an important connection between meaning and use, for anyone who knows the meaning of a term will in general and therefore know its use, and *vice versa*. Rather it is to point out that an appeal of this kind to use does not, by itself, exhaustively explain what there is to meaning.

Use theorists have two possible replies to this point: one is to say that looking at the use of expressions goes far enough towards giving their meaning to count effectively as having done so; the other is to say — one can let questions of meaning fall where they will, what is important is how expressions are used (and misused), and this is what the use theory focuses upon. But neither reply is wholly satisfactory, for it is manifest that one can investigate the uses to which certain kinds of expressions are put — only consider such words as 'good' or 'mind' — and on either count still find one has philosophical difficulties to resolve concerning them.

SPEECH-ACTS

The above point can be spelled out in a general way by concentrating attention on the idea, integral to the use theory, that a chief factor in giving an account of the use (and hence the meaning) of an expression is to look at *what the expression is used to do*. This is the 'speech-act' aspect of language use; 'Stop that!' is standardly used to give an order, 'Where is it?' to ask a question, 'It's on the table' to make a statement, and so on. Ordering, questioning, and stating are speech-acts, and so are promising, appraising, agreeing, denying, criticising, commending, and the like. Austin drew a distinction in this regard between 'illocutionary' and 'perlocutionary' acts:[92] the former are those in which a speech-act is performed in virtue of the use of an expression — 'I promise' constitutes the act of promising, for example, and 'I do thee wed' constitutes the act of wedding oneself to whomever 'thee' picks out; and the latter are those acts performed by means of, or through, the use of an expression — a command is issued by use of 'Get out', and an appraisal or commendation can be made by use of 'I like it' or 'It's good'. Better examples still are 'He protested against her actions' and 'By protesting against her actions he stopped her' the former is the illocutionary, the latter the perlocutionary, case.[93]

The idea is that to show how an expression is used to perform certain speech-acts is to state something about the meaning of that expression. Hare, for example, associated the function of the word 'good' with the speech-acts of commending and evaluating; 'the primary function of the word "good" is to command'.[94] Strawson likewise, in his criticism of Austin's view of truth, held that the word 'true' has its uses in 'confirming, underwriting, admitting, agreeing with, what somebody has said', and that the problem of truth is the problem of how the word 'true' is used.[95]

This general pattern of analysis has been criticised by Searle among others.[96] The pattern in question has this form: with regard to some word W, it is held that

   1) W is used to perform speech-act A

and

   2) the meaning of W is given or explained by 1).

This seems to suggest that at least part of the meaning of W depends upon the fact that its literal occurrence in the sentence containing it characteristically gives rise to the speaker performing speech-act A by its use. As it stands, this view is easily shown to be false, for one can find ready counter-instances.[97] Suppose W is 'good' and the sentence in which it occurs is 'This is a good car'. Then the speech-act in question will be the act of commending or approving the car. However, one is obviously *not* commending anything when 'good' occurs in the sentence 'Is this a good car?', despite is occurrence being literal. Here 1) does not hold water, and neither therefore does 2).

Perhaps, however, this is to be a little harsh, for a defender of the analysis will say that something more general is intended, to this effect: that the point is not that 'good' is used in *every* case to commend, but that its presence in sentences characteristically shows that the relevant speech-act, *viz.,* commendation, is 'in the offing'. For example, 'Is this a good car?' can be viewed as having the force of 'Do you commend this car?', which explains what 'good' is doing (what it means) in 'Is this a good car?'[98]

But this will not do either. Searle offers the following sentences containing literal occurrences of 'good' in which the speech-act of commending is neither performed nor in the offing:

   3) If this is a good electric blanket, then perhaps we ought to buy it.

   4) I wonder if this is a good electric blanket.

   5) I don't know whether it's a good electric blanket.

   6) Let's hope that it's a good electric blanket.

That none of 3)-6) constitutes commendatory speech-acts, or has them in the offing, can be seen by comparing them with —

   3a) If I commend this electric blanket, then perhaps we ought to buy it.

   4a) I wonder if I commend this electric blanket.

   5a) I don't know whether I commend this electric blanket.

   6a) Let's hope I commend this electric blanket.[99]   •

What the comparison shows is that the speech-act analysis of meaning, in relying upon a similarity of function between 'This is a good electric blanket' and 'I commend this electric blanket', is mistaken because the similarity of function 'is not preserved through the permutations of linguistic context in which each of these expressions can be placed without alteration of the literal meanings of the component words'.[100] Whatever way, therefore, one tries to construe the speech-act analysis of given words, it simply fails to yield an account of their meaning. The argument here is quite general: no identification of the meaning of a word with a speech-act (other than words which are expressly speech-act words themselves, like 'commend') will do. Consider another example; on Strawson's view, 'p is true' roughly means 'I confirm that p'; but 'if p is true then q is true' does not even roughly mean 'If I confirm that p then I confirm that q'. The pattern of analysis which this exemplifies is accordingly impugned in general. It shows that philosophically problematic words like 'good' and 'true' cannot be explained by focusing attention on their connections with performative verbs like 'commend' and 'confirm', because the sense in which 'good' is used to commend and 'true' is used to confirm differs markedly from the sense in which 'commend' is used to commend and 'confirm' is used to confirm.[101]

It is important to be clear about what work these criticisms do and do not do. One thing which is *not* being denied is that words are sometimes used to perform speech-acts, or that there are specifiable cases in which explaining the use of a word is to be done by showing what speech-act it is used to perform. What *is* being denied is that one gives the meaning of a word W by showing what speech-acts a speaker performs by using W. Schematically, the criticism is this: in terms of the use theory, the meaning of a word is taken to be (or in large part, *at least,* to be) its use. Accordingly it is thought that questions of the form 'What does W mean?' should be rephrased as 'How is W used?' (This is very clear in Strawson's criticism of Austin on truth as discussed in the preceding chaper.) The next step is then to ask what acts are performed by the use of W. But the foregoing discussion shows that answers, even correct ones, to questions about what speech-acts are performed by uses of W, are *not* answers to questions about the meaning of W.[102] A word like 'good', in other words, makes different contributions in different sentences uttered on different occasions, on some of which the sentences may be used to perform different speech-acts; to select one of these latter as somehow specifying the meaning of 'good' is obviously partial and mistaken.

A defender of the use theory might accept this criticism and choose to settle for the view that speech-act analysis does not tell the whole story about use and hence meaning; but he might then go on to say that such analysis plays *a part* in giving an account of use — and hence meaning — in general. But this simply returns the discussion to its starting-point, where the complaint was that the notion of use is too general and vague to be of help; that, in other words, the use theory is so far programmatic that it is not even clear how we are to begin filling in the details. Quinton and Strawson defended the theory's generality, as noted above, and their defence of it is strongly supported by Wittgenstein's own view that it is a radical mistake to try to construct a systematic theory of meaning. But these defences of the use theory's generality will not do because, as it turns out on reflection, the idea that there can be no systematic theory of meaning is belied by the facts. The facts in question are that anyone able to use a language *ipso faco* has the ability to understand a potential infinity of sentences, most of which, of course, he has never heard before; a point not only emphasised by theoretical linguists like Chomsky but by Wittgenstein himself. And this fact can only be explained by the hypothesis that the speaker has an implicit mastery of rules governing the use of words in the language. But then, if there are general principles of this kind, they can surely be unearthed and stated explicitly, or at any rate an attempt can be made in the direction of specifying them. Any success enjoyed by such an enterprise would precisely consist in the formulation of, or an approach to the formulation of, a complete theory of meaning for the language in question. [103] This thought − a compelling one − runs directly counter to the spirit of the use theory at least as it stands in its original sources in Wittgenstein and the 'ordinary language' school; for there the idea had been that an unsystematic and piecemeal demonstration of the uses of expressions in specified contexts was the right way to settle questions of meaning. This approach is shown by the foregoing considerations to be mistaken. It does not, however, show that use is irrelevant to questions of meaning; far from it.

The notion of a systematic and general theory of meaning for a language, just suggested, leads on to the topic of the next chapter, and accordingly this is a suitable point to leave discussion of earlier options in the pursuit of an account of meaning. Of the theories discussed in this chapter, the verificationist and use theories in particular provide materials which it is useful to carry forward.

NOTES

1. cf. Chomsky, N., *Cartesian Linguistics,* New York, 1966; *Language and Mind,* New York, 1968.
2. cf. Katz. J. *The Philosophy of Language,* New York, 1966.
3. Lehrer, K., and Lehrer, A., *Theory of Meaning,* New Jersey, 1970.
4. Some philosophers, like Lehrer and perhaps Bernard Harrison, would disagree with the characterisation I am giving here.
5. Wittgenstein, L., *Philosophical Investigations* (tr. Anscombe, G. E. M.) London, 1963,55 119, 133.
6. Russell, B., *The Principles of Mathematics,* Cambridge, 1903, p.47.
7. Strawson, P. F., 'On Referring', in Feigl *et. al., op. cit.,* p.40.
8. ibid.
9. Russell, *The Analysis of Mind,* London, 1921, p.191.
10. cf. Alston, *op. cit.* p.2 .
11. Strawson, 'Identifying Reference and Truth Values', *Logico-Linguistic Papers,* London, 1971, *passim.*
12. Austin, J. L., 'The Meaning of a Word', in Feigl *et. al., op. cit.,* p.232.
13. That is, I take it for the purposes of the following discussion that one can talk of *terms* referring, even if it is only because they have a referring *use* (i.e., such that speakers alone refer, but by their use.)
14. cf. e.g. Donnellan, K., 'Reference and Definite Descriptions' and 'Speaking of Nothing' in Schwartz, S. P., *Naming, Necessity and Natural Kinds,* Cornell, 1977, p.13 *et seq.* and p.216 *et seq.*; Kripke, 'Identity and Necessity', in Schwartz *op. cit.,* p.66 *et seq.*; Putnam, H., 'Is Semantics Possible?' and 'Meaning and Reference', in Schwartz *op. cit.,* p.102 *et seq.,* and p.119 *et seq.*
15. Putnam, *op. cit.,* p.103.
16. Donnellan, *op. cit.,* p.46 *et seq.*
17. Kripke, *op. cit.,* p.62 *et seq.,* esp. pp.72-4.
18. cf. ibid., p.88 *et seq.*
19. cf. the discussion in chapter 3 above.
20. cf. Putnam 'Meaning and Reference', *op. cit.,* p.119 *et seq.,* esp. p.127-9.
21. Kripke, ibid.
22. Donnellan, 'Speaking of Nothing', *op. ct.,* p.216 *et seq.*
23. Evans, G., 'The Causal theory of Names', in Schwartz *op. cit.,* p.192 *et seq.*
24. Donnellan, ibid.
25. cf. Dummet M. A. E., *Frege,* Duckworth, 1973, p.40.
26. Mill, J. S., *A System of Logic,* London, 1886, I.ii.3.
27. Putnam, 'The Meaning of "Meaning" ', in Gunderson, K., (ed.), *Language, Mind and Knowledge,* Minnesota, 1975; cf. pp.104-5.
28. cf. Schwartz, in Schwartz *op. cit.,* pp.39-40.
29. Locke, J., *Essay Concerning Human Understanding* III.2.1.
30. cf. the relevant papers in Pitcher, G., (ed.), *Wittgenstein: Critical Essays,* London, 1966.
31. Locke, *Essay,* III.7.1.
32. cf. Winch, P., *The Idea of a Social Science,* London 1958.
33. Although not by Pavlov himself; his work only became known outside Russia comparatively late.
34. This view is to be found in the literature – particularly the early literature – of behavioural psychology.
35. cf. e.g., Bloomfield, L., *Language,* London, 1935.
36. An account of meaning which turns specifically on the utterer's intentions in

communicating something to his audience is given by Grice, H. P., 'Utterer's Meaning, Sentence Meaning, and Word Meaning', in Searle, J., (ed.), *Philosophy of Language*, Oxford, 1971. Strawson has defended this approach to meaning too; cf. his *Logico-Linguistic Papers*, op. cit., and particularly his 'Meaning and Truth', the Inaugural Lecture at Oxford, reprinted in Honderich, T., and Burnyeat, M., *Philosophy As It Is*, London, 1979, pp.519-39.

37. cf. Morris, C., *Signs, Language and Behaviour*, New Jersey, 1946, esp. chapter 1; and Osgood, C., *Method and Theory in Experimental Psychology*, New York, 1953, chapter 16.

38. Quine, W. V. O., *From A Logical Point of View,* Harvard, 1953, Essays II, III, and VII.

39. cf. chaper 8 below.

40. Quine, *The Roots of Reference,* La Salle, 1973; see also *Word and Object* chapter III.

41. cf. ibid., pp.3-4; pp.35-7.

42. ibid., pp.37-49; pp.62-8.

43. ibid., p.67 *et seq.*; pt.III *passim*.

44. cf. Wilks, K., *Physicalism*, London, 1978.

45. Strawson, Lectures in Oxford 1977-9. (Unpublished.)

46. Schlick, M., 'Meaning and Verification', in Feigl and Sellars *Readings In Philosophical Analysis* New York 1949.

47. Ayer, A. J., *Language, Truth and Logic,* 2nd Ed., London, 1946.

48. Ayer, 'Introduction', in Ayer (ed.), *Logical Positivism*, London, 1959, p.10.

49. ibid.

50. Hume, D., *Enquiry Concerning Human Understanding,* §XII Pt. III.

51. Strictly speaking, Wittgenstein viewed mathematical propositions as identities, but the view is the same in net.

52. cf. Ayer, *Language, Truth and Logic,* Preface to the 2nd. Ed., *passim*.

53. ibid.

54. Feyerabend, P., *Against Method*, London, 1975.

55. Waismann, F., 'Verifiability', *Proceedings of the Aristotelian Society* 1945.

56. Ayer, *Logical Positivism*, p.15.

57. ibid.

58. Schlick, ibid.

59. Bridgman, P. W., *The Logic of Modern Physics* New York 1960.

60. Schlick, ibid.

61. cf. Quine, 'Two Dogmas', *op. cit.*

62. Wittgenstein, *Philosophical Investigations,* 421.

63. ibid., 43.

64. ibid., 23.

65. ibid., cf. 10, 27, 30, 32.

66. ibid., cf., e.g., 11, 17, 274, 556, 559.

67. ibid., e.g., 5, and also 6, 8, 398.

68. ibid., e.g., 402.

69. ibid., e.g., (respectively) 103, 108, 421.

70. ibid. 66 ff.

71. cf. Alston, W. P., 'Meaning and Use', *Philosophical Quarterly,* 1963, reprinted in Feigl *et al., New Readings* New York, 1972, cf. p.243.

72. Quinton, A. M., 'Contemporary British Philosophy', in O'Connor, D. J., (ed.), *A Critical History of Western Philosophy,* London, 1964, p.525 ff.; reprinted in Pitcher, *Wittgenstein, op. cit.,* pp.11-12.

73. Strawson, 'Review of the *Philosophical Investigations'*, *Mind,* LXIII, 1954; reprinted in Pitcher *op. cit.*

74. cf Alston *op. cit., passim*; and Pitcher, G., *The Philosophy of Wittgenstein*, New Jersey, 1964, chaper 10 *passim*.
75. Pitcher *op. cit.*, 1964, p.230.
76. Alston *op. cit.*, p.245.
77. Wittgenstein, op. cit., 19, 23, p.226.
78. ibid., p.223.
79. cf Pitcher *op. cit.*, 1964, p.243.
80. Wittgenstein *op. cit.*, 7.
81. Quoted in Malcolm, N., *Wittgenstein: A Memoir*, Oxford, 1958, p.93.
82. Wittgenstein, *op. cit.*, 132.
83. ibid., 38.
84. ibid., 109.
85. ibid., 309.
86. ibid., 664
87. ibid., 90.
88. ibid., 243-315, 350-1, 398-421.
89. cf. chapter 4 above.
90. Austin, J. L., *Sense and Sensibilia*, Oxford, 1962; *passim*. Ayer is the main target in this work, but not the only one; Price and Warnock are also in the firing-line.
91. cf. Pitcher *op. cit.*, 1964, p.252.
92. Austin, J. L., *How To Do Things With Words*, 2nd. Ed., Oxford, 1975, cf. Lecture VIII *passim*, p.94 *et seq*.
93. ibid., p.102.
94. Hare, R. M., *The Language of Morals*, Oxford, 19 2, p.27.
95. See above, chaper 6.
96. Searle, J., cf. e.g., 'Meaning and Speech-Acts', *Philosophical Review* 71, 1962; reprinted in Lehrer and Lehrer *op. cit.*, p.149 *et seq*.
97. ibid.
98. ibid., pp.151-2.
99. ibid., p. 152. Searle points out that 'commend' is doing duty for many verbs, but that ' "good" is used to commend' means '. . . commend, praise, approve, express satisfaction' and the like. So 'commend' here must be taken as 'commend etc.'
100. ibid.
101. ibid., p.153.
102. ibid., p.154.
103. cf. Dummett, M. A. E., 'Can Analytic Philosophy be Systematic, and Ought it to be?', *Truth and Other Enigmas*, London, 1978, pp.450-1.

8 Truth, Meaning, Realism and Antirealism

INTRODUCTION

The last chaper contained informal discussions of some 'traditional' theories of meaning, together with certain contemporary extensions of them. In this chapter I look in some detail at major approaches to the question of meaning, beginning with a discussion of truth-conditional semantics, and going on to discuss the wider issue of whether meaning can indeed be accounted for in terms of truth-conditions, where truth is understood in an objective 'realist' sense, or whether an alternative conception, 'antirealist' in character, is required to serve as the key concept in the theory of meaning. The discussion in this chapter as a whole may be seen as arising from the question, what should a theory of meaning be like?

The proposals and counter-proposals which follow are of the very first importance in contemporary philosophy, because whichever option one chooses, profound metaphysical consequences flow from it. In the next, concluding, chapter I shall take up and discuss certain of those consequences.

TRUTH AND MEANING

An idea which has been current since Frege, and which has, for the most part, grown in persuasiveness as it has received more detailed investigation, is that the meaning of a sentence can be given by stating the conditions under which it is true. In addition to Frege, this view has been held by, among others, Wittgenstein, Carnap, Quine, and − as its chief apologist and most recent proponent − Davidson.

It will be recalled from chapter 2 that Frege took the view that names have both references and senses, and that sentences, as a species of complex *names*, have as their references either The True or The False; which is to say that sentences are, in Frege's view, the names of truth-values. The thought or sense expressed by a sentence is determined by the conditions under which the (sentence)-name designates The True; and the sense of this name 'is the sense or thought that these conditions are fulfilled'.[1] Wittgenstein in the *Tractatus* gave a more direct expression of this idea – 'To know the meaning of a sentence is to know what is the case if it is true',[2] and Carnap later did likewise – 'To know the meaning of a sentence is to know in which of the possible cases it would be true and in which not'.[3] It is this basic idea which Davidson, in particular, has been concerned to work out in detail.

A point I have had frequent occasion to iterate in earlier chapters is that by investigating language one thereby investigates the world. Davidson puts the same point by saying that 'In making manifest the large features of our language, we make manifest the large features of reality'.[4] Accordingly, in his view, 'what we must attend to in language, if we want to bring into relief general features of the world, is what it is in general for a sentence in the language to be true.'[5] Before looking at the details of Davidson's proposals, it is interesting and valuable to note how they relate to the work of Frege, Tarski, and Quine, all of whom greatly influenced the truth-conditional theory of meaning Davidson has been concerned to develop.

Frege stressed the importance of showing how the semantic constituents of sentences determine the truth of those sentences, and he suggested ways in which an account of his kind could be applied to regions of natural language. He did not think in terms of a general truth-theory for natural language, however, because he took natural languages to be defective and recalcitrant; and accordingly he proposed, and effected, the construction of an improved language, for which he deivsed a notation whose syntax clearly reflected the interpretation intended for it. This language he believed to have the same expressive power as important tracts of natural language. However, in part because of his pessimism over natural language, and in part because of the artificiality of certain of his innovations – as, for example, treating sentences as names – Frege's work cannot, in Davidson's view, be applied directly to the matter of investigating meaning – and metaphysics – in natural language as such.[6]

An essential ingredient in Davidson's theory was provided by Quine; namely, the demonstration, as Davidson views it, of how an holistic approach to the problem of language-understanding furnishes the empirical foundations needed by the theory. 'If metaphysical conclusions are to be drawn from a theory of truth in the way that I propose,' Davidson says, 'the approach to language must be holistic,' that is, must treat the language inclusively and as a whole, a whole whose properties are no mere functions of the properties of its parts.[7] Quine did not himself see holism as having the metaphysical import which Davidson attaches to it, for he did not make truth-theory central either to the question of language's ontological significance, or to the matter of investigating language's logical form. Moreover he shared Frege's view that the purpose of devising a regimented language is to improve on natural language, rather than to find a tool for its investigation. Indeed Quine went further than Frege, taking it that regimentation not only makes for better language but also better science. Accordingly Quine's metaphysics attach to his logic and not to natural language; Davidson, by contrast, sees logic as a device for exploring natural language itself.[8]

The inspiration for Davidson's proposals derives from Tarski's work on truth. The Tarskian theory consists in an enumeration of the semantic properties of the items in a finite vocabulary, together with a recursive characterisation of the infinity of sentences which can be generated from that vocabulary; which characterisation turns on the 'subtle and powerful concept (satisfaction) which relates both sentences and non-sentential expressions to objects in the world'.[9] The details of Davidson's application of Tarski's work, together with extensions and modifications of it to account for indexicality and other problematic features of natural language, are described below. What is important for Davidson's purposes is that use of Tarski's notion allows the truth-theory for natural language to do what is centrally required, *viz.*, to reveal and articulate *structure* in the language, which is just what is required if a systematic and comprehensive theory of truth for the language is to yield the results on meaning and metaphysics which we are eager to obtain.

The first task, then, is to look at the substance of Davidson's proposals, in order to see how a truth-conditional approach to meaning unpacks in detail. It will then be necessary to take up and explore a question which is, effectively, begged by the foregoing remarks: *Is* truth the right concept to employ at the centre of an attempt to investigate meaning (and metaphysics) in natural language? And if it is not, what alernative concept should be employed? The work recently done by Dummett is of crucial importance in this connection.

DAVIDSON'S PROPOSALS

Davidson begins by observing that any adequate theory of meaning must satisfy four conditions:

(i)   it must enable us to 'give the meaning' for each sentence of the natural language L we are studying;[10]

(ii)   it must show how the sentences of L are semantically compounded from the finite stock of L's words by means of L's rules for combining those words;[11].

(iii)   it must show that its demonstration of how sentences of L mean is based on the same stock of concepts as L's sentences themselves;[12] and

(iv)   it must be empirically testable.[13]

None of these requirements is particularly controversial; but the claim that a theory of truth for L will satisfy them *is* controversial, the more so because Davidson holds that a theory of truth for L will also amount to a theory of L's logical form, and, further, will reveal the ontological presuppositions of our language, and in this way, as noted, lead to the discovery of metaphysically exciting results.

Davidson insists that any adequate theory of meaning must make it clear how the meanings of sentences in any L depend upon the meaning of their constituent words. Unless sentence-meaning is a function of word-meaning in this way, it is difficult to see how anyone could learn L. Speakers of L have a creative ability to construct and comprehend sentences they have never encountered before; which is to say, from L's finite stock of words, and the rules governing their combination and use, an (at least potentially) infinite stock of sentences can be produced and understood by L's speakers. To say that an adequate theory of meaning must give an account of this is to say, on Davidson's view, that such a theory must yield all sentences of the form

(1) s means m

where 's' is a description of some sentence which specifies its structure, and 'm' is an expression which denotes that sentence's meaning. But appeal to the notion of a sentence's meaning is, says Davidson, unhelpful, as is reformulating (1) as

(2) s means that p

where 'p' is the sentence described by 's'; since 'means that' is obviously no less problematic than the notion of something's being 'the meaning' of a sentence. Accordingly Davidson reformulates (2), using an arbitrary predicate 'T' to replace 'means that' by 'is T iff'. In (2) the idea was that 'p' is a sentence which means the same as the sentence described by 's', but since the appeal to meaning is obscure, a more perspicuous surrogate needs to be found. If the conditions on 's' and 'p' as just given (namely, that 's' is a structure-specifying description of the sentence 'p') are held in view for the use of the arbitrary predicate 'T', then (2) can be reformulated as

(3) s is T iff p.

Now, any predicate which satisfies this condition is, Tarski-style, a materially adequate *truth* predicate; and this is exactly what Davidson wants, because in his view what a theory of meaning should provide is just such a definition for just such a truth predicate.[14] This comes down to saying what is not exactly new, namely that the meaning of a sentence is to be given by stating its truth-conditions; the difference is that the demand is made with the added muscle of Tarski-style constraints on those truth-conditions.

Although the basic model for Davidson's truth-theoretical approach is afforded by Tarski's semantic theory of truth, the approach is not too closely tied to that model. For Davidson's purposes it is sufficient that the required species of truth theory entails a statement of the conditions under which every sentence of L is true. Take as an example the simplest case, that of an unambiguous declarative sentence free from indexicals and demonstratives (that is, free from references to particular times, places, and utterers, or objects picked out demonstratively by terms such as 'this' and 'that'). Then Davidson's demand is for a theory which will entail an infinite number of biconditional statements of the form

(4) s is true iff p.

Note how this is a reformulation of (3); the arbitrary predicate 'T' has disappeared in favour of 'true', and we have an explicit truth-conditional form. Bear in mind that 's' is a structural description of a sentence, and 'p' (where the object language is contained in the metalanguage in which the description 's' occurs) is that sentence itself. (Where the object language and the metalanguage differ, 'p' will be replaced by a translation of the sentence described by 's'.)

It is important for Davidson's purposes that the number of non-logical axioms in a truth theory must be finite; for if it were not, that is, if we take as axioms of the theory every instance of (4), then requirement (ii) specified above would be violated. In this way Davidson excludes trivial theories with infinite axiom schemata, and restricts attention to Tarski-style truth theory.

So much for the bare bones of Davidson's proposal. Now let us see what its point is supposed to be.

Something it is important to grasp in understanding Davidson's proposal is that 'is true iff' is not intended merely as a perspicuous alternative reading of 'means that'. For one thing, 'is true iff' and 'means that' are not synonymous. The context following 'is true iff' is truth-functional, whereas the context following 'means that' is not. The difference is crucial; if 'means that' were truth-functional, all true sentences would mean the same. What Davidson is arguing for is an elimination of the 'obscure' idiom of meaning, and its replacement by the more tractable extensional idiom of truth and truth-conditions.

This follows Quine's separation of semantic notions into two groups, the first consisting in theories of reference, that is, exensional theories turning on or essentially involving notions like 'designates', 'saisfies', and 'is true'. and the second consisting in theories of meaning, that is, intensional theories turning on or essentially involving notions like synonymy and analyticity. Quine's view is that theories of reference are more philosophically promising, and in 'better shape', than intensional theories, which are infected by the uncomfortable obscurities of the concept of meaning itself.[15]

Accordingly, Davidson writes:

The theory of meaning will have done its work if it provides, for every sentence 's' in the language under study, a matching sentence (to replace 'p' in 's means that p') that, in some way yet to be made clear, 'gives the meaning' of 's'. One obvious candidate for the matching sentence is just 's' itself, if the object language is contained in the metalanguage: otherwise a translation of 's' in the metalanguage. As a final bold step, let us try treating the position occupied by 'p' extensionally; to implement this, sweep away the obscure 'means that', provide the sentence that replaces 'p' with a proper sentential connective, and supply the description that replaces 's' with its own predicate. The plausible result is
(T) s is T iff p
What we require of a theory of meaning for a language L is that without appeal to any (further) semantical notions, it places enough restrictions on the predicate 'is T' to entail all sentences got from schema (T) when 's' is replaced by a structural description of a sentence and 'p' by that sentence.[16]

The phrase 'sweep away the obscure "means that" ' indicates a revisionist line in Davidson's semantical programme which accords with the revisionary line to be found in Quine. It is not at all fortuitous that in Quine's work, notably in *Word and Object,* the point is iterated that 'ascent' from ordinary ways of talking to the more exact idioms of logic, or logic-informed discourse, provides a better purchase on philosophical problems, despite the fact that in making the ascent from the informal to the formal mode, not all that is contained in the informal mode is preserved; which is to say that the more formal way of doing things is not, except in a methodological sense, a substitute for the informal way, since the formal and informal discourses are not synonymous. Rather in this way, Davidson is saying that leaving 'means' behind and looking to truth for a solution to semantical problems constitutes an ascent of sorts, which does not merely substitute for talk of meaning, but provides a different and more tractable way of handling the set of issues hitherto associated with talk of meaning. The 'bold step' which consists in 'treating the position occupied by "p" extensionally', thus accords with Quine's view of the matter, and makes for what Davidson thinks to be an at least promising attempt to overcome the difficulies inherent in Quine's second and unhappy group of semantic concepts by concentrating only on notions in the first and happier group.

Still, these considerations do not settle much; they are rather general. It remains necessary to ask *exactly* what reasons there are for thinking that supplanting talk of meaning by talk of truth will result in a satisfactory semantic theory. Let us retrace a few steps.

The passage quoted from Davidson above issues in the conclusion that what is wanted of a theory of meaning is that it should so place constraints on the predicate 'is T' that the theory will entail all (T)-sentences, bearing in mind that (T)-sentences are biconditionals in which 's' is in every case a standardised structural description of 'p'. This is to say that what is wanted of a theory of meaning appears to be precisely what is supplied by Tarski's proposed criterion of adequacy for any formal truth definition. The predicate 'is T' and the truth predicate are coextensive; 'isT' will apply to nothing other than all the true sentences of L. Accordingly, in Davidson's view, 'a theory of meaning for a language L shows "how the meanings of sentences depend upon the meanings of words" if it contains a [recursive] definition of truth-in-L',[17] the idea being that we must demonstrate how the truth-conditions for sentences are determined by the semantic features of the constituents of those sentences together with the semantic significance of their structure.

The requirement, remember, is that a theory of meaning should supply pairings between sentences of the object language with sentences of the metalanguage, in a way which will 'give the meaning' of the object language sentences. Davidson argues that it is more fruitful to sweep away intensionality (that is, talk of 'means' as in 's means that p'), and make the context extensional (that is, truth-functional). If we ask, how should this be done? the most obvious answer is that we should employ the biconditional form, since the aim is to arrive somehow at equivalence of meaning between s and p. We could try 's≡p' for this purpose, but 's≡p' is ill-formed; for 's' is effectively a name, so that the biconditional here says something like 'Roger if and only if snow is white'. The biconditional is a *sentential* connective; 's' therefore must be turned into a sentence by predicating something of it. Let us take an arbitrary predicate 'X' and attach it to 's'; the biconditional now becomes a well-formed '(s is X) ≡ p'. And here is where the trick is turned: the metalanguage sentence p is intended somehow to 'give the meaning' of s. If it does so, ' . . . is X' and the Tarski truth predicate are at least coextensive; and therefore, because no other reading of '. . .is X' readily suggests itself, it is highly convenient to interpret it as 'is true'. [18]

But this way of substituting talk of truth for talk of meaning, although plausible on the face of it, is not strictly an argument which settles that Davidson's proposal is the right way, or even the best way, to give a theory of meaning. In fact, as it stands, the proposal will not do. To see why, it is necessary to look at an important supplementary element in Davidson's thought, concerning the notion of *interpretation*.

Davidson argues that in interpreting someone else's discourse, whether his discourse consists in another language or one's own, we require a way of telling when a sentence 'p' of the metalanguage has the meaning possessed by the sentence uttered by that someone else and described by 's'. An empirical test of whether the Tarski condition is met by some such sentence as '*Schnee ist weiss* is true iff snow is white' is to check whether speakers of German hold true '*Schnee ist weiss*' if and only if snow is white. The idea, according to Davidson, is that one discovers the meaning of a speaker's utterances by invoking a notion of what the speaker *holds true*; meaning is discovered by holding the speaker's beliefs constant. A principle is employed here, the 'principle of charity', which states that speakers generally agree upon what is in fact the case. Davidson's views in this respect are holistic in the same way as Quine's; the idea is that the basic unit of interpretation is the language as a whole, which echoes the epistemological thesis, insisted upon by Quine, to the effect that beliefs are not individually testable, but that the corpus of beliefs as a whole is the unit to which verification and falsification apply.

Now, where Davidson's proposal goes awry is that whereas this notion of *interpretation* or *translation* is one which Tarski justifiably employed in defining the truth predicate (it is a condition on 's is true iff p' that p be a translation of s, with homophonic, i.e., same-language, translation as the simplest case), it cannot do for a theory of meaning, for if we are setting out to construct a theory of meaning, translation must be the *consequence* of, and not an integral part of, the theory of meaning itself. Accordingly it appears to be a mistake to think that use of a Tarski truth predicate does the work we require of a theory of meaning; we do not, at any rate as yet, have a reason for selecting *truth* as the key concept in such a theory. Why, therefore, truth?

I shall return to this question in a more general way shortly. There are other problems in Davidson's proposal to look at first.

PARADOX AND OTHER PROBLEMS

If the appeal to truth is considered, for the moment, unexceptionable, what other difficulties does Davidson's proposal face?

Tarski, it will be recalled from chapter 6, was deeply pessimistic about the relevance of his theory to natural languages. Davidson evidently is not. Two features of natural language particularly troubled Tarski; one is that their semantic closedness leads to paradoxes, and the other is that they are too amorphous, confused, and changeable to admit the application of formal techniques. It is important therefore to see what Davidson has to say about these problems.

On the first head – the paradoxes – his reply is that Tarski's point 'deserves a serious answer, and I wish I had one'; nevertheless 'I think we are justified in carrying on without having disinfected this particular source of conceptual anxiety',[19] for these reasons. In Davidson's view, paradox arises because of the over-generous scope of the quantifiers in natural languages; but, he says, for one thing, this fact does not exclude our being able to give an explicit definition of true-in-L for any natural L, and for another thing, attention can anyway be restricted to those fragments of natural languages where the risk of paradox is minimal.[20]

On the second head – formal specifiability – Davidson admits that, if it were true that natural language would have to be refined out of all recognition in order to admit the application of formal techniques, then that fact would be 'fatal' to his project,[21] for the task of the theory of meaning is not to reform but to describe L. His response is to waive pessimism –

Let us look at the positive side. Tarski has shown the way to giving a theory for interpreted formal languages of various kinds; pick one as much like English as possible. Since this new language has been explained in English and contains much English we not only may, but I think must, view it as part of English for those who understand it. For this fragment of English we have, *ex hypothesi,* a theory of the required sort.[22]

Tarski's doubts centred upon the fact that natural languages are growing and changing, and contain a plethora of features which are difficult to formalise, such as vagueness, indexicality and ambiguity. Davidson thinks that although a certain amount of 'tidying up' will be necessary before Tarski's truth theory can be grafted on to natural language, nevertheless by starting from a tractable fragment and extending outwards bit by bit, any difficulties in applying the theory can be overcome. (Davidson observes 'it's good to know we shan't run out of work'.)[23]

One of the problems facing a Davidsonian programme – indexicality – might, for example, be handled as follows. The presence of indexicals in natural language simply requires viewing truth as a predicate of utterances rather than sentences, and relativising application of the predicate to speakers and times. Then the extended T-schema will require the theory to entail such sentences as ' "I am tired" (s,t) is true iff s is tired at t'.[24] For demonstratives ('this', 'that'), the account to be given is that 'this is X' is true iff the object picked out by the speaker's use of 'this' satisfies '. . .is X' at the time of utterance.[25] And so on for like cases.

Nevertheless, Davidson early admitted the extent of the task facing his proposal: 'But it must be allowed that a staggering list of difficulties and conundrums remain'.[26] On some of the issues he lists, Davidson has since claimed progress, particularly with respect to propositional attitudes, quotations, adverbs,[27] proper names,[28] imperatives,[29] mass terms, and comparatives.[30] Nevertheless the progress that has been made has depended upon assuming the validity of Davidson's approach as a starting-point, and although success on these and other items in Davidson's 'staggering list' would count towards a vindication of the approach, the question remains whether selecting truth as the key concept in the theory of meaning will do. To that question I now return.

WHY TRUTH?

One reason why truth might serve as the key concept in the theory of meaning is that, on the face of it, it provides for an empirically testable theory. This is the fourth requirement, listed above, on a satisfactory theory of meaning. Davidson claims that this is where his own approach does best. The claim merits assessment.

The truth-conditions approach 'has been characterised', says Davidson, 'as issuing in a flood of sentences each giving the truth-conditions of a sentence', so to test the theory 'we need only ask, in selected cases, whether what the theory avers to be the truth-conditions for a sentence really are. A typical case might involve deciding whether the sentence "snow is white" *is* true if and only if snow is white'.[31] The decision procedure is quite straightforward: all that is required is the ability to recognise as true the T-sentences entailed by the theory. For the simplest cases 'it is no harder to test the empirical adequacy' of the theory 'than it is for a competent speaker of English to decide whether sentences like " 'snow is white' is true if and only if snow is white" are true'.[32] In Davidson's view this is analogous to the empirical checks available on a theory of generative grammar; a grammar provides, in potentially infinite numbers, entailments of sentences of the form 's is grammatical', and the chief method of checking the grammar's correctness is to test its deliverances against the 'linguistic intuitions' of speakers.[33] For the semantic theory the homophonic case is straightforward; in the case where metalanguage and object language differ, testing the theory involves determining whether the right- and left-hand-sides of the biconditional have the same truth-value. As noted, Davidson's choice of technique for this enterprise is the method of 'radical translation':

We will try to notice under what conditions the alien speaker assents to or dissents from a variety of his sentences. The relevant conditions will, of course, be what we take to be the truth-conditions of his sentences. We will have to assume that most of his assents are to true, and his dissents from false, sentences − an inevitable assumption since the alternative is unintelligible.[34]

It would indeed seem plausible to think that an empirically testable theory of meaning is best grounded on appeal to assent and dissent patterns, since these appear to carry relatively little theoretical burden;[35] and there is a manifest connection between truth and the notions of assent and dissent. Accordingly, this connection might be argued to count as a good reason for forging links between truth and meaning of the kind suggested.

Is it, though, a good reason? First, it is needful to note that it will be a *good* reason only if the truth theory in question is Tarskian. Part of what Davidson maintains is that a truth theory should issue in an account of logical truth, equivalence, and entailment for the object language. It happens that practically any theory which entails T-sentences for each sentence in a given language will say (in the metalanguage) that the logical truths of the object language are true; but this is trivial, or at least will hardly amount to a theory of the object language's logical form. Tarskian theories, however, show how the truth conditions of sentences depend upon those of their parts, and in doing so entail not just that certain sentences are true, but that every sentence *of a given form* is true; which class of sentences can therefore be specified as the object language's logical truths. The merit of Tarskian truth theories is that they entail generalisations, based on a notion of sentence *structure*, about true sentences; which is what entitles them to be plausible candidates for theories of logical form. Accordingly Davidson holds that his choice of theory 'entails not only that [given] sentences are true but that they will remain true under all significant rewritings of their logical parts'.[36] The connection with testability then goes through: 'It is hard to imagine how a theory of meaning could fail to read a logic into its object language to this degree; and to the extent that it does, our intuitions of logical truth, equivalence, and entailment may be called upon in constructing and testing the theory.'[37]

What is wrong with this, however, is that speakers' intuitions turn out to be the *only* test for the theory. In the absence of anything else, the theory may as well be reconstrued as a theory about speakers' intuitions, one which sets out to describe and perhaps to explain them; but then it is extraordinarily puzzling to know why such a theory should have the idiosyncratic and restricted form proposed by Davidson, particularly when, on the face of it, a theory of semantic intuition would be better allied to a theory of syntactic intuition, in marriage with which latter a Davidsonian truth theory constitutes a somewhat improbable partner. Certainly a Davidsonian theory could not propose itself as the simplest or most natural theory of speakers' intuitions, and that raises a question-mark over the idea from the outset.[38]

However, that cavil may be left aside. Other suggsted reasons for thinking that the appeal to Tarski-style truth does the required trick are these. Even although the claim that 'the meaning of sentences is given by their truth-conditions' is very vague, indeed 'too vague to be of any use as it stands' as one commentator put it,[39] it is not clear that there is any obvious alternative. Tarskian truth theory has the independent merit of precision, particularly in the sense that it shows how the truth-conditions of sentences are determined by the truth-conditions of their constituent items. What is required, it will be remembered, is that the meaning of sentences should somehow be explained as a function of the meanings of their parts; by substituting talk of Tarskian truth for meaning, the requirement that this form of explanation be given becomes sharply realisable. Moreover, if we employ Tarskian notions, *system* can be added to precision, for the Tarskian device equips us to deal with a potential infinity of sentences in the language for which we are trying to construct a theory. Despite the fact that statements of truth-conditions in the form of T-sentences are individually all but trivial (Davidson himself calls them 'snow-bound trivialities'), the point is that the Tarskian device provides a way of proving *all* the near-trivial T-sentences, showing not just what the truth-conditions of a given sentence are but how they are determined.[40] We might accordingly allow ourselves to be encouraged by the thought, or inclined towards the thought, that an appeal to truth — specifically, to Tarskian truth — will serve us well in this area.

These however are only *inclining* reasons.[41] Perhaps the absence of a fully compelling reason results from too exclusive a concentration on the notion of truth itself. Perhaps what should be looked for instead is how, in a more general survey of what a theory of meaning should be like, the notion of truth plays a part. Certainly, despite early enthusiasm over the unlocking powers of truth as a key concept in talk of meaning, it is now at least clear that it is not a *sufficient* condition for a sentence s to 'mean (in L) that p' that 's is true (in L) iff p'; something more has to be said.

TRUTH AND A THEORY OF LINGUISTIC BEHAVIOUR

One way that the appeal to truth might be vindicated, then, is to see how it fits into a more general theory. McDowell offers such an approach.[42] The idea is that we begin by locating the place of a theory of meaning in a more inclusive theory of behaviour, and in doing so uncover the links between truth and meaning. One benefit of this tack is that it removes the uncomfortable need, manifest in any theory which *starts* with truth, to give from the outset a rich enough and sound enough characterisation of truth to enable it to bear the load of theory it must go on to carry. Doing so is not easy. For one thing, there are no compelling reasons, as noted above, why we should start with truth anyway; and for another, it would not be satisfactory to begin with an axiomatic definition of truth, or any notion of truth relativised for its intelligibility to a given language, because the threat of circularity reduces the value of using such a notion of truth to explain meaning.[43]

Accordingly, McDowell's proposal is to start with the idea that seeing how sentences of a metalanguage and its object language are to be paired must be treated as a component in a theory describing 'what is involved in understanding a language'.[44] That component of a theory of understanding will be a theory of *sense*, and it will need to be worked out in conjunction with a theory of *force*,[45] the point of which is to provide us with the means to identify linguistic actions (making assertions, giving commands, asking questions) and therefore the types of propositional acts they consist in (assertion, command, question); and additionally to correlate an indicative sentence with each imperative, question, and so on, so that their propositional contents are clear. The theories of sense and force will then, in combination, and with neither of them being primary, fit into a wider picture of speakers' behaviour, both linguistic and non-linguistic, in such a way that the speakers' behaviour can be rendered intelligible in the light of their beliefs, desires, and other propositional attitudes. 'Understanding linguistic behaviour, and hence understanding language,' McDowell says, 'involves no more than a special case of understanding what behaviour, in general, involves.'

The connection between s and p in the incorporated theory of sense can be seen, then, to play this role: 'p' contributes to an unpacking of the propositional content of acts performed by use of 's'. Accordingly the way 's' and 'p' are to be paired invites attention. The theory has to show how 'p' specifies the propositional content of 's', and evidently what we require is that the pairing device be such that 'p' says the same thing, performs the same (or can be used to perform the same) propositional act, as 's'. Placing 'is true iff' between 's' and 'p' acceptably does the trick.[47] 'That the truth predicate is insertable is a discovery: the general ruminations about the role of a theory of meaning within an explanation of behaviour can be appreciated *before* the adequacy of the truth-predicate is realised'.[48] The minimal idea of the truth predicate as a disquotation device is all that is required to see that 'truth is what a theory of sense is a theory of', which is *not,* note, to say that '*sense* is what a theory of truth is a theory of'.[49]

Why should the truth predicate be invoked here? Is it the only available way of pairing 's' and 'p'? These questions can be recast as: why 'iff', and why '. . .is *true*' (rather than some other predicate)? The reply is that 'iff', as an extensional connective, makes the proof theory unproblematic, for it is after all equivalence between 's' and 'p' which is being sought, either of sense or (at an earlier stage) of the propositional acts performed. And ' . . . is true' is invoked, according to Platts, because

(a)This does indeed give us the doctrine that the meaning of a sentence is given by stating its truth-conditions . . . (b)We build a bridge with the least theoretically loaded evidential base, and so ease the route to an empirical theory of meaning. (c)We obtain a connection with Tarski's work on truth, a connection that replaces vagueness by precision . . . and . . . provides he essential systematic structure within a theory of meaning.[50]

In McDowell's proposals, the question of precisely what is to fill the gap in 's . . . p' could be left open by using an unspecified predicate 'f' thus: 's is f iff p'; but the requirement that the theory of sense should interact with the theory of force ensures that an acceptable theory of sense will remain acceptable if 'f' is replaced by 'true'.[51] Nevertheless, as McDowell points out, a concept of truth as such does not *have* to be involved in setting up the theory of sense, and a theory of force need not even be 'sensitive' to the syntactic form of what fills the gap between 's' and 'p'; so the theory of meaning, couched in terms of a general theory of linguistic behaviour, does not turn upon an *initial* obligation to elucidate truth.[52] Still, the Tarskian truth predicate fits the bill as a replacement for 'f' and brings with it all the benefits listed by Platts. Indeed, because 'true' will substitute acceptably for any 'f' in terms of this theory, it will remain that the theory of sense will specify truth-conditions for sentences, as Frege thought, whether directly or by 'justifiable conversion' of any 'f' into 'true'.[53]

These considerations lend strength to the idea that an appeal to truth is appropriate. Indeed, the appeal to truth appears, on the foregoing, to be more than merely appropriate − it appears to be powerful and suggestive. Nevertheless it must be borne in mind that it is not *forced*; that is, we are not compelled by the foregoing considerations to employ the concept of truth, we are merely given a number of persuasive reasons why we might use it. It is note-worthy that the foregoing arguments mix together reasons why the concept *can* be used with reasons why it *should* be used, as though the fact that it *can* be used counted towards reasons why it should. Presumably, the argument is this: the fact that the concept of truth *can* be used counts as a reason why it *should* be used in view of the precision, system, and so forth, which the well-defined Tarskian recursive notion offers. That is a reasonable point, so long, again, as one does not take it to settle that use of such a notion of truth in the theory of meaning is inescapable.

It should by now be obvious that the question of the place of a concept of truth in the theory of meaning is crucial. And indeed this is precisely where the fur is made most to fly in the contemporary debate on meaning. The reason why is set out by Dummett.

TRUTH AND REALISM

In Dummett's view, any theory which has it that the meaning of sentences, in a given class of sentences, is to be specified in terms of truth-conditions, is equivalent to *realism* concerning the subject matter of that class of sentences.[54] Realism is the thesis that the world is determinately constituted, that is, has its character in-dependently of any knowledge or experience of it, so that sentences about the world are either determinately true or false in virtue of the way things are in the world, whether or not we can come to know how things are in the world and thus whether or not we can come to know those sentences to be true or false. On a realist thesis, the truth-conditions of sentences in a given class of sentences may transcend our capacity to recognise whether or not they obtain. On a first approximation, then, realism with respect to a given class of sentences may be characterised as the thesis that the principle of bivalence holds for that class, whether or not we can tell what truth-value any sentence has. The 'principle of bivalence' is the principle that there are precisely two truth-values, namely 'true' and 'false'; the principle states that every sentence in a given class of sentences determinately possesses either one or other of them.

Drummett objects to the idea that meaning is to be accounted for in terms of a realist notion of truth precisely because such a notion places many sentences of the language beyond our capacity to *recognise* whether they are true or false. A transcendent notion of truth will not do, in Dummett's view, because what a theory of meaning must tell us is what speakers of a language *know* when they know (that is, understand) their language; and in telling us what speakers know, the theory must show how that knowledge equips speakers to derive every aspect of the use of sentences from whatever conditions govern the sense of those sentences. On Dummett's view, a realist theory fails to account for this connection between knowledge and use. Schematically, his argument is as follows (I give a more detailed account of it shortly).

A theory of meaning must tell us, as just noted, what speakers of a language L know in knowing what L's sentences mean. Therefore the theory must be a theoretical representation of propositional knowledge implicitly possessed by L's speakers; and it must show how that knowledge enables L's speakers to *use* L's sentences, that is, how L's speakers are able to apply their knowledge in the specific practical capacities constituting use of sentences of L. Therefore, if truth is taken to be the basic concept in the theory of meaning, then the theory must explain how knowledge of truth-conditions connects with actual language use. The demand that this connection be made plain is justified by two requirements on any acceptable theory of meaning: one is that we must be able to tell what counts as a speaker's *manifestation* of his knowledge of the meanings of L's sentences; and the other is that because language is a tool of communication, sense must be public, and accordingly what it is speakers know in knowing their language must not only be publicly observable in their linguistic behaviour, but also acquireable in public contexts. And this is where Dummett's objection to a theory of meaning based on a realist (that is, a transcendent) notion of truth comes in; for in his view, such a theory simply cannot satisfy the demand that these requirements be met.

The reason is this: If knowledge of truth-conditions is held to consist in an ability to know when a given sentence is true or false, that is, to recognise whether or not the sentence's truth-conditions obtain, then the connection between knowledge and use is un-problematic, for we have here a practical capacity connecting the conditions of sense for sentences (their truth-conditions, construed as decidable or recognisable) and the use to which those sentences can be put. Because *being able to recognise* whether or not truth-conditions obtain constitutes a practical mastery of a procedure for settling what truth-value a sentence has, 'understanding a sentence' comes down to having this recognitional capacity; thus, grasp of the sense of a sentence determines and is determined by the uses to which the sentence can be put — the connection between knowledge (knowing the meaning) and use is manifest. However, if truth-value is construed as a possibly recognition-transcendent property of sentences, as in the realist view it is, then what account is to be given of what it is to know the truth-conditions of sentences whose truth-values we are not able to establish? It is plainly impossible to associate grasp of the transcendent truth-conditions of certain sentences with the possession of an ability to recognise what their truth-values are, precisely because their truth-conditions are *transcendent*. For such sentences, then, we have no way of saying how knowledge of their truth-conditions can be manifested. But if we cannot say this, the theory does not show how sense and use connect — how, that is, sense and use determine each other. Accordingly any theory of meaning based on a transcendent concept, as in the case of a realist theory of meaning, is useless.

This is *not* to say that the notion of truth is irrelevant to the theory of meaning. Dummett holds that what is needful is a revised notion of truth; truth is to be thought of as a product of the verification procedures we employ in exercising our capacity to establish truth-value. To construe truth in this way is to reject realism.

Now, Dummett's proposed alternative conception of sense in terms of verification 'would', says McDowell, 'require a novel, anti-realist conception of the world: if truth is not independent of our discovering it, we must picture the world either as our own creation or, at least, as springing up in response to our investigations. So verificationist objections to a truth-conditions conception of sense would have far-reaching metaphysical implications.[55] Dummett's arguments against realism in the theory of meaning — particularly if they have anything like the consequences McDowell suggests — demand and indeed merit fuller treatment. Accordingly, armed with the foregoing paragraphs as a sketch-map, I shall go through Dummett's views now in more detail.

WHAT IS IT TO KNOW THE|TRUTH-CONDITIONS OF A SENTENCE?

Philosophical questions about meaning, Dummett holds, 'are best interpreted as questions about understanding: a dictum about what the meaning of an expression consists in must be construed as a thesis about what it is to *know* its meaning'.[56] Accordingly if truth is taken to be the key concept, then a truth-conditions theory is to be construed as one which states that to know the meaning of a sentence is to *know the condition for it to be true*. But what is it to know the truth-conditions of a sentence?

It has to be remembered that whatever knowing the truth-conditions of a sentence (=understanding that sentence) is, it has to depend upon an understanding of the words constituting the sentence and the significance of their arrangement. The problem therefore is: 'what is it that a speaker knows when he knows a language, and what, in particular, does he thereby know about any given sentence of the language?[57] Any theory offered in reply to this question will constitute a theoretical representation of a practical ability, *viz.*, the ability to speak the language. That theoretical representation will consist in a set of deductively connected propositions, and will be an explicit setting-out of the speaker's linguistic knowledge. Of course, the speaker will not himself have *explicit* knowledge of these propositions, but it is enough to attribute *implicit* knowledge to anyone who has mastery of a given practice, because we should not require that someone knows how to do something – for example, ride a bike or speak a language – only if he can spell out the underlying theory.[58] And if what is being attributed to the speaker is *implicit* knowledge, the theory of meaning 'must specify not merely what it is that the speaker must know, but . . . what counts as a *manifestation* of that knowledge,'[59] for if the theory did not do this, it would fail to be an account of the practical ability it is supposed to be a theory *of*. Thus at least some individual propositions of the theory must be correlated with specific practical linguistic abilities. (The demand that every proposition of the theory should do this would, however, be too strong.)

A distinction between *sense* and *force* is implicit in, and very important to, any theory of a meaning such as the one under consideration. The 'force' of an utterance, to reiterate, consists in the linguistic act effected by means of the utterance – asserting, asking, commanding, and so on. Without a sense-force distinction we should not at all know how to go about constructing a systematic account of language.[60] Now, in Dummett's view, 'someone who knows, of a given sentence, what condition must obtain for it to be true does not yet know all that he needs to know in order to grasp the significance of an utterance of that sentence'.[61] If we supposed that someone's knowing the truth-condition were enough, we should be smuggling in a notion to the effect that speakers understand how a sentence's truth-condition determines its conventional significance; but the point of a theory of meaning is to make *explicit* the presumed connection between a sentence's truth-conditions and the linguistic act performed by a use of that sentence. For one thing, a particular sentence can be used to perform different lingustic acts on different occasions, and it needs to be made clear how the truth-condition relates to the significance of each use; evidently therefore a theory of meaning will have to offer, in addition to an account of how the meaning of a sentence can be given by stating its truth-conditions, a supplementary account of those principles, relating to the notion of truth, which anyone has to grasp if he is to be able to derive the use of a sentence from the condition for its truth.[62]

Accordingly, any theory of meaning which takes truth as its basic notion will consist of two parts, a) a theory of reference couched within a theory of sense, and b) a theory of force giving us an account of the different linguistic acts which can be performed by utterances of the language's sentences. The core of part a) of the theory of meaning, which Dummett calls a 'theory of reference', will be a theory of truth, consisting in an inductive specification of the truth-conditions for sentences of the language. It is better called a theory of *reference* because, while some of its *theorems* will state the truth-conditions of sentences, its *axioms,* which govern individual words, will assign references to those words. The surrounding theory of sense specifies what a speaker knows in knowing the theory of reference, by correlating the speaker's practical linguistic abilities to certain propositions of the theory.[63] This characterisation of a theory of meaning shows that knowledge of truth-conditions is not *all* a speaker has to know; but it is all that a speaker has to know *specifically,* in connection with any given sentence, because the rest of what he has to know is *general* in nature, *viz.,* a set of general principles which enable him to derive every aspect of a sentence's use from its truth-conditions. This will be how things stand with any theory of meaning which has it that there is a single feature of a sentence − in this case, its truth-conditions − such that awareness of it amounts to a grasp of the sentence's meaning.[64]

And now the question to be asked is 'whether the concept of truth is the right choice for the *central notion* of a theory of meaning . . . or whether we need to employ some other notion in this role'.[65] On Dummett's view, so long as the notion of truth is taken for granted, it seems obvious that it is indeed the right notion to serve as the basis of a theory of meaning; but the moment we cease to take truth for granted, and subject it to investigation, the intuitive sense of its aptness for the role vanishes.[66]

This becomes apparent when we note that if we ask what analysis should be given of the notion of truth, or if we ask where we get the notion from, what we are effectively asking is: where, in the process of mastering a language, does a grasp of the notion of truth come in? One thing is immediately clear: if truth is to be the basis of a theory of meaning, we cannot think of it as being introduced stipulatively, for to so introduce it we should have to have mastery of a large fragment of the language already. If we wish to say that learning a language is learning what it is for each sentence of the language to be true, then we must be able to state what it is to know that a sentence is true without assuming prior understanding of the sentence – to do otherwise would make the theory circular.[67] Of course, in many cases the meaning of a sentence *can* be given by purely verbal means, and in such cases it is quite appropriate to do so by stating under what conditions the sentence in question is true – indeed, there seems no other way. But in such cases the speaker's knowledge of the sentence's truth-condition is *explicit* knowledge, and his being able to come to understand a sentence in this way presupposes a large measure of antecedent language mastery on his part. It would plainly be circular to hold that a speaker's understanding of his language consisted in an ability to specify the meaning of a sentence in other words, that is, by equivalent sentences of the same language; therefore mastery of the lower or more primitive levels of language cannot be explained in this way.[68]

The difficulty at issue is not how to specify what counts as a speaker's recognition that a sentence's truth-condition is satisfied. This is not our difficulty because, provided that a sentence's truth-condition *can* be recognised by a speaker to be fulfilled, we can in general find one or another way of saying what constitutes the speaker's recognition of that fact. This however restricts us to those few cases where the condition for a sentence's truth can indeed be recognised to obtain; which is to say, where the sentence's truth-value is in practice or in principle *decidable* – that is, for which a speaker has an effective procedure which, in a finite time, will enable him to recognise the sentence as true or false. Rather, the difficulty at issue is that *natural language is full of sentences which are not effectively decidable.*[69] Quantifications over infinite or un-surveyable domains (for example, the future), subjunctive conditionals, and references to inaccessible regions of space-time, are examples of cases where, for the sentences used, there is no effective procedure for determining whether the truth-conditions of the sentences in question are satisfied or otherwise. For any given such sentence we *might* discover a way of recognising whether its truth-condition is satisfied or not; but that is not the point. The point is that for any such sentence 'we cannot *equate* a capacity to recognise the satisfaction or non-satisfaction of the condition for the sentence to be true with a knowledge of what that condition is,' because

by hypothesis, either the condition is one which may obtain in some cases in which we are incapable of recognising the fact, or it is one which may fail to obtain in some cases in which we are incapable of recognising that fact, or both: hence a knowledge of what it is for that condition to hold or not to hold, while it may demand an ability to recognise one or another state of affairs whenever we are in a position to do so, cannot be exhaustively explained in terms of that ability. In fact, whenever the condition for the truth of a sentence is one that we have no way of bringing ourselves to recognise as obtaining whenever it obtains, it seems plain that there is no content to an ascription of *implicit* knowledge of what that condition is, since there is no practical ability by means of which such knowledge may be manifested.[70]

The problem at issue here, it will be recalled, concerns the theory of sense, conceived as the 'shell' around a theory of reference (a theory of truth) constituting the 'core' theory. It is the task of a theory of sense, as noted, to relate the core theory to the speaker's mastery of his language. Now what the speaker learns, in learning his language, is a practice; and part of that practice is the acknowledgement of sentences as true or false. Accordingly what the speaker knows, which enables him to use his language, must be manifestable in his practice; but 'knowing the condition which has to obtain for a sentence to be true is not anything which [the speaker] *does*, nor something of which anything he does is the direct manifestation'.[71] So, although in some cases we can ascribe knowledge of truth-conditions to speakers, in crucial cases we cannot; and consequently we 'fail to attain a genuinely explanatory account' of a speaker's language-mastery if we attempt to do so in terms of knowledge of *truth*-conditions.[72] This is Dummett's chief point against theories of meaning based on a realist or transcendent notion of truth.

The task in hand, to reiterate, is to answer the questions: what is it to know the truth-conditions of a sentence? Is truth the right choice as the central concept in the theory of meaning? To make further progress on these issues, Dummett suggests that we need to clarify what is involved in ascribing truth to statements. Doing so involves a short detour.

Consider the principle (call it 'principle C'): 'If a statement is true, there must be something in virtue of which it is true.'[73] Principle C underlies the correspondence theory of truth, and it is regulative, in the sense that having chosen our notion of truth for various classes of statements, we conclude from that to the nature of reality (that is, we do not *first* settle what there is in the world and *then* settle what, on that basis, makes statements true; but the other way round). In Dummett's view, the force of C is felt when we consider apparent violations of it, as, for example, with counter-factuals alleged to be true despite there being nothing we should accept as grounds for their truth. Dummett cites the example of theological claims about the behaviour of free-willed beings whom God *might* have created, but chose not to, because He knew *how* they would behave if created. Many object to such a notion on the grounds that there is nothing which could make the counterfactual true; and what this objection comes down to is a claim that a counterfactual cannot be '*barely* true', that is, cannot be true unless there is some other statement, not involving the subjunctive conditional, in virtue of which it is true.[74]

Why should anyone think that a counterfactual might be barely true? Presumably because he thinks it is logically necessary that either it or its negation should be true, without there necessarily being any grounds, of the kind we usually base assertions of counterfactuals upon, for either's truth. Now, it would be mistaken to think that *all* pairs of counterfactuals are determinately either true or false, but we are disposed to think *some* pairs are so, because we readily equate the truth of certain ordinary statements with the truth of certain associated subjunctive conditionals. Consider for example the case of ascribing abilities to people. Suppose we say of someone who has never learned any language but his own, 'Michael is good at learning languages'. (Call this statement 'A'.) There are three possible attitudes to the question 'must A be either true or false?': (i) It is not necessarily either; (ii) linguistic ability must correlate with or consist in some feature of brain structure, whether or not we know what it is; Michael either does or does not have that feature; therefore A must be either true or false, even if we cannot know which; and (iii) linguistic ability need not have to do with brain structure, but people either have or fail to have such ability none the less, so statement A must be either true or false. Upholders of all of (i)-(iii) agree that the truth-value of A depends upon the truth-value of the associated subjunctive conditional (call it 'B'): 'if Michael were to try learning a language, he would easily succeed', A being true if B is, false if B is false; so the question 'must B be either true or false?' coincides with the question whether the law of bivalence holds for A itself. Upholders of (iii) are committed to believing that B is barely true, if true; upholders of (ii) maintain bivalence for A but, disliking the idea that counterfactuals can be barely true, make A's truth depend on another statement, one which says something about brain structure. Upholders of (i) share with upholders of (iii) the belief that there need be nothing which helps in determining A's truth-value, and with upholders of (ii) they share a dislike of allowing bare truth to counterfactuals; so 'they escape the dilemma by rejecting the law of bivalence'.[75]

A vast range of expressions in our language may be said to be introduced by reference to some sort of conditional, including every expression for testable properties and measurable quantities. We regard tests and measurements as revealing how things are in themselves, independently of any tests or measurements; and proceed therefore to assume that property- or quantity-ascribing sentences are determinately true, independently of whether relevant tests and measurements were or could be carried out. In assuming this, 'we are adopting a realistic attitude to the property or quantity in question', which shows, Dummett says, how 'the notion of truth we take as governing our statements determines, *via* the principle C, how we regard reality as constituted. We may, in fact, characterise realism concerning a given class of statements as the assumption that each statement of that class is determinately either true or false'.[76] Accordingly, theses (ii) and (iii) are different versions of realism about human abilities, and (i) is a rejection of such realism. It is *antirealism*.

Thesis (ii) is a reductionist thesis. Reductionism need not be a strong thesis to the effect that statements of one class, call it M, must be translatable into statements of another class, call it R; it need only be a thesis to the effect that the truth-value of M statements is related to that of R statements, like this: for any statement A in M, there is a family $\overline{A}$ of sets of statements in R such that, for A to be true, it is necessary and sufficient that some set in the family of statements $\overline{A}$ be true.[77] On such a notion of reducibility, 'bare truth' can be characterised thus: a statement A is barely true if a) A is true and b) there is no class of statements, not containing A or trivial variations of it, to which any class containing A can be reduced. While (ii) represents a reductionist realism, (iii) is a naïve realism;

'naïve realism' is a thesis which, for a given class of statements *M, combines realism concerning *M with the notion that the statements in *M are barely true (that is, there is no other class of statements to which statements in *M can be reduced). 'Our view of the constitution of reality – our metaphysical position – depends,' says Dummett, 'on which are the classes of statements of which we take a realist view, that is, for which we assume the principle of bivalence, and in part on which are those which we admit as capable of being barely true.'[78]

We can now, at last, see what is involved in ascribing, to a speaker, knowledge of a sentence's truth-conditions; this was the question Dummett was concerned to deal with from the outset. If a sentence s is usable to make statements not capable of bare truth, then any utterance of s is true only if there is a class of statements, R, the members of some appropriate subset of which are true. Grasp of s's truth-conditions will depend on an implicit grasp of how s's truth relates to that subset of R. This relation could be displayed within the truth theory (the theory of reference): if the theory is expressed in a metalanguage which is an extension of the object language, the (T)-sentence for s will be non-trivial (will not have s on the right-hand-side of the biconditional). Alternatively, if there is an obstacle to giving a translation of s in the object-language, the theory of sense (which explains what a speaker's grasp of the truth theory consists in) will have to make the dependence of s on R explicit. Either way, there is nothing problematic about the notion of a grasp of s's truth-conditions here.

However, where s can be used to say something barely true, the associated (T)-sentence will be trivial; so in this case the theory of sense takes the whole burden of explaining a speaker's grasp of s's truth-conditions. The model we use in such cases is the reporting of observations; if someone is able to tell, by looking, that one tree is taller than another, then he knows what it is for one tree to be taller than another, and therefore knows what condition must be satisfied for the truth of 'this tree is taller than that tree',[79] There are therefore two basic models for explaining what it is to grasp truth-conditions. One model, unproblematically, has to do with the possession of explicit knowledge, that is, the ability to *state* the condition for any s's truth; but this model will not serve, for the reasons given earlier, if we wish to base a theory of meaning on the notion of a grasp of truth-conditions. The other model has to do with the possession of a capacity to recognise whether or not the sentence is true. But this, in turn, does not stretch far enough, for the reason that there are plenty of cases where we cannot observe whether or not some s is true.[80]

In Dummett's view, we come to think of our mastery of effectively undecidable sentences (for example, counterfactuals,
quantifications over infinite or unsurveyable domains, references to
inaccessible regions of space-time, and so forth) by means of a
sometimes surreptitious, sometimes explicit, appeal to the observational model. That is, we 'try to convince ourselves that our
understanding of what it is for undecidable sentences to be true
consists in our grasp of what it would be *to be able to use* such
sentences to give direct reports of observation.'[81] We cannot give
such reports, of course, but we know what powers a superhuman
observer would require in such cases; accordingly we tacitly assume
that our understanding of the truth-conditions of undecidable
sentences consists in our knowing what powers a superhuman
observer would need. This line of thought is associated with another
regulative principle, to be set alongside principle C, governing the
concept of truth: 'If a statement is true, it must be in principle
possible to know that it is true.' (Call this 'principle K'.) C and K are
closely related, because if one could not *know* the truth of a given
statement, how could there be anything which *makes* the statement
true? Thus 'even the most thorough-going realist must grant that we
could hardly be said to grasp what it is for a statement to be true if
we had no conception whatever of how it might be known to be
true'.[82] Thus the realist is obliged to extend the observational model
(that is, the model for decidable sentences) to cover the case of
undecidable sentences, in the way just suggested.

This account is offered as a 'diagnosis' by Dummett of the
motives we have for extending our concept of what it is to grasp the
truth-conditions of sentences, at the primitive level, to our
supposed grasp of truth-conditions at less primitive levels of
language. These motives, however, do not justify that extension;
and therefore employment of a transcendent concept of truth 'fails
to answer the question how we come to be able to assign to our
sentences a meaning which is dependent upon a use to which we are
unable to put them'.[83] In fact, such an account is indistinguishable
from one which has it that 'we treat certain of our sentences as if
their use resembled that of other sentences in certain respects in
which it in fact does not; that is, that we systematically misunderstand our own language'.[84]

Dummett earlier asked (cf. above) 'whether the concept of truth
is the right choice for the *central notion* of a theory of meaning . . .
or whether we need to employ some other notion in this role'. On
the basis of the foregoing, the answer is that truth is the wrong
choice, and some alternative notion *is* required. What notion
should this be?

THE ANTIREALIST ALTERNATIVE

The difficulties identified in the preceding section arose from our assuming a realistic interpretation of all sentences of our language – that is, the difficulty arose from our assuming that all statements, made by use of those sentences, are determinately either true or false, independently of whether we can know them to be so. Assuming bivalence for decidable statements is unproblematic; the difficulties in question arise because the principle of bivalence is applied to undecidable statements, and therefore we find ourselves 'unable to equate an ability to recognise when a statement has been established as true or false with a knowledge of its truth-condition'.[85] In some cases, as noted, a speaker's knowledge of a sentence's truth-condition can be represented as *explicit* knowledge, in the sense that the speaker can *state* the sentence's truth-condition; but when this is not the case, we do not know how to explain what constitutes the speaker's implicit knowledge of a sentence's truth-condition, because that knowledge cannot be exhaustively explained in terms of the actual use we make of that sentence.

The solution is to abandon bivalence. If we do not do so, we are bound to attribute to ourselves a grasp of a concept of truth which transcends any knowledge we might manifest in our actual use of language. If we abandon bivalence for any class of sentences, we must fashion a semantics for them which is not formulated in terms of truth-conditions; and, says Dummett, 'it is probable, though not certain, that the outcome will be that we can no longer acknowledge a classical logic as governing them'.[86]

There is, in Dummett's view, a prototype available for a semantics which does not take the notion of objectively determined truth as its central concept. The prototype is the intuitionist account of the meaning of mathematical statements. The fundamental intuitionist idea is this: an understanding of mathematical statements does not rest on our having to know, whether or not we can come to know, what has to be the case for those statements to be true. Rather, it rests on our having an ability to recognise, with respect to any mathematical construction, whether or not it constitutes a *proof* of a given statement. Thus the assertion of a mathematical statement is not to be interpreted as a claim that the statement is true, but, instead, as a claim that there is a proof of it, or that a proof of it can be devised. Correlatively, one understands any mathematical *expression* if one knows how it contributes to determining what counts as a proof of any statement in which it occurs. On this line it is guaranteed that a grasp of any mathematical statement or expression is fully manifestable in a mastery of the use of mathematical language, because that grasp is directly connected to use.[87]

Taking this tack does not commit us to the view that *every* intelligible statement must be effectively decidable. Understanding a statement consists, not in being able to *find,* but in being able to *recognise,* a proof of it when one is offered; and understanding the negation of a statement similarly consists not in finding, but in being able to recognise, a proof of the negation. Thus since the intelligibility of statements does not guarantee that we have a decision procedure for them, our understanding of them consists in an ability to recognise proofs when they are found. (It follows that the Law of Excluded Middle is not generally valid for mathematical statements.)[88]

Such a theory, Dummett holds, 'generalises readily to the non-mathematical case. Proof is the sole means which exists in mathematics for establishing a statement as true: the required *general* notion is, therefore, that of *verification*'.[89] On a verificationist view, understanding a statement consists in being able to recognise what verifies it, that is, in being able to recognise what conclusively establishes it as true. This does not mean that we must have, in every case, a way of deciding the truth-value of statements; it means only that we must be able to recognise, when it happens, that the truth of a statement is established. 'The advantage of this conception,' says Dummett, 'is that the condition for a statement's being verified, unlike the condition for its truth under the assumption of bivalence, is one which we must be credited with the capacity for effectively recognising when it obtains; hence there is no difficulty in stating what an implicit knowledge of such a condition consists in — once again, it is directly displayed by our linguistic practice.'[90]

If one accepts the verificationist alternative, a couple of points need to be borne in mind. One is that such a theory must take account of the interlocking nature of language, along lines suggested by Quine.[91] Quine, it will be remembered, proposed a verificationist account of language shrived of the positivist notion that the verification of a sentence should be represented as the occurrence of sequences of sense-experiences. This latter notion applies only to sentences on the periphery of the 'web' of language, where, in Quine's metaphor, language impinges on the world; in the case of the verification of sentences within the web, by contrast, inferential procedures will be involved — and mathematical theorems will form a limiting case in consequence of involving *only* inference. Thus there will be a coherence flavour to the verification of non-peripheral sentences, since the relevant procedures will involve recognising their interconnections.[92]

Another point is that the theory is a generalisation to language from intuitionistically-conceived mathematics, and therefore the differences between language and mathematics must be remarked. For example, one difference is that in mathematics the notion of understanding a statement does not involve *both* an ability to recognise a proof of it *and* an ability to recognise a refutation of it, since there is available within the theory a uniform way of explaining negation. There is however no such analogous procedure for ordinary language; thus the meaning of a statement will here have to be regarded as given by the simultaneous provision of means for recognising both its verification and its falsification, under the constraint that such means should exclude the possibility that the sentence can be both verified and falsified at once. There are other differences, but in general 'all will,' says Dummett, 'remain within the spirit of a verificationist theory of meaning, so long as the meaning of each sentence is given by specifying what is to be taken as conclusively establishing a statement made by means of it, and what conclusively falsifying such a statement, and so long as this is done systematically in terms only of conditions which a speaker is capable of recognising'.[93]

It should be noted that, in Dummett's view, adopting a verificationist approach to meaning by no means excludes the concept of truth from any role. On the contrary, truth remains important, Dummett holds, because we require it to give an account of deductive inference, which we recognise as valid just in case it is *truth-preserving*. In any theory of meaning, the dependence of the sense of sentences upon their structure will manifest what we consider to be the most *direct* way of establishing their truth; but the theory must also take into account not only the fact that we assert many statements on inconclusive grounds, but also that there are *indirect* ways of conclusively establishing the truth of statements – the conclusions of deductive inferences exemplify this. The notion of a statement's *truth* is thus needed to allow the possibility of there being conclusive but indirect procedures for establishing statements; and evidently, such a notion cannot be equated with verification.[94] Dummett admits that it is far from easy to explain exactly what account should be given of the notion of truth in terms of a verificationist theory of meaning; all that is immediately clear is that it must be explained somehow in terms of our capacity to recognise statements as true, and not in terms of conditions which transcend human capacities; and this means that whatever verificationist notion of truth we come up with is bound to involve the failure of bivalence for many sentences which are normally interpreted in a realistic manner.[95]

ANTIREALISM: SOME OBJECTIONS AND DEFENCES

One immediately apparent objection to the proposed antirealist alternative sketched above concerns its programmatic nature; nothing detailed or specific has been offered in place of the truth-based theory of meaning it criticises, and moreover it seems to raise as many problems as it exposes in the rival conception. Strawson, for example, argues that in order to clarify what is at issue between realism and antirealism, the antirealist proposals have to be more fully explained:

> we need to know *at least* what is to count as falling within the range of 'recognisable situations'; what is to count as conclusive verification; *whose* capacity in fact or in principle to do the recognising is in question; what importance, if any, to attach to the disjunction: in fact or in principle; and what 'in principle' means.[96]

It should be remarked straightaway that defenders of an antirealist approach, like Dummett and Wright, would be the first to acknowledge that the proposed alternative is no more, as yet, than a *proposed* alternative. 'We have,' Dummett says, 'more grasp of what a theory of meaning given in terms of truth-conditions looks like than on a general form of a theory of meaning of any rival kind; indeed, the retort that equally formidable difficulties face the construction of any rival theory is entirely just . . . I am not *certain* that meaning is *not* to be explained in terms of truth-conditions.'[97] However, the difficulties which face a truth-based theory are difficulties of *principle*; although we know what the theory would look like, we do not know whether it can be made to work. The foregoing discussion strongly suggests it will not work. Alternative theories, in which the central concept is not truth, have not so far had enough detailed work devoted to them. Nevertheless, 'on our present exceedingly imperfect comprehension of these matters, reflection should make us admit that a verificationist theory of meaning is a better bet than a thoroughgoing realistic one'.[98] One task is to see whether a verificationist alternative can meet some of the criticisms levelled against it.

An obvious objection to the antirealist proposal is that it is revisionary. If we abandon the assumption of bivalence, it becomes necessary to frame our semantic theory for given classes of sentences in terms which do not involve truth-conditions, and it is accordingly probable that classical logic cannot be acknowledged as governing those sentences. Now, our ordinary practice is to accept classical forms of inference; so a theory which demands the substitution of an alternative logic will not be purely descriptive of our linguistic practice, but will involve us in having to revise that practice. This would seem to be a weakness in the antirealist alternative, because it is quite clear that if we have competing but equally viable theories, the one which justifies accepted practice, and therefore is in no sense revisionary, is the preferable one. However 'we have no ground,' says Dummett, 'to assume in advance that our language is in every way perfectly in order'.[99] Indeed, Frege held that many features of natural language, such as vagueness and the existence of singular terms lacking a reference, render it impossible to devise a coherent semantics for language as it stands, and similarly Tarski held that the semantically closed character of natural language makes for inconsistency – the paradoxes exemplify this. Whether or not Frege and Tarski are right, their apprehensions about natural language cannot be dismissed *a priori*; the possibility remains not only that language may require adjustment, but that the conventionally recognised principles of inference we employ may need to be reassessed – these possibilities are implicit in the very idea that language should be amenable to systematic description by a theory of meaning which sets out to determine each sentence's use, construed as a function of the sentence's internal structure. 'There can be no guarantee,' Dummett says, 'that a complex of linguistic practices which has grown up by a piecemeal historical evolution in response to needs felt in practical communication will conform to any systematic theory.'[100]

The charge of revisionism thus does little damage, at least in prospect; and in any case, as noted earlier, Davidson's variety of a truth-conditional semantics is itself somewhat revisionary, in a different way – although it is not clear that some of the 'tidying up' which Davidson says natural language may need is too far different in kind from the adjustments envisaged by Dummett.

More trenchant an objection to Dummett's proposals is offered by McGinn,[101] who fastens on an admission made by Dummett to the effect that a wholly inclusive or 'global' antirealism may not be possible. 'There are,' Dummett says,

Truth, Meaning, Realism and Antirealism 249

a number of reasons for doubting whether global antirealism is coherent, for instance, behaviourism is one species of antirealism, namely the rejection of realism concerning mental states and processes; phenomenalism is another species, namely the rejection of realism concerning physical objects and processes; it immediately occurs to us to wonder whether it is possible to consistently maintain an antirealist position simultaneously in both regards.[102]

McGinn's argument is that the species of antirealism mentioned by Dummett are jointly inconsistent; that antirealism in either case coupled with realism in the other case is likewise inconsistent; and that therefore the only alternative is to be a realist with respect to both. His argument proceeds as follows.

Let statements about material objects and statements about mental events be called, respectively, 'M-statements' and 'P-statements'. (This usage recalls Strawson's talk, in *Individuals,* of 'material predicates' and 'person predicates'.) According to McGinn, antirealism about M- and P-statements is the view that such statements possess whatever truth-value they do possess 'in virtue of the truth-value of statements drawn from certain other classes of statements not trivially different from the given (statements)'.[103] An antirealist attitude to M-statements can he says, be characterised as *phenomenalism,* and antirealism about P-statements *behaviourism.*[104] Thus M- and P-statements are subject to a reductive thesis, which is a thesis to this effect: a sentence s of a given class K if reducible to (is true in virtue of) some sentence s' of a class R iff necessarily s is true (or false) just in case s' is true (or false); it is a logically necessary and sufficient condition for a sentence of K to be true (or otherwise) that some sentence, or set of sentences, of R be true (or otherwise).[105] The reductive antirealist theses in question have it that M-statements are true or false according to the truth-value of statements about experiences (call them E-statements), and P-statements likewise according to the truth-value of statements about behaviour (call them B-statements.) E- and B-statements are the 'basal statements' for M- and P-statements respectively,[106] and therefore are those statements which are *barely true.*[107] The first step in McGinn's argument is then to say that phenomenalism and behaviourism cannot be jointly affirmed; they

offer competing proposals as to what statements comprise the basal truths; phenomenalism takes E-statements, a subclass of P-statements, as basic, while behaviourism takes B-statements, a subclass of M-statements, as basic . . . Since a statement that is basal for one antirealism is derivative for the other, it is plain enough that a vicious regress is generated by the conjunction of the two doctrines; and this, of course, effectively frustrates the reductive ambitions definitive of each antirealist thesis.[108]

The next step is to see whether an antirealist attitude towards either class of statements, conjoined with a realist attitude to the other, is feasible.

The answer, according to McGinn, is that neither conjunction is feasible, because of the 'independence thesis'. This is the 'fundamental thesis of realism',[109] and has it that M-facts are not reducible to (that is, are independent of) E-facts, and P-facts are not reducible to B-facts. For realism precisely consists in a commitment to the view that there can be recognition-transcendent facts; therefore, in realist terms, it is possible for M-facts to obtain without there being any experiences had of their obtaining, which is to say that it is *not* necessary for the truth of any M-statement that some E-statement be true. Moreover, since no set of E-statements ever entails the truth of an M-statement, it is also not a sufficient condition for the truth of an M-statement that some related E-statement be true. And similarly for P- and B-statements.[110] Now, this independence of M- from E-statements, and P- from B-statements, cuts both ways; to say that an E-fact is not necessary for an M-fact is to say that the latter is not sufficient for the former, and to say that the former is not sufficient for the latter is to say that the latter is not necessary for the former. Thus the independence is symmetrical, and 'implies realism as much one way as the other'.[111] 'So,' says McGinn,

it begins to seem that realism about M- and P-statements implies realism about E- and B-statements, under the independence formulation. But now E- and B-facts are just subclasses of P- and M-facts, respectively; and if we are prepared to admit these in unreduced realist fashion, there can be no objection of general principle to admitting the rest.[112]

One can assess the weight of McGinn's argument against antirealism without going into its further details.[113] The central point is his identifying antirealism as a species of reductionism. This is a mistake. One does not have to hold to any variety of reductionism to be an antirealist and since this is so, the apparent difficulty of a vicious regress evaporates.

This is to say that, whereas it is true that objections to realism have often taken the form of reductionism, nevertheless it is incorrect 'to make rejection or acceptance of such a thesis a touchstone of whether one adopts or repudiates a realistic interpretation' of some given class of statements.[114] The motive for regarding reductionism as the touchstone in this regard is that it is frequently the preface to a further move; namely, the observation that there may be no statements of the reducing class which determine that some statement of the given class is either true or false, and accordingly no guarantee that the principle of bivalence holds for that class. It is realising *this* fact which motivates rejection of realism; but although a familiar way of making the point proceeds by way of a reductive thesis — as just shown — it does not have to do so. For, accepting a reductive thesis does not inevitably lead to a rejection of realism — one need not take the step of denying that bivalence holds for the given class, simply because it does not follow from a reductive thesis alone that bivalence fails for that class. One has to look at cases. For example, anyone who holds that if a statement ascribing a mental state to someone is true, then it is so in virtue of a neurophysiological state of that person, is likely to place a realist construction on the mental-state-ascribing statement by the criterion of realism just reiterated, *viz.,* that bivalence holds for such statements. Conversely, rejecting realism does not require prior commitment to reductionism, for one might hold that a given class of statements is such that bivalence fails for it *and* it is irreducible.[115]

In Dummett's view, all four combinations are possible: 1) one may take a realistic view of a class of statements, and yet regard it as subject to reducibility ('sophisticated realism'); or 2) one may construe the class realistically but deny its reducibility ('naïve realism'). Again, 3) one may deny realism of a class of statements *because* of a reductionist thesis ('reductive antirealism'); or one may deny realism with respect to the class while holding it to be irreducible ('outright antirealism').[116]

The term 'reductionism' itself has to be handled with care, for it usually means the thesis not only that the truth-values of statements in a given class depend on the truth-values of statements in the reducing class, but that it is at least in principle possible that the former be translatable into the latter without remainder. Now, one may accept some kind of reductive thesis without being a reductionist in this strong sense. For one thing, one may hold some kind of reductive thesis and also hold that statements of the reducing class are unintelligible independently of those in the given class. Or, one who holds a species of reductive thesis may take it that there is no way of settling *which* statements of the reducing class determine, either way, the truth-value of some statement in the given class. Or again, one may be a species of reductionist and hold either or both of the views that the truth (if it is true) of a statement in the given class depends upon the truth of an infinite set of statements in the reducing class, or, alternatively, guarantees the truth of only one out of an infinite number of statements in the reducing class — so that, in either case or in both taken together, actual translation may be impossible. (Indeed this is one reason why many philosphers reject reductionism whether or not they hold to some sort of reductive thesis otherwise')[117]

These considerations do enough to show that it is insufficient to define antirealisms with respect to M- and P-statements as reductive theses without qualification (McGinn says, 'the reductive ambitions *definitive* of each antirealist thesis'), since it is open to an antirealist to advance one or another construal of the reductions, or no construal at all; and either way his doing so will affect that account to be given of the relation between the two classes of statements in question. The matter is evidently complex. In any case, there appears to be an allied manoeuvre which undercuts the debate entirely.[118] This is to observe that phenomenalists, for example, have not always construed E-statements as a subclass of P-statements, as in the case of Russell's 'neutral monism', in which sense-data, as the fundamental atoms of the universe, are constituents of both material objects *and* mental events. Moves along these lines, or along related lines suggested by a metaphysical view of this stamp, for a different ordering among statements as to which are basic and which dependent, would remove the appearance of conflict McGinn identifies. Again, it depends on cases; one needs to see particular arguments. But such thoughts show that the antirealist does not appear to be without recourse in principle in setting out to construct a global version of his views.

Moreover, a point McGinn admits is that scepticism is invited by the 'independence thesis' which he employs to show that a mixture of antirealism and realism will not do. Epistemological scepticism turns precisely upon the observation that there at least appears to be a gap between a) the evidence we have for asserting M- and P-statements, and b) those M- and P-statements themselves, such that possession even of the best evidence for the assertion of either kind of statement is consistent with its falsity. If this is so, then on any given occasion we cannot be sure that possession even of the best evidence for some M- or P-statements entitles us to assert it. On an antirealist view, by contrast, the very sense of M- and P-statements is constituted by their assertibility conditions, that is, the evidence relevant to our asserting or denying them; and accordingly the sceptical gap is closed. One would be entitled to take this as a very good reason for preferring the antirealist to the realist account in general. [119]

One final matter may be noted. It will have become clear by now that Dummett frequently characterises realism about a given class of statements as the thesis that the principle of bivalence holds for that class. He also states that realism is the thesis that statements in a given class are determinately either true or false independently of our having any capacity to recognise that they are so. Indeed, he equates these two theses. Now, it is clear that anyone committed to bivalence will *ipso facto* be committed to the view that the truth-conditions of some sentences will be recognition-transcendent; but it has been pointed out by McDowell that the converse does not, at least automatically, hold.[120] Following Wright, let us call someone who holds the principle of bivalence a 'classical realist', and one who holds that truth value can be recognition – transcendent a 'bare realist'.[121] Then McDowell's view is that the bare realist is not, at least obviously, committed to classical realism, even although the classical realist's position commits *him* to bare realism as well. In McDowell's view, noting that such a separation can be made between bare and classical realism allows for the possibility that the antirealist's reservations *about bivalence* can be conceded, while preserving the workability of a realist conception of sense in which recognition-transcendent truth plays a role.

This is not, however, a problem for the antirealist position. For one thing, despite the apparent independence of bare from classical realism, it is excessively difficult to see what a bare realist would wish to object to in classical realism, since it is more than merely consistent with his position, but indeed is one powerful way of unpacking what the bare realist might mean by talk of the recognition-transcendence of the truth-conditions of sentences in some class. In any case, what it is about classical realism to which the antirealist most objects is precisely its bare realist core; so whether or not the antirealist charge should, or should not, most appropriately be couched in terms of a rejection of bivalence, it remains that the ultimate target is bare realism. Dummett's attack lies chiefly there.

THE PROBLEM OF THE PAST

An issue which sharply points the conflict between realist and antirealist attitudes to meaning, and which introduces refinements into our understanding of both positions, concerns statements about the past. Evidently, a realist will regard such statements as determinately either true or false whether or not we can come to know them to be so, whereas an antirealist will deny this. A consideration of the debate on this topic illustrates both positions and brings certain of their features into clearer focus.

It is clear from the foregoing sections that Dummett's two main arguments consist in challenges to the realist to explain these two things: a) how a speaker could learn or acquire his language if doing so involves forming a conception of what it is for recognition-transcendent states-of-affairs to obtain, and b) what counts as a manifestation of the speaker's implicit knowledge of his language if that knowledge involves conceptions of what it transcends his capacities to know. Call the first the *acquisition* challenge, the second the *manifestation* challenge. This latter is the more fundamental of the two. If the antirealist challenge rested only on the acquisition argument, then if a realist could show that our understanding of statements really *is* best conceived realistically, we should have to rest content with the mystery of how that understanding was achieved – fortified perhaps by the hope that someone ingenous enough will one day suggest a solution. The manifestation challenge, however, directly threatens to unseat the realist in his attempt to offer an account of what it is to possess and employ a language. This is demonstrated by the arguments reported in the last section but one, where the manifestation issue figures very largely.

Nevertheless the acquisition challenge remains important, especially taken in tandem with the manifestation challenge, since one powerful way of showing what it is to have (to manifest possession of) a concept is to show what goes into acquiring it. Dummett's arguments for an antirealist attitude to statements about the past rest heavily on the acquisition issue, regarded as being crucial, in just this way, to the manfestation issue.

The antirealist argument about the past goes like this.[122] We learn the use of past-tense statements by learning to recognise what counts as justification for the assertion of such statements. For example, we recall witnessing a certain event, and our early training in the use of the past tense includes learning how past-tense statements work as expressions of such memories. Now, for an antirealist, there can be no leap *from* what goes into our understanding of such statements *to* a notion of what it would be for such statements to have a determinate truth-value independently of anything which could now or later justify their assertion. Therefore the only notion of truth for past-tense statements which we can have acquired in learning how to use them, is a notion which coincides with the notion of conditions for justifiably asserting such statements. 'What we learn to do,' Dummett says,

is to accept . . . the occurrence of certain conditions which we have been trained to recognise, as conclusively justifying the assertion of a given statement [about the past, and] certain other conditions as conclusively justifying its denial. In the very nature of the case, we could not possibly have come to understand what it would be for the statement to be true independently of that which we have learned to treat as establishing its truth; there was simply no means by which we could be shown this.[123]

The thesis which Dummett ascribes to the realist is 'truth-value link realism', which has it that a past-tense statement uttered now is true if and only if an appropriate present-tense statement uttered at that past time, would have been true at that time. The realist's claim is that it is our understanding of the truth-value link which gives rise to our understanding (our being able to use) past-tense statements. The antirealist, as Dummett indeed grants, has to concede that the notion of a truth-value link is 'a fundamental feature of our understanding of tensed statements', so that denying it, or arguing that it involves an incoherence, would amount to the claim that our use of tensed statements is in general incoherent.[124] The point however is that the antirealist resists the temptation to infer, from the role the truth-value link plays, the conclusion that past-tense statements, made now, are 'true in virtue of some past fact, if "past fact" means something other than that by means of which we can recognise the statement as true'.[125]

One can see the crux of the dispute in terms of certain models. 'What the realist would like to do,' says Dummett, 'is to stand in thought outside the whole temporal process and describe the world from a point which has no temporal position at all'; from this point of atemporal privilege the realist wishes to survey all temporal positions 'in a single glance', regarding different points of time as standing in a temporal order of precedence among themselves, with the privileged point of temporal description having no relation to any of them.[126] The antirealist, by contrast, 'takes more seriously the fact that we are immersed in time: being so immersed, we cannot frame any description of the world as it would appear to one who is not in time'.[127] It is tempting − but misleading − to characterise the respective positions like this: the antirealist says the past 'exists only in the traces it has left upon the present', whereas for the realist 'the past still exists as past, just as it was when present'; which is why, in his view, describing things 'as they actually are in themselves' will involve treating all points of time alike, detached from the particular perspective which an observer, immersed in time, is obliged to take.[128] In Dummett's view, the antirealist considerations are faithful to the fact that we are temporal creatures; the realist thesis, on the other hand, seems simply inadequate to account for our mastery of tensed statements. Accordingly the former is to be preferred.

It would seem natural for a realist to respond by defending the notion of truth-value links, taken together with his characteristic acceptance of the recognition-transcendence of the truth-conditions of statements in a class of statements which are in part understood by means of them. The most trenchant reply to Dummett, offered by McDowell, does not however do so. Rather, McDowell rejects the intelligibility of talk of truth-value links as well as antirealism; and offers instead a middle way — which Wright has dubbed 'M-realism' — as the correct account.[129]

On this view, a realist (let us call him a 'link-realist') who appeals to truth-value links to meet the antirealist's acquisition challenge, is committed to a notion of truth-conditions as being always inaccessible. Such a realist is trying to respect the antirealist view that speakers could only have learned the use of these or those kinds of statements by having appropriate circumstances available to them in training; but he does so by refusing to allow that the circumstances available to the trainee are *truth-conditions* of the utterances the trainee is learning to make. This is, the link-realist distinguishes between assertibility-conditions and truth-conditions; allows that the former, but not the latter, must be available in training; and thus views the obtaining of truth-conditions as 'something which, in itself, transcends what is accessible to awareness'.[130] But a realism of this kind — link-realism — is, McDowell says, 'impotent' to do what its upholders require of it.

To see why, it is first useful to note the similarity between statements about the past and statements about what is going on in others' minds. Another's pain, on the link-realist view just presented, is essentially concealed from us behind a screen of behaviour. Others' behavings might count among the circumstances available to a trainee in his learning how to ascribe various kinds of sentience to others, but they are not themselves the truth-conditions of sentience-ascribing statements. Here, as with the past, the truth-conditions are inaccessible.[131] Now, it is precisely the antirealist's point that it is unintelligible to claim that a notion of inaccessible states-of-affairs should enter into an account of language mastery. The link-realist's reply, in connection with the other-minds issue, goes something like this: 'You can see how a person can have the idea of what it is for someone to be in pain — when the someone in question is himself. So, the sentence "he is in pain" uttered in circumstances which fix a reference for the pronoun "he", is to be understood as saying, of that other person, that he is in the very same state.'[132] And the link-realist's account of past-tense statements is similar. 'You can see,' the link-realist says, 'what it is for rain to be falling. Well, a sentence like "it *was* raining" is understood as saying that that very circumstance obtained at some past time.'[133] What the link-realist is suggesting is that a kind of 'projection' of understanding is effected by means of the truth-value link.

McDowell's objection to these link-realist manoeuvres is that, far from solving the problem posed by the antirealist, they simply ignore it. If someone simply cannot see how the past obtaining of some circumstance enters into the meaning of a statement, or cannot see how another's being in pain (when his being in pain is inaccessible to us) enters into the meaning of some form of words, then his doubts are not settled by simply and baldly reasserting that past circumstances, or others' inaccessible mental states, *do* enter into the meaning of such statements. Yet this is precisely what the link-realist does.

If link-realism and antirealism were the only options, in McDowell's view, then antirealism would win the dispute hands down on the above considerations. But McDowell has another option, a species of realism which meets the antirealist challenge without appeal to the notion of truth-value links.[134] This middle-way realism (hence Wright's label for it as 'M-realism', 'm' for 'middle') is as follows.

M-realism differs from link-realism in having it that satisfaction of the *truth*-conditions of past-tense and other-minds statements *is* sometimes available to us; and it differs from antirealism in having it that we understand the possibility that both kinds of statements can be true in virtue of the obtaining of states-of-affairs which are inaccessible to us. (This commitment to a statement's being true in virtue of recognition-transcendent circumstances is of course what makes M-realism, distinctively, *realism*. Let us call this central and characteristic feature of any realism, *viz.*, invocation of possibly recognition-transcendent truth-conditions, *bare realism*.[135]) Thus McDowell characterises the M-realist view of other-ascriptions of sensation like this:

what warrants the assertion that another is in pain, on one of the relevant occasions, is the detectable obtaining of the circumstance of that person's being in pain: an instance of a kind of circumstance – another person's being in pain – which is available to awareness, in its own right and not merely through behavioural proxies, on some occasions, including this one, although, on other occasions, the obtaining of other instances can be quite beyond detection.[136]

Similarly, M-realism about the past is the view that

what warrants the assertion, on one of the relevant occasions, that, say, some event of a specified kind occurred in the past is the obtaining of a circumstance which consists simply in such an event's having occurred: an instance of a kind of circumstance which is available to awareness, in its own right and not merely through traces going proxy for it, on some occasions, including this one, although, on other occasions, the obtaining of other instances can be quite outside our reach.[137]

What is essential to M-realism, then, is the idea that if and only if the generally non-effectively decidable truth-conditions for the kinds of statements in question *can* on occasion be accessible to us, can we acquire a genuinely bare-realist conception of what it is for those truth-conditions to be satisfied. That is, the M-realist says: the circumstances which justify the making of assertions are of a kind which are sometimes available to awareness and which are sometimes not available to awareness; 'thus [the M-realist] enables himself to think of [these circumstances] as actually *being* truth-conditions, realistically conceived'.[138] The link-realist represented truth-conditions as wholly inaccessible; the antirealist demands that the assertion-justifying circumstances in question must be available to awareness *whenever* they obtain. The M-realist steers a middle course between both positions, satisfying the antirealist's acquisition challenge while yet remaining a realist. For he concedes that to learn how to use sentences of the relevant kinds, the trainee must have access to circumstances which justify use of those sentences; but he holds that those circumstances are the *truth*-conditions of those sentences, and are such that although they sometimes *are* accessible, they often are not; and so the notion of recognition-transcendent truth-conditions is retained, and with it a distinctively realist approach to the question of meaning.

Moreover, not only does M-realism meet the antirealist's acquisition challenge, McDowell claims, but it meets his manifestation challenge too. This challenge, to reiterate, is that since linguistic competence is a practical capacity, it should be observable in (manifestable in) linguistic behaviour. Dummett requires that it be *exhaustively* so manifestable. On McDowell's view, the challenge is reasonable, so long as the 'exhaustively' is dropped; the M-realist's response to this challenge is to say: a conception of the circumstances which are the truth-conditions of given sentences manifests itself on those occasions when linguistic behaviour is a response to the detectable obtaining of a truth-condition when it *is* detectable, even although in general such circumstances are not always detectable. The conception of appropriate circumstances in question is that of a *kind* of circumstance; the M-realist

claims the right to ascribe [possession of the conception of utterance-justifying circumstances] on the basis of behaviour construable as a response to *some* instances of the kind, in spite of the admitted fact that *other* instances, on his view, are incapable of eliciting any response from the possessor of the conception.[139]

At first blush, McDowell's proposals recommend themselves strongly, precisely because they consist in a defence of realism which appears to meet the antirealist challenge in both its forms. On reflection, however, it might be thought relevant to ask, as Wright in effect does, whether McDowell is not trying to have his cake and eat it. Let us look at his proposals from both sides – that is, from the link-realist side and the antirealist side – and ask whether, on the one hand, he is fair to link-realism (for if not, he may not in fact have distanced himself far enough from it for his own purposes), and, on the other hand, whether M-realism really does succeed in satisfying the antirealist demands over acquisition and manifestation.

In Wright's view, McDowell is unfair to link-realism in several ways, the chief of which is his holding that a link-realist cannot without embarrassment acknowledge what the M-realist holds, namely that we can, on occasion, non-inferentially see that certain circumstances in fact obtain. The link-realist invokes truth-value links because he holds that the truth-conditions of the relevent kinds of statements are inaccessible, and therefore he holds that understanding such statements involves a 'projection' into the past or other minds by means of the truth-value link. Nevertheless even on the M-realist view, in which sometimes-accessible circumstances are admitted, there is going to have to be just such a projection: for the trainee is going to have to advance somehow from cases where assertions are justified by detectable circumstances to those where there are no detectable circumstances available. But, now, is this not precisely the place to invoke the notion of a truth-value link to make such a projection intelligible? If it is supposed, on M-realist lines, that observing certain kinds of manifest evidence (say, a contorted facial expression together with a bleeding wound) *is* observing that another is in pain, how does one bridge the gap from such a case to, say, understanding that stoicism is possible – 'that, indeed, in special circumstances a man's pain may go unreflected in anything he does or the overt state of his body?'[140]

The point here is that it is a mistake to take it that appeal to truth-value links *presupposes* a commitment to the view that the truth-conditions of the relevant kinds of statements are always recognition-transcendent. McDowell takes it that this is so, and denies the value of link-realism on that ground. What in fact the appeal to truth-value links presupposes is only that there is *no essential connection* between the realisation of those conditions, on the one hand, and on the other hand a speaker's ability to recognise that they are realised. But *this* presupposition is 'exactly the characteristic belief of bare realism': and accordingly link- and

M-realism are a good deal closer than McDowell supposes. This, as will become apparent, results in there not being the advantages which McDowell claims for M-realism over link-realism.[141]

It is important to see how extensive the class of statements is, whose truth-conditions can, in the M-realist view, be available to awareness on some occasions. McDowell talks of circumstances which are available 'in their own right' and the not via 'proxies', that is, which are non-inferentially available. Such a view is consistent with a notion of *criteria* in Wittgenstein's sense; criteria are not symptoms or traces from which some state-of-affairs can be inferred, nor are they truth-conditions, for they are defeasible – in the sense that one can recognise that criteria are present (facial expression, bleeding wound) for the ascription of pain, and yet one can also recognise that there may be no pain present (the person displaying the pain-behaviour might be acting).[142] Now, a notion of criteria has certain advantages over an M-realist notion of 'available truth-conditions', for claims we make on the basis of criteria can be withdrawn consistently with our still holding that the criteria were in fact satisfied. The M-realist, therefore, has to maintain not just that inference via proxies is not always involved when use of a statement is justified, but, more strongly, that those occasions best suited to teaching use of such a statement involve *more* than mere satisfaction of criteria – they must involve the actual realisation of truth-conditions; for if this were not so, then experience of the relevant circumstances would be experience of circumstances whose occurrence is consistent with the falsity of the statement whose use is being learned.[143]

This suggests that M-realists are committed to believing that there can be situations in which someone is indefeasibly warranted in claiming that things are thus-and-so regarding the past or other minds. But one has to tread carefully here; for it is highly doubtful that indefeasible warrant can ever be claimed for contingent statements, since we are always open to making errors of judgement, perception or understanding, and are therefore rarely, if ever, in a position to claim *indefeasible* warrant for what we assert. Accordingly, it looks as if one would be better advised either to give up the M-realist idea that *truth-conditions* can obtain detectably, or to construct an account of what it is for them to obtain detectably which does not involve our being indefeasibly certain of the statement whose truth-conditions they are.[144]

An account of this latter kind might be modelled on the fact that some classes of statements – for example, effectively decidable mathematical statements – are such that there is a procedure one can follow which, provided it is followed correctly and no other mistakes occur, *settles* that the opinion one arrives at is bound to be correct. Indeed, having such a procedure for certain statements *just is* what it is for the statements in question to be effectively decidable.[145] But the certainty we arrive at in these cases is not indefeasible; and this is not because we do not have the truth-value-conferring circumstances fully available to us, but because it is in general not possible for us to be sure that the relevant procedures have been implemented perfectly − that is, without perceptual, ratiocinative, or other kinds of error infecting the carrying-out of the procedure.[146]

At any rate, on this model, the notion of 'detectably obtaining truth-conditions' is the notion that there is a procedure of the above sort available for deciding the statement whose truth-conditions they are. Now, a clear case of statements for which there *cannot* be detectably obtaining truth-conditions as thus specified, is the class of unrestrictedly generally quantified contingent statements, that is, statements about matters-of-fact upon whose quantification there are no limits. For whatever procedures we carry out in an effort to determine the truth-value of such statements, it is always consistent with our best efforts that we may form an incorrect opinion of their truth-value − a falsifying instance may be just around the corner. And the trouble is that statements about the past and other minds fall into this very category.[147]

Because this is so, the M-realist is faced with a serious difficulty. On his account, learning the use of statements whose truth-conditions in general transcend our capacity to recognise that they do or do not obtain, is meant to be based on occasions when they happen to obtain detectably. But if there is no indefeasible warrant available to the learner on such occasions, not only is it unclear what his grasp of the statement's *truth-conditions* consists in, but he has still somehow to make something like the link-realist's leap of projection to the non-detectable cases.

Other considerations reinforce this point. Consider the M-realist replies to the antirealist's two challenges. On the manifestation issue, McDowell's argument was that it is unreasonable to demand that the knowledge which underwrites a speaker's practical competence with his language should be *exhaustively* manifestable; it is, he says, enough that the speaker should manifest his knowledge on occasions when he has the *chance* to display it. Thus the M-realist wishes a) to credit the speaker with recognitional capacities which he may, if it so happens, never get the opportunity to display. At the same time, the M-realist centrally wishes b) to credit the speaker with an understanding of what it is for truth-conditions to obtain *un*detectably. What McDowell's response to the manifestation challenge comes down to, in effect, is an equation of a) and b). But in Wright's view, McDowell has not made out a case for this equation. On the M-realist arguments presented, the most that can be done is attribution of a) to speakers; yet what the antirealist demands by way of the manifestation challenge is an answer to b).[148] In other words, the problem of the projection from a) to b) remains unsolved.

The M-realist response to the acquisition challenge fares no better. It turns, once again, on there being detectable obtainings of truth-conditions; but it is still left unclear how the learner gets from such cases to those in which the truth-conditions obtain undetectably. Wright offers this example: suppose you are a language learner. You are confronted with a number of different cases in which another person pulls faces, groans, bleeds, and so forth; and you are told that in each case it is true that the person is in pain. But now you are told that other people, who behave completely differently, are or may also be in pain. 'Wouldn't there be a temptation to think you had misunderstood the original examples, that the distinctive behaviour had nothing to do with being [in pain]?', Wright asks, 'and if you were reassured about that, would you not then be constrained to think that the concept of being [in pain] had a breadth to it which the original examples had not made clear?'[149]

One can leave the realist-antirealist debate about other minds and the past at that point, not because it is resolved either way, although the antirealist case appears to be very strong (and it is interesting to note how far the realist feels impelled to make concessions to it); but because, for one thing, the debate remains open, and for another, the apparent strength of the antirealist case suggests that it is high time to turn back and address the issue of what metaphysical consequences flow from antirealism if it turns out to win the day in the argument about meaning. I do this in the next chapter.

NOTES

1. Frege, G., *Grundgesetze* 1.32.
2. Wittgenstein, L., *Tractatus Logico-Philosophicus* 4.024
3. Carnap, R., *Meaning and Necessity* Chicago 1956 p.10.
4. Davidson, D., 'The Method of Truth in Metaphysics' in French. P. A., *et*

al., *Contemporary Perspectives in the Philosophy of Language* University of Minnesota Press 1979, p.294.

5. ibid.
6. ibid.
7. ibid.
8. ibid., pp.296-7.
9. ibid., pp.297.
10. Davidson, 'Truth and Meaning', *Synthese* 17, 1967, p.308; 'Theories of Meaning and Learnable Languages', *Proceedings of the 1964 Congress for Logic, Methodology, and Philosophy of Science,* Amsterdam, 1964, p.387; 'Semantics for Natural Languages, *Linguaggi Nella Societe e Nella Technica,* Milano 1970, p.179.
11. Davidson, 'On Saying That', *Synthese* 19, 1968, p.131, reprinted in Davidson, D., and Hintikka, J., *Words and Objections,* Hingham, Mass., 1969; 'Theories of Meaning and Learnable Languages' *op. cit.,* p.387; 'Semantics for Natural Languages' *op. cit.,* pp.177.
12. Davidson, 'Semantics for Natural Languages' *op. cit.,* pp.178.9.
13. ibid., p.183; 'Truth and Meaning' *op. cit.,* p.311.
14. cf. 'Truth and Meaning' pp.309 *et seq.*
15. Quine, *From A Logical Point of View,* Cambridge, Mass., 1961.
16. Davidson, 'Truth and Meaning', p.309.
17. ibid., p.310.
18. cf Platts, M., *Ways of Meaning* London: Routledge & Kegan Paul Ltd., 1979, pp.54-6.
19. Davidson, 'Truth and Meaning', p.314.
20. ibid.
21. ibid.
22. ibid., pp.318-20.
23. cf. ibid.
24. ibid., p.319.
25. ibid., pp.318 .20
26. ibid., p.320.
27. ibid., and 'The Logical Form of Action Sentences', in Rescher, N., (ed.), *The Logic of Decision and Action,* Pittsburg 1968; also cf. 'On Saying That' *op. cit.*
28. Burge, T., 'Reference and Proper Names', *Journal of Philosophy* 70, 1973.
29. Harman, G., 'Moral Relativism Defended', *Philosophical Review* 1975.
30. Wallace, J., 'On the Frame of Reference', *Synthese* 22, 1970, and 'Positive, Comparative, Superlative', *Journal of Philosophy* 69, 1972.
31. Davidson, 'Truth and Meaning' *op. cit.,* p.311.
32. Davidson, 'Semantics for Natural Languages', *op. cit.,* p.185.
33. ibid., pp.185-6.
34. ibid., p.184; cf. 'Truth and Meaning' p.313.
35. In fact, it can be argued (and I shall later show this) that the notions of assent and dissent are a deal more complicated than Quine and Davidson would wish them to be − to an extent, indeed, that generates results quite contrary to those they seek. Cf. below; and Grayling, A. C., *Epistemological Scepticism and Transcendental Arguments,* D.Phil. Thesis, Oxford 1981., chapter 4.
36. Davidson, 'Truth and Meaning' *op. cit.,* p.318.
37. ibid.
38. Stich, S. P., 'Davidson's Semantic Program', *Canadian Journal of Philosophy* Vol. VI No.2, June 1976, §7.
39. Platts, *op. cit.,* p.57.
40. ibid.

41. For more detailed discussion see Foster, J. A., 'Meaning Truth Theory'; and Loar, B., 'Two Theories of Meaning', both in Evans, G., and McDowell, J., *Truth and Meaning,* Oxford, 1976.

42. McDowell, J., 'Truth-Conditions, Bivalence, and Verificationism' in Evans and McDowell *op. cit.,* p.42 *et seq.* For a theory in some respects similar to McDowell's cf. Loar, *op. cit.*

43. McDowell *op. cit., p.43.*

44. ibid., p.44.

45. ibid.

46. ibid., pp.44-5.

47. ibid., p.46; and cf. Platts, *op. cit.,* p.61.

48. Platts, ibid.

49. McDowell, p.47; cf. Platts, ibid.

50. Platts, p.62.

51. McDowell, p.46.

52. ibid., pp.46-7.

53. ibid., p.47.

54. Dummett, M. A. E., see especially 'What Is A Theory of Meaning?' (II), in Evans and McDowell *op. cit.,* and variously in *Truth and Other Enigmas,* Duckworth, 1978.

55. McDowell, *op. cit.,* p.48.

56. Dummett, 'What Is A Theory of Meaning?' (II) *op. cit.,* p.69.

57. ibid.

58. ibid., pp.69-70.

59. ibid., pp.70-1, my italics.

60. ibid., pp.72-3.

61. ibid. p.73.

62. ibid., pp.73-4.

63. ibid., p.74.

64. ibid., pp.74-5.

65. ibid., p.76, my italics.

66. ibid., p.78.

67. ibid.

68. ibid., pp.79-80.

69. ibid., pp.80-1.

70. ibid., pp.81-2.

71. ibid., pp.82-3.

72. ibid., p.83.

73. ibid., p.89.

74. ibid., pp.89-90.

75. ibid., p.91.

76. ibid., p.93.

77. ibid., p.94.

78. ibid.

79. ibid., p.95.

80. ibid., pp.96-8.

81. ibid., p.99.

82. ibid., p.100.

83. ibid.

84. ibid., p.101.

85. ibid.

86. ibid., p.103.

87. ibid., cf. especially pp.103-10, where Dummett sets out an account of

intuitionistic semantics for mathematical language; see also 'The Philosophical Basis of Intuitionistic Logic' *Truth and Other Enigmas* (henceforth TOE), pp.216-26. for an exceptionally clear and vigorous account of all these issues.

88. Dummett, 'What Is A Theory of Meaning?' (II) p.110.
89. ibid., my italics.
90. ibid., p.111.
91. cf. Quine, 'Two Dogmas', *op. cit.*
92. Dummett, ibid.
93. ibid., p.114.
94. For other reasons why Dummett thinks we need a concept of truth cf. chapter 9 below; and Dummett's 'What Does The Appeal To Use Do For The Theory of Meaning?' in Margalit, A., (ed.), *Meaning and Use,* Reidel, 1979 p.123 *et seq.*
95. Dummett, 'What Is A Theory of Meaning?' (II), pp. 115-16. Dummett goes on to consider a theory of meaning with falsification as its central concept (pp. 117-26), and then talks specifically about the notion of force and how the passage from knowledge of meanings to use is forged (pp. 127-37.) For his discussions of truth cf. 'Truth' in TOE and chapter 13 of *Frege* Duckworth, 1973; also the forthcoming William James Lectures delivered at Harvard in 1976.
96. Strawson, P. F., 'Scruton and Wright on Anti-Realism', *Proceedings of the Aristotelian Society* 1976-7, p.17. Cf. Wright's reply: 'Strawson on Anti-Realism' *Synthese* 40, 1978, p.283 *et seq.*
97. Dummett, 'What Is A Theory Of Meaning?' (II) pp.67-8, my italics.
98. ibid., p.137.
99. ibid., p.103.
100. ibid., p.104.
101. McGinn, C., 'An A Priori Argument For Realism', *Journal of Philosophy,* 1979, p.113 *et seq.*
102. Dummett, TOE, pp.367-8.
103. McGinn, *op. cit.,* p.116.
104. ibid.
105. ibid.
106. ibid.
107. ibid., p.118.
108. ibid., pp.118-9.
109. ibid., p.119.
110. ibid., pp.119-20. These observations recall the sense-data debate and the issue of phenomenalism in general.
111. ibid., pp.121-2.
112. ibid., p.122.
113. The further details are interesting, and spell out the second step in the argument in greater detail.
114. Dummett, 'Common Sense and Metaphysics', in Macdonald, G., (ed.), *Perception and Identity,* Macmillan, 1979, p.4. Cf. also TOE, pp.361-2.
115. Dummett, 'Common Sense and Metaphysics', pp.4-5.
116. ibid., p.5.
117. ibid., pp.5-6.
118. The following suggestion owes itself to Michael Luntley of Linacre College, Oxford. Cf. his 'The Real Antirealism and Other Bare Truths', B.Phil. Thesis Oxford 1981, chapter 1.
119. I have written on this issue at length elsewhere; cf. Grayling *op. cit.,* especially chapters 3-5.
120. McDowell, 'Truth-Values, Bivalence, and Verificationsim' *op. cit.,* pp.54-5.
121. Wright, C., 'Realism, Truth-Value Links, Other Minds, and the Past' *Ratio*

Vol.XXII No.2., December 1980, pp.112-132.
122. Dummett TOE, pp.362-3.
123. ibid., p.362.
124. ibid., p.364.
125. ibid., p.373.
126. ibid., p.369
127. ibid.
128. ibid., p.370
129. McDowell, J., 'On "The Reality of the Past" ', in Pettit and Hookway (eds.), *Action and Interpretation*, Cambridge, 1978.
130. ibid., p.132.
131. ibid.
132. ibid.
133. ibid., p.133.
134. ibid., p.135.
135. Wright, C., 'Realism, Truth-Value Links, Other Minds and the Past', *op. cit.*, p. 121
136. McDowell, ibid., pp.135-6.
137. ibid., p.136.
138. ibid., p.135.
139. ibid., p.139
140. Wright, *op. cit.*, p.121.
141. ibid.
142. ibid., p.123
143. ibid.
144. ibid., pp.123-4.
145. ibid., p.123.
146. ibid., pp122-4.
147. ibid., pp.124-5.
148. ibid., pp.126-8.
149. ibid., pp.129-30.

9 Some Consequences and Commitments

INTRODUCTION

In the preceding chapters I have tried to present a detached account of some of the main issues in philosophical logic. Impartiality is appropriate in a survey of problems conducted by means of a survey of the literature on those problems. In this concluding chapter, however, I shall, in connection with a couple of interesting topics arising out of the foregoing discussions, indicate my preferences. Doing so has two virtues. One – the most important – is that it illustrates what kind of line one must take through these various problems given a certain starting-point in the theory of meaning. The other virtue is that it permits me to quit the fence and declare an interest, in the light of which any unwitting bias in the preceding chapters can be tested.

First, I shall look at the metaphysical consequences of anti-realism, and then comment briefly on truth, and more briefly still on essentialism, to show what it looks like to make one set of choices among the philosphical options already discussed. The route I choose is premissed on the selection of an antirealist approach to questions of meaning, as constituting the most plausible view of what a theory of meaning should be like. This is a choice which the discussion in the last chapter seems to me to force.

THE METAPHYSICS OF ANTIREALISM

McDowell, it will be recalled, observed that if we accept a conception of sense in terms of verification, then such a conception 'would require a novel, antirealist conception of the world: if truth is not independent of our discovery of it, we must picture the world as our own creation or, at least, as springing up in response to our investigations. So verificationist objections to a truth-conditions conception of sense would have far-reaching metaphysical implications'.[1] One thing McDowell is wrong about, in saying this, is that the required antirealist conception of the world would be 'novel'; for neither of the two options which seem to me to flow from antirealism is novel, but has been an option for quite some time. So much will become apparent shortly. He is however right that antirealism has metaphysical implications; Dummett says 'the whole point of my approach . . . has been to show that the theory of meaning underlies metaphysics'.[2] Now, this remark salutarily reminds us that realism, no less than antirealism, has metaphysical implications; one might be forgiven for thinking that McDowell's observations were intended to suggest either that antirealism is metaphysically consequential where to be 'metaphysical' is to be in a species of intellectually unhealthy state, or (and more weakly) that in so far as both realism and antirealism are attended by metaphysical implications, those of realism are unexceptionably orthodox or even anodyne, whereas those of antirealism are revisionary and implausible.[3]

What are the competing metaphysics of realism and antirealism? To get clear on this question it is necessary to investigate what options an antirealist has, for, so far, it is not entirely obvious what they could be. First however it is instructive to look at the metaphysics of realism. This at least is a fairly straightforward matter. There is no better short statement of realist metaphysics – so I quote it in full – than that provided by Platts, writing with his characteristic verve and charm. Realism, he says,

> embodies a picture of our language reaching out to, connecting with, the external world in ways that are (at least) beyond our present practical comprehension. It embodies a picture of an independently existing, somewhat recalcitrant world describable by our language in ways that transcend (at least) our present capacities to determine whether those descriptions are true or not. It embodies a picture of our language, and our understanding, grappling with a stubbornly elusive reality. Perhaps, with effort, we can improve our capacities to understand that world, to know that our characterisations of it are true. If we succeed in so doing, we do not bring that world into being, we merely *discover* what was there all along. But that reality will always exceed our capacities: we can struggle to achieve *approximately true* beliefs about that reality, approximately true beliefs about the entities and their characteristics which, independently of us, make up that reality. But we have to rest with the approximate belief, and ultimately to resign ourselves to (non-complacent) ignorance: for the world, austerely characterised by our language, will always outrun our recognitional capacities.
>
> I find this conception of the world profound, sympathetic, and (healthily) depressing.[4]

This characterisation undoubtedly articulates what lies beneath – and not too far beneath – the ordinary common-sense view of the world with which we are familiar. Moreover our familiarity with such a view is precisely a function of the obvious realist commitments our everyday talk leads us to make; for there does not appear to be a reasonable way of explaining what someone believes about the world, when he says something quite ordinary like 'the cups are on the table', other than by crediting him with a realist conception of the world and therefore language. So much seems inescapable. For in making such a statement, one is implicitly claiming that there are objects existing independently of one's talk or experience of them, and that it is in virtue of their so existing that language has the sense (and, hence, thought the character) it does have.

Nevertheless, far from settling that the realist picture is the right one, these considerations do something quite else: they startle us, in thinking carefully about language and the world, because when we do so it quickly becomes apparent that there is a profoundly mystifying, and very considerable, gap between that realist picture, on the one hand, and on the other hand the ways we could have come to possess it and the ways in which we could show that we possess it. This indeed is precisely what the antirealist's acquisition and manifestation challenges are designed to show; and Platts acknowledges as much: 'the picture, like the realistic truth-based semantics which prompts it, is open to serious challenge [from verificationism]'.[5] The discussions in the preceding chapter are discussions of that challenge.

If the antirealist challenge cannot be met, we are bound to take seriously the metaphysical consequences of antirealism. What are these consequences? It seems to me that there are two main options: *relativism* and *idealism*. Each merits discussion in some detail.[6]

RELATIVISM

There is a distinction to be drawn between moral or cultural relativism, on the one hand, and cognitive relativism on the other. The former concerns the difference between cultures, or between different historical phases of the same culture, with respect to religious, social, and moral values and practices; that is, with respect to what might be called the 'superstructure' of a culture's conceptual scheme.[7] Cognitive relativism concerns the 'infrastructure', the level of basic beliefs about the world, such as that there are perception-independent, reidentifiable and individually discriminable objects or events, occupying space and time, interacting causally, bearing properties of various kinds – and so on. On the face of it, cultural relativism presents few philosophical difficulties, because our being able to recognise that another culture, or historical phase in our own culture, differs from our own in these and those respects, presupposes an ability on our part to gain access to the alien culture and recognise the differences *as* differences; which means that there must be enough in common between our own and the alien culture to allow us that access. These points are best made by thinking of a conceptual scheme as a language or set of intertranslatable languages, and as access between cultures (schemes) as effected by translation between the languages in which they consist.[8]

It is, however, just this point which has been denied most hotly by philosophical proponents of relativism, on grounds furnished by an objection which goes as follows: The appearance of accessibility is misleading, because what we have done is, far from gaining entry to the alien scheme, merely reinterpreted it in a systematic way into the terms of our own scheme; and this is the best we can ever hope to do, because translation is not possible above a certain highly indeterminate level. By failure of translation such relativists do not mean the empirically false thesis that no language can be rendered into another, but the philosophical thesis that (to employ Quine's terms) synonymy relations cannot be established above the level of stimulus-meanings of sentences, these being native speakers' patterns of assent and dissent to them; and therefore although we might come to use a term of a foreign language in the correct assent-dissent pattern, we can never be quite sure which of alternative translations of the term exhaustively captures its sense, for its stimulus-conditions underdetermine what precise construction is to be placed upon it. Thus 'gavagai' might mean 'rabbit' or 'temporal slices of rabbithood', and so on, without our having means to reduce the indeterminacy.[9]

What underlies Quine's thesis of the indeterminacy of translation, and its yet more extreme variants like Feyerabend's views on meaning variance,[10] is the problem about theory -ladenness of observation. If all discourse is theoretical, then there is no Archimedean point to step upon from which subscribers to one scheme can neutrally compare an alien scheme. If the problem of translation proves to be intractable, it follows that relativism is true; and Quine's view, that a difference of language marks a difference of ontology, is substantiated. Accordingly the issue of theory-ladenness and its consequences for translation need to be investigated.

What the thesis of theory-ladenness comes down to is the denial, by its proponents, of any distinction between theoretical and observational terms. The consequence of the Positivist's debate on whether there can be an observation language, *protokolsätze*, or some form of theory-neutral description of experience, was that there can be no such thing, precisely because the notion of observationality is *itself* theoretical,[11] forming part of a theory of reductive analysis; so there is no way out, on either count of whether a) there can be a neutral observation language into which different theoretical languages can be translated for comparison, or b) whether certain sets of theoretical statements (for example, about physical objects) can be reduced to observational statements (for example, about sense-data); for the distinction required to license such translations trades upon the possibility of there being formal criteria of synonymy by means of which the translation is such reductive exercises can be effected. And this is what is denied; Quine holds that there can be no such formal criteria of synonymy, because any such criteria would be constructable only by reference to our knowledge of what things in the world the terms in question apply to, and therefore cannot be independent of our theories about the world.[12] Accordingly, because the synonymy relations will themselves be theory-infected, appeal to them in reduction vitiates the reductive enterprise.

The truth of the claim that there can be no observation term-theoretical term distinction rests therefore on the denial of the possibility of synonymy. It is on the basis of this latter, as noted, that it is then denied that the meaning of an expression in some natural language L_1 can be stated in another natural language L_2, and that therefore, because the conceptual scheme is the language, failure of translation amounts to radical relativism. Feyerabend takes this position further by claiming that because, within a single scheme, all the concepts employed are theoretical, shifts in theory constitute conceptual change and therefore change in meaning; for example, inventing finer ways of calibrating temperature results, in Feyerabend's view, in change in the meaning of 'temperature'.

Now, these relativist considerations may appear to be a natural corollary of antirealism. Feyerabend's thermometers afford a case in point. If the sense of a term is fixed by its conditions of assertion, evidently changes in these latter — as with finer calibrations of temperature — constitute changes of sense, and this is what Feyerabend means (or must at least mean) by a 'change of meaning'. More generally, if, as Quine's arguments suggest, we can never have a determinate grasp of the conditions for assertion of expressions in languages other than our own — and therefore cannot grasp the sense of those expressions except indeterminately — then relativism is true, each language is its own conceptual scheme, and speakers are locked within their own conceptual schemes. And all this seems to be, as noted, one way of spelling out the consequences of antirealism in the theory of meaning. These arguments also give the lie, of course, to the view that moral or cultural relativism is philosophically unproblematic; we do not, if relativist arguments are right, have access of any genuine kind to other cultures or phases in the history of our own.

Relativism, however, is not only unattractive, but demonstrably false. First I shall demonstrate its falsity, and then show how anti-realism has no part in it.

What sense attaches to the idea that, despite our being sealed-off from an alien language or conceptual scheme, we can recognise it *as* a language or conceptual scheme? Surely, in order to recognise the alien language as a language, we must have access to it in some way? The idea here is that nothing could count for us as a language unless it were recognisable as such to us; and that whatever differences there are, in outlook or opinion, between ourselves and speakers of another language, they would, in order to be *recognised* as differences, have to occur against a wide background of mutual comprehensibility, and a wide range of shared beliefs and assumptions. This idea strongly suggests that relativism cannot be true, and indeed furnishes the materials for an argument to show that it is *not* true; for it turns on the notion that the criterion of languagehood is: translatability into our own language. This seems a startling notion at first blush, but it can be shown to be correct. Moreover, the translatability in question must be more than the indeterminate translation allowed by Quine, since indeterminate translation is more than merely consistent with, but indeed gives rise to, relativism, as noted above. The argument against relativism proceeds as follows.

Schematically: a language is a conceptual scheme. If we are to recognise the language as a language, we must be able to recognise the presence of a certain range of beliefs, specifically empirical beliefs, underlying the speakers' employment of their language. Evidently what these beliefs are is the important issue, and what features or devices of the language they reveal themselves in will constitute those features or devices the presence of which will enable us to recognise the language as a language. The task is to specify these.

It is fruitful to think of a language (a scheme) as 'organising' or systematising the world over which our experience ranges, or, if one prefers, that experience itself.[13] If a language (scheme) organises the world or experience, then the ontology at issue is puralist.[14] Accordingly the language must contain individuative devices (and thus concepts of individuals) and predicative devices (and thus concepts of properties) as does ours; for otherwise noting failure in coexstensivity of predicates between our own and the alien language would not be possible. Accordingly, at least part of the languagehood criterion is that if anything is a language it contains devices for individuation and for ascribing properties to the individuals individuated, which devices can be recognised as such in a way exactly parallel to our understanding the same linguistic features of our own language. The translatability of the alien tongue will indeed rest upon this; for not even recognising assent and dissent patterns, after the Quine model, would be possible unless we recognised that (taking the simplest cases) what the assent or dissent is relative to is a claim that here or there is something x, or that x is or is not something F. At the base of a model of discourse which is built upon the idea, surely right, that at its simplest communication rests upon pointing out, agreeing upon, or denyng, as the case may be, such matters as these, is the notion that an x can be marked off from the rest of the perceptual field, and that something can be said about x, i.e., that some property can be ascribed to it (or denied of it), such as that it stands in a certain relation (to, say, y), or is spotted, or is of a certain kind, or is about to pounce. Evidently, a wholly uninterpreted discourse would be one just in virtue of our failure to recognise certain strings of sounds or marks as what might on the foregoing be called individuative and predicative claims, for – the reason noted – our failure in this respect would deny us purchase on what is to count as assent or dissent. It follows that being able to recognise a language as such comes down to being able to recognise certain of its features as individuative and predictive in function.

It is important to notice at this point how taking such a view marks an advance over the Quine-Davidson line. Quine allows that for a certain range of sentences, *viz.,* 'observation sentences' falling on to the periphery of the web of language, meanings can be grasped by 'pure ostension'. Mass terms are good examples; 'water' can be learned ostensively by conditioning or induction. In contrast, terms of divided reference like 'rabbit' cannot be mastered without mastering the principles of individuation governing them, yet these cannot be mastered by ostension; therefore indeterminacy enters the picture, for if one cannot tell, in connection with 'gavagai', where one leaves off and another begins, e.g., whether 'gavagai' picks out rabbits, undetached rabbit parts, or rabbit stages, then appeal to reference is of no avail in accounting for however much of meaning of 'gavagai' we grasp, and in consequence we have to rest content, in trying to do so, with indeterminate 'stimulus-meaning'.[15] This alone on Quine's view is what enables us to get our translation manual started. (Reference proper, for Quine, is something which only bound variables do, because in order to circumvent the problem of referential opacity, i.e., to ensure that reference is successful, it must be restricted to a connection between bound variables in a canonically regimented language and the values which those variables take in the selected domain of discourse[16].) But this will not do; for all that the stimulus-conditions for 'gavagai' tell us is that 'gavagai' is assertible when current stimulation includes a rabbit, and that native speakers never dissent when 'gavagai' is offered in the presence of one. But this is to know for too little about the assertibility-conditions of 'gavagai' to permit *any* translation of the term, for it may be, as some widely different set of circumstances might show, that 'gavagai' means something like 'creature which yields white meat', and may therefore also apply to chickens. Unless the translator had a way of focusing on what the term contrasts with in native usage, i.e., on what it is for something to be '*not* gavagai', he could not render the term. Among the complexities known to a speaker about the sentences of his own language are some of the implications which use of them carry; in particular, interpreting a sentence (e.g., 'this is not red') involves knowing that it implies a certain closed field of options, having the force of 'this is (some other colour)' rather than, say, 'this is liquid' or 'this tastes pleasant'.[17] Unless the translator knew what remained open by a case of dissent to 'gavagai', the expression would be wholly opaque; yet to know the force of such a denial would be to know a principle of individuation for gavagais, for the simple reason that the translator would know, in knowing what was left open by denials, *ipso facto* where one gavagai left off and another begun. Accordingly, for any sort of interpretation to get going, what must be known to the translator is the reference of the relevant terms. And the notion of reference here is not particularly arcane; the reference of a term is just the object which use of the term (if it is a singular term) picks out or individuates, or the objects which the term (if it is a general term) collects.

If it is granted that references must be perspicuous across languages for translation to be possible, it follows that the extension of at least many simple predicates, or, at any rate, the intersection of the extension of such predicates as between the languages, is determinable; for referential scrutability allows the direct enumeration of lists of objects satisfying a predicate in a way which would permit correct application (and withholdings) of a predicate in L_1 by a speaker of L_2. It follows that for some expressions paired from L_1 and L_2 there will be a semantic feature of the pairing suspiciously like our pretheoretical grasp of intralanguage synonymy; 'la plume est rouge' and 'the pen is red' is a case in point. Evidently, if such a relation obtains between sentences of different languages, it does so in a way both richer and more determinate than is allowable on Quine's view of stimulus-synonymy; and this is as it should be, for the perspicuity of reference and accessibility of predicate-extensions across languages would be expected to generate together a number of unquestionable matchings of this kind as a direct consequence. This is not (or not directly) a point about intralanguage synonymy in the sense of intersubstitutivity of terms or expressions in sentential contexts *salva veritate*; rather, holding for present purposes to the level of complete sentences of a given class, *viz.,* sentences expressing perceptual judgements, it is a point about statement synonymy within and across languages. It will be recalled that in 'Two Dogmas' Quine[18] attacked *both* the analytic-synthetic distinction *and* reductionism on the grounds that they are closely linked and mutually supportive, depending as they do on the possibility of extricating factual from semantic considerations and considering their bearing on the truth-conditions of a given statement separately, which, if it were possible, would make reduction a feasible enterprise in that we could display the factual component of truth-conditions independently of the purely semantical features of sentences made true (or false) by them, and we could give an account of analytic statements as constituting a degenerate class wholly dependent for their truth-value on semantical considerations alone. Quine's attack was an attack on Positivist verificationism, to which this 'extricability thesis' was fundamental.[19] Statement synonymy on the Positivist view consists in the fact that because the meaning of a statement is its method of verification, any two statements with identical empirical conditions of confirmation or disconfirmation are synonymous. This demands that unique ranges of sensory events are identifiable for individual statements which, as the case may be, verify or falsify the statements in question; and it is this in which the reductionism of the view consists and which Quine finds objectionable. His holism or 'organic' verificationism is opposed precisely to this 'molecular' verificationism.[20] But it is by no means clear that what Quine takes to follow from the adoption of a holistic view *does* follow, specifically in connection with indeterminacy at the level of observation statements. Here, on his view, the stimulus meanings of observation sentences, construed as the ordered pair of assents and dissents prompted by given stimuli, underdetermine the translation of such sentences from L_1 to L_2 in the way noted; but for the reason that the range of options left open by dissents must be determinate — again, as noted — this degree of indeterminacy would prevent any translation at all. Quine's notion of stimulus-meaning as it stands will not therefore do, and the added requirement that the force of dissents be available to the translator is precisely a requirement for determinacy. This has two results: it entails that sentences indeterminate in L_2 will reflect indeterminacy in L_1 in the way described by Dummett, [21] i.e., that if a sentence of L_1 has competing renderings in L_2 then this will be because speakers of L_1 themselves attach competing interpretations to the sentence in L_1, and this feature of the sentence's ambiguity or underdetermination will be reflected in L_2; and secondly, it entails that the assertibility-conditions for unambiguous sentences of L_1 will be known to a speaker of L_2 if he can translate it, in such a way that for at least some sentences of L_1 the speaker of L_2 can recognise the assertibility-conditions for the sentence to be identical to its translation in L_2, and so stand in a relation of statement-synonymy to its L_2 translation. [22]

It is important to note how this notion of statement-synonymy unpacks. It trades upon the fact that determinacy of reference and predicate extension must be available to the translator if he is to translate at all. This if he knows that a term α in L_1 refers to all and only what the term α in L_2 refers to, and a predicate F introduces a particularly property designated ϕ in L_2, then the sentence Fa in L_1 is synonymous with the L_2 sentence $\phi\alpha$. It is to be borne in mind that, in the most general terms, understanding (knowing how to use) a sentence involves knowing all of (a) what terms correlate with what features of a perceptual environment, (b) how to recognise such features, and (c) in what ways things can go wrong with either (a) or (b), and chiefly the latter. Knowing, at least implicitly, these things is to know how to use, i.e., understand, the sentence. To assert as it were *across* languages, it might seem that what has to be known is extra information under (a), e.g., that 'plume' corefers with 'pen', 'voiture' with 'motor-car', and so on; but matters are somewhat tighter than this, for knowing (a) is *ipso facto* to know all of (a)-(c); displaying mastery of a term presupposes mastery of all three conditions. Because understanding a sentence of L_1 involves the same as understanding a sentence of L_2, knowing extra information about terms (or rather, just knowing more terms) which apply to certain features in perceptual environments is to know how things

must be for their use to be warranted. This strengthens the requirement of option-closure connected with negation. For it is a corollary
of these conditions that one has failed in grasping the sense of an
expression if one does not know what alternatives are left open by
dissent to a term, for all one would know in such a case is *that* use of
the term was inappropriate, not *why* or *how*, and this violates the
conditions for mastery.

This is not to say, however, that unique ranges of sensory
evidence are or have to be available for the confirmation or disconfirmation of a sentence in order for it to be *assertible,* although
they would be available on each occasion of an undefeatedly
warranted use of such a sentence. What the speaker has to know is
what circumstances would warrant use of the sentence; if there are
such circumstances, the sentence is assertible. The conditions for
understanding a sentence do not require that for every understood
sentence there is an occasion on which a speaker was actually
warranted in its use. A difficulty may appear to arise here: it
follows, most clearly in connection with option-closure, that understanding a sentence involves understanding other sentences, or
more generally a portion at least of a language. This would seem to
require of a translator that he knows other sentences of L_1 before he
can understand whatever sentence of L_1 is in question. Not so; in so
far as he is a *translator*, he knows L_2, and the sentence of L_1 at issue
can be placed in the context of what can be said in L_2 on the topic in
hand. This affords an alternative means of marking the sense in
which, for a language to be recognisable as a language, it must be
accessible, i.e., translatable into a familiar idiom.

The foregoing arguments show that relativism is false, for if
languages=schemes, and any language, to be recognisable as such,
is translatable into our own, then there is only one conceptual
scheme. It is now necessary to show that antirealism has no part in
relativism; and this is best done by considering the 'meaning-
variance' thesis advanced by Feyerabend (cf. above).

Feyerabend's thesis about meaning-variance, demonstrated by
means of the thermometer example, rests upon two mistakes to the
effect that a) the sense of a term is grasped only through possession
or mastery of such facts as would *inductively* justify application of
the term, so that change in the nature of facts involves a change of
sense, because these facts constitute the term's assertion conditions; and b) that any such change involves change of reference too.
(This latter part of the mistake makes illegitimate use of something
arguably right, *viz.,* that sense provides the route for reference for
terms picking out abstract objects like temperature.)

The mistakes here are easily spotted. It is evident that being able to understand what improving our understanding of some phenomenon consists in demands *continuity* of reference to the phenomenon, to ensure that modifications in our concept of it are intelligible – which is to say that improving, extending, or refining our understanding of something x cannot entail that *ipso facto* we cease to mean x by y instead, for then we should not have been improving or extending our grasp of x at all. An alternative example may help to clarify the point; electrons for Bohr and electrons for contemporary physicists are, as we say, 'two different things', and yet understanding the recent history of particle physics demands an important minimum of continuity of reference for the term 'electron', and therefore some degree of overlap of sense; otherwise it would not be possible to talk of a change or improvement in our understanding of electrons. This ties in with the earlier part of the mistake; for to know that it is a finer way of calibrating *temperature* which has been found, the sense of 'temperature' cannot have changed, and therefore cannot turn solely upon the various procedures by which temperature is measured; rather, talk of temperature is appropriate when what is at issue is, independently of the alternative ways we measure it, simply the degree or intensity of sensible heat of a body or the air. It would be absurd, and yet a direct consequence of Feyerabend's views, to hold that if I say 'it was 21° Centigrade, or 69.8° Fahrenheit yesterday, I am talking about two different things. If someone came up with a new temperature-scale based on letters of the alphabet, and a new kind of thermometer, and presented it to me with the request to say what the instrument measured, my failure to tell him would mean neither that I misunderstood 'temperature' (and certainly not because the term had 'changed its meaning' owing to the innovations present), nor that what a mercury thermometer measures in Fahrenheit units is different from what the new alphabetical thermometer measures. Again, that the new thermometer measures temperature is something we grasp independently of any particular knowledge of how temperature is measured; the sense of the term is fixed in quite general ways involving an ability to perceive sensible differences in heat – 'hotter' and 'colder' form the scale which counts, and that must be invariant with respect to sophisticated means of dealing with temperature; they are, so to say, the appearances which the sophistications must save. Accordingly, Feyerabend's mistake is to identify inductive instrumental facts and assertibility conditions, and incorrectly takes changes in such facts to entail correspondent changes in sense, which if he is right would so far dislocate our conceptual scheme as to make the notion of conceptual change itself meaningless.

That it is a mistake to identify inductive instrumental facts and assertibility conditions can be shown by considering the following. Earlier it was noted that on an antirealist approach, understanding sentences is to know how to recognise when one is warranted in using them. What we wish to show now is that the kind of verification at issue can be neither such as to *entail* some assertion, nor to stand to it as *inductive* warrant; for what one recognises as warranting use of a particular sentence is that these are the conditions for the sense of the sentence, and this does not constitute an entailment relation (for the statement made by use of the sentence is defeasible); but yet is stronger than merely contingent conditions fixing the sentence's epistemic value. That this latter is the case may be seen by considering an example.[23]

A chemical experiment is conducted by X in which a piece of blue litmus paper is immersed in a solution S. It turns red, and X concludes that S is acidic. Y, observing the experiment, does not see why this should follow. But X is justified in holding S to be acidic, for this just is one of the ways one is justified in saying that S is acidic − it has turned blue litmus paper red. Evidently it is not that Y fails to understand 'S is acidic'. He may indeed be well able to give account of what an acid is; it may just be that he does not know about acid's effect on litmus paper.

Accordingly, understanding a sentence must consist in a grasp of what would *non-inductively* justify asserting it; we should not say that anyone does not understand a sentence just because he lacks such information as could inductively justify its use. Possession of warrant for the use of a sentence may then be informatively described (as Wright describes it; cf. chapter 8 above) as consisting in the knowledge that the evidence is a *criterion* for the use of the sentence. The usefulness of employing such a notion is clear. What, say, a philosophical sceptic wishes to know, is what account can be given of *evidence,* granted that the justification we have for asserting some statement p on the basis of evidence e is just that e is evidence for p. E's being evidence for p is either a contingent or a necessary matter; if e is contingently evidence for p, we could only come to know that it *is evidence* for p by experience; but this renders our notion of evidence vulnerable to sceptical attack. By contrast, if grasping the sense of p *is* to know that e is evidence for it, that is, that e is the (or a) criterion for p, then it is necessary that e is evidence for p − we know that e is evidence for p *a priori*.[24] Learning a language is, crucially, to learn when saying what is appropriate; to talk of a criterial ('meaning-connection') relation between occasions for the use of sentences and those sentences themselves is to say that we do not discover *post facto* that these sentences are assertible in those circumstances; it is impossibly difficult to see how, if this is how things are, anyone could ever come by a language. (Denying that we know the assertibility-conditions for sentences only *a posteriori* is not to deny that we are ever wrong; our claims are defeasible, which is why one needs to invoke the notion of a *criterion* in this connection, rather than some stronger relation.[25])

These arguments show that antirealism has no part in relativism. It is particularly interesting to note this in view of the fact that, in some moods, Dummett appears to countenance relativist consequences for his views.[26] If relativism is not after all an option for antirealism, what of idealism?

IDEALISM

There are different species of idealism. What is common to them is the notion that the world is in some sense dependent on being known or conceived by subjects of experience, including − in some variations − God; such that the idea of a world's existing independently of any thought of it is unintelligible. At different pounts in the history of modern philosophy from Berkeley onwards, idealism has been given competing articulations, which accounts for the variety of its forms. In recent philosophy, phenomenalism has been the closest to a form of idealism among theories of knowledge (and, hence, theories of the objects of knowledge)'.[27]

It is important to emphasise this last point, namely that idealism takes its rise from epistemological considerations, and in particular from *empiricism* in epistemology. If one takes seriously the idea that what can be known about the world rests on a foundation of empirical experience, or in some way arises primarily from empirical experience, then *what* can be known is, clearly, subject throughout to the conditions of empirical experience − unless somehow one can find a respectable way of starting from, but going beyond, experience, so that statements about the world can be validated in a way which does not involve essential reference to experience itself.[28] Ordinary realist presumptions are based upon the view that this can be done, and most recent epistemology has been devoted, indeed, to the effort to substantiate these ordinary realist presumptions by arriving at conclusions based upon, but transcending, empirical considerations. On the whole such efforts have failed, as the continuing force of sceptical arguments shows.[29]

If, therefore, reference to the empirical conditions governing the concepts we habitually employ and apply is inescapable, an anti-realist attitude to language seems inescapable too; for antirealism is the thesis that the sense of our discourse is determined by the empirical conditions of it acquisition and use, and our everyday concepts of the world are applied in – one might say, embodied in – our discourse.[30] Antirealism is an attitude to language which takes epistemology, and in particular empirical epistemology, seriously; it is for this reason that some form of idealism, minimally conceived of as the idea that the conception of the world's existing independently of any experience of it is unintelligible, appears to be a natural consequence of it.

The question is, idealism in what sense? The general characterisation given above of what is common to different forms of idealism applies to antirealism concerning the language we use to talk about the world; but it is not clear that this forces commitment to any of the familiar specific forms of idealism espoused, variously, by Berkeley, Hegel, or the 'Absolute Idealists' like Bradley and Bosanquet. These varieties of idealism are strong theses which purport to establish the falsity of the view that there is an experience-independent world (in the ordinary realist sense), by substantiating the view that the world is a collection of ideas (as in Berkeley) or is a seamless and eternal whole (the 'Absolute', as in Bradley); and such views stand at enough of a distance from the premiss, *viz.*, that talk of the world makes essential reference to experience, for a good deal of argument, and mostly tendentious argument, to be required to bridge the gap.[31] In order to get quite clear on these issues, we should have to (and here cannot, for lack of space) pick a way through a forest of details. What I choose to do instead is to cut directly across them to a line which seems to me most promising.

It is important to note, first, two general constraints on what kind of theory would be acceptable; these constraints apply as much to realism as to any antirealist thesis. For one thing, we have to take seriously the idea that empirical experience is in some sense centrally important to any conception we form of the world, and therefore any discourse about the world we employ; for otherwise we should find ourselves in the situation of having to lay claim to justified beliefs about contingent matters with only such epistemic capacities as would consist in rational excogitation from first principles, or some kind of epistemological intuition, or – in Descartes' fashion – an appeal to the goodness of God. Secondly, we have to take seriously the fact that our ordinary thought and talk is realist, and that there would be no means of making sense of the concept of experience itself, unless we had available to us an operable distinction between what is objective and what is subjective in experience. (This point becomes clearer in due course.) The first constraint pleases the antirealist and presents a problem to the realist; the second pleases the realist and − on the face of it − presents a problem to the antirealist. Indeed, the two constraints pull against one another, and the tension between them can be seen as constituting one of the fundamental reasons − if not *the* fundamental reason − for there being a philosophical problem about knowledge of this deeply puzzling kind.

A fruitful way of articulating the possibilities for antirealism construed as a species of idealism is to consider certain important distinctions and ideas owing to Kant,[32] who regarded his *transcendental idealism* as a thesis equivalent to *empirical realism*. The term 'transcendental' in this context has to do with the notion of experience's setting limits to what the understanding can do; the connection with antirealism is plain, for, in this latter view, having a proof or verification procedure sets limits to what can be said: sense *must* be explained in terms of the constraints imposed by the methods available to us for acquiring and manifesting knowledge of language.[33]

Now, Kant had it that phenomena − that is, the objects of experience − are transcendentally ideal but empirically real, by which he meant that the ordinary distinction between appearance and reality is a genuine one, but has to be drawn *within* experience itself. Transcendental idealism is *not* concerned with the relation between perceptual experience, on the one hand, and its objects, on the other, in anything like the sense familiar in traditional epistemology, where the relation in question is conceived of as one obtaining between subjects, whose empirical self-awareness is immediate, and objects whose existence has to be inferred from the immediate subjective data of consciousness. This latter thesis Kant called 'empirical idealism', and he held that it has two forms: 'problematic idealism' (exemplified, for Kant, by Descartes) in which the existence of outer objects is taken to be dubious but demonstrable, and 'dogmatic idealism' (exemplified by Berkeley) in which the assumption is that the existence of outer objects is false and logically impossible. Kant's transcendental idealism, by contrast, constitutes an empirical realism because it turns on the notion that experience of outer objects is truly immediate, and that only by means of it is inner (or subjective) experience possible. What Kant meant by this touches on the heart of his transcendental philosophy, contained in the 'Transcendental Deduction', the purpose of which is to show that it is a necessary condition of having experience that that experience should in part be experience of objects which exist independently of any particular acts of awareness of them.[34] Rather than go through the metaphysical and transcendental deductions offered by Kant, one can demonstrate what *kind* of argument this is, and what kind of result it yields, by looking, for example, at an analogous argument, concerning the necessity of other-ascribing states of consciousness if one is to be able to ascribe them to oneself. The argument here owes itself to Strawson.

Strawson argued that one can self-ascribe states of consciousness only if one is able to other-ascribe them (and that the fact that this is so defeats scepticism about other minds). For, in order to doubt the existence of other minds, the sceptic must employ the concept of other minds itself, which can only be done if he distinguishes between 'my states of consciousness' and 'others' states of consciousness'; and this can only be done, in turn, if others exist, because the identification of conscious states can only be effected by reference to particulars of a special kind, *viz.*, persons, the concept of which – in turn again – demands that there be criteria for distinguishing one person from another, for otherwise the identification of states of consciousness would not be possible. So one can talk of '*my* experiences' only if one can talk of others' experiences; this is possible only if there are criteria for distinguishing between persons; and since one *does* talk significantly about one's own experiences, there must be such criteria. Then if there are such criteria, bodily behaviour constitutes logically adequate grounds for ascription of states of consciousness to others. Hence sceptical doubts about the existence of other minds are idle, for to so much as formulate such doubts, a sceptic would have to employ the discourse whose very conditions of employment legitimise what he wishes to call into question.[36]

This kind of argument is called a 'transcendental argument', and the aim of such arguments in general is to show what are the necessary conditions of some given conceptual practice or, more usually, of our conceptual scheme as a whole. An argument about *objects* can be reconstructed along closely similar lines.[37] It is, roughly, that if we think, as we do, of the world as a coherent spatio-temporal system of material things, then it is a condition of having this conceptual scheme that we unquestioningly accept the continued unperceived existence of at least some of these things in at least some cases; for, if we suppose that we never reidentified objects, we should effectively be committing ourselves to the notion that each new stretch of observation or experience ranges over discrete and independent spatio-temporal systems. But if this were so then no question would arise as to the identity of a material item in one system with an item in another. To *doubt* that material things continue to exist unperceived makes sense only if the two systems are not independent; but then it is precisely a condition of a unified system that there should be satisfiable, and commonly satisfied, criteria for the identity of at least some material items in one sub-system with some items in the other. Hence one cannot be sceptical about the unperceived continuous existence of objects.[38]

Now, it would be a mistake to take it that this argument establishes the existence of objects independently of any experience. What it shows is that it is a necessary condition of the experience we have that we are committed to believing that objects continue to exist unperceived; we must have and employ the concept of perception-independent particulars if experience is to be coherent.[39] Nothing follows as to there being anything which answers to that concept independently of the entertainment of that concept by experiencing subjects. At first blush, this seems rather a lame conclusion, for it settles nothing as to whether *there are* objects independently of experience. But the whole point is that the desire to secure this latter result is misguided. For, if it is a necessary condition of the coherence of our conceptual scheme that we must believe that there are perception-independent objects, and if there is only one conceptual scheme, as the anti-relativist arguments earlier demonstrated, then a belief in the perception-independent existence of objects *is a condition of experience in general.* And this is all that either can be or needs to be shown. The realist wishes to go further than this, to derive a result about objects as *really* real, as existing *wholly* or *absolutely* independently of any experience whatever; but the demand that this be done is, literally, senseless — which is to say, no sense attaches to, or can attach to, talk of entities for whose existence nothing whatever could count as evidence, that is, for talk of which nothing whatever could count as a means of acquiring and displaying the warrant for such talk. Contemporary realists therefore can be characterised as 'transcendental realists' in Kant's sense, as opposed to 'empirical realists' which is what contemporary antirealists are; for realists are committed to the view that the notion of a) the perception-independent existence of objects is equivalent to — that is, entails and is entailed by — b) the notion of thought- or experience-independence of objects in general; whereas in fact, although b) entails a), a) does not entail b), and empirical realism is the view that whereas a commitment to a) is demanded by the nature of experience itself, nothing either does or needs to follow as to b). Kant put matters like this: whereas an object is 'nothing to us' unless it is or can be 'thought' by us, nevertheless what it is to 'think' an object carries with it, as a condition of the necessary connectedness of experience without which having such a concept would be impossible, the concept of the object's independence of *particular* acts of perceptual awareness of it; but this is far from a claim to the effect that objects are wholly independent of thought or experience in the way the realist wishes to hold.[40] The general point at issue is well made by Strawson:

If we accept the conclusion that experience necessarily involves awareness of objects conceived of as existing in time independently of any particular states of awareness of them, then we must accept it without reservation. We have no extraneous standard or scheme in terms of which we can give an esoteric sense to the question whether such objects *really* exist, as we must empirically conceive of them as existing, independently of our perceptions. The question can be understood only in the sense of the scheme itself to which we are committed and in that sense it admits of but one commonplace answer. The philosophical achievement consists in showing that the answer is not merely a commonplace, though it is that. It consists in showing the place of this commonplace in any intelligible conception of experience we can form, in showing that it holds such a place even if we take the conception of experience to the last point of abstraction it can reach before distintegrating.[41]

It is important to note that what I am borrowing from Kant is a deliberately bowdlerised version of his views, for nothing of his 'transcendental psychology' is here being invoked. In terms of Kant's project in the first *Critique*, the transcendental psychology plays a crucial role; but it is incredible, and best dispensed with.[42] This means that the notion of transcendental idealism in particular needs to be understood in a way which makes no appeal to Kant's doctrines of apperception and the transcendental self. For present purposes, transcendental idealism is the thesis that the world, as the orderly collection of accusatives of empirical experience, is everywhere and always conditioned by the nature of empirical experience — which is just to say that the sense of any discourse about the world is always essentially relative to the conditions under which that sense can be mastered and manifested in discourse, in that *grasp* of sense consists in the possession of verification procedures in the way discussed earlier. Transcendental idealism is therefore not an adventurous thesis of the kind typically suggested by talk of idealism; it simply iterates the point that there is no understanding the world or language in any way which dispenses with reference to the conditions under which the world is known or language publicly mastered and used.

This, in turn, means that questions about what there is *independently* of any talk or experience are strictly unintelligible. The point is not that there *is* no world existing independently of experience, but that there is no senseful way in which one can talk of a world lying beyond or outside experience; neither, indeed, of the locutions 'there is an experience-independent world' and 'there is not an experience-independent world' strictly makes sense, for there is all and only the world as it is experienced or experienceable, and nothing can count as senseful comment outside the limits which the conditions of senseful discourse impose.

To grasp this point fully one needs to perform an intellectual Gestalt of sorts. Pre-philosophical assumptions, and much philosophical tradition, both strongly lean towards the idea that there are subjects of experience and, existing independently of them, objects of experience. There are two ways this dualism can be understood. It is evident that criteria are needed for understanding the difference between what it is for something to be a subject of experience (an experiencing subject) and what it is for something to be an object of experience. According to the assumptions and the tradition of realism, the obvious way to mark the difference is to conceive of the objects of experience as existing wholly independently of experiencing subjects. But this is highly problematic, for the reasons given; and in any case the subject-object distinction can be accommodated within terms even of a Berkeleyan idealism, thus: concepts of what in realist terminology would be called 'subjective' and 'objective' elements in experience may be characterised as belonging, say, to two different conceptual categories in the idealist's scheme, such that concepts in the 'objective' category, call it the O-category, like concepts of tables and trees, differ from those in the 'subjective' category, call it the S-category, like one's own images, memories and desires, in virtue of such features as that O-concepts are far less tractable to one's willings than S-concepts; that they are linked together in more determinate fashion than S-concepts, so that their relations may be represented as law-like; that thoughts intending O-type accusatives differ in *quality* from S-type ones, perhaps − in Humean fashion − by being more 'forceful' and 'vivid', say; and so on. Then for allocation to the relevant class of the kind of reference the idealist takes his concepts to have, it will be possible to state that some concept is of such-and-such a kind just according to whether it satisfies the criteria for a concept to be of that kind in general; and such criteria appear, on this sketch, to be readily and naturally available in the course of experience itself, without any reference to an external world. This is not of course seriously intended as an argument in favour of a traditional-idealist account; rather, it shows that having a grasp of a subject-object distinction need not essentially depend upon commitment to realism. Now, the point which it requires a conceptual Gestalt to grasp is this: from an antirealist point of view, realism is premissed on a strictly un-intelligible commitment to the existence of an experience-transcendent reality, to say which is also to say or imply that a *denial* of realist claims about such a reality is equally unintelligible. Accordingly, what one has to see is that *both* sides of the dispute are futile: straining after a sense for questions (and denials) about whether the world is '*really* real' is just beside the point.[42]

What, then, of the constraint, noted earlier, that any theory must take account of the fact that ordinary thought and talk is realist? Indeed, the very idea of 'publicly available' conditions being required for language-learning is a realistic idea. Some account of the pervasive realism of our everyday conceptual scheme is required.

In line with the foregoing thoughts, what has to be said is this. The idea that the world is independent of particular acts of awareness of it, or independent of the relation in which individual perceivers stand to it, has to be construed as an idea which has a special status in our conceptual scheme. The proposition 'objects exist un-perceived' might best be regarded as a 'grammatical' proposition in Wittgenstein's sense; a 'grammatical proposition' is one which it makes no sense to doubt, and therefore, in an important way, no sense to assert or to claim to *know*.[43] The most fruitful way to characterise a belief enshrined in a grammatical proposition is to say that it is a presupposition of our thinking, talking, and acting as we do, such that to doubt that it *is* a presupposition is not to do something merely false, but unintelligible. An analogy is provided by the example of the man who prays, attends church, reads devotional literature, is sane, and is neither a dissimulator nor a sociologist conducting a hermeneutic experiment. To doubt or deny that such a man believes in the existence of at least one divinity is to fail to, or to refuse to, understand his practice or whatever asser-tions he may issue relevant to his practice.

Now, to put matters in this way is to say that a belief in the existence of objects is a necessary condition of our thought and talk. To say this is tantamount to saying that realist assumptions are necessary to our conceptual scheme; that, in effect, we are bound to be epistemological (or ontological) realists, if our thought and talk is to be coherent. But saying 'we are bound to be realists' is thus to make an antirealist point; for the claim is not a claim as to the *truth* of a realist view of the world, but a claim to the *necessity of taking* a realist view, with nothing following, because nothing *can* follow, as to the truth or falsity of such a view. This is precisely the force of saying that antirealism is an empirical realism (and *ipso facto* a transcendental idealism) in Kant's sense.

No doubt these considerations appear at first sight to be no more than an effort to both have and eat one's cake; it is always difficult to grasp alternative routes between the Scylla and Charybdis of entrenched conceptual oppositions such as those jointly repudiated here, *viz.*, traditional realism and traditional idealism. What I find most interesting in this is the powerful way some aspects of Kant's thought apply to contemporary concerns.

Two points need to be noted before this discussion is left. One is that neither of antirealism's chief proposers, Dummett and Wright, explicitly commits himself to any form of idealism. Wright indeed repudiates any idealist consequences for his views;[44] Dummett is consistently chary − not to say, equivocal − as to what outcome antirealism forces; the closest he comes is to say: '[the antirealist view] has profound metaphysical repercussions; it means that we cannot operate, in general, with a picture of our language as bearing a sense that enables us to talk about a determinate, objective reality'.[45] The foregoing is a partisan view therefore. The other point is that there are connections between relativism and idealism in at least the sense that both deny sense to the idea of a common co-ordinate reality existing independently of the point of view of (some given) experience. As a way of arriving at this conclusion, however − and, moreover, at this as a wholly general conclusion − relativism is particularly unconvincing, and brings with it infections of the concept of sense itself.[46] Some form of idealism is a much more promising option.

THE ELIMINABILITY OF TRUTH

On the basis of the foregoing thoughts, a claim can be made out to the effect that the concept of truth is dispensable, at least as far as these issues are concerned. One might argue as follows.

Dummett has it that a concept of truth remains important in the theory of meaning, and gives two reasons. One, already noted, is that it is required for our understanding of deductive inference and therefore our concept of indirect conclusive proof. The other reason is as follows.

Frege said that grasping an assertoric utterance involves three levels of understanding: The first concerns the *sense* of the sentence, grasping which consists in grasping the condition for its truth: the second concerns grasp of a notion of *force* for utterances, that is, being able to tell whether it is an assertion, command, question, and so on; and the third concerns mastery of *point*, that is, being able to divine the speaker's particular intention in issuing an utterance of just such-and-such a sentence with just such-and-such a sense and force. A concept of truth is required to keep these three levels apart, for to do so we need, on Frege's view, to have the *contrast* between a) the idea of a statement's being true, and b) someone's having grounds for taking it to be true.[47] If the distinction between the first and second levels is denied, all three levels collapse into one; but if by means of a concept of truth the second and third levels can be kept apart, all three levels stay apart.[48] On Dummett's view (cf. above) a sense-force distinction is vital if we are to be able to give a systematic account of language; therefore, a concept of truth is required to keep apart these three levels in what it is to understand utterances.

It seems to me, however, that the less obscure notion of *warrant* will better serve our purposes both in these two cases and generally; and it is on its superiority as the central notion of a theory of meaning that the argument to the eliminability of truth rests.

'True' and 'false' undoubtedly have several useful roles in colloquial discourse, and certain specific roles in formal contexts; but if the following suggestions are correct, they are otherwise redundant. To see why, let us take a minimal characterisation of warrant as what attaches to a speaker's use of a sentence when he has grounds, yielded by a verification procedure of a kind which bestows sense on his sentences, for asserting (or otherwise — depending on force — employing) that sentence on a given occasion. Then we can say that a statement like 'the dome of the Radcliffe Camera will be visible from All Souls in 2084 AD' is assertible, for we know what verifying situations it can be employed in, but until 2084 AD its assertion will not be warranted, because the relevant actual verifying situation will not be available until then. Accordingly, since it is probable to some degree that that situation will become available, the statement itself is probable to that degree. On this basis, we can say that statements about the past, future, or currently unavailable regions of space, are always probable to some degree for a speaker on an occasion, and that statements about speakers' present perceptual environments are alone what can be undefeatedly (or defeatedly) warranted.

In talking of *warrant* for the use of sentences by means of which to talk about the world, we are talking about the way our beliefs entitle us to make the judgements we are accustomed to making daily. This is the same thing as tracing out the structure of our beliefs and showing how, by virtue of that structure, they bear the weight of our epistemological claims; under constraints of consitency or coherence among these, a belief structure which can be shown to justify our ordinary claims is thus far *rational*. Now, it is a standard view that rational systems of belief are rational just in virtue of their being truth-directed, and successfully so, and that the rules by means of which beliefs can be seen truth-directedly to support — or otherwise variously relate to — one another are the rules of logic. Truth theories indeed form the basis of logical systems, which is why, on the standard view of these matters, truth is regarded as the fundamental notion for understanding justification under species of the rationality of a belief system. On this view, then, knowledge of truth-conditions is something we must have prior to being able to talk about justification or warrant. A certain initial plausibility attaches to this view, for we know that we cannot hold both the belief that, say, something is green and nothing is green in the same system of beliefs, and we take it that knowing this derives from knowing the truth-conditions for the sentences 'some particular thing is green' and 'nothing is green'. But despite this appearance of plausibility in behalf of the truth-conditional approach, matters are otherwise. One can recognise a system of beliefs as rational — that is, as consistent and as having relations of consequence or support between its members — without being able to furnish an adequate specification of the truth-conditions for the sentences expressing those beliefs; indeed, it is not even necessary to our recognising that some belief is justified on the basis of certain others, or that two or more beliefs are consistent or inconsistent with respect to one another, that we believe the sentences expressing the beliefs to be true or false (still less 'objectively' true or false). Thus an account of justification can be given without depending on an assumption to the effect that understanding truth is crucially prior to understanding justification or warrant. It is in this sense that the notion of truth is eliminable, for what is to be understood as truth is more than adequately usurped by talk, instead, of warrant. Indeed, in view of the obscurity which attaches to the notion of truth — something which chapters 5 and 6 above may have suggested — its replacement by the more perspicuous idiom of warrant marks an advance in its own right.

The notion of indirect conclusive proof then comes down to the notion that the conclusive verification of a given statement proceeds by way of verified statements alone; any statement the satisfaction of whose verifying conditions proceeds entirely via the verification of other statements is *ipso facto indirectly* verified. Given a relation of consequence among statements, successfully deducing one from other statements comes down to seeing that the deduced statement is a) a consequence of the other statements, and b) wholly verified via them. This characterisation is exceedingly general, but once again the point is that it can be stated without reference to truth. For one requires only the notion of a *value* which a statement might possess – say, the value 'warranted' – for an account of the relation of consequence needed here: deductive inferences are value-preserving, such that if the premisses are individually warranted and it is a contradiction to assert the conjunction of the premisses and the denial of the conclusion, then the transition from premisses to conclusion is valid. Evidently, the notion of warrant is by no means coterminous with the concept of truth, nor is the denial of warrant coterminous with falsehood; warrant and its denial have the same content as provability and its negation in intuitionistic logic.

Similarly, one can hold apart the notions of sense and force by saying that to grasp *sense* is to grasp the notion of under what conditions, in general, employment of a sentence is warranted, and that to grasp *force* is to grasp (in the case of assertion) that the warrant is on the given occasion claimed to be available, or (in the case, say, of interrogatives) that it is being asked whether warrant is on the given occasion available – and so on.

The virtue of eschewing the concept of truth is that it is, confusedly, festooned with competing interpretations, as earlier chapters showed; and yet at the same time carries irreducibly realist connotations. Warrant, at least, is a straightforward verificationist notion, and there can be no doubt what is intended by its use. Whereas truth is transcendent, warrant is (in the anatomical sense) sublime. In connection with the concerns of this and the last chapter, it is therefore, in my view, strongly to be preferred.

A CONCLUDING COMMITMENT

If essences are not accessible to our recognitional capacities, then an antirealist must take exception to them. It would seem that the essentialism discussed in chapter 3 tends to be strongly realist in character; Kripke says '*whatever* it is' in connection with the essence of a kind. There are of course ways of employing possible-worlds talk which does not trade on essentialism, but it is doubtful that they are anything like as useful as essentialism-involving ways, and accordingly it is doubtful whether the success of antirealism in the theory of meaning would leave possible worlds talk (and, consequently, the 'casual theory of reference', CTR, touched upon in chapter 7) in very good shape. I mention this more or less in passing, to show what result might have to flow when one chooses one or the other of these two commitments; namely, that whichever one chooses, it is probably incompatible with the other. Remarking this also shows that, on the whole, possible worlds talk and the CTR assume a realist interpretation of the sense of the relevant discourse − not, in the case of the CTR, the sense of referring expressions, since on this view they have none − but the circumambient discourse as a whole. It is worth noting this because it demonstrates how far-reaching are the philosophical consequences of plumping for one or another way of dealing with meaning. That is a point which has had to be made often in the course of these chapters; and it explains why, in contemporary philosophy, the question of meaning looms so large.

NOTES

1. McDowell, 'Truth-Values, Bivalence, and Verificationism', in Evans and McDowell, *op. cit.,* p.48.
2. Dummett, TOE, p.xi.
3. It is interesting to remark, in passing, a curious irony here. It is that, as a consequence of Logical Positivism, the term 'metaphysics' was for a time a pejorative. One dismissed a philosophical position out-of-hand by describing it as 'metaphysical'. If one places the stronger of the two possible constructions on McDowell's remarks, then it turns out that verificationism, once wielded by its espousers as a weapon for deflating metaphysical pretensions, has become a target for that pejorative charge itself. Of course, contemporary antirealism differs substantially from its forebear, but the continuities are substantial too; it is entertaining to note these odd cycles of philosophical temper. All this, however, by way of aside.
4. Platts, *Ways of Meaning,* pp.237-8.
5. ibid., p.238.
6. I have elsewhere discussed the following issues in much greater detail than is possible here; cf. Grayling, *op. cit.,* chapters 3-5, *passim,* esp. chapters 4 and 5.
7. For 'conceptual scheme', cf. ibid., chapter 4, esp. pp.144-96.
8. cf. Davidson, 'On The Very Idea Of A Conceptual Scheme,' *Proceedings of the American Philosophical Society,* 1974, *passim,* and Grayling, ibid., p.171, *et seq.*
9. cf. Quine, W. V., *Word and Object,* chapter 2, *passim.*
10. Feyerabend, P., *Against Method,* London, 1975.
11. cf. the discussion of Neurath and Positivism in chapters 5 and 7 above.
12. cf. the discussion of Quine on synonymy in chapter 3 above.
13. For 'organises' cf. Grayling ibid., chapter 4, *passim,* esp. p.190, *et seq.*
14. That is, the language (scheme) ranges over an ontology of more than one different and discriminable item.

15. cf. Quine, *Ontological Releativity and Other Essays,* New York, 1961, p.31., *et seq.*

16. cf. ibid., p.124.

17. cf. Harrison, B., *Introduction To The Philosophy of Language*, London, 1979, pp.116-17.

18. Quine, 'Two Dogmas of Empiricism', *op. cit., passim.*

19. Dummett calls Quine's rejection of this thesis 'the inextricability thesis'; thus the coining here. cf. Dummett 'The Significance of Quine's Indeterminacy Thesis', TOE p.375, *et seq.*

20. Dummett's coinings, ibid., p.379.

21. ibid., pp.4-5, *et seq.*

22. It is an unavoidable complication that, however demarcated, sentences in a language have different degrees of theoreticity. For more rather than less theoretical sentences, underdetermination and therefore same-language indeterminacy will be greater than for more rather than less observational sentences. The first entailment speaks to the former more than to the latter, and *vice versa* for the second entailment. Observational or perceptual statements are what chiefly concern me here, however, and my remarks centre upon them unless qualified.

23. This example is drawn from Phillips, C., 'Constructivism and Epistemology', *Philosophy* vol. 53 No.203, 1978; cf p.55.

24. ibid.

25. cf., ibid.; and Grayling, *op. cit.,* chapter 3, *passim.*

26. cf. Dummett, 'On The Reality Of The Past', TOE p.373, *et seq.*; and 'Common Sense and Physics', in MacDonald (ed.), *op. cit.,* pp.20-1.

27. Classical phenomenalism attempted to construe statements about physical objects as exhaustively translatable into sets of experiential statements. It differs from idealism in taking not ideas but sense-data as the primary entities (in some versions, sense-data are independent of experiencers).

28. I discuss these issues at length in Grayling *op. cit.,* chapters 2 and 3 *passim.*

29. One standard way of dismissing these issues is to say (as does Mackie) that the simplest hypothesis available to us to account for our experience, is the hypothesis that there is an external world. What is wrong with this, however, is that the simplicity of our hypotheses is always consistent with their falsity.

30. cf. chapter 7 above, where the relation of thought and language is discussed.

31. In the case of the Absolute Idealists, the argument is: appearances in the sensible world are contradictory; reality cannot be contradictory; therefore the sensible world is not real. cf. Bradley's *Appearance and Reality, op. cit.*

32. I cannot hope to give here a proper account of Kant's views. Note that what I say is in no way premissed upon any of Kant's transcendental psychology.

33. Note that 'transcendental' here differs from 'transcendent' in talk of 'transcendent truth conditions'; the former concerns what is *within* the limits of experience, the latter concerns what is *outside* them.

34. Kant A85/B117 *et seq.*; cf *Prolegomena* § 18-30; and Strawson *The Bounds of Sense,* London, 1966, Pt.2, chapter II, *passim.*

35. Strawson, *Individuals,* chapter 3, *passim*; cf. p.106.

36. This argument requires further discussion; see Grayling, *op. cit.,* pp.216-19.

37. This argument also comes from Strawson; cf. *Individuals* pp.35-6. It is very celebrated, cf. the discussion and references (particularly to Stroud) in Grayling, *op. cit.,* pp.219-29.

38. cf. Strawson, ibid.

39. cf. Grayling for more detailed discussion of this and what follows.

40. cf. Kant A104; and Strawson, *Bounds of Sense,* p.73.

41. Strawson, ibid., p.262. Although this reads as a manifesto for my equation of antirealism and empirical realism, it is certain that Strawson would *wish* to resist the idea that his remarks should be read as supporting a thesis which could be construed as idealist in any way — although on the strength of this passage I do not see how he can make out a claim to that effect.

42. Strawson's enterprise in *Bounds of Sense* is the effort chiefly to preserve what is valuable in Kant *without* the transcendental psychology. Note also that Kant's doctrine of the noumenon falls entirely out of account too.

43. Grayling, *op. cit.,* chapter 5 for a detailed account of this.

44. Wittgenstein *On Certainty,* cf. e.g., 83, 105, 162, 211, 354, 411, 415.

45. cf. Wright, *Wittgenstein on the Foundations of Mathematics* Duckworth 1980 pp 199-222 *passim*.

46. Dummett, 'What Does the Appeal to Use do for the Theory of Meaning?', in Margalit, A. (ed.), *op. cit.,* p.135. In some moods, as noted, he appears to accept relativist consequences; in others, as in *The Interpretation of Frege's Philosophy*, Duckworth, 1981, he talks constantly of 'idealism or other forms of antirealism'. (This book came to hand too late for me to use it in preparing this volume; however it makes no substantial changes to Dummett's position on antirealism.)

47. For further discussion of the issues touched upon here, see the papers by Rescher, N., Blackburn, S. and Margolis, J., in French, P. A., *et al.* (eds.), *Midwest Studies in Philosophy* Minnesota, 1980. Hilary Putnam has written on these issues too; cf. his *Meaning and The Moral Sciences,* London, 1978, esp. Pts. 3 and 4.

48. Dummett, in Margalit, pp.125-6.

49. ibid., pp.127-8.

Index